W9-ABB-481

THE ESO™ ECSTASY PROGRAM

THE ESO™ ECSTASY PROGRAM

Better, Safer Sexual Intimacy and Extended Orgasmic Response

Alan P. Brauer, M.D. and Donna J. Brauer

WARNER BOOKS

A Warner Communications Company

Copyright © 1990 by Alan P. Brauer and Donna J. Brauer
All rights reserved

Warner Books, Inc., 666 Fifth Avenue, New York, NY 10103
 A Warner Communications Company

Printed in the United States of America
First printing: February 1990
10 9 8 7 6 5 4 3 2 1

Library of Congress Cataloging-in-Publication Data

Brauer, Alan P.
   The ESO ecstasy program : better, safer sexual intimacy and
extended orgasmic response /Alan P. Brauer and Donna J. Brauer.
      p.   cm.
   Includes bibliographical references.
   ISBN 0-446-51410-1
   1. Sex instruction.   2. Orgasm.   I. Brauer, Donna.   II. Title.
HQ31.B7718   1990
613.9'6—dc20   89-40046
                                                           CIP

Designed by Giorgetta Bell McRee
Illustrations by Vincent Perez

To the many researchers and professionals whose investigations made our work possible—we acknowledge our debt and respect. To the more than five thousand people who attended our weekend workshops or participated in relationship training at our medical center in Palo Alto, and to the many *ESO* readers who took the time to respond to the book's questionnaire, often sending detailed personal letters, we express our appreciation for your willingness to share your experiences, which helped provide the information on which the Ecstasy Program is based.

CONTENTS

1
GOALS

We have schools for truck driving, schools for hotel management, schools for nuclear physics, dancing, tennis, and ancient Greek literature, but few schools anywhere teach interpersonal relationships, intimacy, romance, sensuality, or sexuality. Assistance in improving sexual interaction is available primarily to the sexually troubled.

We would like to change that situation.

In this book, as in our earlier book *ESO*, our purpose is to help you to improve the quality and strength of your intimate relationship, to increase your sexual pleasure, and to experience enhanced orgasm if you choose.

Anyone, man or woman, with or without a partner, can learn to experience sexuality and orgasm more pleasurably. Orgasm is totally safe. There are no known harmful side effects to having orgasm. Orgasm can improve by becoming more frequent. It can improve by becoming more intense—by feeling more powerful, more bodily, more electric, fuller or deeper than it has felt to you before. Orgasm can become more emotionally satisfying, more spiritual, more ecstatic. It can improve by lasting longer—by being experienced not for the usual eight to ten seconds but for twenty seconds, a minute, ten minutes, or even half an hour or more.

The most successful outcome we hope for you is that by reading and following the Ecstasy Program, your satisfaction with your intimacy, sexuality, and orgasm will increase.

We're Alan and Donna Brauer. We're husband and wife, physician and co-therapist, happily married, monogamous, parents of two children, with a thriving medical and counseling center in Palo Alto, California. In 1983 we published a best-selling book entitled *ESO [Extended Sexual Orgasm]: The New Promise of Pleasure for Couples in Love.* Many people purchased *ESO* to improve their relationships. It's gratifying to find that people seem to benefit from our work because of its underlying dedication

1

to improved relationships developed by following the principles of clear communication, equal compromise, and keeping agreements.

Our work focuses on effective communication between men and women in the widest sense of that word, mental and physical, encompassing everything from the silent signals people send each other, to talking to each other, to making love. Clear communication is crucial to maintaining a relationship. In our practice we find it's the area that usually breaks down first. It's rare that both partners in a relationship agree that they have even fairly good communication. By reading this book and following the Ecstasy Program you will almost certainly improve the quality of your communications.

LEARNING PLEASURE

We're specialists in behavior modification. This is a relatively new and effective psychological technology for changing feelings and experience through a deliberate process of modifying actions and thought. Over the years we've helped people deal with a great variety of problems: intractable pain, erectile dysfunction, early ejaculation, lack of orgasm, substance abuse, smoking, insomnia, high blood pressure, overweight. In every case our approach is similar. It's based on solid scientific evidence. We select small steps toward change that are easy to see and do right now, today or tomorrow. Small, deliberate steps practiced regularly become a new habit. Several desirable new habits together can result in major improvements in how someone's life works and how it feels to that person and those close to him or her.

Even physical responses can be changed this way, by arranging to give our patients more real-time information about the behavior they want to improve so that they can monitor the change. A blood-pressure gauge, for example, gives real-time information that people with high blood pressure can use to learn to lower blood pressure voluntarily. Orgasmic response, like almost any other bodily system, can be monitored in progress so that changes can be observed, brought under conscious control, and trained.

A woman who is preorgasmic, for example, can learn to have orgasm. If she wishes, she may then progress to multiple orgasm and from there to continuous extended orgasm. A man who pursues intercourse or self-stimulation directly and briefly to ejaculation can learn to experience increasingly extended periods of emission-phase orgasm before voluntarily going on to ejaculate. He can also learn to experience multiple ejaculatory orgasm with minimal wait states (so-called refractory periods) between episodes. Both partners can learn to stimulate each other separately to these highly pleasurable experiences by hand, orally, and in intercourse. Eventually both partners can learn to stimulate each other to extended orgasmic response mutually and simultaneously. *The ultimate limit to the sexual pleasure two people can create together appears to be determined only by their time, interest, and energy levels.*

As long as you both agree to what you're doing, there's no right or wrong way to have sex. The Ecstasy Program is a structure that encourages honest communication, allowing you to decide together what you may want to explore or do differently. Following the program will allow you to gain more information and knowledge.

Through training in the Ecstasy Program you can learn to move more efficiently to higher levels of sexual experience than you have ever achieved before. A reasonable *minimum* goal to set for yourself is at very least to double your present levels of sexual pleasure. If you're now enjoying sex once a week, you can almost certainly double that frequency if both partners want to do so. If you're having two sexual interactions a week, you might aim for three or four times a week or even every day. Similarly, if orgasm now lasts for four to twelve seconds, it is possible to double that time to twenty seconds or longer, increasing the time you experience that intense pleasure by 100 percent. Women who have never or rarely experienced an orgasm may want to learn to have orgasm. Women who ordinarily experience only one orgasm during a sexual interaction have the possibility of experiencing at least two or more. These are *minimum* goals, we emphasize; you may well progress faster and further to truly extended, deeply pleasurable intimacy and sexuality.

RESTORING LOST LUST

Some people think lust is a dirty word. In fact, lust is important to a relationship. Lust is sexual desire for another person that is purely physical. If you don't try to analyze it, lust is like magic. It usually starts with a mental picture followed by attention to another person's body. People who don't usually visualize easily may first become aware of lust as a physical response such as erection in men and vaginal lubrication in women. Lust is specifically sexual interest in another person. Some call it chemistry. It doesn't necessarily include any personal interest in or love for another person, which is probably why it's intimidating to some people. There may be a forbidden component to it—a sexual situation where there is a risk of discovery or that occurs at an unusual location or time of day. There may be a brief, unusually exciting sense of vulnerability and freedom.

In the early stages of a relationship, lust may be important for motivating continued interest and growth if the relationship is growing in other areas as well. If trust, communication, and intimacy are improving, lust may be the engine. Some researchers feel that lust is in fact biochemically induced. To the extent that it manifests itself as thoughts that result in sexual arousal, it probably is, since sexual arousal is partly a chemically mediated process.

Nevertheless, it's useful to recognize that lust normally begins in the mind with thoughts and pictures which are then translated into physical reactions.

Lust usually surges early in a relationship and then fades over time. A recent Ann Landers survey of 141,000 people aged 17–93, divided more or less equally between men and women, found that 82 percent felt that sex after marriage was much less pleasurable. Couples usually miss lust when it fades and dream of finding some way of making it return. Searching for it is sometimes the reason one or both partners stray to other relationships.

Deliberately spending more time together sexually, playing together with the goal of increasing mutual pleasure, can often help to compensate for the missing electricity of lust. The Ecstasy Program is designed to do just that.

Lust deliberately stimulated is different from the spontaneous lust that appears early in a relationship, but it's equally powerful and pleasurable.

BASIC PRINCIPLES
FOR A BETTER RELATIONSHIP

Throughout this book, woven into the structure of the program and each exercise, are the four basic principles for improving intimate relationships:

1. Be deliberate to allow more spontaneity.
2. Alternate giving and receiving.
3. Learn sensitivity to subtle differences of timing and pressure.
4. Make compromises and keep agreements.

Let's look at these principles one by one.

Be Deliberate

Love is central to the ideal intimate relationship. But love is never enough to sustain intimacy over a long period of time. Partners need deliberately to pay attention to other fundamentals that are necessary to keep their relationship vital: commitment, compromise, caring, touching, and sexuality.

The idea that sexual pleasuring in particular can be learned by deliberate application bothers some men and women. They contend that sex should be spontaneous and "natural," the automatic outcome of love, and that introducing deliberate training may make sex self-conscious, less "real," less pleasurable. By this reasoning, deliberate sex means there's less love between partners.

But no matter how strong or deep the love, love by itself doesn't sustain growth and improvement in a couple's sexual experience. That's simply a fact, based on extensive clinical observation. Sexual pleasure is not spontaneously maintained in a long-term marriage. It has to be nurtured, continuously.

In fact, learning any skill requires self-consciousness—literally. One of the functions of consciousness is to focus attention on new experiences so that learning can take place. Once the learning has been accomplished, the experience then becomes habitual and "spontaneous." An Olympic skier skis "spontaneously" well because she has devoted years to deliberate, "self-conscious" learning. You dance well, swim well, sing well, because you spent hours and years practicing, self-consciously learning your skills a step at a time.

Spontaneity can also be understood as a measure of timing. Something done spontaneously is as much a decision as something done with forethought. But the time frame is shorter for the "spontaneous" event. You decide to raid the refrigerator now rather than wait until mealtime. You decide to make love not tomorrow night but as soon as you can tear off your clothes. It's a decision either way. It seems more impulsive only because the decision-making process is compressed.

Deliberation furthers spontaneity. An obvious example is personal hygiene. Unless you and your partner deliberately pay attention to daily personal hygiene—washing, bathing or showering, and shaving—you won't be comfortably positioned to allow unplanned or less planned lovemaking. Often, what appears to one partner to be spontaneous actually represents deliberateness on the other partner's part. The bedroom is pleasantly arranged for lovemaking when you walk in because you or your partner deliberately set it up that way earlier in the day.

Learning extended orgasm is a deliberate practice that results in reexperiencing spontaneity at a more intensely pleasurable and more intimate level. Learning to have better, deeper, longer orgasm is also entertaining, a structure of exercises and games that leaves plenty of room for pleasure and intimacy. Not the least of the pleasures involved are the deep satisfactions of self-discovery and achievement, mutually shared.

Sometimes people find it difficult to apply the four basic principles for improving pleasure to themselves and their behavior. We'll offer exercises that show you how and teach you to make the necessary improvements gradually, and we assure you that if you overcome your reluctance to be deliberate about things that you normally do in your life without a great deal of thought, you'll be amply rewarded.

If you want something to happen in your life—a baby, a promotion, a new car, for example—but you aren't deliberate about the steps necessary to make it happen, the odds are good that it *won't* happen. This precept is especially true in your personal relationships. Personal relationships don't stand still. They're dynamic, constantly changing. If you aren't developing your relationship, if you're simply maintaining the status quo, the forces that pull people apart are almost certainly at work and your relationship is probably deteriorating. Eventually one or the other of you, or both of you, is likely to find it unsatisfactory.

Alternate Giving and Receiving

Couples often begin making love by stimulating each other manually at the same time. This simultaneous stimulation is certainly pleasurable. But it's more difficult to concentrate on the quality of stimulation you're supplying your partner if you're trying at the same time to focus on what your partner is doing to you. Your attention is divided.

Focusing your attention on two experiences at once is hard to do. One experience inevitably gets more attention than the other. If, for example, you want to become sexually aroused in the course of your mutual foreplay (meaning erect if you're a man, engorged if you're a woman), focusing your attention on arousing your partner while your partner focuses his/her attention on arousing you may slow the process considerably.

We suggest in addition to simultaneous stimulation that you sometimes deliberately take turns at arousal, designating one partner in turn as the giver and the other as the receiver. This concept, giving and receiving, applies to other areas of your relationship as well. We'll be suggesting that you and your partner agree on trading giving and receiving at specific times in play, communication, sensuality, and sexuality.

Practicing this separation of roles allows each of you to concentrate on giving and receiving in turn without dividing your attention between the two. You can focus on taking pleasure or on giving pleasure (both of which, we should emphasize, are pleasurable experiences in themselves!). In this way you learn how much and how often you enjoy giving and how much and how often you enjoy receiving. You also learn your partner's preferences.

Learning about yourself helps you teach your partner your preferences. Since none of us can read minds, the only way we can learn what our partners want is to be told or shown. Partners have to know what they want themselves before they can tell us or show us. The more your partner knows what you prefer, the better he/she can please you. Such knowledge develops into intimacy.

Many people resist deliberately becoming givers or receivers because of past habits, training, or cultural expectations. A man may feel he should always be active, always in charge, always the one who decides what to do next. For such a man, reversing roles even for a short time may be a challenge.

Similarly, a woman may feel uncomfortable telling a man what she wants or what he should do next sexually. We're not advocating any basic change in roles. We're merely proposing that you explore the advantages of focusing your attention on each other serially rather than simultaneously during brief, designated periods of time. We think you'll be pleased by the increased intensity of feeling and the freedom that this flexibility makes possible.

Learn Timing and Pressure

Whether you're making an investment or telling a joke, timing is crucial. Variations in the timing of what you do in everyday life have a great deal to do with the outcome. Try soft-boiling an egg for ten minutes. Try swinging at a pitch before the ball is over the plate.

As with timing, so with pressure. How intensely you apply pressure on a car's accelerator determines how fast the car will go. How intensely you press yourself at work or your child at school can partly determine success.

In sexual areas, issues of time and physical or emotional pressure are equally significant and equally important to understand.

We touch each other in subtly different ways to communicate friendship, affection, sensuality, or sexuality. People respond differently to different degrees of touch. Different people respond differently to the same degree of touch as well. People have different requirements of timing and pressure that they've learned from past experience to interpret as pleasurable. And men and women seem to differ in their requirements as well.

Many people stimulate their partners with the same timing and pressure they prefer for themselves. That's logical enough, since what they're doing is essentially applying what they know. But their partners may not prefer such timing and pressure. They may prefer faster or slower stroking. They may prefer less pressure or more. Pressing too hard or not hard enough, stroking too fast or not fast enough, can even be disruptive and distracting. Men frequently prefer rapid, heavy stroking. Women frequently prefer slow, softer stroking. In the Ecstasy Program we direct you to exercises that allow you to explore these differences deliberately and to discover your partner's preferences and your own. Sexual technique is an important element in creating optimum sexual response. It can be learned through instruction, observation, and practice.

Make Compromises and Keep Agreements

This may be the most important principle of all. In a healthy, growing relationship the overall balance of adjustment and settlement of differences needs to be approximately equal on both sides. There are probably some issues that each of you feels so strongly about that no compromise is possible—insisting on maintaining an exclusive relationship, for example, or refusing to tolerate a partner's physical abuse, or use of drugs or alcohol. Some beliefs are simply nonnegotiable and need to be clearly articulated.

But most differences between partners—leisure activities, for example, child-rearing, spending, friendships, work—are negotiable. A regular pattern of imbalance, where one partner makes self-serving decisions at the expense of the other, will create resentment, anger, and resistance. Checkbooks and relationships need to be balanced regularly. The more accommodating partner needs to learn to become more assertive about his/her preferences. The more rigid partner needs to learn that sensitivity to his/her partner's needs will return more happiness to both.

We suggest that, just as businesses do, when couples make agreements they put those agreements in writing to reduce later arguments about what they agreed to do. Keep a file of your agreements.

Agreeing to complete the exercises in the Ecstasy Program is important. If, after you've done so, you find that a particular exercise doesn't work for you, then you have the freedom to rule out doing that activity again outside the program. But at least you'll have given the process a fair try, and you may find that it allowed you to learn more about your and your partner's preferences. You'll be more aware of your differences in the techniques of timing and pressure, giving and receiving, deliberateness, agreement and compromise. That awareness will be valuable in itself. The exercises are designed to help you learn about yourselves and each other; you do not necessarily need to make them permanent parts of your repertoire.

BECOMING A SEXUAL INVESTIGATOR

We encourage you and your partner to become sexual investigators, to examine the unexamined areas of your relationship with the intention of improving it. Much of the Ecstasy Program is devoted to activities designed to help you conduct that mutual investigation comfortably, safely, and productively.

When you awaken the investigator in you, you can learn first to observe and then to change your patterns of thinking, feeling, and behaving that involve sexuality. The first step to such change is to *measure* the behavior. If you can measure or quantify a behavior, you can learn to control it.

The behaviors and thoughts you'll be measuring in the Ecstasy Program will include details that you may not have noticed. For instance, you'll be asked to pay attention to how you go about coming to a decision to have sex on a particular occasion. Who initiates sex and in what way? Is there overt agreement? Does sex just seem to "happen"? We'll show you a variety of ways to achieve mutually acceptable agreement on this important issue. Learning to do so will require awareness and deliberateness at first.

Noticing the subtleties of your orgasmic contractions or those of your partner is another example. Once you've observed these contractions, you're then in a position to enhance them.

MEASURING YOUR RELATIONSHIP'S SEXUAL HEALTH

One basic measure of the health of your relationship can be whether you make love as often as each of you would like and whether your lovemaking meets your needs and expectations. When people have problems, they usually make love less than one or both of them would like. Natural reductions in frequency of lovemaking due to work, parenting, illness, medications, aging, differing biological needs and energy levels, and differing belief systems or religious orientations may also influence such change. But it's a good general rule that a relationship has problems that need to be addressed if a couple was satisfied earlier in their relationship with their level of sexual interaction and now one or both no longer are. Improvement will usually mean finding a middle ground where both individuals agree on fair compromise. We'll help to provide some common ground.

DIFFERENCES BETWEEN MEN AND WOMEN

Before couples can find increased intimacy and pleasure, male sexuality must recognize the equality of female sexuality. The great barrier between man and woman is often the man's fear of the depth and intensity of female sexuality. Because power and aggression are neutralized through sexual pleasure, one primary defense men have used historically against loss of dominance has been the denial, repression, and control of female sexuality. This reduction of sex to mere release from physical tension should not be confused with real sexual pleasure and the intimacy from which it flows, which is incompatible with dominance, power, aggression, violence, and pain. It's through a mutual sharing of pleasure that sexual equality between men and women will be realized.

The aim of this book is to provide a structure that can enable men and women to achieve greater sexual equality by realizing that the development of their individual sexual potentials is dependent upon not only *taking* pleasure but also *giving* pleasure.

For a man, that means learning from his partner what her needs are and not trying to dominate her with his power, strength, ego, or will. It means, for example, asking his partner if she would like to have sex, finding out what she feels like doing, stopping when she wants to stop, and focusing on her pleasure and reactions rather than her orgasm.

For a man, it also means seeking more physical and emotional pleasure from the sexual process. It means changing his definition of "good sex." Good sex is not merely an orgasm for his partner and an ejaculation for him. Rather, good sex happens when a man's partner feels he has paid enough attention to her pleasure for a sufficient time and when he in turn has accepted and experienced a sufficiency of pleasure from her.

For a woman, sexual equality means being assertive enough to arrange a romantic and sexual encounter during which she experiences as much pleasure as she desires. It means, further, being able and willing to pay sufficient attention to her partner to allow him to experience as much pleasure as is possible for him at any particular time.

WHY THE ECSTASY PROGRAM?

ESO, our first book, was a general overview of sexuality, including discussions of sexual problems, resistances, and increasing sexual potential. In that book, we suggested to couples that if they both wanted to do so, they might reach for the ultimate goal, which is extending sexual orgasm.

The Ecstasy Program is more structured. Half a million people used *ESO* to examine their love lives and to explore the possibilities for creative improvement. We heard from nearly a thousand of them by letter and worked with thousands more during the professional training seminars we teach throughout the United States. We learned from what we heard. The Ecstasy Program in this book draws on the manual we developed for our seminars. We've put together what we consider to be achievable goals for many couples to help them improve their relationship in many areas of communication, and especially sexually.

Every couple's sexual relationship is unique. Broadly speaking, we've observed three kinds of sexual relationships among couples: the Maintainers, the Enthusiasts, and the Dissatisfied.

The vast majority of couples are Maintainers. They feel that their sexual interactions are adequate. They're not especially exciting, but they're not a problem or a worry either. Maintainers aren't actively seeking ways to change or improve their sexual experience. They're more often struggling to fit physical intimacy into their busy lives. Given the right circumstances, though, Maintainers can become motivated to work on their sexual relationships and improve them. For Maintainers—couples who are functioning well, are happy to be together, and have at least one or more sexual interactions per week, who communicate comfortably and courteously, who are satisfied or only mildly dissatisfied with the amount of intimacy they are experiencing—we suggest a twelve-week program.

Enthusiasts are in the minority. They actively seek out ways to intensify and extend their sexual intimacy. For these ambitious couples—who presently enjoy several sexual interactions per week and exciting lovemaking—we suggest considering an accelerated program of approximately eight weeks.

The Dissatisfied feel they have problems, either as individuals or as couples. They may never have functioned as they believe they should. Their level of sexual functioning may have deteriorated. Or they may have long-standing difficulties. For the Dissatisfied, who are having difficulties, we suggest a slower and less demanding version of the Ecstasy Program that might require six months or more to complete. We suggest that the Dissatisfied consider agreeing to follow the Ecstasy Program through Week Five, taking several weeks to complete each week's assignment. They can then evaluate their interest and capacity to continue with the remaining seven weeks of program exercises.

Ecstasy Program techniques can be utilized effectively by people without regular partners; we describe how to modify the program for those men and women as well in Chapter X: Singles.

We assume that most readers are heterosexual. For same-sex couples, the information and many of the exercises work equally well. Please transpose the appropriate gender as you read and follow the program.

PROBLEMS THAT MIGHT INTERFERE

The Twelve-Week Ecstasy Program isn't for everyone. Anger, when it is frequently present, broad-ranging, and deep-seated, particularly if the woman is angry with the man, may make following the program structure difficult. If several weeks of trying to follow the program exercises seems to result in greater anger than before, you should probably stop. The information in this book may still be of value to you in other, less structured ways.

If either one or both partners have a persistent problem with sexual functioning, they shouldn't try to follow the full twelve-week program sequence unless and until those problems have been resolved. The likeliest problem a man might have is with unreliable or persistently absent erection. The likeliest problem a woman might have is with orgasm. Some women may never have had orgasm, a condition called preorgasmia. Some women may have had orgasm in the past but may not be having orgasm at present by any means—by partner- or self-stimulation—a condition called secondary nonorgasmia.

We advise women who experience physical pain during intercourse to have a gynecological examination by a doctor before going beyond the exercises of Week Seven. Couples with this problem may need to modify or eliminate exercises in Weeks Eight through Twelve that include intercourse.

Couples who have sex very infrequently—less than once a month or so—should take at least two or three real-time weeks for each week's exercise and should proceed only through Week Five. When they've completed Week Five, they should discuss their progress and may then consider agreeing to continue with Week Six exercises and beyond. Please consult the section "Solving Problems" for more specific suggestions and instructions.

Couples should not undertake the Ecstasy Program if one partner feels excessively pressured or coerced by the other to change sexual attitudes or behavior. If one partner threatens to leave the other unless they follow the program, or implies other negative consequences, or refuses to allow the other to stop or modify the structure, then following the program is likely to be harmful rather than helpful. You can't force your partner to love you or to give you pleasure, or to have sex; love and pleasuring are voluntary, gifts freely exchanged. Coercion taints, sours, and ultimately destroys them.

Most couples, even those with significant sexual problems, can reasonably follow the exercises through Week Five, allowing even a month or more if necessary to practice each week's assignments.

A few people should postpone learning extended orgasm for physical reasons. Men and women who have serious heart disease, who have recently suffered a stroke, have acute injuries, a serious chronic illness, or men with prostate infections or cancer should talk with their doctors first. A guideline: Anyone who is able to perform moderate exercise is likely to be able, from a physical standpoint, to practice program training.

Couples on the verge of breaking up, couples with serious relationship problems, may need counseling first. If following the steps of the Ecstasy Program seems to make your problems and relationship worse rather than better, that's a sign that you may need outside help.

Individuals with lifelong sexual problems may benefit from counseling for those problems before beginning program training.

Singles without partners who have strong negative feelings about self-stimulation may be uncomfortable following the singles program. Read through that program first, and then decide.

LEARNING AND UNLEARNING

Most men and women—and most sex experts as well—think of orgasm as an experience that lasts for six to twelve seconds. Some acknowledge the possibility that women sometimes can have a rare mega-orgasm of up to sixty seconds' duration. Before you will be able to experience extending your orgasm, you must know and believe that it is possible to do so.

A few couples have experienced extended orgasm by chance. For many reasons, they have rarely been able to repeat the experience. Most couples don't have the knowledge and don't spend enough time making love to discover how to expand and extend their orgasms reliably.

Many couples, we find, average only two or fewer sexual interactions per week after they've been together for several years. There are several reasons this reduction in frequency occurs. One of the most important is the differences they brought to the relationship, differences in gender, culture, energy levels, taste, philosophy, belief, and profession, all of which affect their ability to resolve problems in a courteous and caring way. Such differences become barriers to intimacy.

Improving sexual communication, we feel, is centrally important to a relationship. For women, satisfactory sexual intimacy—feeling sexually desired, attractive, wanted—is a form of security. For men, it's a form of approval.

Sometimes a woman will refuse to become sexual in a relationship because she feels intimacy and caring are not growing and improving, but decreasing. Communication and understanding are then also deteriorating, so she may feel it would not be honest to respond to her partner and allow him to think everything is okay. She may build up resentment toward him for not giving priority to the survival and improvement of the relationship. She intuitively knows that growth is important in the relationship. If it isn't growing, it's probably deteriorating. Unless a woman feels cared for and kindly toward her partner, she may find it very difficult to respond to his sexual overtures. Her negative thoughts and feelings toward her partner interfere with her ability to respond in an honest, caring way and cause her not to want to get involved more physically. She thinks of lovemaking as good, courteous communication and affection. It's a continuum across the day and the evening, not just something that happens at night in bed. It's a state of mind and a pattern of attentive behavior. Discovering a love note, receiving an "I love you" phone call or a small bouquet are important communications that build and maintain a woman's sexual desire.

Many men, by contrast, can turn desire on or off. Men more easily than women can separate having sex from making love, and making love from having sex. Most women have difficulty separating making love and having sex.

Difficulties a man experiences in a relationship can manifest themselves in sexual dysfunction. If a man feels judged by his partner, inhibited, insecure, intimidated, fearful, or rejected, such feelings can reveal themselves in early ejaculation or an erection problem. The connection is usually unconscious; most men aren't even aware of it. Each person enters a relationship with different personal habits and preferences. What they've seen, where and how they've lived, the previous intimate relationships they've sustained, all go into determining their style of intimacy. That style isn't necessarily the best for them or for their partner. Fortunately, more functional habits for enhancing intimacy can be learned.

SEXUAL DYSFUNCTION

The Ecstasy Program is primarily addressed to Maintainers and Enthusiasts. We've tailored our discussion to the needs of Maintainers and Enthusiasts simply because one book can't deal with everything and there are many books already available that discuss persistent dysfunction, including our previous book, *ESO*. This limitation doesn't mean we believe that presently dysfunctional couples are not able to gain more sexual pleasure, or can never learn to enjoy extending orgasmic response. However, if either partner believes a problem may exist, first consult the Appendix on "Solving Problems" and follow the recommendations in the section that applies. It may also be useful to read some of the additional self-help books recommended in the section on page xxx, "Further Reading." If the problem persists, we suggest considering seeking assistance from a mental health professional experienced in working with sexual dysfunctions.

Regardless of an individual's or couple's level of functioning or dysfunctioning, improvement is always possible. It depends upon your willingness to work patiently with your partner, to seek and accept positively small alterations in experience, and to think about seeking professional help.

What exactly is a sexual dysfunction? Quite simply, it's the difference between what a person is currently experiencing and what he feels he *should* be experiencing. That is, it's basically a gap between ideal expectation and present reality.

In our therapy practice we've helped many hundreds of sexually dysfunctional couples. We believe that a good therapist can help overcome persistent sexual problems, even when there is some contributing physical cause, as long as both partners are willing. Many sexual problems or dysfunctions—even some of physical origin—can be improved to some degree by applying the principles, procedures, and information described in this book. If you suspect any physical causation—such as pain, medication side effects, diabetes, chronic fatigue, or alcohol effects, consult a knowledgeable physician first. It's important to remember that very frequently even those who have chronic physical conditions that affect physical functioning can learn at least partly to compensate by deliberate, additional attention to sexual interactions. Take as much time as you need to proceed through Weeks One through Five. At that point, if both you and your partner feel pleased with your progress, you may agree to continue with additional weeks, again taking as much time as you need for each week's assignment.

In the past decade, sex therapists have observed a distinct change in the kind of problems people bring to them for help. During the 1970s, the first decade after the research of Masters and Johnson helped establish sex therapy as a respectable profession, the common dysfunctions accounted for more than half the problems therapists addressed—in men, impotence and premature ejaculation; in women, lack of or infrequent orgasm, infrequent or painful intercourse.

In the 1980s, however, fewer couples sought therapy for the common dysfunctions. Today we usually see couples complaining of discrepancy of desire, a knot of psychological problems deeply entrenched in the interactions of the relationship that lead one or both partners seemingly to lose interest in sex. The change has occurred, we think, because so many sexual self-help books, newspaper and magazine articles, television programs and talk shows are available today. People are wiser about sex than they used to be and are treating the common dysfunctions themselves.

The couples whom therapists see today are challenged by more serious relationship issues. Quite often the sexual problem is only the most obvious symptom. By the time such couples seek therapy, the sexual issues have been ignored for so long that they're massively apparent. Often there's so much anger involved that the partners have stopped wanting to live together. As therapists, we have to uncover and attempt to treat a whole list of relationship problems before we deal directly with sexual differences.

Despite these caveats, we emphasize again that the Ecstasy Program outlined in this book can help almost any couple improve their intimacy, romance, communication, shared pleasure, and, of course, sexual satisfaction.

Those who have been very depressed or extremely anxious for many years, those who honestly know that they don't want to or may be afraid to change their sexual relationship or who are fundamentally opposed to making sex more deliberate or are simply fearful of making change in their lives, and those who feel that their present experience is good enough, may want to read through this book for information without committing themselves to practicing its programs.

However, people who are simply skeptical or who have some doubts should consider proceeding with the program anyway, keeping an open mind. We've seen dramatic changes in attitude at our weekend professional seminars. Often, the partners who originally doubted have been the happiest of all. But no partner should bully another into tackling the Ecstasy Program. Where there is a discrepancy of desire to improve sexual intimacy, one possible solution can be to participate in the Ecstasy Program, allowing the partner with the less intense sexual desire to set the pace. Under those circumstances, allowing two or three weeks for each program week may work best.

Otherwise, the path to learning extended response can be a delight and a challenge to young and old. Try it. It's the real thing—pleasure at one of its highest levels. Success in extending orgasmic response isn't the main object, however. Improved communication, intimacy, and overall pleasure are your reasonable goals.

THE ECSTASY PROGRAM IS ADDITIVE

One of the important and unique features of the Ecstasy Program is that you need not give up any sexual activity you are now enjoying. The Ecstasy Program is entirely additive. Although it's quite probable that you will find yourself modifying your present habits after a number of weeks of following the assigned exercises, it's not necessary to do so. The choice is yours.

A NUTS-AND-BOLTS WORKBOOK

The Ecstasy Program is engineered to be a nuts-and-bolts workbook. This approach may be as good as, or perhaps can be better than, having your own personal therapist. You wouldn't pay a therapist hundreds of dollars and ignore his advice. You'd give the therapist's program a reasonable try. The Ecstasy Program has improved the relationships of hundreds of men and women who have followed its structure. It can improve yours as well.

The structure we describe has been carefully engineered to provide a safe emotional foundation within your relationship. Trust is continually addressed. The limits we've built into the Ecstasy Program are designed to help you feel safe as you venture into the openness of deeper intimacy and the joy of freer, more intense sexual interaction.

Men and women may rightly ask what's in the program for them. Here's a breakdown:

If you're a woman, you can expect the possibility of:

1. Receiving more courteous *communication* from your partner. You'll learn to assist your partner in understanding your thinking and needs. In some important ways, your needs are definitely different from his.
2. Getting more romantic *attention* from your partner. More attention usually results in greater affection, trust, and intimacy.
3. Enjoying a longer, more leisurely *time* of lovemaking.
4. Experiencing more sexual *pleasure*. When communication is better, when you're enjoying more attention, when your relationship is growing, you'll find yourself trusting more and will allow yourself to feel more sexual pleasure. Orgasmic expression depends on having an attentive, sensitive, caring partner whom you trust sufficiently to allow yourself to let go. You'll learn more about your own sexuality and your partner's, and possibly you'll have deeper, longer-lasting orgasmic response.
5. Increasing your *self-esteem* by improving the quality of the time you and your partner spend together.

If you're a man, you can expect the possibility of:

1. Experiencing more *variety* in your sexual interactions.
2. Enjoying *orgasm more frequently*. Depending upon age and past habits, men are generally satisfied with sexual release three or four times a week. Frequency and efficiency are more important to most men than quality and amount of time spent at sexual play, which are more important to women. Men certainly enjoy improved sexual quality, but they are often far less motivated than women to seek such changes.

3. Winning more *approval* and support from your partner. Because of the deliberateness, the clear communication, and the agreement structures we've built into the Ecstasy Program, you can experience the security of not feeling rejected sexually. Sustained absence of a partner's approval can often lead to erection problems and loss of sexual desire. These difficulties undermine a man's self-esteem and affect other areas of his life negatively. Positive approval has the opposite effect. The exercises in this book are designed to help identify subtle, negative communication habits and to neutralize their impact on the couple's interaction.

4. Extending the length of your orgasm. Men and women both can expect to receive *a fair exchange*. Through the Ecstasy Program, the man assures his partner of his time and attention for at least one long (one to two hours) period of lovemaking, usually on a weekend. In return, the woman agrees to have several briefer interactions (ten to fifteen minutes), usually during the week.

MAJOR REQUIREMENTS

In return for these benefits, the Ecstasy Program poses some major requirements. These are:

1. Agreeing to follow the program even if you're skeptical of its rewards. It's normal to feel some apprehension about the extent of the commitment of time we'll be asking of you and whether you will be able to keep your end of the bargain. The more positively you support your commitment, the more likely you'll be to achieve your goals.

2. Allocating two to three hours per week to the exercises.

3. Following the procedures assigned as honestly and completely as you can.

4. Keeping agreements you make. Don't make any agreement that you feel you are not likely to be able to keep. If your partner appears to break an agreement, use the Communication Exercises to express your observation of that situation, your feelings about it, and a suggested plan for improvement.

5. The ability to recognize and the willingness to push through the

inevitable mental resistances that come up for nearly everyone as they follow the program's exercises. For instance, you may resist and feel uncomfortable at first with the deliberateness of scheduling an hour of sexual time, believing sex should be spontaneous. Acknowledge this to yourself (and to your partner). Then make and keep to your schedule anyhow.

II
BETTER ORGASM

The oldest description of orgasm we have located in world literature appears in an early Chinese book, *Nu-chieh* (*The Ideal Woman*), which poetically characterizes female orgasm as "fire inside the Jade Pavilion." In modern America the informal name for orgasm is "coming," but in Elizabethan England it was "dying," in Victorian England "spending." To the French in past centuries orgasm was *le petit mort*—the little death.

Writers have worked to describe the complex feelings of orgasm. Two of the most famous descriptions of sexual response occur in the novels of D. H. Lawrence and Ernest Hemingway. In *Lady Chatterly's Lover* Lawrence compares Lady Chatterly's sexual passion to the depth and motion of the sea:

> And it seemed she was like the sea, nothing but dark waves rising and heaving, heaving with a great swell, so that slowly her whole darkness was in motion, and she was ocean rolling its dark, dumb mass. Oh, and far down inside her the deeps parted and rolled asunder, in long, far-traveling billows, and ever, at the quick of her, the depths parted and rolled asunder, from the centre of soft plunging, as the plunger went deeper and deeper, touching lower, as she was deeper and deeper and deeper disclosed, and heavier the billows of her rolled away to some shore, uncovering her, and closer and closer plunged the palpable unknown, and further and further rolled the waves of herself away from herself, heaving her, till suddenly, in a soft, shuddering convulsion, the quick of all her plasm was touched, she knew herself touched, the consummation was upon her, and she was gone. She was gone, she was not, and she was born: a woman.

Hemingway made the earth itself move in response to Robert Jordan's and Maria's ecstasy in *For Whom the Bell Tolls*:

Then there was the smell of heather crushed and the roughness of the bent stalks under her head and the sun bright on her closed eyes and all his life he would remember the curve of her throat with her head pushed back into the heather roots and her lips that moved smally and by themselves and the fluttering of the lashes on the eyes tight closed against the sun and against everything, and for her everything was red, orange, gold-red from the sun on the closed eyes, and it all was that color, all of it, the filling, the possessing, the having, all of that color, all in a blindness of that color. For him it was a dark passage which led to nowhere, then to nowhere, then again to nowhere, once again to nowhere, always and forever to nowhere, heavy on the elbows in the earth to nowhere, dark, never any end to nowhere, hung on all time always to unknowing nowhere, this time and again for always to nowhere, now not to be borne once again always and to nowhere, now beyond all bearing up, up, up and into nowhere, suddenly scaldingly, holdingly all nowhere gone and time absolutely still and they were both there, time having stopped and he felt the earth move out and away from under them.

Gilbert V. T. Hamilton, a physician and pioneer American sex researcher, published in 1929 a study of one hundred married men and one hundred married women, *A Research into Marriage*. "The word 'orgasm,' " Hamilton explained there, "is used to designate the spasmodic, highly pleasurable feeling with which the sex act ends for both men and women. . . . Women do not discharge semen at such a time, of course, but with that exception, their orgasm . . . is essentially similar to that of men." Hamilton found four women among his sample of one hundred who, he wrote, "will have anywhere from two or three to a score of orgasms to the man's one"—evidence that female orgasm is not "essentially similar" to male—but chose to discount that evidence; these multiple orgasms, he thought, were "not fully satisfying," "incomplete," and "spurious, probably clitoridal, minor climaxes."

The most popular American source of sexual information before the work of Alfred Kinsey and of William Masters and Virginia Johnson was probably T. H. Van de Velde's *Ideal Marriage*, first published in the United States in 1926. Van de Velde encouraged tenderness and mutuality between partners but was also responsible for the enduring myth that the ideal orgasm is mutual and simultaneous. "In normal and perfect coitus," the Dutch physician wrote, "mutual orgasm must be almost simultaneous; the usual procedure is that the man's ejaculation begins and sets the woman's acme of sensation in train at once."

Another early marriage manual, *The Sex Technique in Marriage*, by the woman physician Isabel Emslie Hutton, was more poetic but not much more helpful. "Orgasm varies in intensity," Hutton wrote, "but it is always an unmistakable throbbing, ecstatic sensation that pervades and thrills through every fiber of the being; it is especially concentrated in the organs of generation, spreading in pleasurable waves over the body, and following this, there is a general feeling of fitness and well-being."

Definition based on extensive evidence began with Alfred Kinsey's famous and controversial 1948 study, *Sexual Behavior in the Human Male*. Kinsey and his colleagues interviewed thousands of men and women for their studies of human sexuality. They were concerned with recording existing behavior rather than idealizing, changing, or enhancing it. Male orgasm as Kinsey defined it "involves a series of gradual physiologic changes, the development of rhythmic body movements with distinct penis throbs and pelvic thrusts, an obvious change in sensory capacities, a final tension of muscles, especially of the abdomen, hips, and back, a sudden release with convulsions, including rhythmic anal contractions —followed by the disappearance of all symptoms."

By contrast, Masters and Johnson found by direct observation that male orgasm is a two-stage process. In the first stage, they wrote in *Human Sexual Response*, "a sensation of ejaculatory inevitability develops for an instant immediately prior to, and then parallels in timing sequence, the first stage of the ejaculatory process. . . . This subjective experience has been described by many males as the sensation of 'feeling the ejaculation coming.' From the onset of this specific sensation, there is a brief interval (2 to 3 seconds) during which the male feels the ejaculation coming and no longer can constrain, delay, or in any way control the process."

Ejaculation takes place, Masters and Johnson observe, "during the second stage of the ejaculatory process," when the semen is propelled from the urethra in the area of the prostate gland up the penis and out. During this second stage "the male subjectively progresses through two phases: First, a contractile sensation is stimulated by regularly recurring contractions of the [urethral sphincter muscles]. Second, a specific appreciation of fluid volume develops as the seminal plasma is expelled under pressure along the lengthened and distended [penis]."

Masters and Johnson observed female orgasm as well. They describe "a brief episode of physical release" but also note "a rare reaction" in some women they term "status orgasmus" characterized by either "a series of rapidly recurrent orgasmic experiences between which no recordable plateau-phase intervals can be demonstrated or by a single, long-continued orgasmic episode. . . . Status orgasmus may last from 20 to more than 60 seconds."

More recently, J. H. Bancroft defined orgasm as a complex mind-body process involving the interactions among multiple changes in genitals, muscles, heart, and respiratory systems, with accompanying physical sensations and alterations in consciousness.

A new school of thinking about sexual response argues that orgasm is mostly a mental phenomenon, an electrical brain discharge. Changes in the rest of the body are the result of the brain's activity. A small but growing body of brain-wave research supports this theory that orgasm originates in, and is defined primarily by a reaction in, the brain. The fact that orgasm in both sexes can occur during sleep, with no physical stimulation, supports this theory.

Considering how prominent the subject of orgasm is in the psychological and popular literature, it's surprising that there isn't more laboratory study devoted to the subject.

What all of these descriptions (and many more like them from other researchers and authors) have in common is the unspoken assumption that orgasm is fixed and unchanging, an immutable natural endowment. In fact, the scientific study of orgasm only began with Masters and Johnson, less than twenty-five years ago, and relatively little investigation by observation has been done since then. Despite some additional knowledge about physical reactions, the essential nature of orgasm still remains more mysterious than understood.

Since some might argue that orgasm is best left a mystery, what's the value of searching for understanding of the relationships among the component responses? The more we know about the specific functioning parts—how they look and feel—the more we can learn to control the individual component responses. We can do so by changing behavior (the things you do), thinking (your mental and emotional state), and the environment (what's around you). If a primary trigger mechanism shows up, either a physical or a mental trigger that sets off all the other responses, we may be able to influence the orgasmic process more directly and easily.

A new, important discovery about orgasm is that by focusing attention deliberately on the component elements of sexual response, such response can be intensified.

An extensive and rapidly growing body of scientific research in the field of biofeedback and relaxation training is demonstrating that individuals can influence many physical and mental processes that until just a few years ago were believed to be beyond voluntary control, except perhaps by masters of spiritual disciplines. It's now within most people's ability to learn to lower their blood pressure and heart rate, to alter breathing patterns, to increase or decrease muscular tension, to direct blood to specific areas such as the hands to warm them, to diminish the activity of the skin's tiny sweat glands, and to alter their brain-wave states by changing their process of thinking and attention. Acquiring abilities such as these usually results in achieving an emotional state that feels better and is more balanced. These self-regulation skills are among those that can trigger the body's natural relaxation response, which helps reduce the physical and emotional effects of stress and pain. They can usually be learned in eight to twelve weeks by any motivated person in an organized biofeedback or relaxation training program. At our center in Palo Alto, California, we have individually trained more than ten thousand people in measurable stress-control skills.

Although we all have the natural ability to switch on our relaxation response, the process usually isn't spontaneous. Most people need training and practice in order to master it.

Just as the relaxation response can be learned, so can the orgasmic response. Those who do not experience it can train themselves to do so. Those who wish to extend or intensify their orgasmic response can learn to do so. This may be surprising information to many people. We were skeptical about the discovery ourselves. Our laboratory and clinical experience, however, continues to confirm it. Other investigators are also beginning to identify and support these concepts.

PROBLEMS BETWEEN MEN AND WOMEN

The work of Masters and Johnson did focus attention on female orgasm, however. In the 1970s, that focus led to greatly increased discussion of the number of orgasms a woman could achieve and who is responsible for giving them to her. The issues of the decade for women were learning how to have orgasm and then how to have it more frequently. For men, the issue was learning how to delay ejaculation in order to facilitate their partners' response. The *duration* of both male and female orgasm—a measure with great potential for pleasure for men and women alike—continued to be neglected.

Delaying ejaculation is only one aspect of extending orgasm. The literature of sexual guidance is heavy with discussions of how to help a man delay his eight seconds of ejaculatory orgasm long enough to permit his partner to begin her ten seconds of orgasm. Most men can move readily from arousal to orgasm and ejaculation. This natural reflex permits our species to reproduce. Kinsey found that nearly 80 percent of the men he studied ejaculated less than two minutes after entering a partner's body. Morton Hunt found in 1974 in a follow-up study along Kinsey lines that the average duration of intercourse among Americans had increased to ten minutes. Men were learning to last longer in order to "give" their partners more time for orgasm. In his book *Beyond the Male Myth* the writer Anthony Pietropinto discovered that an amazing 80 percent of four thousand males interviewed judged their sexual satisfaction according to their success at "giving" their partners at least one and preferably more orgasms in intercourse.

Men learning to value their partners' pleasure along with their own is a wonderful idea, but the single-minded pursuit of female orgasm could well be exacting a price from men. Mutual pleasure and mutual pleasuring, both partners experiencing the maximum sensation they can allow themselves to feel, should be the real and freeing goal of lovemaking. Unfortunately, men appear to be the neglected sex in bed these days, blocking sensation in order to retard ejaculation, learning not to enlarge their pleasure but to narrow and contain it. Although emission-phase orgasm as an entity distinct from ejaculatory orgasm is an established fact of male sexual response, one researcher at a recent World Conference on Sexology declared bluntly that "most men don't have two orgasms. They experience a localized genital response, not the total body response which is female orgasm." If so—and our clinical practice certainly corroborates the researcher's observation—that's a sad loss of pleasure and of potential intimacy between men and women.

It's not necessary for a man to close off sensation to become aware of his body, to learn to control it and to increase pleasure. Men are just as capable of experiencing heightened, extended response as women. In the context of the Ecstasy Program they can enjoy that total body response without worrying about their partners' response because partners take turns stimulating each other, trading off roles as giver and receiver so that each in turn may be free to concentrate fully on him or herself. The result of that temporary trading off of roles, perhaps paradoxically, is increased intimacy. Most of that increased intimacy comes from better communication, but part of it comes from a welling up of gratitude and trust at the gift of pleasure one partner is giving another. If men are paying more attention to pleasuring their partners but women aren't returning the favor in kind, the likeliest outcome is that men are becoming disappointed, frustrated, and perhaps bored. Those are destructive emotions. They're also unnecessary.

One of the commonest sexual problems couples encounter in established relationships (ongoing for several years or more) is male difficulty in becoming aroused. Either erection occurs less reliably in the first place or it's more difficult to sustain. The man may have had no concern with arousal at the beginning of the relationship. It was still new, different, exciting, and adventurous. Man and woman were probably spending more total sexual time together. From the woman's point of view it seemed that all the man had to do to achieve hard erection was to look at her or stimulate her.

Now he has difficulty. The woman doesn't know why. She conjures up all sorts of reasons, blaming her partner or blaming herself. She worries about her attractiveness. She wonders if he really loves her. She thinks he's avoiding intimacy. She thinks he's working too hard or away from home too much and not spending enough time with the family.

The man, for his part, may feel that his hands are tied. He knows he can stimulate himself to erection, but he doesn't feel he's allowed to do so in front of his partner—even if she might have no objection. Men are conditioned to believe that their penises should operate automatically in all sexual situations. Women often believe that as well.

There aren't many situations in a man's experience where he does not feel free to use his hands to correct a problem. If a tire's flat, he can change it. If a report needs to be written, he can write it. If a child is about to fall down, he can catch it. But if his penis doesn't erect when he thinks it should, he doesn't believe he's allowed to stimulate it. And it often doesn't occur to his partner, who thinks his erection problem is a relationship problem, to volunteer to stimulate him or to suggest that he stimulate himself.

Even if the man asks his partner to stimulate his penis directly, this request may consciously or unconsciously represent to her a change in their relationship and worry her. The woman may resist this change, resenting giving more effort to lovemaking when the very problem he wants her to solve seems to be dramatic evidence of the relationship's decline. He wants her to stimulate his penis. She wants him to love her more. It seldom occurs to either partner that one path—the path of openness, good communication, and mutual pleasuring—might lead to the satisfaction of both wishes.

Such extremes of miscommunication—ships passing in the night in a sea full of icebergs—are all too common. They're especially tragic because they're based on a misunderstanding. The fact is, without deliberate effort at renewal, arousal declines as relationships mature and partners become more familiar. It's not a question of loving each other less. It's a question of psychological and biological noise drowning out the signals. That's why it's important—increasingly as a relationship matures—for couples to move toward allowing and encouraging the woman to take more equal sexual initiatives and the man to open himself up to accepting pleasure his partner actively provides.

ORGASMIC VARIETY

Women want more than brief intercourse. We frequently hear complaints from women clients that their men are preoccupied with intercourse to the exclusion of other forms of sexual pleasuring, content to end a sexual encounter as soon as they've ejaculated. Not having orgasm during intercourse is less likely to frustrate a woman than a partner's indifference to bringing her to orgasm by *some* means during lovemaking. She probably measures his caring not in orgasms but in the time, patience, and sensitivity he demonstrates to her needs and feelings.

A woman's orgasm can vary greatly in subjective intensity and perceived pleasure. Many different factors enter into that perception: time of day, energy level, her partner's attention and technique, how much time pressure she's under, and especially her mood. How she feels about herself and her partner can have substantial influence. If she feels close to her partner, loving, appreciative, and attractive, she'll usually allow herself to build to higher levels of arousal and orgasm.

If, on the other hand, they've recently argued or even if she's been emotionally injured recently in another close relationship—with a child, a relative, or a close friend—if her mood is negative or her self-esteem is low, she may still have an orgasm, but she's likely to perceive it subjectively to be less satisfying. Even if her partner spends a considerable amount of time stimulating her, she may resist building the muscular tension and vascular engorgement that prepare the way for greater pleasure. That's why, once again, openness, communication, and shared knowledge are crucial. All orgasms don't feel the same. You can't judge satisfaction in men or women according to how many orgasms they have.

Having said this much, we also want to say that we aren't simply proposing better *verbal* communication between partners as a solution to these and the many other tangled problems that develop in intimate relationships. Verbal communication is crucial, and the Ecstasy Program includes valuable exercises designed to improve it. But equally crucial is *physical* communication—increased touching and holding, increased sensual pleasuring, increased and more skillful sexual stimulation, stronger and if possible longer orgasms. You'll certainly spend a great deal more time kissing if you decide to follow the Ecstasy Program. You'll also spend more time making love and having orgasm in a more loving context where each of you feels rewarded with greater pleasure and intimacy for the time and energy devoted to the other's pleasure. We ask you to do more than talk. We ask you to learn to stimulate each other, to become more aware of the communication of messages via timing and pressure by learning more about your partner's wishes and body language. We hope you'll learn to take pleasure in yourselves as well, more extensively and intensively than you may ever have before in your lives.

ORGASM AND ECSTASY

Orgasm is one of the most intense, positive physical experiences possible. Ecstasy is the most intense psychological experience possible. The ultimate mind and body experience is the blending of orgasm and ecstasy.

The state of sexual ecstasy at the highest level is a sense of surrender and merging with your partner.

But ecstasy is not a state you can aim for directly. Paradoxically, the harder you try, the less likely you are to achieve it. Ultimately you must let go and allow it to happen. You can increase the probability, however, simply by knowing it exists as a real possibility. Sexual energy is a part of your fundamental life energy. Some people manifest that energy at very low levels. Virtually no one can experience all his/her potential; all who are motivated can experience more of their sexual possibilities.

Following the Ecstasy Program can help you to learn the art and skill of deliberately creating the conditions that can allow the safe release of more of your blocked sexual energy. Sexual energy is more than physical and emotional pleasure. Unlocking it increases vitality, enthusiasm, and creativity. Freeing sexual energy improves physical health and makes us feel and act more alive.

III
BETTER COMMUNICATION

Orgasm is learned. That revolutionary truth was implied years ago in the work of Alfred Kinsey. "It is doubtful," Kinsey wrote, "that any type of therapy has ever been as effective as early experience, premaritally, in reducing the incidence of unresponsiveness in marital coitus and in increasing the frequency of response to orgasm in coition."

Many men and women, however, and many professionals as well, continue to believe that inhibited sexual response is a sign of neurosis even in the absence of other symptoms. The fact that sexual response is learned rather than "natural" implies that education, rather than poor mental health, is more often at fault. For many years, for example, it was an item of faith among mental health professionals that women experienced two distinctly different kinds of orgasm, one induced by stimulating the clitoris, one induced by vaginal intercourse. "Clitoral" orgasm was considered superficial, inferior, and infantile—probably because it's usually induced by manual stimulation. "Vaginal" orgasm, by contrast, was considered profound, superior, and adult—probably because it's usually induced by penile stimulation.

Nothing shocked the professional mental health community more, and called forth more outrage, than Masters and Johnson's discovery by actual observation of numerous volunteer subjects that the two supposedly distinct female orgasms were in fact one. The pioneer St. Louis sex researchers laid the myth of distinct clitoral and vaginal orgasms to rest in *Human Sexual Response*, summarizing:

> There may be great variation in duration and intensity of orgasmic experience, varying from individual to individual and within the same woman from time to time. However, when

32

any woman experiences orgasmic response to effective sexual stimulation, the vagina and clitoris react in consistent physiological patterns. Thus, clitoral and vaginal orgasms are not separate biologic entities.

We suspect that most couples have not approached their full potential for mutually shared, intimate pleasure because of misinformation and lack of information. In our books and in the weekend training seminars we conduct for health professionals we have worked to change that picture.

Women in particular are still conditioned from childhood not to be sexually assertive even within socially sanctioned relationships. Both men and women are taught that men, not women, are authorities on sex. With no instruction, each man is somehow expected to understand each woman's unique sexuality as well as his own—which he is also supposed to have puzzled out without advice or instruction. This wonder of intergender understanding is expected to occur without direction from the woman herself—because if she's decent and respectable she's supposed to be sexually innocent and naive. Nor can the man comfortably ask his partner for information. She may not know what she wants him to do to stimulate her. And if he's "really a man" he's supposed to know already.

Within this closed, destructive system the woman can't tell her partner what would bring her pleasure. In the first place, she's expected to be too innocent to have found out herself. In the second place, telling him would ostensibly devastate his ego. Not surprisingly, many women subscribe to the romantic expectation that a man who really loves her will automatically know what she wants and how to give it to her. Unfortunately, many women themselves do not know what they want, let alone how to get it.

In one study, 78 percent of women who were classified as sexual romantics—who subscribed to an idealized, mystic vision of romantic love—were found to be low-orgasmic, whereas 70 percent of women who were classified as sexual realists—who valued conscious sexual cooperation—were high-orgasmic. These data suggest that conditioning, training, and communication make a dramatic difference in female orgasmic response. (Our own clinical experience convinces us that they make a dramatic difference in male orgasmic response as well.)

Some women are taught to be dependent and passive in their relationships with men. Women confined within such polarized relationships sometimes attempt to gain a measure of control by way of resistance, negatively. Negative control sends a clear message that even though the woman can't have what she wishes, no one can force her to do what she doesn't want to do. Rather than accept oppression, such women choose, consciously or unconsciously, to be or to become unresponsive sexually, depriving their partners—but also themselves—of pleasure.

Men in turn find themselves caught in a similar trap. Not knowing how their partners prefer to be stimulated, but feeling the responsibility of pretending to be expert, they go through the motions of foreplay and then quickly take their own orgasm in intercourse. Or they stimulate their partners to orgasm once or several times but seek and accept no stimulation other than intercourse themselves. Either way their experience of pleasure and of intimacy remains impoverished. Even when a woman tells her partner what she wants or explains what she doesn't like, she may do so in a way that irritates him and can block his acceptance of her guidance. The woman may interpret this interaction as neglect, thinking her man "isn't listening."

There's a way out of this vicious circle: learning openness, trust, and mutual pleasuring in a controlled, graduated program that makes both partners equals and respects both partners' needs.

The Ecstasy Program is designed to serve those ends. It's intended to provide a structure on which to learn to explore and improve intimacy. In the end, we hope you'll incorporate what you found valuable in the program into your day-to-day interactions. More sexual pleasure and the possibility of longer and deeper orgasm are the physical rewards the Ecstasy Program offers. But deeper intimacy and a strengthening of trust are the interpersonal goals it fosters. Though the program is highly structured, you'll find it's anything but mechanical. You'll laugh with it and cry with it. If you follow it faithfully, you'll emerge from it changed— and almost certainly happier.

INCREASING SEXUAL PLEASURE

Any committed, reasonably stable relationship can serve as the starting point for the mutual exploration of trust and of sexual pleasure.

There are two basic ways to increase pleasure. One is to increase the number of channels through which you experience pleasure. Many men, for example, focus all their attention on genital stimulation and have never explored or experienced the more diffuse and subtle satisfactions of stimulation directed at the rest of their bodies—scalp, back of neck, inside of elbows and hands, nipples, belly, buttocks, inside of thighs, back of knees, feet. The entire surface of the body is a sensing organ; with sufficient stimulation to sensitize and prepare it, the entire body can feel orgasm.

The other basic way to increase pleasure is to increase the intensity of the sensations you experience through the channels you already use. Focused, conscious attention on the maximally sensitive areas of the genitals can produce enhanced response. Prolonged stimulation of one partner by the other and the possibility of extended orgasm are perhaps the ultimate techniques for this approach to increasing pleasure. The Ecstasy Program trains you in both approaches.

SHARING SEXUAL INFORMATION

Rationale

If you've discussed with your partner the ideas we've presented so far in this chapter, you've already begun the process of opening up your relationship to new experiences and new pleasures. The questions that follow are designed to help further that process. Ensure a time and place of relative privacy, without distraction. You will need thirty to forty minutes. Turn off any TV and put down your newspaper or magazine. One partner asks the question and the other answers, taking less than two minutes for each question. Take turns asking and answering each question. Listen to your partner's answer and ask one or two related follow-up questions if you want more information. Don't discuss any answer for at least thirty minutes. Don't let your discussion deteriorate into argument. Listen with an open, accepting mind for the new information you'll be hearing about your partner's feelings, experiences, and wishes. It will help you get to know your partner better—even if you may have been together for years, you may find yourself revealing experiences and feelings you've never shared before.

The questions:

1. What did you learn about sex from your parents?
2. What do you *wish* you had learned about sex from your parents?

3. Describe what you remember of your first experience of sexual intercourse with your current partner. Include feelings, inhibitions, fears, and concerns as well as joy, pleasure, and humor.

4. Describe one or two of your better or more memorable sexual experiences with your current partner.

5. Describe one or two uncomfortable or embarrassing sexual experiences with your current partner.

6. Describe a fantasy of a perfect romantic evening with your partner. Be specific about the setting, the mood, how you're dressed, how your partner might approach you verbally and physically. Keeping in mind that this is a fantasy, not a request, tell him/her how you might like him/her to act.

7. Suggest safe times and places for your partner to talk to you about sexual concerns—before dinner, for example, after dinner, alone in the living room, watching TV, just before bedtime in your bedroom, after sex.

8. How can your partner make it easier for you to discuss your sexual concerns? By letting you know ahead of time when he/she would like such a discussion to take place? By making sure his/her statements are expressed calmly and neutrally rather than angrily or as accusations? Without manipulation, self-righteous justification, or blaming? By dealing more with the present and avoiding bringing up long stretches of the past?

9. Are there particular words that you object to or prefer to use when talking about sex with your partner? How do you prefer to refer to the following activities and anatomical parts: intercourse, fellatio, cunnilingus, orgasm, ejaculation, penis, vagina, intercourse, breasts? Some prefer more romantic language—"making love," "cleavage," "kissing your penis," "kissing your vagina," "coming," "love nest." Others prefer slang terms or relish the plain old "four-letter" words that some people consider offensive. Tell your partner which words you prefer to use. If you generally prefer anatomical or romantic terms, are there some times when you may prefer slang/earthy terms? If so, when?

10. Describe how you have sabotaged, or might sabotage in the future, your partner's discussion of sexual concerns—for example, by acting bored, impatient, or angry, by not paying attention, by responding with criticism, by being defensive or sarcastic.

Preferred Sexual Times

Write down your answers to the following questions:

1. How often do you currently have sex?
2. How often would you prefer to have sex?
3. When—days of the week, time of day, specific situation—do you usually have sex?
4. Is sex conditioned to particular circumstances such as "after the kids are asleep" or "Saturday night"?

Discuss your answers with your partner. Are they similar? If not, discuss your different viewpoints *without anger or judgment.*

Be as honest as you can in recording your ideal or preferred frequency and arrangements, even if you don't believe your partner will agree. It's important at least to communicate what you would prefer, even if you negotiate a different arrangement. Some couples already enjoy a higher frequency and may find that still more interactions suit them even better. A general pattern that seems to be a stable compromise for many couples is two or three brief sexual interactions spaced through the week in the morning or evening and one or two hour to hour-and-a-half interactions on weekends. Other couples may prefer fewer interactions and be perfectly satisfied. Older couples, particularly, may find that they both desire and require less frequent interaction. Even so, it's our experience that older couples who are so inclined can enjoy sexual interaction four, five, or even more times per week. There's no physical reason not to do so even for couples in their sixties, seventies, and beyond. Older couples often have the substantial advantage of more free time with fewer outside pressures.

IDENTIFYING PRIORITIES

Very few of us are aware of how we specifically allocate our time outside of our hours of work and sleep. If you decide to commit yourselves to the Ecstasy Program, you'll need to find time for its exercises. You can begin that process now, and continue your discussions with your partner, by making a few estimates and going over them together.

Following is a list of the ways that people commonly spend their time. Under "Current" make a rough estimate of the number of hours per week that you spend, on the average, at each activity. Under "Ideal" estimate the number of hours that you would ideally wish to spend at this activity. Remember that there are 168 hours in a week. Don't worry if your numbers don't add up precisely.

IDENTIFYING PRIORITIES

	Current	Ideal
Job, including travel time		
Eating		
Sleeping		
Child care		
Dressing and personal grooming		
Watching TV		
Housework		
Education/study		
Hobbies/sports		
Talking to your partner alone without distractions		
Shopping		
Talking on telephone		
Visiting friends		
Movies and entertainment		
Reading (newspapers, magazines, books)		
Listening to music		
Sexual interactions		
Other		
Total		

Do any of these numbers surprise you? Are you surprised at the amount of time you spend in sexual intimacy compared to other activities?

Show your list to your partner and discuss it.

SEX BY REQUEST

Rationale

The idea of never denying sex to their partners frightens some people. They use withholding sex as a weapon for self-defense and punishment and don't want to disarm. But using sex as a weapon creates enormous distrust and resentment in the victim. So the weapon eventually turns back emotional injury to the user. No one wins that war.

Sexual activity can't be separated entirely from the rest of life. Feelings that arise in day-to-day living find their way into sexual relations. Couples can develop more consistency and greater pleasure in their relationship by understanding these connections.

Withholding sex because of emotional conflicts such as anger and jealousy makes a relationship more insecure. Sex withheld unpredictably and inconsistently tends to promote distrust and resentment. It detracts from the quality of sexual interactions when they do occur. Agreeing to sex by request, in contrast, separates sexual negotiations from emotional negotiations and helps partners learn which is which.

Some people fear that always agreeing to a partner's request for sex might turn sexual demands into a weapon. It's important for each person to be sensitive to the other's preferences and not deliberately cause irritation or anger by the timing or manner of their request. This is especially important for the partner who has the higher sexual desire level. Do not, for instance, suggest sex when your partner is obviously pressed for time or engaged in activity that you know he/she will not want to interrupt.

Others fear that sex is somehow addictive. They fear that if they don't restrain their sexual impulses, their sexuality or their partners' may spiral out of control. If sexual withholding has been a part of your relationship, your partner is likely to ask to make love more often when your habitual sexual restraints are set aside. Partly that's a way of testing a newfound agreement. Partly it's a way of establishing a new pattern of lovemaking free of control. Partly it's a response to the novelty of the arrangement.

But sex isn't addictive. To the contrary, the problem for most sexually active couples—even couples skilled at ESO—is finding time for regular sex in the midst of all their other activities. Not one of the several thousands of people we have worked with has, to our knowledge, ever become "oversexed," unable to control his/her sexual impulses, as a result of following the Ecstasy Program.

Finally, some people fear saying yes because they don't enjoy sex. Once a week, once a month, is more than enough for them. Since sexual interaction is a learned skill, that's a vicious circle. You can't improve or even maintain what you have without practice. Neither can your partner.

Agreeing not to deny your partner sex builds trust by freeing each other of rejection. You accept your partner's sexual needs as your responsibility; your partner accepts yours. Women in particular learn the pleasure of asking for lovemaking when they want it. That's something many women don't trust their partners enough to do.

Men who believe they're sexual failures if they don't anticipate all their partners' needs find that mutual sexual responsibility frees them from that pressure. When they grow beyond feeling threatened, they discover that it's flattering to be asked.

Exercise: Sex by Request

An effective way to build trust in a relationship can be to make an agreement with your partner to say yes to any reasonable requests to have sex at a particular time. The requestor should allow the partner some flexibility to negotiate a modification in the time requested.

The agreement to do this exercise should be limited to a defined period of time—initially, one week. After the first week, when you've evaluated how this agreement works in your relationship, you can agree to extend the arrangement for an additional week or two.

Set ground rules in advance for any unacceptable timing requests that you anticipate your partner might make, e.g., "not after eleven P.M. or before dinner when our daughter is at home." If the request is inconvenient at the time that your partner makes it, you should offer an alternative time. "I'd like to finish what I'm doing right now," you can say, "but I'd love for us to have sex about an hour after dinner tonight." Or you might agree to a brief interaction. That can be a reasonable compromise if time is a problem. "I have a time concern. Would a ten-minute quickie be okay?"

This exercise is concerned more with changing the timing of your usual sexual pattern than with altering your frequency or basic style.

If you make an agreement not to withhold sex when requested according to these ground rules, keep that agreement. It's better to say no than to say yes and act no. Otherwise you'll be teaching your partner not to trust you in this area of your relationship.

If you have a significant discrepancy in your sexual frequency, and the difference has been a problem for you, we strongly advise you to avoid abusing the agreement. Simply agreeing to this exercise will not eliminate that difference. The exercise will work best if sexual requests don't significantly exceed your present frequency.

THE BUSINESS OF LOVE

Most couples don't realize that their relationships need regular maintenance. Men and women who agree without question that a house needs regular attention to its plumbing, that its exterior has to be repainted periodically, that cars need tuning, and that children need monitoring to stay alert and happy seldom deliberately set aside time to work on their relationships. In our experience, unexamined relationships inevitably deteriorate. There's no consistent mechanism for communicating the emotional changes that everyone experiences in the course of living and growing.

When we work with couples at our medical center, we often ask them to get together for what we call "business meetings" to discuss the nuts and bolts of their lives together—not only the bills and how to pay them but more personal issues as well. We ask them to think together and talk together about how their relationship is going and what they'd like to do to improve it. We do this partly to give them a format for solving problems and partly to encourage them to create a rational context for their emotional lives, just as they probably have created a rational context for their work lives and their personal financial lives.

At our center we assign the exercise of regular business meetings once a month, allowing one hour for the meeting. It should be in a calm, private setting where you will not be interrupted. Each of you prepares an agenda prior to the meeting, including problems and issues you want to discuss, and one of you volunteers to keep notes during the meeting. The notetaker can be the same person each time, or you can alternate.

The initiator can write down the topics that are relevant and any specific questions he/she may have about them. The other partner reviews the topics as well and asks the initiator to include any additional ones on the agenda. During the time between meetings, each partner can keep a separate list of proposed topics as ideas occur, or the designated initiator can keep one for both. Agenda items need to be defined in terms of identifiable and objective issues that are potentially resolvable or can lead to some practical plan of action. Here are some suggestions:

1. Children: issues of discipline, time spent with them, both parents being consistent, school problems
2. Household: chores, maintenance, shopping, meal preparation
3. Finances and spending: budget, possible purchases, unbalanced spending by one partner
4. Transportation and cars: maintenance
5. Social activities: upcoming events, time spent as a couple with others, time spent individually with others
6. Vacations, planning holidays, and romantic overnights
7. Number of sexual interactions: number and time agreed upon per week for the next month
8. Interpersonal relationships: individual problems with each other, differences, annoying personal habits or behaviors
9. Agreements: review and possible revision of those previously made

Agenda topics to be avoided are those that attack or judge the other or involve complaints about complicated or unresolvable matters—"I want to discuss your laziness," for example, or "This apartment is too small. I want our own house. Why can't you make more money?" These issues can be refined to remove the elements of attack or to break down the problem into smaller, definable parts. One item, for example, might be "Ways in which I would like more help with household chores." Another might be "Brainstorming for possible ways to increase our income so we can save for a house."

Concerns should be addressed honestly and reasonably. Any expression of emotion should be governed by the same unwritten rules that apply to a corporate business meeting. Those include addressing each other in a civil manner, avoiding name-calling, sarcasm, loud speech or threats, and maintaining a relatively neutral tone of voice. Both sides should present what they see as problems and what they view as alternatives. Then a decision should be made to select an option that you both can agree on. If it turns out that an option doesn't work, then the issue should go on the agenda for discussion at the next meeting to identify a new option.

No business could survive without business meetings among the principals. There are few things in life as important as your personal relationship with your partner. A structure in which to embed that relationship, a format with goals, is a far healthier way to sustain it than simply living it from day to day, blindly hoping it will stay happy or improve.

The evaluation questions in this chapter and the exercises that form part of the Ecstasy Program can help you explore your relationship during these "business meetings."

WHO MAKES DECISIONS?

Consider now which one of you decides on the activities that characterize your relationship. What percentage of joint activities does each of you decide? Which one of you takes responsibility for planning? Is the pattern of responsibility different now from the beginning of your relationship? In what ways has it changed? Who makes most of the decisions? Who decides on the frequency of sex?

On the following table, each of you estimate the percentage (100 percent, 75 percent, 50 percent, 25 percent, 0 percent?) that matches the approximate percentage of responsibility that you currently share in doing housework, household maintenance, family activities, social activities, setting the frequency and type of sexual activities, and determining the preponderance of budget and spending. Then estimate the percentage you would ideally prefer to have as your relative level of responsibility.

Now discuss your estimates of each of these categories. Please put particular emphasis on any categories that are not fifty-fifty and those where there's a difference between current and preferred percentages. See if you can reach agreement about changing your share of responsibility or your partner's share. Remember to use good communication techniques. Keep your communications relatively neutral in tone. Use "I" statements rather than "you" statements. Don't pass judgment on your partner. State clearly and calmly the changes you would like to make and the reasons for doing so. Consider putting this subject on the agenda for your next business meeting.

Who Decides or Does What?	Man		Woman	
	Current %	Preferred %	Current %	Preferred %
Housework				
weekly laundry				
weekly shopping				
weekly cleaning				
weekly cooking				
Household maintenance				
Outside maintenance				
Automobile maintenance				
Family activities				
Social activities				
Budget/bill paying				
Spending				
Frequency of sex				

JEALOUSY

Jealousy in long-term relationships is not usually the result of obvious threats such as the discovery of an affair. Rather, jealousy usually stems from a feeling of exclusion and insecurity. What are the mechanics?

In ongoing relationships where overt infidelity isn't involved, jealousy often results from seemingly minor, unspoken, nonverbal communications. Glancing at the opposite sex, for example, the timing of such glances, spending considerable time at a party with someone your partner considers an attractive rival, flirting either verbally or nonverbally, can all provoke jealousy. The jealous partner feels excluded from these interactions.

For example, a man glances at the rearview mirror after driving past an attractive woman. His partner in the passenger seat watches his eyes. His curiosity bothers her because looking at other women is something he does frequently. Even though he isn't communicating with the woman he's looking at, he's shifting his attention from his partner to her.

Such behavior tends to make one partner feel excluded. It's read as discourtesy, rudeness, and even insult, feelings that understandably lead to a loss of self-esteem and a lack of trust. Men sometimes experience this kind of jealousy as well.

If behavior that provokes jealousy occurs rarely—once a month or less for a few seconds when an unusually attractive man or woman is present—it's probably not a significant issue.

Men are often unaware of what such behavior means. If confronted they'll usually deny they've been rude. There's a natural curiosity to observe what's different and unique. We are all basically curious about how others would be with us and we with them.

Couples need to come to reasonable agreement and compromise about behavior that provokes jealousy. It's another area where good, productive talk can clear the air. In the instance we described above, the solution might be for the man to acknowledge his behavior and ask his partner to help him monitor it. "Susan," he might say, "I'm noticing my eyes wandering to a very attractive woman and I'm tempted to keep looking at her. I'm trying to be discreet and courteous, but I may have some difficulty. Would you be willing to tell me how I'm doing?"

MEN AND SEX

Some men, especially those whose personality is what psychologists call Type A, resist some of the exercises and techniques we offer in our Ecstasy Program. Type A personalities are impatient. They usually feel themselves to be constantly pressed for time. They're focused on trying to have more, now, quickly. The Ecstasy Program exercises require, on the other hand, that you deliberately slow things down, at least in the beginning.

Type A men are also often oriented toward early ejaculation. "It feels good," they tell themselves, "so let's get there as fast as we can." Statements that many men make, especially Type A's, are: (1) Don't waste time, (2) Time is money, (3) Work is the only activity that truly satisfies. These widely held beliefs will definitely impede extending orgasmic experience. For that matter, they may impede *any* intimate experience.

A frequent but misplaced male sexual belief is that the main purpose of sex for the male is to ejaculate. Many men truly believe that sex ends with ejaculation. Unfortunately, their partners may come to the same conclusion by default.

Women generally are oriented more than men toward the extended pleasures of romance, sexual foreplay, and passion, with orgasm as a pleasurable culmination. Women want more, rather than less, time spent with their partner. Thus, initially at least, women understand and assimilate the principles of the Ecstasy Program better than men do. Men, on the other hand, are often the ones who buy our book and bring it home in the first place, acting out a fantasy of improving sexual response beyond usual limits. Both attitudes have a place in the Ecstasy Program.

Training for increased orgasmic time and intensity gives the man many ways to delay and control his ejaculatory response, with the ultimate goal of extended pleasure for both himself and his partner. The techniques we teach for delaying and controlling ejaculation offer the Type A male a variety of constructive activities on which to focus his restlessness. A man working at arousal is paying attention to the ebb and flow of his feelings and sensations, noticing his breathing, counting exhalations, tightening or relaxing his sex muscles, and keeping aware of time. This complicated agenda usually gives even impatient men enough to do.

Men seem to worry more than women about "winning" at sex. Sometimes this competitive instinct has actually encouraged men to continue Ecstasy training when they might otherwise have given way to impatience. Ecstasy training can be highly challenging. At times you have to juggle many different physical and mental activities all at once. Type A men can find in the program the multiple challenges they need in order to feel satisfied with what they are doing. Because the Ecstasy Program is systematic—so much of this, so many of that—the analytical part of the mind finds satisfaction in keeping track. The cognitive restructuring (thought retraining) that goes along with the program will ultimately help the fast-track male to relax and enjoy the sensual experience—without blunting his mental alertness at the office, we might add.

Orgasm can become routine for men. When it does, some men shift their attention to their partners. Men who want to be known as great lovers tend to quantify their goals. They aren't happy with their performance unless their partners have multiple orgasms—so many groans of pleasure, so many hours in bed. Their own orgasm dwindles to an afterthought, a spasm at the end of a job well done.

In the Ecstasy Program we encourage such men to shift their attention part of the time from such outwardly directed goals, important though they can be, to receiving and taking more pleasure for themselves. Just as women in recent years have begun to demand greater equality in the work place and more say in their lives, perhaps it's time for men to expect more equal pleasure from intimacy.

The notion that women are able to experience greater sensual arousal than men is a myth. Pleasure is subjective, and a man enjoying the floating bliss of extended orgasm is experiencing no less ecstasy than a woman who is similarly aroused.

It's essential for men to set a higher priority on pleasure if they want to experience better orgasms. As much as women do, men have to learn to become comfortable with themselves and their own feelings in order to experience the truly overwhelming pleasures of sexuality.

A man whose ego is tied up with being the provider, the active partner, the decision-maker, may not have much attention left over for his own feelings and sensations. When orgasm first approaches after a minute or two or three or four, it's over all too quickly. To extend that momentarily pleasurable sensation across longer and longer stretches of time, a man has to focus on his feelings until he can diffuse them across his entire body (which the program trains him to do). In the process, he'll experience the subtleties of sexual arousal in himself as well as his partner, coordinate the process of breathing and muscle tension, and learn to pattern the various forms of sexual stimulation.

The secret of winning a man's interest in extending orgasm is to present it as a challenge. That's one reason why we've consistently quantified the exercises in the Ecstasy Program. These are the numerical, analytical aspects of doing any task that men respond to, because they're familiar from everyday life.

We've found, too, from years of therapeutic practice, that men aren't comfortable with vague, amorphous concepts. They like practical challenges to which they can commit themselves enthusiastically. Tense those muscles! Exhale now! Count! These are instructions men like to follow. If they do, they'll win more pleasure for themselves even as they give more to their partners.

HIDDEN SEXUAL ENERGY

Men and women accrue sexual tension. That sexual energy creates effects that may express themselves in a variety of nonsexual ways. When sexual tension builds up, it requires attention, nonsexual as well as sexual, for release. For men, sexual tension usually becomes apparent in relatively conscious physical ways and can often be released by ejaculation—with a partner or by self-stimulation, or even in nocturnal emission. Women, however, often do not experience the build-up of sexual tension on a conscious level and therefore do not seek its physiological release. They also tend to be more restricted by cultural taboos against self-stimulation and expectations that encourage sexual passivity. Women may experience sexual tension not as unexpressed sexual energy, but instead as frustration, irritation, anxiety, disappointment, depression, anger, or rage—almost any negative emotion. On occasion, these emotions may lead a woman to withdraw her attention from her partner. More frequently they seem to be expressed as emotional accusations, demands, complaints, criticisms, whining, nagging, and sometimes even physically destructive outbursts such as throwing objects or even hitting.

Men usually react to these discourteous behaviors by temporarily losing respect for their partners and withdrawing emotionally. This response is precisely opposite to what it ought to be. Solving the problem of negative sexual tension often requires that the man give his partner *nonsexual* attention. Loving and listening may reassure her and sufficiently relieve her tension to allow her to express her sexual energy more directly and effectively in physical, intimate interaction. When the woman's sexual tension level is too high, therefore, it's generally best to reduce it by giving her nonsexual attention first.

Men can do so by showing their partners sufficient interest to discover what they want at the moment. A man can tell his partner that he hears and understands her frustration and would like to know what he can do at that moment to assist and cooperate with her. Signs of physical affection (holding her hand, looking into her eyes) may show her he's caring, as long as she doesn't interpret these physical signs as a preliminary to sexual interaction. When her negative feelings subside, she may be more inclined to accept a sexual overture.

A man must carefully consider timing and pressure in these situations. If he pushes to have sex when his partner is upset, nagging, or angry, especially at him, he's likely to provoke her further. He needs first to reduce her negative feelings through loving attention before he can approach her sexually. This extremely important and fundamental strategy is one that many men apparently don't know or practice frequently enough.

ERRONEOUS SEXUAL BELIEFS

Following are some common but erroneous beliefs that may burden you and your partner. If they do, discussing them is a good way to talk about your sexual relationship.

Besides talking them over, you should observe your own behavior from day to day for evidence that you may be acting on such erroneous beliefs. Sometimes our behavior is hidden even from ourselves until we make a point of observing it.

Exercise: Examining Common Sexual Beliefs

Designate a five- or ten-minute period to discuss your attitudes toward the beliefs we describe below. Ensure relative privacy, and eliminate outside distractions. As with all communication exercises, conduct this discussion honestly, calmly, and courteously. Ask your partner if he/she has observed you acting out these beliefs from day to day.

1. *If my partner loves me, he/she will know instinctively what I want sexually.* Such an expectation implies we can read each other's minds, which we can't. Because sexual response is learned, and learned casually and personally rather than in school, each of us responds to a unique pattern of stimulation. The only way a partner can learn that unique pattern is to be shown and told.

2. *Sex should happen naturally and spontaneously.* Feelings are natural; ways of expressing them are learned. Sexual response is natural in a reflex-limited way; enlarging and extending sexual response is learned. An analogous bodily urge we aren't ashamed to train is hunger: we could survive and even thrive on a monotonous diet of plain, cold, tasteless, uncooked food, but we prefer flavor, warmth, variety, and subtlety. Eating becomes a pleasure we can enjoy ourselves and share with others. It's the same with sex.

Planning and agreeing to have sex at a particular time, making a date for sex, seems cold-blooded and mechanical to some people. But sexual behavior is learned. The learning occurs in much the same way as swimming or any other human activity. Some people can learn to swim, for example, without any instruction. Novice swimmers splash around inefficiently, but they manage to avoid drowning by doing what comes naturally. An Olympic swimmer swims more skillfully by devoting a great deal of attention to learning and practicing. Is swimming natural or learned? It's both. So is sexual behavior.

3. *All or nothing at all.* Many men and some women believe that kissing, cuddling, and caressing must inevitably lead to intercourse and orgasm. A corollary belief is that arousal without orgasm is invariably unhealthy. Another is that intercourse is the only "real" sexual experience; everything else is either foreplay or perversion. In fact, it's valuable to learn the pleasures of touching and caressing for their own sake, to expand the range of sensual response. For that matter, intense sexual response without any direct genital stimulation at all is possible and has been demonstrated. Orgasm can occur by stimulation of erogenous zones only, or without any physical stimulation at all, during sleep.

4. *Sex is for bedtime.* Sex may not be best at bedtime, though that's when most people have it. It's certainly more convenient to make love at bedtime, since you're undressing and getting into bed anyway. But pleasures aren't always pleasures when you're tired and stressed. Saving sex for bedtime implies that everything else you do in your life is more important and sex comes last. That's not necessarily a message you want to communicate to your partner.

5. *I owe her an orgasm.* According to this belief, men must work hard to "give" their partners orgasm. Such a grim, focused goal turns sex into work. The man assumes that orgasm is his to give and that he's unmasculine if he fails to deliver. The woman assumes that orgasm is required and that she's implicitly questioning his masculinity if she fails to deliver. Belief number five sets the stage for belief number six.

6. *I owe him an orgasm.* Some women and a few men fake orgasm. That puts them at a double disadvantage. Faking orgasm doesn't lead to orgasm. It also doesn't communicate to their partners their need to change from unsuccessful to successful techniques of stimulation.

APPRECIATIONS AND RESENTMENTS

Rationale

This exercise is one of the most important in the Ecstasy Program! Read it several times. Ask your partner's agreement to do the exercise and start doing it immediately, every day, even if you "don't have time," even if "it seems silly," even if you "can't think of anything to say."

Expressing yourself to your partner is not the same as communicating with your partner. Communication requires feedback—communication in return—or at least acknowledgment of receipt. Merely talking to your partner doesn't mean that he/she understands you or agrees with you or even that he/she heard what you said. When attention is focused elsewhere, a person simply may not be processing what you're saying. Even if the words are being processed, your intent might not be clearly understood. An essential first step in communication is determining if you have your partner's attention. That means that when you start a communication process, your partner needs to give an observable indication of listening early in the process. Similarly, your partner needs to acknowledge at the conclusion of the communication process that he/she heard and understands what you said.

To help you communicate more effectively, we offer here an exercise designed to foster good communication. *Appreciations* and *Resentments* are little thoughts and feelings that too often in a relationship remain unspoken, or are spoken in such a way that your partner filters them out. From doubt or hesitation or simply from preoccupation with other activities, we hold many feelings inside of us, frequently delaying expressing them past the time when doing so would be appropriate.

You may think in the morning, "Jane is certainly considerate, marshaling the kids off to school while I enjoy the morning paper." But you may not tell your partner how much you appreciate those few quiet minutes to yourself that she makes possible.

Or you may think, "I hate the way Don flirts at parties." But to avoid starting an argument, you may avoid telling your partner of the hurt you feel and what specific behavior initiated that feeling.

The Appreciations and Resentments Exercise is one of the most important exercises in this book. You have to like each other and be able to talk to each other if you're going to enjoy adequate lovemaking regularly and for the long term. Appreciations and Resentments is a safe way we've devised to allow you to share information that you would like your partner to know.

Some of that information will be uncomfortable to share and to hear. But if it exists in your partner's mind, it's part of reality, and it's better to know that reality. Unspoken, it will accumulate in a mental file labeled "Negative experiences of my partner," and when that file is loaded, some otherwise innocuous act will set it off. Then you'll find out about all the contents of the file, all at once, in a manner that's likely to be considerably more uncomfortable than if you'd learned of it in smaller segments as the feelings occurred. Generally speaking, what you don't know about your partner's feelings is more damaging to a relationship than what you do know. Knowledge, even of negative conditions, can at least be worked with and usually worked through.

Some of the information you'll be sharing—expressions of appreciation you may not have made before or often enough—will give pleasure. You don't have to wait until you start the Ecstasy Program to begin practicing Appreciations and Resentments. Whenever you begin communicating in this safe, structured way, your relationship is likely to improve.

No one tires of being appreciated. Everyone likes approval and honest compliments. Six months ago you may have told your partner how much you enjoy her sense of humor or how much you admire his strength, but all of us love to hear those things more often. In the beginning, when you were dating, you complimented one another a lot, didn't you? Appreciation warmly, honestly, and openly expressed, binds a relationship together, and we never really outgrow our need for it.

Resentments can be harder to express, but unexpressed, they fester. They accumulate into major arguments. They sabotage agreement and poison trust. They need to be communicated regularly and honestly so that your partner knows how you feel. No one can read your mind. You have to communicate in order to be understood. The Appreciations and Resentments Exercise encourages that communication by enforcing regularity and providing a context designed deliberately to be as neutral as possible.

In therapy we find that many couples resist practicing this exercise. It requires discipline and hard work. It may open what looks at first to be a can of worms. But if there are worms, they need to be looked at; otherwise, they'll grow and become even more unattractive and difficult to deal with later. Based on our extensive experience as counselors, we assure you that you will find it extremely difficult to improve your sexual relationship unless you improve communication across your entire relationship. You can expect such improvements if you practice Appreciations and Resentments. Doing this exercise exactly as described, without any deviation—*ever*—is like having a therapist on hand to help you full-time.

The Communication Exercise

The basic Communication Exercise goes like this:

Appreciation:
You say: "[Your partner's name], there's something I'd like to tell you."
Your partner responds: "Okay, I'm listening."
You state an appreciation.
Your partner responds: "Thank you."

Resentment:
You say: "[Your partner's name], there's something I'd like to tell you."
Your partner responds: "Okay, I'm listening."
You state a resentment.
Your partner responds: "Thank you."

An Appreciation must include:
Objective report—a brief, factual description about the matter or situation:

a. when it occurred;
b. what you observed and/or heard, i.e., your perceptions;
c. your positive feelings.

A Resentment must include:
Objective report—a short, specific, factual description about the matter or situation:

a. when it occurred;
b. what you observed and/or heard, i.e., your perceptions;
c. your negative feelings;
d. how you would have preferred your partner to have acted or how the situation might have been handled differently or better.

If you want to discuss any appreciations or resentments you must wait at least thirty minutes and then ask your partner for explicit agreement to do so. You may not circumvent this rule by expressing an appreciation or resentment on a subject or situation about which your partner has expressed one within the past twenty-four hours.

Face your partner. Make and keep eye contact. Avoid excessive body movements and facial expressions, such as rolling your eyes, sighing, grimacing, shaking your head.

Use "I" statements about your feelings rather than "you" statements. Avoid using the words "always" and "never." Make only statements: don't ask questions. Be specific and brief.

Use a neutral tone of voice. Avoid detectable emotions such as anger, judgment, or sarcasm. Feelings should be conveyed only by the words themselves.

Beltline rule: Some issues are intrinsically unresolvable or destructive to verbalize. If you discover such an issue, agree to avoid bringing it up.

Follow this format and these rules exactly, with no deviations.

Subject matter should start, preferably, with current concerns: things that happened today, yesterday, or within the last week. You may, however, bring up matters from any time in the past (unless they fall under the "beltline rule" you have both agreed to). Or you may choose to mention a general pattern you've observed in your partner. It's preferable, but not essential, that a particular resentment have some connection with, or relationship to, the preceding appreciation.

Here's an example of a complete round of Appreciations and Resentments.

You might begin by mentioning small things:
You say: "Susan, there's something I'd like to tell you."
"Okay, I'm listening."
"When we were watching TV last night, you were playful and a little silly. You were fun, and I love it when you show that positive, emotional side."
"Thank you."

That's an appreciation. Follow it with a resentment:
"Susan, there's something I'd like to tell you."
"Okay, I'm listening."
"This evening I was late and forgot to stop at the grocery store. You attacked me with accusations of never listening to you, being lazy, selfish,

and acting like my father. You raised your voice and you brought up three or four situations from the past that had nothing to do with getting the groceries. The more I tried to reason with you, the angrier you became. When negative emotion controls you, I close off and nothing gets accomplished. I felt you were being unfair, emotional and illogical. What I'd like you to be willing to do in the future when you're feeling upset is to tell me in a more logical way and stick to the subject."

"Thank you."

More general problems can be good subjects for Appreciations and Resentments:

"Tom, there's something I'd like to tell you."

"Okay, I'm listening."

"Yesterday we went to your parents' house for the holiday. I like your parents and enjoy being with them and with you."

"Thank you."

"Tom, there's something I'd like to tell you."

"Okay, I'm listening."

"When we spent the entire holiday with your family, I felt my family was left out. They've told me more than once that they'd like us to spend more holiday time with them. I felt disappointed and annoyed with you for not arranging more fairly to distribute the holidays between our families. I'd like you to be willing to alternate or split those days more equally in the future. I'd like to discuss this problem at our business meeting next week."

"Thank you."

Resentments may include things you've observed, things you've heard, feelings you've felt, things you would prefer had happened differently. Be sure to state your Appreciations and Resentments in a *neutral*, not an emotional, angry, nagging, or sarcastic tone of voice. Express your emotions in words, not in nuances. That way your partner will hear the *content* of your message clearly and won't be distracted by the tone.

An important guideline for the Resentments part of the exercise is to use "I" statements when you're describing your feelings, rather than "you" statements. Stick to talking about a behavior you didn't like, rather than condemning your partner's entire personality. Rather than stating, "You're a stupid idiot," say, "When you sped through that stop light, I was shocked at your poor judgment." Avoid the words "always" and "never." An example of a Resentment pattern to avoid is: "You *never* put the top back on the toothpaste tube." Such statements will immediately put your partner on the defensive and will probably start an argument. He may rebut you with times he has capped the tube and attack you back with some irritating habit of your own.

Try to maintain continuous eye contact during the Appreciations and Resentments Exercise. Face each other. Avoid nonverbal signals. Don't roll your eyes, sigh, shake your head, or grimace. Body language conveys meaning as certainly as tone of voice does.

The "beltline rule" applies during Appreciations and Resentments: Don't hit below the belt. Some issues are inherently not resolvable and are therefore destructive to verbalize. For example: "I resented having to give up my education so that you could attend law school." "I've never felt the same about you since I found out about your affair with X." However you feel about such resentments, if you have agreed despite your feelings to do the Appreciations and Resentments Exercise, then you should avoid bringing them up in that context. If your relationship is to be healthy, such questions will someday have to be resolved. A structured exercise isn't the time, though the increased trust and intimacy this form of communication engenders may make it possible to confront them at a later time.

You may, however, bring up issues that allow some possibility of improvement and do not carry with them purely destructive connotations:

"Bob, there's something I'd like to tell you."

"Okay, I'm listening."

"The party tonight was certainly lively. That new couple we met might be fun to see again. I was glad you encouraged us to go."

"Thank you."

"Bob, there's something I'd like to tell you."

"Okay, I'm listening."

"At the party you were talking to that cute blonde on the patio for a long time. When I came over, you seemed to ignore me and continued talking to her without including me. In the future in a situation like that I'd like to have you put your arm around me or take my hand, introduce me, and include me in the conversation."

"Thank you."

On another subject:

"Dave, there's something I'd like to tell you."

"Okay, I'm listening."

"The new audiovisual system is complex and impressive. I appreciate your effort and thought in putting it together."

"Thank you."

"Dave, there's something I'd like to tell you."

"Okay, I'm listening."

"The new system is so complicated that I get confused trying to run it. Sometimes I wish we just had a plain old stereo. I'd really appreciate your slowly going over the system another time or two with me and writing down simple instructions until I understand it."

"Thank you."

Spontaneous Appreciations and Resentments can make things go more smoothly immediately. For example:

"Gail, there's something I'd like to tell you."

"Okay, I'm listening."

"I value and respect the work you do to keep up the house and take care of the kids when you have a job. Sometimes I wonder how you manage to do it all."

"Thank you."

"Gail, there's something I'd like to tell you."

"Okay, I'm listening."

"Your tone of voice just now when you asked me to clear the dishes felt critical and impatient, so I put off doing it. I realize you may feel overburdened this evening. If you'd ask me nicely, I'd respond with more enthusiasm."

"Thank you."

The point of Appreciations and Resentments is safe communication. It's safe because you've agreed in advance to listen and to acknowledge but not to argue. It also builds trust. We've seen too many couples communicate only their resentments. They hardly ever compliment each other.

Choose a neutral time to practice the Appreciations and Resentments Exercise. Schedule a specific time of day and stick to it. Working couples often discover that after dinner is a comfortable time for them to practice Appreciations and Resentments. But any time of day that's mutually acceptable will do. We suggest you schedule at least two complete rounds a day, every day. They'll take about five minutes each for a total of ten minutes per day, seventy minutes per week.

Appreciations and Resentments often brings up important and powerful subject matter that merits further discussion. To preserve the emotional safety and trust that go along with communicating in this structured way and to allow the exercise to become a "safety valve" for the stresses your relationship inevitably experiences, you and your partner must agree to delay that further discussion. If you wish to discuss a particular appreciation or resentment, please agree: (1) to wait at least thirty minutes, (2) to ask your partner's permission, and (3) to respect absolutely your partner's right to refuse to discuss at that moment what they've told you. At least thirty minutes later, if you wish, you can ask again.

Appreciations and Resentments is not only a powerful tool for communication between partners, it's also valuable to each of you personally, because it encourages you to acknowledge and formulate feelings you may only partly have realized you feel. People often have trouble talking about their feelings. They tend to be vague. Appreciations and Resentments can help you to be more specific about your needs and desires, which helps you understand yourself as well as communicate with your partner. After a few weeks you'll discover how powerful this exercise is.

You're likely to encounter resistance to doing Appreciations and Resentments. "This is ridiculous," your partner will say to you. "I don't know why we have to go through this charade. We communicate fine." Or you'll find yourself thinking, "I don't have any resentments today." Such resistance is common.

People claim, for example, that they have nothing to say. But even people who have known each other for only a few minutes can usually find qualities they like or don't like about each other. Couples who have been together months and years have a vast stockpile of appreciations and resentments available—thousands of past experiences to draw from, plus all of the new feelings that come up each and every day.

Similarly, some people resist doing the Communication Exercise by claiming they already communicate well with their partners. But Appreciations and Resentments is different from even exceptionally open informal communication because the former is structured. It compels candor even as it holds anger and estrangement temporarily at bay. So there's great value in doing it, even for partners who already communicate well. Even if doing the Appreciations and Resentments Exercise seems embarrassing and valueless at first, please practice it for at least four weeks before you pass judgment. We are convinced that the resulting openness and the new information you acquire about your partner will surprise you.

Ideally, you and your partner should takes turns initiating this exercise so that each of you gets used to being both giver and receiver. One of you—often the woman—will tend to be more enthusiastic about it. To counterbalance that tendency, take turns initiating it. Women sometimes feel that men don't communicate well enough with them and care enough about improving their relationship. If this is the case, a woman will probably appreciate the Communication Exercise even more if her partner initiates it. We encourage you to experiment with a full month of Appreciations and Resentments, initiated the majority of the time by the man, and watch what happens.

The Dumping Exercise

This exercise can help reduce or eliminate arguments. All of us periodically need to unload, to "get things off our chest" to a sympathetic, nonjudgmental ear. Often, however, the person we unload our feelings on responds by trying to help by explaining, defending, or rationalizing the situation or the people we're complaining about. Or the partner receiving the dump may take the contents personally and counterattack, escalating the situation to an argument. The receiving partner, in other words, gets trapped in the experience rather than simply listening. The Dumping Exercise avoids these problems. It prepares partners ahead of time and protects them from feeling ambushed.

Unlike the Communication Exercise above, strong emotion is permitted in the Dumping Exercise, no positive counterbalance is necessary, and no solution or preferences for action or change need be stated.

The Exercise

When you want to complain, get angry, whine, receive sympathy, talk like an undeserving victim, express fear, or simply describe an individual situation that is troubling you, without expecting feedback or help, consider "dumping" on your partner according to the following guidelines:

1. Dumper asks the partner: "May I dump on you?"
2. Dumpee responds: "No, not now. Perhaps in an hour." (Partner must give an alternate time.) Or, "Okay, I'm listening."
3. Dumper "unloads" whatever is bothering him/her, emoting, swear-

ing, shouting as much as he/she wishes. Suggested time limit is five minutes.

4. Dumpee listens attentively—making eye contact, nodding, shaking his/her head, communicating sympathy and understanding.

5. When the dumper is finished, the dumpee says, "Thank you." There is *no* further discussion about the content of the "dump" unless the dumpee asks, "Is it okay to talk about your dump?" If the response is "no," the dumpee must honor that preference unless and until the dumper agrees to discuss the dump at a later time.

IV
THE BASICS

Before we present the Ecstasy Program structure, we'd like to prepare you with some basic information you should know and put into practice as you proceed through the weekly exercises. As with Chapter III, the information here can serve as a starting point for talking more specifically about your sexual preferences. Discuss it together.

ANATOMY

Knowing your partner's sexual anatomy and your own is especially important for extended orgasm, since we'll be asking you to teach each other effective stimulation. For instance, men may not be familiar with the area on their own bodies we call the "external prostate spot"; women may not know about their "inner trigger" area.

Female Anatomy

The major labia normally rest closed over the other parts of the female genitals, protecting them. *Labia* means "lips." That's more or less what they look like under their protective padding of pubic hair. When a woman becomes sexually excited, her major labia (outer lips) become engorged with blood, expand, and flatten against her groin. This causes her genitals to become more open and exposes their sensitive inner structures.

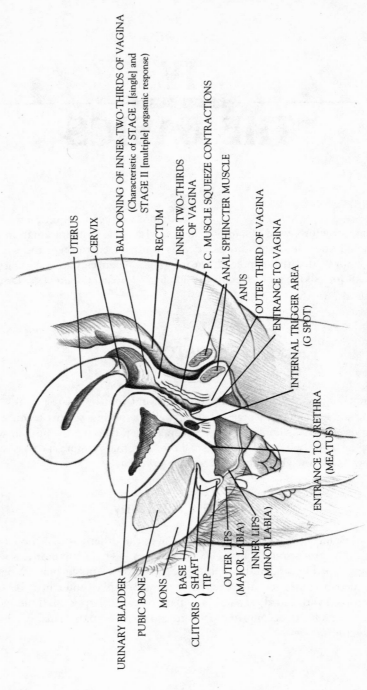

UTERUS

CERVIX

BALLOONING OF INNER TWO-THIRDS OF VAGINA
(Characteristic of STAGE I [single] and
STAGE II [multiple] orgasmic response)

RECTUM

INNER TWO-THIRDS
OF VAGINA

P.C. MUSCLE SQUEEZE CONTRACTIONS

ANAL SPHINCTER MUSCLE

ANUS

OUTER THIRD OF VAGINA

ENTRANCE TO VAGINA

INTERNAL TRIGGER AREA
(G SPOT)

ENTRANCE TO URETHRA
(MEATUS)

INNER LIPS
(MINOR LABIA)

OUTER LIPS
(MAJOR LABIA)

CLITORIS { BASE
SHAFT
TIP

MONS

PUBIC BONE

URINARY BLADDER

FEMALE ANATOMY

The minor labia (inner lips) also normally rest closed. With sexual excitement they lengthen, thicken, and swell with blood until they sometimes protrude well past the outer lips. When a woman approaches orgasm, the inner lips change color, depending on skin color and whether she has had children, to bright red or even to a deep wine.

The clitoris, with its hood, its glans, consisting of shaft and tip, appears at the upper junction of the inner lips. When a woman is sexually stimulated, the glans clitoris engorges with blood and enlarges at least enough to smooth out the wrinkles in its covering of skin, much like a miniature penis. In a minority of women the glans may enlarge to double its normal size. However little or much it swells, its changes follow along with the changes in the length and thickness of the inner lips. As a woman reaches high levels of sexual arousal and approaches orgasm, the entire exposed body (glans) of the clitoris—shaft and tip—retracts inward and down toward the vagina until the glans is entirely hidden under the clitoral hood. If arousal then decreases, the clitoris reappears. If arousal increases again, the clitoris retracts again. The clitoris has a root, buried beneath the surface, which is often responsive to stimulation by pressure from outside or from inside the vagina.

Downward from the clitoris and within the shelter of the inner and outer lips is the small opening of the urethra. The urethra is the tube that leads outward from the bladder and carries away urine.

Downward from the urethral opening is the opening of the vagina. The vagina serves for sexual intercourse and for birth. Normally the barrel of the vagina is collapsed upon itself so that its walls are touching all along its length. A woman's first physical response to sexual stimulation is vaginal lubrication. The walls of the vagina produce lubricating fluid—finely filtered blood plasma—by a process similar to sweating.

With continuing arousal the vagina opens and lengthens. It produces more lubrication. The uterus—the womb—elevates inside the body, making a tentlike space above the bottom of the vaginal barrel. At the same time, the outer third of the vaginal barrel becomes engorged with blood and actually closes down smaller than its previous opening, which allows it to hold and to feel a penis of any size, from very small to very large.

With the beginning of orgasm the outer third of the vagina pulses in rhythmic contraction. This pulsing is the work of a sling of muscle, the pubococcygeus (*pyub*-oh-cock-sih-*gee*-us), that attaches to the pubic bone in front and the coccyx, or tailbone, in back. This muscle, the "P.C.," surrounds the opening of the urethra and the vagina. It's an important muscle to get to know. We'll discuss training it for increased strength and control during the Ecstasy Program.

An important and little-appreciated feature of female anatomy is an area in the vagina that in many women can help function as an orgasmic trigger. It's not usually sensitive or even detectable except at high levels of sexual excitement. Some sexually experimental couples have known for years of an inner trigger, but it was first mentioned in the professional literature some thirty years ago by a gynecologist, Dr. Ernest Grafenberg. And only in the past several years have sexual investigators and therapists appreciated the important role this area can serve in the orgasmic process.

It's variously called "the twelve o'clock spot," the "Grafenberg spot," the "G spot," or the "inner trigger." It's an area of tissue in the upper front wall of the vagina, varying in size from shirt button to coat button, just behind the pubic bone, which is the bone you can feel above and toward the front of the vagina. The G-spot trigger area is located on the vaginal wall about one and a half to two inches in depth at the twelve o'clock position. Sometimes it's more toward the eleven or one o'clock position.

It normally can't be easily felt. The best time to locate it is immediately after a woman has had orgasm. It's then already somewhat enlarged and sensitive. It often feels like little ridges or tiny bumps. If a partner presses the G-spot trigger area with one or two fingers and strokes it at a rate of about once a second, a woman mentally open to the experience may become more sexually aroused. Experiment with alternating lighter and firmer pressure. Be guided by your partner's response.

The next best time to locate the inner trigger is when a woman is near orgasm. If her partner continues clitoral stimulation manually or orally, she may crest over into orgasm when he identifies and strokes the inner trigger.

Pressure on the inner trigger may feel uncomfortable at first. It may produce an urge to urinate. That's not a sign that a partner should stop stimulating the area. He should simply lighten his stroke. After a minute or so of continued pressure and stroking, discomfort—most commonly, the fear of urination—usually gives way to pleasure.

With continued stroking, the inner trigger increases in size, hardens —much as the clitoris and penis do—and is then easier to locate.

What exactly is this inner trigger area? There are several theories. Its sensitivity may be due to nerves from the clitoris that pass through it on their way to the spinal cord. It may be an area surrounding the female urethra which contains a vestigial prostate gland. Gynecologists and pathologists agree that the area does contain some paraurethral ducts that are similar to the male prostate, and as we will discuss later, stimulating the male prostate may help to trigger a deeper and more intense orgasm in some men.

Some women, including those who are unable to locate an inner trigger area in their vaginas, frequently discover other areas within the vagina that are especially sensitive. There are two arousing pressure points that some women and their partners report along the back wall of the vagina, about midway back at the four o'clock and eight o'clock positions (if the clitoris is taken as twelve o'clock). These points are best stimulated with inserted forefinger and middle finger spread apart and with firm rhythmic, probing pressure. Sensitivity may occur at other positions as well. Both partners should seek together to identify an inner trigger area or areas during the Sexual Exploration Exercise that is part of Week Six of the Ecstasy Program.

A significant minority of women report feeling no special sensitivity in the G-spot area, regardless of stimulation. A majority of women, however, do enjoy inner-trigger-area stimulation when they have already arrived at a high state of arousal.

A few women report an uncomfortable sensitivity in the G-spot area all of the time, just as some males report an uncomfortable sensitivity to scrotum, testicle, or external prostate stimulation.

One of our ESO readers wrote to us concerned that she experienced a strong urge to urinate after extensive inner trigger stimulation. That's a frequent early consequence of such stimulation. An urge to urinate is usually a sign that the right area is being stimulated. Before arousal becomes intense, inner trigger stimulation can mislead the bladder into reacting as if it's full. With continued stimulation, this response usually fades, overshadowed by pleasure.

Another ESO reader reports that she enjoys her husband's inner trigger stimulation, but experiences frequent urinary urges for twenty-four hours afterward. This response sounds more like honeymoon cystitis, which occurs in young women who are not accustomed to prolonged vaginal stimulation and which resolves itself with experience. If a woman repeatedly experiences discomfort that continues for a day or more after inner trigger stimulation, she may have developed a urinary tract infection, which may be treated with antibiotics by her doctor. If the condition recurs, it may be necessary to discontinue inner trigger stimulation. We've seen such reinfection only rarely, however.

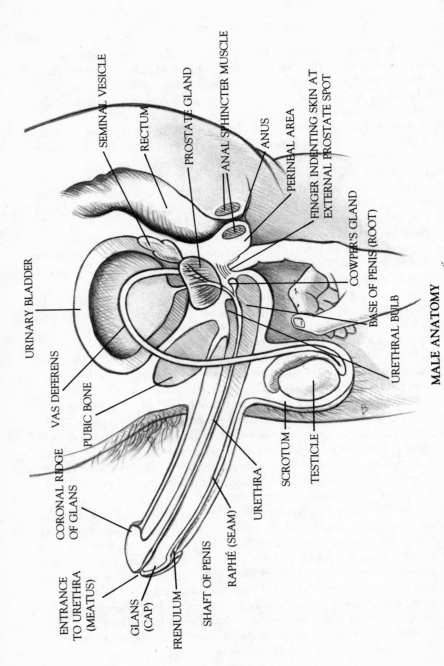

MALE ANATOMY

SEMINAL VESICLE
RECTUM
PROSTATE GLAND
ANAL SPHINCTER MUSCLE
ANUS
PERINEAL AREA
FINGER INDENTING SKIN AT EXTERNAL PROSTATE SPOT
COWPER'S GLAND
BASE OF PENIS (ROOT)
URETHRAL BULB

URINARY BLADDER
VAS DEFERENS
PUBIC BONE

SCROTUM
TESTICLE

CORONAL RIDGE OF GLANS
ENTRANCE TO URETHRA (MEATUS)
GLANS (CAP)
FRENULUM
SHAFT OF PENIS
RAPHÉ (SEAM)
URETHRA

66

Male Anatomy

The male penis in its unaroused state is a short, soft tube of spongy tissue that provides a channel for emptying the bladder of urine. The male urethra runs along the length of the underside of the penis. The penis itself is not a muscle and contains no muscles, nor any bones. Two to three inches of it is rooted inside the body in the pubococcygeus musculature. The suspensory ligament attaches these muscles, which surround the penis base, to the pubic bone. Specific exercises assigned throughout the Ecstasy Program can strengthen that musculature and help make erections harder and more pleasurable.

In men who haven't been circumcised, the head of the penis—the glans—is covered by a loose tube of skin called the prepuce or foreskin. Circumcised males have had their foreskins surgically removed, leaving their glans permanently exposed.

The question continues to be debated, but has not been resolved, whether circumcision diminishes the sexual sensitivity of the glans penis. The uncircumcised have no greater incidence of irritation, local infection, or genital cancer, nor does the presence of the foreskin appear to influence the incidence of uterine cancer in their partners. As a result, parents are deciding more frequently not to circumcise their sons.

The penis erects with sexual stimulation. Valves close down in veins that would normally return to the body the blood carried by the penis and its arteries. The organ increases in length and thickness as its spongy tissue fills with blood.

With increasing arousal the glans swells to several times its unaroused state and sometimes darkens in color. Erection occurs in newborn baby boys as well as in men ninety years old. It occurs a number of times every night during sleep in every healthy male. Erection is a man's first physical response to sexual stimulation, as vaginal lubrication is a woman's. At ejaculation, semen spurts with an average of three to twelve contractions from the urethral opening in the penis, sometimes in a dribble, at other times with enough force to propel itself outward several inches, or even a foot or more. Younger men generally ejaculate with more propulsive force than older men. Higher and longer-sustained levels of sexual arousal frequently result in more forceful ejaculation than brief encounters do.

Aroused or unaroused, different penises vary in thickness and length. The size differences are largely hereditary. They don't necessarily correlate with body size. A large man may have a small penis; a small man may have a large penis. Penises do tend to withdraw into the body with lack of sexual use, as some sexually inactive older men have discovered.

Some men experienced in ESO have reported measuring some apparent permanent increase in the length of their penises. These reports are quite surprising, since sexual researchers generally agree that permanent penis enlargement isn't possible. One controlled study at a large medical clinic in England, however, in 1975, reported permanent increases in length and girth using specific exercises. Of the approximately 1,600 self-report questionaires returned by weekend seminar participants, ESO readers, and clients at our center, 110 men practiced in ESO reported measuring apparent persistent increases in penis length of from a quarter of an inch up to an inch.

We offer this information certainly not as proven fact but as an interesting possibility. How could such increases occur? The penis is rooted within the body; two to four inches of its length lie behind the pubic bone, attached to it by a suspensory ligament. It could be speculated that repetitive, forceful pressures over a period of months might gradually stretch this ligament, loosening it, and freeing the extra length, allowing the penis to move forward. The reverse is recognized in older males, where a lack of stimulation may gradually result in retraction of the penis inward, resulting in apparent diminishment in size. The Ecstasy Program, particularly the Learning to Extend Orgasmic Response Exercises with the man in receiving position, involves frequent, prolonged, and maximum erection, pulling forward of the shaft and head of the penis, and pressure forward at the base of the penis inside the body, by his partner, over a period of months. Further stimulation comes from the exercises we'll be recommending to strengthen the sex muscles and muscles at the penile base. Such types of stimulation could possibly encourage the penis to extend a short distance farther outside the body.

A man can track changes in penile length during program training by measuring his erect penis along the top, at a 90 degree angle from pubic bone to tip. If penis size is of interest to you or to your partner, this possibility of increase could be a fringe benefit of following the Ecstasy Program and practicing the techniques regularly over a period of months.

In our experience, most men overemphasize the value of a large penis. The great majority of women count many other qualities in a man much more important than the size of his penis. And couples who regularly experience ESO, in particular, enjoy such high levels of sexual satisfaction and such correspondingly high levels of sexual self-confidence that any concern they may once have had about penis size becomes minimal.

Below and behind the penis is the scrotum. The scrotum is a sac of skin that contains the testicles, the two walnut-sized glands where sperm are nurtured. The scrotum, and the two cords that support the testicles, raise and lower the testicles against and away from the body to regulate their temperature. Sperm die if they're kept at body temperature for very long, which is why the wives of men who wear tight undershorts sometimes have difficulty getting pregnant.

With sexual arousal a man's testicles swell. Along with the thickened, engorged scrotum, they draw up against the body as he approaches orgasm. Men under fifty usually don't ejaculate until their testicles are fully drawn up against their bodies. Men over fifty may not experience full elevation of both testicles. Some men with low-hanging testicles find that although their scrotum lifts, it never actually pulls the testicles against the body.

Behind the scrotum and toward the anus, but inside the body, is a gland known as the prostate. It surrounds the male urethra directly in front of the urinary bladder. It supplies the majority of the clear fluid that bathes the swimming sperm that the testicles produce and that is expelled from the body at ejaculation.

The prostate in the male, like the inner trigger areas in the female, is often highly sensitive to stimulation, especially when there is already excitement with erection. A man's sexual arousal can often be increased simply by massaging his prostate with a finger inserted through the anus into the rectum! The prostate can also be stimulated less directly—but more easily and comfortably—by applying pressure to the area between the back of the scrotum and the anus, in the valley of skin known as the perineum (pear-ih-*nee*-um). We call this important pressure point the "external prostate spot." Not every man finds this stimulation arousing at first. The closer a man is to orgasm, the more likely he is to find prostate stimulation pleasurable. Some men may not enjoy this stimulation at any time. One caution: if a man knows he has a prostate infection, or if there is continued pain when pressure is applied, he should consult a physician.

There is some medical evidence that men who go through life with a low frequency of orgasm and ejaculation are more likely to suffer from prostate enlargement and prostatic cancer than men who are sexually more active.

A man in an advanced state of sexual arousal will often produce a drop or two of clear fluid from the urethra prior to ejaculation. This preseminal fluid heralds the approach of the emission stage of orgasm.

SIMILARITIES

Male and female sexual anatomy look dramatically different, and they are—one is almost the reverse of the other—but in terms of how the genitals develop, they're very much alike. The male and female genitals evolve from the same tissues in the developing fetus.

The male scrotum and the female major labia (outer lips) develop from the same fetal tissue. The shaft of the penis and the shaft of the clitoris correspond. So, most importantly, do the glans penis and the glans clitoris. Remember these similarities when you stimulate your partner. They'll help you understand where your partner is sensitive and how that sensitivity feels.

The similarity between the glans penis and the glans clitoris partly explains why many women don't have orgasm during intercourse. When a man's penis is thrusting in a woman's vagina, he's directly stimulating *his* most sensitive organ but only indirectly stimulating hers. Only about one woman in three is regularly orgasmic with intercourse. That's another reason why the Ecstasy Program involves direct clitoral stimulation initially.

Just as male and female genitals correspond anatomically, so also do male and female sexual response patterns correspond. The sequence of response begins with sensitivity and engorgement in the front of the genitals and moves progressively to the middle area of the genitals and then to the posterior area.

In the man, the front part of the genitals that becomes responsive initially includes the glans penis or cap, the most sensitive part of which is the frenulum on the underside, and the penile shaft and base. In the woman, the front area includes the clitoris hood, the clitoris body, and buried root.

As stimulation and arousal progress, the man's middle genital area becomes more engorged and sensitive. This area consists of the base of the penis inside the body, the scrotal sac, and the testicles. In the woman, it consists of the outer and inner vaginal lips—the labia majora and minora. The deeper genital structures in this middle zone include, for the man, the area behind the scrotum and in front of the anus—the perineum, which includes the external prostate spot. The middle zone for the woman includes the inner trigger areas of the vagina.

If stimulation and arousal continue to still higher levels, the posterior area of the genital structures becomes engorged and sensitive to stimulation as well. For both men and women, surface structures in this area include the anus and surrounding areas of the anal musculature; inner structures include the rectum for men and women both and, for the man, the prostate.

It's important that both partners know about this sequence of engorgement, from front to middle to rear. Stimulating a middle or posterior area too soon during sexual arousal may make your partner uncomfortable. It may require five to ten minutes of stimulation at each step of the way to condition the next area for arousal, beginning with the front and moving toward the rear.

Some men and women are interested in experiencing anal stimulation but may be uncomfortable with initiating or allowing it. They may be reluctant because of hygienic or religious concerns, or they may have experienced premature or excessively vigorous stimulation in the past. Middle and posterior areas are best stimulated when the front genital areas are aroused and fully engorged. For men this means having a full erection. For women it means having full inner and outer lips with an enlarged, sensitized clitoris. It also means being psychologically receptive. Make sure the anal area is well washed before stimulating it.

One more comment about anatomy: each of us is different, from our unique fingerprints and the unique sizes and responses of our genitals to our unique patterns of orgasm. "There is nothing more characteristic of the sexual response," Alfred Kinsey concluded after interviewing thousands of men and women, "than the fact that it is not the same in any two individuals." That's because the body's central organ of sexual response is the brain.

A small minority of women can have orgasm with breast stimulation alone; most cannot. Some men and women experience a red, rashlike flush on their upper bodies with orgasm; others do not. Some men stop thrusting at the onset of ejaculatory orgasm; others continue thrusting through ejaculation. There are patterns common to all, and there is much of sensation and pleasure that can be learned. It's worth remembering always that your partner is first of all an individual, is first of all a human being, and is more like you than different—in experiencing problems as well as pleasures.

PHYSICAL EXERCISE

The Ecstasy Program is energetic, but it isn't strenuous. You don't have to be an athlete to advance through it and to do it well. On the other hand, better physical conditioning will improve your ability to give your partner pleasure and to take pleasure yourself.

We suggest that both men and women, in addition to the exercise built into the program, follow a regular schedule of at least moderate overall physical conditioning for general physical well-being and maintenance. Depending upon your age, your present condition, and your general health, such a program may include walking, jogging, bicycling, jumping rope, aerobics, martial arts, group or individual calisthenics, or swimming.

If physical exercise is to be of significant value, it's best done regularly—at least three times a week, fifteen or more minutes at a time if your health permits. But exercise sessions don't have to be that long. Even five or ten minutes of moderate calisthenics or exercise against resistance can make a large difference in your physical stamina and sense of well-being within a month or two.

A study by James White of the University of California at San Diego compared middle-aged men who followed a prescribed exercise program three hours a week for nine months with a group of similar men who didn't exercise. The exercise group had significantly more sexual drive, arousal, and orgasms.

Note that upper-body exercises, particularly arm exercises that work the biceps and triceps, can give a man more endurance for prolonged manual stimulation of his partner's clitoris and vagina. So, too, a woman in better physical condition will find it easier and more comfortable to stimulate her partner at length and vigorously.

You don't have to become a bodybuilder. You don't have to pump iron. But you'll feel better and have more pleasure sexually if you practice regular moderate physical conditioning.

SPACE AND SOUNDS

Lovemaking is best when both partners are naked. That means the room you choose for lovemaking should be warm. If turning up the furnace isn't possible, consider using a space heater. Unless you live alone, the room where you make love should have a door, and the door should have a privacy lock. If it doesn't, have one installed. Interruptions don't enhance lovemaking.

Most people make love on a bed. You may want to provide a special sheet to protect your sleeping sheets from the lubricants you'll use and from your own fluids. You don't have to change the sheets. Just put the special sheet on top. Making love on the floor, on pillows can be an arousing variation. Create a nest, a comfortable place. Be deliberate about it.

For mood as well as for privacy, you'll probably want a source of pleasant sound in the early stages of lovemaking. Uninterrupted music is best. Consider using an automatic-reverse tapedeck or the automatic replay control on a compact-disc player. A radio will serve. Some people like to leave on their TV. That's less satisfactory because picture and sound can distract you from giving your partner your undivided attention.

Sex is mainly a silent process. Sexual talk can sometimes be arousing. Conversation often tends to diminish arousal. The time to talk is before and after.

Extended orgasm is a partial exception. It's possible then to talk briefly without stopping orgasm. When a person is experiencing extended orgasm, there's such a deep impression of feeling and sensation that it's possible to divert for a brief conversation while orgasmic contractions continue. The spiritual joy of verbally sharing your ecstasy usually more than compensates for any possible leveling of orgasmic climbing.

PLEASURE SOUNDS

While we discourage much verbalizing during lovemaking, we strongly encourage nonverbal sounds to communicate your levels of arousal and pleasure directly to your partner. To make such communication possible, you need to discover what sounds you produce spontaneously during arousal. If you're silent throughout sex, that's a type of sexual resistance. Making no sexual sounds during lovemaking is a learned control that limits pleasure. If you're thinking about not making noise, you're not completely letting go. Extended orgasm involves learning to let go completely, learning to abandon yourself to sensation. One way past such resistance is to imagine and create sounds that you would like to make.

Start by practicing deliberately at times when you're not making love. Practice alone; practice together for the fun of it while you're massaging your partner's back, hands, neck, head, and feet. You may feel self-conscious about moaning and groaning deliberately in front of your partner. Blush and giggle if you want to. Practice and familiarity will take that self-consciousness away.

Practice in the shower or bathtub. Respond to the warm water caressing you. Release any sounds that you feel. If you're not sure what you feel, experiment with different sounds anyway for the fun of it.

We suggest that you select a pleasure sound such as *ahhhh* or *ummmm*. Experiment with other sounds as well to find one that's most comfortable. Make the sound as you breathe out and relax, letting go and opening up your sex muscles when your partner is stimulating you (your partner giving, you receiving) or during self-stimulation. Then breathe in without a sound and contract (clench) your sex muscles. Alternate these two responses. You can use your special pleasure sound as well to indicate to your partner that you're climbing toward arousal, that you've reached a wonderful level of arousal where you're happy to stay or that you're experiencing an extra burst of pleasure.

Sounds allow your partner to know what's happening. Volume has a lot to do with it. The louder your partner's sounds are, the more pleasure your partner is experiencing.

Sounds you make contribute to your partner's arousal. He/she will love to hear you express your passion vocally. An important bonus is that the process of making your pleasure sound is likely to stimulate you sexually as well.

One of the benefits of this process—of contracting the sex muscles as you breathe in, then making a pleasure sound and relaxing the sex muscles as you exhale—is that it gives the mind a constructive, pleasurable focus. An additional benefit is that by deliberately breathing, by alternating sex-muscle contraction with relaxation, and by communicating your level of arousal to your partner and to yourself, you gain further skill at learning to control your level of sexual arousal and orgasm. Later, when you learn the Sex Muscle and Breathing Exercise (Week I, page 141), you may find it useful sometimes to add your pleasure sounds when you are practicing it.

Sound has vibration that your body experiences pleasurably. Partly for that reason, we advise that you have music playing early in your sexual encounter to help set the mood. But once foreplay is advanced, your own sounds, without music, will usually add more to mutual excitement.

Sounds that flow from sexual pleasure communicate internal sensations. You may find it better if you both create your own sounds as you move further into arousal.

HYGIENE AND BATHING

Our experience confirms that almost nothing inhibits good sex more than poor hygiene. You've read in other guidebooks that the smells of the beloved are wonderful—and if they're fresh, they probably are. But most Americans are conditioned to thorough cleanliness, especially for oral sex. One way to assure each other that you're clean is to bathe or shower together. If it's impossible to bathe or shower, at least wash your genitals thoroughly.

Men in particular need to pay attention to hygiene. It's one of the most common relationship problems women complain of. Don't be lazy about it. A heavy five o'clock shadow and locker-room armpits and/or crotch are *not* romantic, however manly they may seem. Poor hygiene, like all acts of omission and commission in a relationship, conveys a message: that you don't value your partner enough to respect her sensibilities by preparing yourself for lovemaking.

By bathing together, you turn what could be an interruption into a sensual pleasure of its own. Wash each other's genitals: that helps you to know them. Dry each other afterward and enjoy that pleasure, too. Among other primates, such behavior is called "grooming"; it's one of the most effective behaviors our species has evolved for forming intimate bonds.

We recommend that women douche with warm water to which one or two tablespoons of vinegar have been added (rather than with douching preparations) once a month after menstruation, as a routine hygiene. Some women will feel more comfortable using a warm water and vinegar douche after intercourse, so that semen doesn't drip onto clothing, as it otherwise does even the morning after. We suggest consulting your gynecologist on this matter. If you have a persistent problem with odor or discharge, you should rely on your gynecologist's advice.

Be playful. Showering and bathing together is romantic and fun!

WARM UP—DELIBERATELY

Be deliberate about light levels, candles, incense if you like incense, and any other special arrangements you enjoy—erotic media such as videotapes, for example. One of you should be in charge of preparing a checklist of the things you need. These preparations can be made a part of the ritual, a way that couples can share together. Discuss and agree on the kind of music you both want to listen to. One reason that many people like music during lovemaking is that it provides a background of ever-changing rhythms and intensities to guide body movements. Another is that it serves as a vehicle to focus attention away from distracting nonsexual thoughts.

If deliberate preparation for lovemaking seems foolish, think about the last party you gave. You sent invitations, cleaned house, bought food and drink. You probably showered beforehand and dressed in clothes you don't wear every day. You adjusted lights, put your favorite music on the stereo, set out your better glasses and china and tableware. Your guests arrived. No one mentioned the special preparations other than to compliment you on them. You forgot about them to have fun. You do the same thing when you create a special setting for lovemaking.

Both of you may want to dress for the occasion. Women customarily pay more attention to how they look than men do, who aren't above preparing for love by dumping their underwear on the floor. There's nothing immutable about male indifference to dress. Once men master the sexy illogic of dressing to undress, they even find the idea fun. The way a nice robe or even the bottoms of a pair of silk pajamas drape on a man can make him look provocative. For women a robe, a silk teddy, or a slinky negligee is a familiar and attractive addition.

Dancing together can be a relaxing way to set the stage for lovemaking. Learning to dance is similar to learning the skills taught in our Ecstasy Program. With dancing as with training for extending orgasm, you feel awkward at first. Later you glide effortlessly through the exercises, and the conscious effort disappears. Once you've learned the steps, in dancing as well as in ecstasy, you spontaneously flow together as a couple. Both take practice.

The coordinated movement of your bodies when you dance is helpful preparation for lovemaking, where it's also crucial for you to know where you fit into your partner's body, especially during intercourse. Even in manual and oral stimulation, you don't want an elbow knocking you on the head or a knee jabbing you in the ribs. There's an art to moving bodies in coordination comfortably. Dancing can prepare you for it. We aren't suggesting that you have to become a great dancer to become a great lover. We know from clinical experience that many couples who dance passionately aren't necessarily skillful in bed—and vice versa. We only emphasize that there's a correspondence between dancing and love-making. If dancing helps you set the mood, include a few minutes of it in your preparations.

Kissing is an excellent way to connect with your partner. We'll be assigning specific kissing exercises during the Ecstasy Program, but you can kiss informally during foreplay as well.

Exercise: Loving Eyes

Silent eye contact can help you connect and allow yourself to become more open and vulnerable. Sitting or lying down, facing each other, look intently at one of your partner's eyes. Resist any tendency to talk, giggle, or touch. Allow yourself to be comfortable and relaxed with yourself and your partner. Think peaceful, positive thoughts. Imagine being absorbed by your partner's eyes. Do this for five minutes. At first it's sometimes difficult. It may become very erotic.

Exercise: Dancing Hands

Dancing hands is another useful exercise. Select music that's romantic, slow, and sensual. Sitting facing one another, with "Loving Eyes" (as in the last exercise), hold your hands at chest level with palms toward your partner while your partner does the same. Your palms should almost—but not quite—touch your partner's. One of you leads by moving your hands up, down, sideways, and around at varying speed. The other follows intuitively. After about two minutes, leader becomes follower for two minutes. Continue to alternate silently until you feel connected.

LIGHTING

Light levels can be a problem if partners disagree. Low, warm light is better than darkness for the Ecstasy Program. Observing each other passionately naked is erotic. And whoever is pleasuring needs to see what he or she is doing. The giving partner needs to see the receiving partner's movements and his/her physical responses to touch and stimulation. Seeing the labia swell a little more, noticing the mouth open slightly, the scrotum rise, or the neck arch informs the giver that his/her stimulation is creating continuing arousal. Words, sounds, and touch, of course, provide equally important channels of information feedback. The eyes of the pleasured partner won't always be open, but the eyes of the partner giving pleasure probably will be.

If either of you prefers total darkness during lovemaking, you should both discuss why. Often the reason is self-consciousness about your body. Talk it out. Your partner may not feel the same way you do. If you want to work toward adding light comfortably to your lovemaking, you can. Start with a single candle or a low-wattage light and add additional lighting in later weeks, a little at a time, as you become more comfortable.

EROTIC VIDEOS

Many couples have discovered that erotic videos can help them get in the mood for lovemaking. Women as well as men have found the selective use of erotic videos additive to their experience. Selectiveness is important. Men are usually less particular about the content of the erotic videos they watch. Women are more sensitive to the subject matter of videos, especially those that appear to show women being exploited and treated as objects. Sometimes women feel embarrassed watching other women expose their genitals because they've been taught such exposure isn't proper.

In recent years an increasing number of videos have been created by women or with women viewers in mind. Identifying and locating such videos may help reduce a woman's resistance to viewing erotic media. Consult the "Sources" in the Appendix for product information.

Many women in any case don't feel comfortable viewing erotic videos with their partners. If they watch erotic videos alone and privately, they may in fact find them arousing. But sometimes they resent their partner's reactions. The problem is similar to the problem of jealousy we discussed in Chapter III. Some women worry that their men need to look at other women to turn on, that a man is more attracted to the images of women in the videos than to the living woman at his side.

Help your partner feel safe and comfortable with videos if you find them useful to build arousal. Be sure that you have her agreement to watch them. Allow her to choose them and perhaps even to pick them up at the store. If she objects, let her know that erotic images sometimes help you focus more on sexual thoughts and forget your everyday concerns and worries. Reassure her that you don't need to look at other people making love to become aroused, but that you find videos an efficient way to direct your attention away from analyzing and problem-solving to lovemaking. Women open to new experiences and willing to learn may find that erotic videos can serve the same function for them.

It can also be helpful to experiment with turning the sound off. Sometimes women are offended by the sounds. Instead of watching, a woman may choose to allow her partner to watch the video while she focuses her visual and mental attention on stimulating him with her back to the television.

LUBRICANTS

You should arrange ahead of time any equipment or supplies you want in the room you've chosen for lovemaking—perhaps towels, bathrobes, a carafe of juice or a favorite beverage.

One supply you'll need is a good lubricant. You'll need a lubricant for extending orgasm because you'll be stroking delicate tissues for long periods of time. Natural lubrication, even from women who lubricate extensively during sex, isn't adequate. Neither is saliva. How much a woman lubricates is not necessarily an indication of her level of arousal, her degree of enjoyment, or her orgasmic capacity.

Many couples resist using lubrication. Some believe they have enough natural lubrication. "My partner gets very wet when we make love," some men tell us. "I never have a problem with lubricating," some women say. We explain to our clients who resist using lubricants that we're not suggesting they have a problem, only that lubricants are an enhancement to sexual pleasure—just as a sweater keeps you warm, but it's more fun to wear a cashmere sweater than one of ordinary wool. The penis and the clitoris don't self-lubricate, we explain. That's one reason oral stimulation is so desirable. It supplies lubrication to the clitoris or the penis. Sometimes our clients will insist for many sessions on excluding lubrication. When they finally agree to try using a lubricant, if only to rule it out, most of the time they adopt it enthusiastically as part of their sexual interaction.

These are the ideal qualities of a good lubricant:

1. It's long-lasting. It doesn't dry out quickly. It lasts for at least fifteen minutes of stimulation without replenishment.
2. It remains smooth and slippery for the entire time of use. It doesn't become sticky.
3. It tastes pleasant or at least neutral.
4. It's compatible with condoms, diaphragms, and other latex products if such products are used.

Lubricants that are entirely water-soluble and water-based are compatible with latex. Products containing mineral oil or petrolatum are not fully compatible. Check content descriptions to determine.

If you are currently using a lubricant, rate your lubricant on the above criteria. If you don't use rubber products, then you don't need to apply criterion number 4.

Some of the advantages of using a sexual lubricant are:

1. It enhances pleasure by removing pain associated with dryness and friction.
2. It enhances sensation during manual stimulation of the clitoris and the penis. Even when a woman lubricates quickly and easily, her lubrication is produced exclusively in the vaginal area and may be insufficient to lubricate the clitoral area as well. It needs to be transferred from the vagina to the clitoris. Adding a lubricant ensures that the clitoris receives maximum stimulation without abrasive dryness. Since a man lubricates an insignificant amount at best, it's very helpful to add lubrication during self-stimulation and manual stimulation by his partner.
3. When a woman's lubrication is insufficient, develops slowly, or dries during arousal, an effective lubricant ensures achieving and

maintaining maximum stimulation. It protects the delicate tissues of the labia and can reduce the possibility of urethritis or bladder infections.

4. It eliminates performance anxiety. By adding lubrication a woman need not worry whether she will produce sufficient lubrication.

5. For women who find intercourse painful, who suffer from dyspareuria or vaginitis—problems caused by anxiety or fear of pain in the genital area—adding lubrication is vital.

6. For postmenopausal women, whose decreased estrogen production often results in vaginal dryness, adding lubrication is also vital.

7. Saliva is a good natural lubricant, but it's effective only during oral stimulation. Unlike artificial lubricants, it dries quickly. It's not suitable for prolonged manual stimulation or intercourse.

For couples and individuals who use latex products for birth control or for protection from disease, a non-oil-based lubricant is essential. (For a full discussion of disease protection, see Chapter VII on safer sex.) Unfortunately, most over-the-counter lubricants are far from ideal. KY Jelly, Vaseline Intensive Care Lotion, and other such products dry quickly without nearly continuous replenishment and may become sticky. Several good products are available by mail order, including Astroglide and Creme de Femme. (Consult the Sources section in the Appendix for addresses.)

Couples who don't use latex products have more choices. The ideal lubricant is oil-based rather than water-based. We've found two commercial lubricants that serve well for the longer stimulation times of the Ecstasy Program. One is petrolatum, also known as petroleum jelly. The best known brand of petrolatum is Vaseline. It's a long-lasting lubricant, but it may be difficult to wash off and many people find it too greasy. Some gynecologists advise that it may be unhealthy for the vaginal environment if it remains in the vagina for days at a time. It isn't our first choice.

Unscented Albolene Liquefying Cleanser, a makeup remover, is, in our opinion, the best lubricant for most sexual activities. It feels smoother and more natural than petrolatum. Our experience with many thousands of clients confirms that Albolene seems to be the most sensuous, long-lasting lubricant available. It isn't widely distributed, but if you can find it locally or order it, it's likely to be worth the effort. In contact with the skin, Albolene melts to the consistency of natural sexual lubrication and is longer-lasting. It's also completely tasteless, for those times when you proceed from manual to oral stimulation. Even people who at first resist using a lubricant find that the experience of using Albolene usually changes their doubts into appreciation.

If Albolene isn't available, one practical solution is to make your own lubricant. Use the following basic recipe:

> 2 tablespoons melted petrolatum
> 4 tablespoons melted paraffin
> 1¼ cups mineral oil

Heat to boiling an inch of water in a large saucepan. Set petrolatum in its store container in the boiling water to melt. Measure 2 tablespoons of it into a small saucepan. Melt chunks of paraffin in a second small saucepan or a bowl set in the boiling water and measure 4 tablespoons of it into the saucepan that contains the measured petrolatum. Set the saucepan with the paraffin/petrolatum mixture into the boiling water and add the mineral oil. Stir to mix thoroughly. While liquid, pour mixture into decorative container with a lid. Allow to cool. Makes about 1½ cups.

You can scent and flavor this lubricant—or petrolatum or Albolene, for that matter—by adding flavoring oils while it's still liquid. Almond, coconut, lemon, banana, and vanilla are possible flavorings. Be sure the flavoring you use is an oil, not an extract. Extracts are made with alcohol and won't mix. Two or three drops of flavoring oil are enough. Adding oil of cloves produces a slight warming effect that some people enjoy.

If you dislike lubricants but want to extend sexual pleasure, it will help if you work your way through your aversion. Sex is basically slippery and wet—the body deals naturally in the short term with the problem artificial lubricants solve in the longer term—and it's not ever going to be dry. Your aversion can be alleviated by progressing through small, step-by-step changes.

Start with a lightweight lubricant such as baby oil. Rub it only on your hands. Or ask your partner to rub it only on your hands or on some neutral part of your body such as your arm or your knee. It may take several sessions to become comfortable with that application. When you are, over a period of weeks gradually apply the lubricant closer to your genitals until you're comfortable applying it genitally.

Then gradually increase the viscosity and amount of the lubricant— from baby oil to a cream, from a cream to Albolene—until you're adjusted to using lubricant.

If at any time along the way you feel too uncomfortable, go back one step until a sense of comfort returns. Desensitizing yourself to a lubricant phobia may take several weeks or more. Along the way, talk to your partner about how you feel and practice relaxation.

Adding to the desensitization process, deliberately experience lubricants in a nonsexual setting. Apply lotion to your body after bathing, for example, and pay attention to the pleasant sensations. Give your partner back rubs with a lubricant and allow your partner to do the same for you.

Your partner can take responsibility for sexual lubrication. If your partner applies it to your genitals for you, so that you don't have to touch it, you may feel more comfortable using it in lovemaking.

Using lubrication serves another useful purpose: it clearly communicates that you want to make love, that sex is going to happen and there's pleasure in store. Many men and women are deliberately tentative about approaching each other sexually. They brush shoulders or touch an arm to test the waters. If their partners don't respond, they can then pretend they weren't asking (and go away with their feelings secretly hurt). But when you take out the lubricant, you're stating very clearly what you have in mind. You can't be ignored. If no sex follows, at least you'll both have to face the question of why. Applying lubricant at the beginning of a sexual encounter is often enough to melt any resistance your partner may feel to having sex.

DETAILS

A few small but important details deserve mentioning. One is fingernails. For the Ecstasy Program, a man's nails need to be trimmed very short and with the corners rounded. Unless a man's nails are short, he can cause his partner discomfort. Women may keep their nails long if they only stimulate their partner's prostate externally, in which case they can use the knuckle of a bent index or middle finger to apply local pressure to the external prostate spot.

Some people find that alcohol enhances mood and promotes relaxation. Use it, if you both agree, in moderation. Alcohol in whatever form—wine, beer, whiskey, liqueurs—is an anesthetic, like ether or chloroform. It also causes depression and emotional instability. A man who drinks too much may have serious trouble achieving and maintaining an erection. Stay below the legal driving level. On the average, more than two glasses of wine or beer or two cocktails during any three-hour period before or during lovemaking could begin to have undesirable effects. Don't delude yourself about alcohol. You'd be surprised how many people do. If alcohol use is or has been a problem for you, avoid it.

Marijuana can be problematic as well. It alters the perception of time. For some users, time seems to pass more slowly than usual and pleasurable feelings may seem prolonged. Marijuana also helps some people focus their attention on feelings rather than thoughts.

On the other hand, frequent—daily—marijuana use has been proven in authoritative scientific studies to lower androgens, which are the main hormones determining the level of sex drive—libido—in both men and women. Low androgens in men not only diminish interest in sex; they also adversely affect erection and ejaculation. Daily marijuana use appears to produce as much lung damage as a daily pack of cigarettes. Some users experience episodes of anxiety and paranoia. And marijuana is illegal.

You will have to decide if any benefits of using marijuana outweigh the serious disadvantages. If you decide for marijuana, don't use it every time you make love. *Extended orgasm produces a natural high that is far better than any drug-induced high.* A prolonged state of orgasm stimulates your production of sex hormones. There's also evidence that orgasm increases the pleasurable levels of your body's own natural narcotic, endorphin. Stronger or longer orgasm probably produces greater amounts of these desirable natural products.

V
IN THE MOOD FOR LOVE

The Ecstasy Program presents a carefully structured system of exercises designed to increase your sexual experience. You'll be scheduling those exercises in advance, at the beginning of each of the twelve weeks of the program. Some program exercises involve interacting with your partner sexually.

If sex is scheduled, what happens to romance? You need to learn to create it deliberately, then to forget you did so and let yourself enjoy it.

ROMANCE

Romance is the triumph of self over circumstances, making magic in life. Men usually undervalue it except in the early stages of a relationship, when they want to gain a woman's trust and affection to create intimacy. They've been taught to ignore romance and get the job done. In recent years, though, as women have become more assertive, some men have also begun to wish for more romance.

Romance is setting and mood. It's positive attention to each other rather than to outside matters. It's positive feelings and talk rather than negative. It's taking a positive inventory of your partner—discovering, rediscovering, and enjoying your partner's attractive qualities and setting aside for the moment any criticism. Taking a positive inventory means carrying on an internal dialogue, actively reminding yourself of the many qualities you love and appreciate in your partner.

Romance is compliments, looking at each other with appreciation, listening, touching, hugging, holding hands. It's a formal way into intimacy, an arrangement of symbols and cues. For a period of time you are acting in a selfless rather than selfish manner.

Romance is also—and this may be the reason so many men distrust it—a tacit request, usually a woman's tacit request, for reassurance. "Before I allow you to enter my body, I would like to know that you value me. I would like you to tell me so. I would like you to show me by giving me your attention, even by praising me and declaring your love, if only for this moment. You will lose yourself in pleasure with the gift of my body and my mouth and my hands; is reassurance too much to ask?"

If you think romance is a waste of time, think again. Paying attention to romance will win your romantic partner's warm attention in return. Isn't that what you want?

Creating romance is a social skill. People who are good at it weren't born that way. They learned. So can you.

Romance is important to the Ecstasy Program. You're acquiring new skills, but they aren't merely mechanical. They're an enlarging of your experience of intimacy with your partner. They depend on trust and caring. You don't send your genitals alone into the bedroom. All of you is there. All of you must be considered and all of your partner. So communication, setting, and mood are important when you're following the Ecstasy Program, just as they are at other intimate times. Without them, one or both of you will be distracted or feel used. Neither state is conducive to pleasure.

The way to find out what your partner considers romantic is to ask. The way to let your partner know is to speak up.

We give our clients that advice and they mention mind reading. "He [or she] should already know." In fact, the conditions that encourage someone to feel warm and sexy are as individually specified as most other human preferences. A fire may seem romantic to one person and boring to another. Tastes in music vary across an enormous range.

If neither of you is quite sure what you find romantic, think back to when you were dating. People in the early stages of courtship usually pay more attention to romance. Did you take walks together? Hold hands? Talk—share experiences, make each other laugh? Compliment each other more than you do now? Discuss restoring some of these pleasures to your lives.

Longing for romance—for close, loving attention—and sexual frustration can be mixed up together, especially in women. When women are sexually frustrated and miss the positive romantic attention they feel they need, they can become withdrawn, depressed, or angry. In a word, irritable. This reaction, which is often unconscious, may lead them to start arguments over issues that are seemingly unrelated. That sounds irrational, but it operates by the logic of frustration: at least their arguing makes their partners pay attention, and better angry attention than none at all.

Partners, especially men, need to be alert enough to read such responses accurately. When a man finds his partner deliberately picking a fight, he should restrain his probable spontaneous inclinations to withdraw, defend himself, or attack back. Instead he should give her his positive, romantic, nonsexual, undivided attention, and if she is receptive, he should work *slowly* toward lovemaking—not just sex, but lovemaking.

In the motion picture *Moonstruck*, a middle-aged shopkeeper angrily accuses her husband of eyeing other women, calling him a wolf. With customers looking on, he smiles and replies, "You're the same wonderful girl I married twenty years ago." She immediately melts and coyly lowers her eyes. He's given her what she wanted—romantic reassurance of his love.

Often it's not until after satisfactory lovemaking that a woman (or a man, although we find this syndrome more frequently in women) will recognize the real source of her hostility for what it is—pent-up sexual frustration and a hunger for loving attention. She may not acknowledge those motives, but her partner will still find her to be calmer, less irritable, and ultimately more loving if he pays attention.

Incorporate romance into your daily living. Start in the morning, not ten minutes before sex.

Most romantic arrangements have in common a space of time and a partner's full positive attention. Attention first of all. Call your partner during the day. Let each other know you care. When you come home from work, after you've allowed yourself half an hour or so for practical matters, sit down and talk. Sit down and listen. Pay more attention to what your partner is saying than to what you want to reply. "What did you do today?" Listen supportively while your partner clears away the day's debris. Until the debris is cleared away, you can't come together emotionally.

At such times both of you should emphasize positives, set aside negatives, and postpone discussing problems, unless there's some urgency. You can find other times for criticism, worries, complaints. Imagine you're beginning an evening or weekend date. Compliment each other. Joke. Tease. Kid. Touch. Have fun together. Lighten your heart. *Care.*

Sit down to a romantic dinner. That may mean candlelight and a bottle of wine. It may mean a sandwich on a bench in the nearest park. Eating is a pleasure of its own, one we have shaped to a way of sharing. Eat for the pleasure of the food and pay attention to the partner you're sharing it with.

After dinner you may have to interrupt this pleasant performance you've arranged. Discuss what needs to be done to clear the decks: children put to bed, a telephone call made, a favorite TV show watched, the dog walked. Agree when you'll get back together. Then go ahead and do what you need to do to make possible your space of private, uninterrupted time.

Romantics don't like interruptions. The evening would be smoother without them. But intimacy won't be lost if you both agree to them and know that after they're dealt with, you'll pick up where you left off, and that the goal you're both working toward is clearing time together in privacy to give each other pleasure.

Romance is the deliberate creation of a magical setting, so that the mind is lured away from the problems of everyday life into a place where sensuality, intimacy, and imagination hold sway. At the beginning of a relationship the man will often automatically take charge of setting the stage for romance, making sure the candles are lit, the fire is glowing in the fireplace, the music is soft, and the right kind of wine is on the table.

At the outset, then, it's usually left up to the man to create a shared fantasy that says, "Come and play with me. I'll give you my undivided attention. I'll gaze into your eyes, I'll hold your hand. When I walk past you, I'll touch you. I'll communicate silently across a crowded room. When I'm with you, I'll know where you are at all times, and let you know I know by glances or touches. I'll show you in a thousand ways that I think about you constantly. I'll make your life magic." And since a woman loves magic, she falls in love.

Later, once the relationship is established, men unfortunately tend to lose interest in creating romance. They settle into routine. The relationship is established, they think, so why go to all that trouble when they're already comfortable? Women, who desire romance more than men, are often less capable of creating the proper settings because they've been led to expect, erroneously, that romance just happens, spontaneously, without effort. They didn't notice the man's elaborate efforts before. That's a tribute to his skill even if it's counterproductive now. In this era of more egalitarian relationships, romance is equally the responsibility of the woman.

When a man gets busy with the practical issues of life and doesn't bother with romance anymore, his partner may become angry. There problems begin. To re-create the romance they enjoyed at the beginning of the relationship, both partners have to understand that somebody has to make it happen. They should decide deliberately whose job it is to create the magical settings, who should light the candles, who should arrange the music. That agreement should be included in their weekly agreements to follow the Ecstasy Program. We designate the partner whose turn it is to make these arrangements "the initiator."

It's extremely important to learn to express all of the different aspects of your personality through intimacy—to be able to play together, to be silly, to laugh, but also to give way to the powerful, silent intimacy of romance when you look into your partner's eyes and are lost for a time, the two of you merged into one.

For such intimacy you need to arrange times when you're not around family, children, or friends. Many couples form the habit of creating foursomes with close friends whenever they go out together. Foursomes may be fun, but they're not romantic. Make time for yourselves alone as a couple, at home and away. Periodically just the two of you eat out or go to a movie.

It's crucial to your relationship not to give romantic sexuality second shrift. The magic of romantic attention is crucial to both of you, but especially to the woman. A woman will begin to exclude sexuality from her expectations of life if she doesn't receive romantic attention regularly. Her orgasm, in the proper context, is about herself; it makes her feel beautiful, special, and wonderful. Her ability to respond to her partner and the quality of the life they share affect her orgasm. Without romantic love, she begins to think herself undesirable.

That's why the tried-and-true prescription of getting away occasionally for a weekend makes good sense. Even if the weekend hideaway is a motel down the street, it will automatically define a different time and place—different and potentially magical. Going away together to a private place commits you to giving each other your undivided attention, away from old habits, away from the telephone, away from the press of chores and intrusive obligations. You may want to take a weekend or two away together during the months you work on the Ecstasy Program.

AFFECTION

Affection is also a part of romance, or can be. Physical affection is important. It feels good, it's nurturing, and it's a message to your partner that you're thinking about him or her in a loving way—so loving you want to manifest it physically. Affection may be a touch on the arm, a squeeze of the hand, hand-holding, kissing, or an arm around a shoulder. Any physical confirmation of tender thoughts about your partner is affectionate.

Some of our clients complain that they don't hear "I love you" often enough or receive affectionate physical confirmation of a partner's love often enough. Men and women frequently experience their love on different levels. A man may feel that if he works to support his wife and family, comes home each night, and regularly turns his paycheck over to his partner, he's expressed his love fully and his wife should know it. A woman, on the other hand, may respect and value her partner's work and loyalty and still miss receiving physical confirmation of his personal devotion. Affectionate touch refers to her personally rather than to the family as a unit. Thinking that you love your partner is one thing. Physically walking over to your partner and kissing her or hugging her is a much more personal, intimate, and romantic message of caring. Many of our women clients have told us that "what he says is nice to hear, but what he does is the truth."

We suggest to couples that they make a habit of always kissing each other hello and good-bye when they enter or leave the house for more than a few hours. We advise the person who is leaving the house to look for his/her partner and kiss her/him good-bye. We suggest you consider adopting a habit of saying to each other "I love you" at least once each day, assuming there is some part of you that feels this affirmation to be true. In the morning, if you awaken together, or at night, if you retire together, could be appropriate times to develop this reaffirming bond. Even if you're angry with your mate and don't like him/her at the moment, you haven't stopped loving him/her. There are times in every relationship when you don't like each other. That's a separate problem. You probably wouldn't stay together unless you loved each other, however angry you may be at the moment. Willingness to agree to practice deliberately loving behavior can add importantly to any relationship.

We also suggest that partners returning from work in the evening look for each other when they enter their home and kiss each other hello, prior to doing anything else. Greeting each other in this way sends an important message—that you've been looking forward to seeing each other and place high priority on doing so before you turn to other activities. In many relationships one partner may be in the house for fifteen minutes or more before the other partner even knows of his/her arrival. Some men and women interpret such inattention as indifference.

FINDING TIME ALONE

We strongly recommend that you find time to go away together overnight every two or three months. You can productively plan such mini-vacations at your monthly "business meetings." Ideally, your special overnight should be just the two of you—no children, no friends.

Take your mini-vacation to a destination you both will enjoy. If you disagree about destinations, agree to alternate choices each time.

These retreats into intimacy need not be expensive. You might go camping, check into a quiet motel with a swimming pool on the other side of town, or stay at a pleasant bed-and-breakfast. Hotels and motels frequently offer special weekend discounts aimed specifically at romantic couples.

Avoid long, tiring drives for a single overnight, no more than two hours away. Many people find that driving more than three hours to an overnight destination is tiring. If you leave at noon on Saturday and return at six o'clock Sunday evening, your expenses will be minimal—one night's lodging—and you'll have time prior to leaving on Saturday and again Sunday evening to spend time with your children if children are part of your life. You'll have time to take care of other weekend responsibilities as well.

PREFERENCES

Part of the Ecstasy Program involves noticing what arrangements help you get in the mood for sex. What setting you prefer, what sounds, clothing, music, time of day or evening, air temperature, lighting, which parts of your body are most sensitive to touch, what pressure you prefer your partner to use to touch you, and many other variables are important to making you comfortable and to building arousal. You'll be happier with your experience if you and your partner have taught each other how to prepare for lovemaking. A useful exercise in preparation is making a list of these conditions.

Circle or describe all your special preferences. Add others.

Location: what room, floor, bed, chair, front of fireplace? Describe other settings. _____

_____

Music: types of music, specific pieces or artists. _____

_____

Lighting: bright, dimmer, near darkness, dark, colored lights, candles, lantern, window shades. Other conditions. _____

_____

Clothing: Man _____

Woman _____

Props: pillows, feather, massage oil.

Other props _____

Other preferences _____

_____

_____

Exercise: Wish List for Romance

Share your list with your partner and discuss both lists. Where there are differences, try to arrive at acceptable compromises or agree to alternate arrangements from week to week.

CONVERSATION TIME

Exchanging thoughts and feelings with no particular purpose except to share an experience, feeling, or a humorous reaction—simple conversation—is often overlooked, especially by men, as an essential prelude to lovemaking. If conversation with your partner doesn't always come easy, you can practice it and learn. Here's an exercise we often assign clients:

Exercise: Conversation Time

One of you initiates. Describe to the listener something of interest—a program you saw on TV, read in a newspaper or magazine, or heard as an interesting piece of information on the radio. Recount a recent conversation you overheard at work, in a store, or at school. Talk about your joys, your accomplishments. Take at least several minutes to describe what you heard or what you read and how you felt about it. Don't offer the information as a lesson that you're trying to teach or imply that your partner should learn. Don't interject any subtle jabs or sarcasm. Choose neutral or emotionally positive subjects only. The possibilities are endless.

Reverse the process. The listener now talks about something of interest for several minutes.

TIME OF DAY

Time of day for having sex is an extremely important consideration. It's surprising how often partners disagree on a preferred time of day for lovemaking. Rarely are couples fortunate enough to be able to agree on an optimum time of day for sex and to have sufficient freedom of scheduling actually to fulfill their preferences.

Ask your partner what time of day he/she generally prefers to make love. Find out what his/her second best time of day is. Finally, ask what a least preferred time of day for lovemaking might be. Then volunteer the same information about yourself. After you've each indicated your preferred times of day, discuss them together and find compromises as close as possible to your preferences. It's likely that some compromise with your partner will be necessary. Such compromises are always worthwhile in the long run.

Once you have set a time of day and agreed on how you'll spend that time, seek agreement on the amount of time you'll spend. Leaving the time open-ended leads to differing expectations. One of you may expect a long session of lovemaking while the other expects a quickie. Determining in advance approximately how much time you'll spend at lovemaking helps to reassure partners about what they can expect and what's expected of them. That makes both of you feel more secure. Don't leave the length of your lovemaking entirely up to random chance or uncontrolled spontaneity.

Once you've made time agreements, it's extremely important to keep them. Trust is crucial for intimacy and for increased sexual response. Change agreements about time only with the consent of your partner. If you want to change an agreed time, ask him or her directly. Avoid manipulating your partner with guilt, pity, or anger.

Here's an example of manipulation: "At the party, Greg, you just kept talking and drinking even though I hinted twice that I was ready to leave. You never listen to me or care about what I want. I know we agreed to make love when we got home, but I don't feel like it now. I'm going to bed."

Feeling manipulated and probably guilty as well, Greg replies: "You always use that excuse. Half an hour ago you were dancing and seemed to be having a great time. Where'd all your energy go?"

A better exchange might be: "Greg, we came home later than we planned, it's midnight, and I'm really tired. I had a good time at the party, but I'm not up to our agreed lovemaking. I prefer that we plan a briefer time tomorrow morning or a longer time tomorrow evening. What do you think?"

Greg can then choose a new time or suggest another alternative of his own.

FANTASY

Visualization and fantasy are skills useful in lovemaking. Visualization can be a way of relaxing. Close your eyes and imagine you're somewhere else. On a Tahiti beach listening to the regular, smooth breaking of the waves, warming in the South Pacific sun. In a suite in a Swiss ski lodge on a fur rug before a crackling fire. In Paris between satin sheets in an elegant hotel. Choose someplace that makes you feel good and makes you feel peaceful.

Sexual fantasy as a preparation for lovemaking or self-stimulating involves a variety of visualization techniques. Fantasy can chase away distracting thoughts and resistances. You imagine a desirable sexual experience with your partner or with someone else or you recall a pleasurable sexual experience you've had in the past. Some people fantasize visual pictures more easily than others. Everyone can learn.

If you think you have difficulty fantasizing, try this exercise: Start by closing your eyes and seeing yourself as you are right now, at this very moment, with your eyes closed, doing just what you are doing. Then experience your breathing. Notice your lungs filling and emptying and the sensation of your breath passing in and out your nose. Now, eyes closed, picture the objects in the room around you. Can you see them almost as clearly as if you had your eyes open? Picture yourself in the room among these objects. What are you wearing? Visualize your clothes. Sometimes self-talk can help create a visualization. Start by telling yourself what you'd like to visualize. Be specific. Tell yourself where you are, how you appear, and what you are saying or hearing. Be as colorful, vivid, and three-dimensional as you can. Sight, sound, colors, and words can create an experience almost as real as if it were actually happening. Experiments by Carl Pribram at Stanford University confirm the virtual identity of imagination and real experience in terms of physically measured responses.

Now change the scene. Visualize yourself on a soft, sandy beach, lying on powder-white sand in warm sun. Then picture someone with you on the beach.

Now switch to a sexual fantasy. Recall in detail a desirable sexual experience with your partner or with someone else. Or imagine a sexual experience that you would like to have at some future time. These memories and experiences may appear to you as snapshots, as movies, as fragmented and impressionistic images. They may involve feelings or words more than visual images.

Keep the fantasy in mind and build on it by adding new details. You can change the setting or add new experiences to real experiences you remember.

Knowing what other people fantasize about can help you learn to fantasize. Everyone has sexual fantasies some of the time. Here are common fantasies, listed in the order of their popularity:

1. *Sex with your regular partner.* Pleasures you've enjoyed together in the past. Pleasures you'd like to enjoy but can't because you or your partner finds them unacceptable. Real experiences with imaginary embellishments. Feel free to invent any activities you think you would enjoy with your partner, however unlikely. They're your private fantasies and yours alone. Visualize what you're doing and focus on the area being stimulated. With your eyes closed, make it larger; fill your entire visual field with it.

2. *Sex with another opposite-sex partner.* Someone you have met or known. Screen stars, sports heroes and heroines, your high school prom king or queen. Since this is fantasy, not reality, it's safe to pick anyone you want. Imagine where you are, what you're doing, what you say to each other. Visualize how your imagined partner looks and how touching and caressing feels. Decide what you would like to do. Mentally write an entire shared scene.

3. *Sex with more than one partner.* A friend as well as your regular partner. A movie star, a famous man or woman. A man may fantasize a woman with full, sensuous lips stimulating him orally while his regular partner watches or joins in. A woman may imagine two men loving her physically at the same time, or a man and a woman. One may be a stranger and the other her regular partner.

4. *Forcible sex.* Fantasies of being taken sexually against your will. Women particularly enjoy this fantasy. It's perfectly acceptable. It has nothing to do with real rape, which is an ugly, violent act of criminal assault. Imagine being kidnapped, or someone breaking into your house. A stranger or someone you know takes you forcefully. Perhaps your regular partner is made to watch. You resist at first, then give in. You may be tied up and totally helpless but become sexually aroused along the way.

5. *Sex with same-sex partners.* Many people fantasize occasionally about having sex with people of their own gender, although they may strongly resist acknowledging these thoughts. People with such fantasies usually don't wish to act them out. If you aren't too threatened to explore this fantasy, picture in detail whom you would enjoy having sex with, what you would do, and where you would do it. Same-sex fantasies aren't an indication of homosexuality, conscious or unconscious. They're simply exercises in human imagination, a normal part of life.

6. *Fantasies left over from childhood.* Vivid memories of fantasies and

experiences may return to you from childhood if you let them. Our first sexual experiences and feelings are often overwhelmingly powerful; you can tap some of that residual emotion by recalling them. They may be only fragmentary: a girl's hair brushing a boy's face; a glimpse of someone naked. You may have thought of playing doctor with another child, or of having sex with an adult. Recall those fantasies now.

Fantasies have great value in sex. They're private, so they affect no one else and depend on no one else, and they actually change body chemistry. They stimulate arousal; they can give you a head start on pleasure with your partner or add stimulation during your sexual encounter. The image comes before the reality and begins preparing the body for that reality.

If you find a fantasy arousing, continue that fantasy. If you find a fantasy neutral or negative, switch to another fantasy until you discover one that gives you pleasure.

Start with a fantasy that feels safe. Mentally write the scene. Tell yourself where you are, the specific setting, whom you are with, and exactly what you're doing. Imagine you're videotaping. What time is it? Where are you? Make the colors as bright as you can. What does your partner (or partners) look like? What do both of you (or all of you) do? Begin dressed and enjoy undressing—even fantasies deserve time for foreplay! Don't rush your fantasy. Extending it will add pleasure and benefit arousal. If you are fantasizing about sex with someone other than your regular partner, choose someone with whom you feel comfortable. If the fantasy works, keep it going. If it doesn't work, change it.

Some people fear they will act out their fantasies. Fantasies are almost always safe. Very few women act out fantasies they believe to be dangerous. Some men may need to be aware of a tendency toward inappropriate aggression or violence in their fantasies. We don't encourage anyone to develop fantasies involving physical aggression or socially unacceptable behavior.

Some people fear that fantasizing is dishonest. They believe they owe their partners 100 percent of their physical and mental attention. They believe fantasizing is disloyal. They think that their partners would feel rejected and excluded if they knew. Sharing fantasies sometimes can increase a partner's excitement. Partners can learn to trust each other enough to share some fantasies. One way to test the water is to share a relatively safe fantasy and see what happens—a fantasy, for example, that involves only your partner and yourself, doing something together that you don't usually do. The sharing can develop from there if you choose. What works for one couple may not work for another, so you can test the sharing. If one of you becomes uncomfortable, stop the sharing process or move it back to safer ground.

Sharing fantasies can help enliven long-standing relationships when partners feel stuck sexually and bored. Fantasies add excitement and may also improve communication. Your partner may find renewed interest. Sharing does require trust and sensitivity. One partner sometimes fears the other may want to act out the fantasy. Generally, fantasies are better kept private.

It's likely, in any case, that you and your partner both use sexual fantasies from time to time. Sometimes your partner's fantasies include you, sometimes not. Feel good about your fantasies—they'll enhance your shared pleasure.

Most of our clients find that regular fantasy helps them break through resistance. Fantasy assists you in removing your attention—your thoughts—from your day-to-day world and focusing them on your specific sexual activity with your partner. It's a tool for increasing intimacy, not a weapon to threaten it. Even in the midst of fantasy, the part of you that keeps track of reality knows whom you're with at the moment and knows you wouldn't be there if you didn't want to be. Replace resistance with fantasy to stimulate yourself to higher levels of arousal. That gives you more pleasure; it also gives your partner more pleasure.

Remember, fantasies are normal and healthy. They don't lead to unfaithfulness. They don't lead to acting them out. You don't even necessarily have to tell your partner about them. You're responsible for what you do in this world, not for what you think.

More on Mental Resistances

You're undoubtedly well aware of your mind's habit of producing distracting nonsexual or negative thoughts—mental resistances to sex—before beginning, at the start of, and even when you're in the middle of lovemaking.

You've also had experience by now with deliberately changing behavior, thoughts, and feelings. Here are suggestions and discussion for applying that experience more specifically to sexual situations.

1. *Controlling thought.* It takes about three seconds, after a thought arises in the brain, to identify the content, decide to change it, and

make the change. The simplest way to change a thought is to reverse it: instead of anxiously thinking, "I'm afraid I'm losing my erection," you can deliberately think, "The stroking on my penis feels really good. More blood is flowing into it and it's becoming more erect." Simultaneously, try to visualize this happening with your eyes closed. Even if a part of your mind doesn't believe what you're thinking, the reversal of self-talk will help change the thought, because we all finally believe what we tell ourselves repeatedly, and two self-talk thoughts can't occupy the same mental space at the same time. Your reversal is founded on a provisional truth: If you continue with self-talk and visualization to direct your concentration, that will assist in creating the desired effect. Your partner can encourage you, too. Make a habit of reversing negative thoughts with positive ones every moment you're in a sexual situation.

A second way to move past a point of resistance is to replace a distracting thought with a neutral thought. The sounds you learned to make, *ahhhhh* and *ummmm*, can fill your attention and drive out distraction. You can design a recurring phrase and repeat it over and over like a mantra: "I'm calm," "My mind is quiet." A neutral thought allows your body's natural responses to reassert themselves. When you're being sexually stimulated, that means a greater sensation of pleasure.

A third way to restructure your thoughts is to switch your attention inward to *feeling* and allow the physical experience of being stimulated to take over your awareness.

Paying attention to good feeling means just that: paying attention to your body and the pleasurable sensation that your partner is creating for you. Some people resist pleasure by telling themselves that their partners aren't stimulating them correctly. Your partner *will* be stimulating you correctly if you teach him/her how to do so. Assuming that your partner isn't causing you pain, whatever stimulation he/she happens to be providing you can potentially be used to build arousal by focusing more mental attention on whatever pleasant sensations are available at the moment and changing any negative self-talk to positive description. Every time you find yourself thinking—especially negative thoughts—switch your attention back to sensation and tell yourself how good it feels. If you're getting any direct physical stimulation at all, you can be getting as much as you need for arousal. Men have erections and ejaculations, and women experience lubrication, arousal, and orgasm, even during sleep, with no physical stimulation whatever.

If you doubt this point, try an exercise. Ask your partner to stimulate you lightly and steadily on your genitals without varying the stroke at all. You may be surprised how aroused you can let yourself become. Use the sensation that's there. It's more than enough to climb on your arousal scale if you decide to let it be.

When you find yourself face-to-face with distracting thoughts, concentrate on a good feeling. Watch your partner stimulating you or close your eyes and sense the feeling you're receiving from his/her touch. If you're completely focused on feeling, you won't be thinking about anything else. Your whole experience will be feeling. In a way your *thought* at that time is to *feel*. That's a strong, positive suggestion in itself.

Your last experience with severe pain is a grim but vivid example of what we mean by "completely feeling." Maybe you smashed your thumb with a hammer. Maybe you stubbed your toe or cracked your shin. When the pain arrived, it overwhelmed thinking. Afterward you probably had a thought or two about it. But before those thoughts came, you were completely aware of pain and only of pain.

In extended orgasmic response training, you're working toward just the opposite state, a state of complete, conscious awareness of pleasure. Any moment you find yourself even for a moment off track, immediately refocus your mind on the pleasure experience you had before you were mentally derailed. The object of Ecstasy Program training is to learn to achieve that state and then to stretch it out second by second, longer through time: to reach a point where you're not thinking *about* anything but simply, consciously, *experiencing* pleasurable feeling.

2. *Constructive communication with your partner.* The moment that you're aware that you'd like your partner to do something different, say so aloud. Your partner can't read your mind. It will take your partner much longer to determine that you had mental resistance if you don't verbally communicate it. Give your partner directions in a brief, positive, constructive manner. Avoid even subtle criticism. Don't say, "Ouch!" or "Couldn't you tell you were hurting me?" Do say, "That felt good, but your fingernails are a little sharp" or "That's getting a little uncomfortable."

3. *Breathing.* Breathing is a good way to work through resistance. Concentrating on deep, regular breathing from the diaphragm, with the stomach rising and falling rather than just the chest, helps bring you back from thought to sensation, to attention to your body. It also helps because many people hold their breath when they're reaching for increased sexual arousal, tightening their muscles and reducing the oxygen supply to the body and the brain.

Breathing also helps because the breathing reflex is complex and many bodily systems involved in sexual arousal are interconnected with it.

Breathing produces relaxation by changing the state of the body's autonomic nervous system. There's anxiety behind each and every one of your resistances, and relaxation reduces anxiety.

4. *Visualization*—fantasy—can be a way of relaxing. We discussed this process at length earlier in this chapter, beginning on page 000.

5. *Suggestion* is another way through resistance. If your partner is struggling with resistance, you can offer positive suggestions. "I love you." "You're so pretty." "You're really wonderful." "Let yourself go." "Breathe—in and out." "Every time you breathe you'll get higher." "Relax." "Trust me." "Yes, yes." "That's it." The right words, suggested quietly and with confidence, can help your partner through.

6. *Monitoring tension.* Tension in the genital area strongly influences your level of sexual arousal. There's always pelvic-muscle activity during sex, with tension either increasing or decreasing, so staying aware of that level of tension is always useful. It won't be distracting; to the contrary, it focuses your attention on the area where you're receiving stimulation.

When you encounter a mental resistance, you can counteract it by tightly clenching your sex muscles, holding the contraction as you slowly breathe in, holding your breath for a second, then relaxing your sex muscles and exhaling. That returns your attention to your genital area, shifting it from the distracting thought to a physical action. It also boosts arousal directly by stimulating the sexual tissues themselves.

7. *Changing position.* Shifting position and making subtle changes in movement can help you work through distracting thoughts. You can tilt your pelvis, arch your back, shift your legs, move to an entirely different position. Movement redirects your attention. Add a pillow. Remove a pillow. Turn to one side. Turn to the other side. Your partner can move along smoothly with you and can usually continue stimulating as you go.

Changing position can be helpful to the stimulating partner as well, particularly the woman. Women generally have less massive upper bodies than men. They also usually prefer relatively light and gentle stimulation. As a result, many women don't realize that men often require substantially more forceful sexual stimulation. This preference for strong and intense direct genital stimulation is often especially true of men in long-standing relationships. It also often applies to men with new partners who may have some performance anxiety. To overcome mental resistances and anxiety, a man may prefer and respond best to a very rapid manual stroke speed of up to four strokes per second. Many men may require this seemingly high rate of stimulation to overcome erection inertia. Once at least a moderate erection has been established, the requirements for direct stimulation, rate, and pressure are usually significantly reduced.

With their more delicate musculature, women usually also tire more quickly than men. For both reasons, they need to compensate by using strategy, by learning to be more efficient, and by developing technical expertise based on knowledge. For instance, a woman may discover that using disorientation techniques is helpful. A man will usually interpret frequent, unpredictable changes in stroke, rate, and pressure, which relieve her fatigue, to be pleasurable teasing. He's likely to attribute such teasing to loving playfulness.

When a woman becomes aware of her fatigue factors, she can learn to shift her body position, arm angle, stroke rate, and hand pressure smoothly to compensate. These changes can be full changes in position, from lying to sitting, or sitting to kneeling, or switching sides (which side of her partner she's working from or which side of her own body she's resting on). They can also involve very slight changes in the angle at which she holds her wrist, or adding stimulation to another area while lightening up on the area she's been stimulating, or switching hands.

The stimulating partner's changes of position may also distract his/her partner from any resistances or intrusive thoughts.

VI

EXTENDED SEXUAL ORGASM

Learning to extend your orgasm isn't automatic. It takes knowledge, cooperation, and practice. The Ecstasy Program will guide you in learning to extend your orgasmic response. So you'll know what to expect, we describe here the three stages of orgasm: brief (Stage I), multiple (Stage II), and extended (Stage III). We'll describe each stage separately, but each is similar in important ways. In the program we'll tell you how to proceed most effectively toward experiencing these intensely pleasurable states.

FEMALE EXTENDED ORGASM

The graph on page 104, Female Orgasmic Response Stages, shows the differences in arousal and response through time of brief orgasm, multiple orgasm, and extended orgasm (Stage I, Stage II, Stage III).

In single, brief orgasm (Stage I), arousal increases with stimulation through an excitement phase to an orgasm of one-second contractions lasting from about three to twelve seconds. Contractions are the vaginal-squeeze, clenching type in the outer one-third of the vagina and reflex contractions of the anal sphincter. Blood, which has been pooling in the pelvic area (vasocongestion) is pumped out and experienced as powerful, throbbing pulsations. Then arousal declines steadily down to baseline, within a few minutes. This is orgasm as Masters and Johnson describe it in *Human Sexual Response*. Sexual researchers William Hartman and Marilyn Fithian have called it discrete orgasm.

In multiple orgasm (Stage II), arousal doesn't decline rapidly to base-

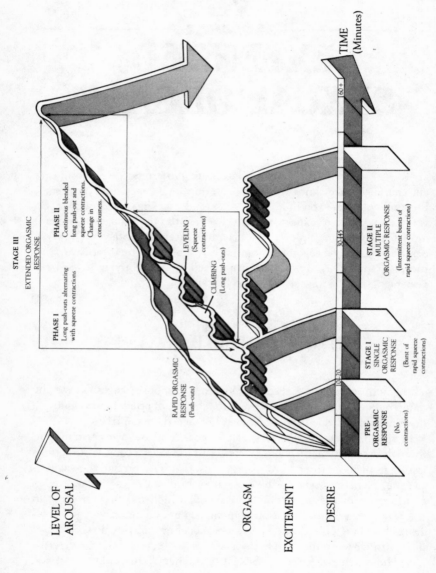

FEMALE ORGASMIC RESPONSE STAGES

LEVEL OF AROUSAL

ORGASM

EXCITEMENT

DESIRE

TIME (Minutes)

STAGE III
EXTENDED ORGASMIC RESPONSE

PHASE I
Long push-outs alternating with squeeze contractions

PHASE II
Continuous blended long push-out and squeeze contractions. Change in consciousness.

LEVELING
(Squeeze contractions)

CLIMBING
(Long push-outs)

RAPID ORGASMIC RESPONSE
(Push-outs)

PRE-ORGASMIC RESPONSE
(No contractions)

STAGE I
SINGLE ORGASMIC RESPONSE
(Burst of rapid squeeze contractions)

STAGE II
MULTIPLE ORGASMIC RESPONSE
(Intermittent bursts of rapid squeeze contractions)

10-20   30-45   60+

104

line after brief orgasm. Instead, the woman's response drops to the high-excitement level for half a minute to two minutes or more. Then, with continuing or renewed stimulation, her arousal level climbs back to orgasm and she experiences another three- to twelve-second burst of vaginal squeeze contractions and anal contractions. Heart rate, blood pressure, and muscle tension throughout the body remain at moderately elevated levels. This process may repeat several times for several minutes—in some women, for thirty minutes or more. After a series of two or more bursts of squeeze contractions, each lasting about three to twelve seconds, arousal returns to baseline. Hartman and Fithian have termed this response multiple discrete orgasm.

Extended orgasm (Stage III) follows a different development. The early phase of this orgasm has been called continuous multiple orgasm by Hartman and Fithian and blended orgasm by other researchers (i.e., Kaplan, Perry, and Whipple). A woman experiences a Stage I orgasm first: desire, excitement, and a burst of rapid squeeze contractions; then moves to Stage III. Or she may experience a Stage II multiple orgasmic response with several bursts of squeeze contractions over several minutes before moving to Stage III orgasm.

Extended, Stage III orgasm has two phases. The first phase is characterized by the occurrence of push-out contractions of the deep pelvic muscles of the uterus and back of the vagina (see page 106). These alternate periodically with squeeze contractions of the outer vaginal muscles. The term "blended" refers to the blending of the squeeze and the push-out sex muscle responses. Compared with the briefer bursts of squeeze contractions, push-out contractions have longer cycles, varying from two seconds to thirty seconds or longer. As push-out contractions continue, they become stronger, are sustained longer, and feel increasingly more powerful. Their intensity and strength vary, depending upon the level of stimulation provided and the woman's ability deliberately to let go of mental resistances. Sex muscle push-outs during extended orgasm are slower and longer-lasting cycles than the bursts of squeeze contractions of Stage I and Stage II orgasm.

The duration and intensity of the deep pelvic contractions depend on the effectiveness of stimulation and on the woman's skill at focusing her attention on genital sensations and on positive sensations and thoughts. The man influences the duration of a contraction when he stimulates his partner, usually manually or orally, in the climbing process we will describe. He can decrease the intensity of contractions by reducing rate and pressure of vaginal and clitoral stroking. The woman climbs to

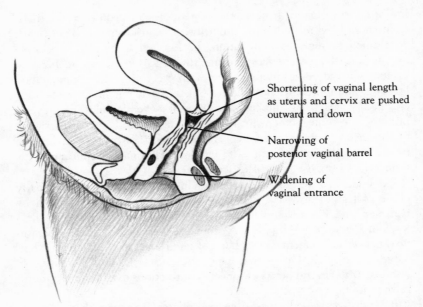

Shortening of vaginal length as uterus and cervix are pushed outward and down

Narrowing of posterior vaginal barrel

Widening of vaginal entrance

PUSH-OUT CONTRACTION OF DEEPER PELVIC MUSCLES
(A Characteristic of STAGE III—Extended Orgasmic Response)

increasingly higher levels of orgasm during push-out contractions. Then she may mentally resist by allowing intrusive thoughts to distract her and level off, the back of her vagina withdrawing subtly from the man's finger and clenching—squeezing—around it instead. During leveling periods, she experiences bursts of squeeze orgasmic contractions for a number of seconds. When the man increases stimulation, she refocuses and climbs again and experiences push-out contractions.

Generally, stimulating the clitoris encourages the squeeze contractions of the outer vagina; stimulating the inner-trigger areas encourages the deeper push-out response. A combination of alternating and simultaneous stimulation of the clitoris and the inner trigger areas is the basic method of stimulation in the first phase of extended orgasm. We also call this phase the "staircase phase" because of the way it looks on a graph—climbing, leveling, climbing, leveling.

The first phase of extended orgasm may last fifteen minutes or more. When a woman finally lets go of enough mental resistances for a sufficient period of time, she enters the second phase of extended orgasmic response, the continuous-climbing phase. This second phase is characterized by smooth, long waves of deep push-out contractions. The anal sphincter muscles are relaxed and open rather than closed or reflexively contracting as in Stages I and II. Her partner influences the intensity and duration of these push-out contractions by the way he stimulates the vaginal trigger areas. Pressure that is too hard, too soft, or off target will result in diminishing or cessation of orgasmic response. Furthermore, what stimulation is effective is not a fixed formula and frequently changes from minute to minute. The dedicated partner must give his full attention to his partner, adjusting his actions to her reactions.

Phase 2, extended orgasmic response, is sometimes referred to subjectively by women who experience it as being on an "orgasmic track" or being "immobilized by pleasure."

To the woman this phase feels timeless. She feels as if she is on a track of continuous and smoothly rising pleasure. Like a meditative state, the feeling is of an altered state of consciousness—floating without effort. In the first phase of extended orgasmic response, the "staircase phase," the woman pushes mentally and constantly reaches for more pleasure. In the second phase, continuously climbing, she has no sensation of effort. This experience can last from several minutes to half an hour or more.

A small percentage of women are able to experience both phase I and phase II extended orgasm with clitoral stimulation alone. They can sustain the push-out response with very light clitoral stimulation. However, vaginal stimulation still usually adds to the intensity of their experience.

We have data from electrical brain recordings that show characteristic changes in brain waves occurring during extended sexual response. The brain-wave pattern appears to be different from other states of arousal and other stages of orgasm. We find a possible shift in activity between the left and right hemispheres of the brain, which become more synchronized with each other. The right side of the brain, which is more involved with intuition and feelings, becomes more active. These changes are similar to those seen in states of deep meditation.

After the woman has enjoyed a few minutes of second-phase extended orgasm, she may need less stimulation to maintain the continuous climb. The orgasmic process becomes more self-sustaining. Light rhythmic stimulation of the vagina alone is usually sufficient to maintain prolonged blended orgasmic contractions. Orgasmic contractions can even continue sometimes for thirty seconds more with no stimulation at all.

Women report experiencing a level of arousal with extended orgasm different from the arousal of brief or multiple orgasm. Each orgasmic burst in a series of multiple orgasms, they say, feels much the same as the last one. But extended orgasm feels gradually and steadily more intense, climbing higher as the stimulation continues.

Sometimes women who have never experienced the extended orgasmic state fear that it could be dangerous for any prolonged period of time to sustain the level of tension that they associate with Stage I or Stage II orgasmic response. However, the extended orgasmic state is a balanced, relatively relaxed state, where heart rate and blood pressure actually decline to near normal baseline, and the total body musculature is relaxed. How long a woman can extend her orgasmic response is potentially limited only by her or her partner's time and interest and energy level.

Women who have learned to extend their orgasmic response tell us that they continue to feel occasional subtle pelvic contractions for up to twenty-four hours after extended orgasmic experience. Which is to say, they continue to be aroused above the baseline state and even feel occasional mild orgasmic contractions as they go about their lives. If they have intercourse the day after an extended orgasm, they may begin orgasm soon after penetration. We call this effect the "rapid orgasmic response." They can catapult right back into extended orgasm again.

We should add that women who regularly experience extended orgasm function better than ever, whatever their responsibilities. And they're healthier, less irritable, more relaxed, and much happier.

Why is it that relatively few women experience extended orgasm without deliberate training and practice? It's possible that toilet training early in life encourages the habit of keeping pelvic sphincter muscles tight. Tight pelvic muscles may be the equivalent of squeeze contractions in the orgasmic response.

A child's earliest muscular training is learning to respond to any feeling of pressure in the pelvic area by automatically tightening pelvic sphincter muscles. A child is strongly rewarded for learning to control his/her sphincter muscles. This control is reinforced throughout life. The inadvertent loss of sphincter control, resulting in accidental urination or defecation, is among the most socially embarrassing events anyone ever experiences. The only acceptable times for relaxing pelvic sphincter muscles are alone in the privacy of a bathroom.

Given this conditioning, if one assumes that the natural orgasmic response is in fact a push-out, the onset of a push-out would immediately be followed by a counter reflex—a squeeze reaction, trying to hold in.

For this reason, a woman may resist or even fear the natural push-out response characteristic of the extended orgasmic response. This learned reflex resistance could equally explain as well males' resistance to experiencing spontaneous extended orgasmic responses.

MALE EXTENDED ORGASM

The graph on page 110, Male Orgasmic Response Stages, shows the differences in arousal and response through time of male single orgasm, multiple orgasm, and extended orgasmic response (Stage I, Stage II, Stage III). Note that Stages I, II, and III each have two phases: emission and ejaculation. In Stage III, the emission phase is extended for many seconds or minutes, or potentially even a half hour or more for some individuals.

Stage I: Orgasmic Response

In single orgasmic response (Stage I), arousal increases with stimulation through an excitement phase to a brief three- to five-second burst of pleasurable internal contractions (emission-phase orgasm), which is experienced as a sense of ejaculatory inevitability—the point of no return. The man knows he's going to ejaculate and can't stop. Several seconds later ejaculation begins, with six to ten strong, propulsive orgasmic contractions and the expulsion of semen, lasting about ten seconds. The anal sphincter muscles reflexively contract at about one cycle per second during ejaculation.

Stage II: Orgasmic Response

Multiple orgasm in the male (Stage II orgasmic response) occurs when a man has a second, similar orgasm after a refractory period of several minutes or longer. This is also characterized by a brief three- to five-second emission phase followed by a three- to ten-second ejaculation phase. Hartman and Fithian have called this response multiple discrete orgasm.

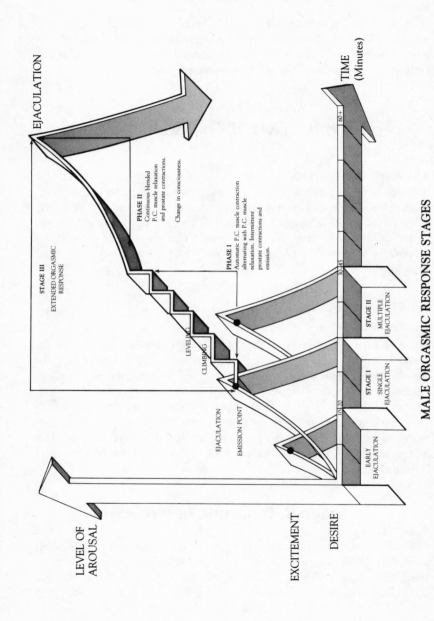

LEVEL OF AROUSAL

EJACULATION

STAGE III
EXTENDED ORGASMIC
RESPONSE

PHASE II
Continuous blended
P.C. muscle relaxation
and prostate contractions.

Change in consciousness.

PHASE I
Automatic P.C. muscle contraction
alternating with P.C. muscle
relaxation. Intermittent
prostate contractions and
emission.

LEVELING

CLIMBING

EJACULATION

EMISSION POINT

EXCITEMENT

DESIRE

EARLY
EJACULATION

STAGE I
SINGLE
EJACULATION

STAGE II
MULTIPLE
EJACULATION

10/20

30/45

60+

TIME
(Minutes)

MALE ORGASMIC RESPONSE STAGES

Stage III: Orgasmic Response

For a man to reach extended orgasmic response (Stage III orgasm) he needs to learn to control the rate of his climbing arousal as he nears the emission phase of his orgasm. Repeated multiple peaking, involving "stop and start" or "fast and slow" stimulation can lead into extended emission phase. The usual three- to five-second emission phase is prolonged in time. At first this extension is merely a second or two. With continued practice, it can be extended to many seconds, a minute, many minutes, even thirty minutes or more.

Unlike a man's process of reaching an extended orgasmic response, a woman is able to move relatively directly through increasing levels of arousal to the onset of squeeze contractions, without the need to hold back or stop stimulation. Whenever squeeze contractions begin, she is then poised potentially to launch into an extended orgasmic response by experiencing the switch to push-out contractions. However, if her partner provides her with teasing, increasing stimulation and multiple peaking for a longer period of time before the onset of the first squeeze contractions, she will be more likely to achieve the greater propulsive force that makes it easier to reach Stage III orgasm. When each of the multiple peaks reaches a little higher arousal level than the one before, greater climbing thrust is created to reach the orbiting velocity necessary to attain entry into extended orgasmic response.

The experience of continuous male orgasm is one of relaxation of the genital muscles with a sense of opening up and pushing out at the same time. The anal sphincter in extended orgasm is relaxed and open, rather than closed or reflexively contracting as it is in brief and multiple orgasm. A man can experience extended orgasm most feasibly when he is receiving his partner's active oral or manual stimulation. He may also be able to learn to experience extended orgasm during intercourse when his partner is experiencing extended orgasm herself. Without the magnified vaginal sensitivity that comes from being in extended orgasm, she may not have the control necessary to maintain him in emission-phase orgasm as she does using her hands and/or mouth.

In male extended orgasm the man moves up to and into first-phase orgasm: the emission phase, where there is hard erection, obvious arousal, and sometimes an intermittent secretion of clear fluid from the penis, which signals the presence of highly pleasurable internal contractions. These contractions are from the prostate and other glands that contribute to semen production. The woman can help her partner reach this phase and extend it to even higher levels of arousal *without cresting over into ejaculation.*

The key to male extended orgasm involves having the man stay as close as possible to the point of ejaculatory inevitability—keeping him in emission-phase orgasm—without allowing him to crest and ejaculate. This is accomplished by creating multiple non-ejaculatory peaks. When a man experiences fifteen or more of these peaks in close succession, they may become blended into a continuous emission-phase orgasm. Self-stimulation is effective to this purpose to a limited degree, but partner stimulation is more effective. The timing and pressure of external prostate spot stimulation is important in extending emission-phase orgasm. Firm pressure applied with a fingertip or finger joint just prior to a peak will help block the ejaculation reflex. External prostate stimulation is equivalent to G-spot inner trigger sensation in a woman. Many men discover it to be remarkably pleasure enhancing. The man uses various ejaculatory-control techniques to assist his entry into emission-phase orgasm. With experience and practice, this first-phase orgasmic response opens out from a narrow, unstable stage to a wide, stable platform of intense pleasure—which can last from a minute or two to thirty minutes or more.

The third type of orgasmic response is Stage III, the extended orgasmic response, which we have also referred to as Extended Sexual Orgasm (ESO).

In Stage III the reflex of ejaculatory inevitability is brought under control by deliberate training and practice. The emission phase of pleasurable internal contractions increases from a few seconds to a minute and then longer.

By learning to control the approach of ejaculatory inevitability, the man will be able to accept increasing amounts of stimulation during emission-phase orgasm. His level of arousal will continuously increase. He'll experience the stimulation as increasingly pleasurable and he'll be able to accept more of it longer without ejaculating. He'll still be using some ejaculatory control techniques himself—breathing, sex muscle exercises, switching attention, for example. During this time he may secrete larger-than-usual amounts of a clear fluid that is more watery than semen. He experiences a state of being pleasurably immobilized. When he ejaculates, his ejaculatory experience will probably be more intense and will also last longer. Instead of six to ten contractions, there may be fifteen to twenty or more. The sex exercises we prescribe in the Ecstasy Program and the testicle-elevation and semen-withholding exercises we describe can increase this intensity and duration. Continuous firm pressure on the external prostate spot during ejaculation can increase the number and intensity of expulsion contractions, which may go on for several minutes of climactic ecstasy.

Eventually, with ejaculation, the man trained in ESO also experiences a refractory period. But with mutual interest and continued, correct stimulation, he can reenter extended orgasm within several minutes. His penis may remain partly or fully erect.

His general level of arousal (and probably his levels of sexual hormones) will remain higher from day to day if both partners keep up their extended orgasmic skills. Then both partners will find even brief sessions of love-making more pleasurable.

Why is it that men don't spontaneously discover the ability to extend their orgasmic response more often? Lack of knowledge is one reason. In the discussion of Extended Orgasmic Response in the woman, we suggested another reason—early bowel training habits reinforced throughout life. For men, a third reason is that extended response requires unlearning still another reflex—the ejaculatory reflex. However, we know from discoveries in the past fifteen years in the medical field of biofeedback that many reflexes that had been believed to be automatic, beyond voluntary control, can in fact be brought under voluntary control through information, training, and practice. This reconditioning includes the orgasmic response.

ALTERED STATES

Extended orgasmic response appears to induce a highly pleasurable state of heightened mental activity. This sexual high is similar to a deep meditative state, with electrical brain activity moving in more synchronous patterns and shifted toward alpha and theta waves, with greater activity in the right side of the brain. Deep relaxation and meditation produce similar brain-wave shifts and patterns. Subjectively, such states induce feelings of peacefulness and harmony and an altered sense of time. The oceanic mental state that extended orgasmic response induces appears to be similar to states described by religious believers who have had visions of God or universal oneness. This common meditative transformation may explain the associations frequently addressed in world literature between sexuality and spirituality.

People usually don't experience sexuality in this heightened way. Most men and women view sex primarily as a physical and psychological release rather than a spiritual revelation. At best, people may achieve heightened mentality along with heightened sexuality very occasionally, and for reasons that are seldom well enough understood to be reproduced.

A woman who attended one of our professional seminars subsequently wrote to us describing such unusual experiences. "The contentment and satisfaction from these orgasms stayed with me for twenty-four to forty-eight hours," she explained; "however, they were few and far between. They were not consistent. And I seemed to have no control over when they happened and when they didn't. It would normally take ten to fifteen minutes for me to 'come down' from the initial high after the orgasm, but the satisfaction would stay twenty-four to forty-eight hours, as though I had been given a shot of some kind of drug." Later, this woman wrote again to tell us that through training guided by our book, *ESO*, she had learned to control and reproduce this heightened sense of well-being.

Another *ESO* reader wrote that extended orgasm felt like a "runner's high." That's an apt comparison. During both extended exercise and extended sexual arousal, the level of endorphins—natural, morphinelike chemicals secreted by the brain—tends to rise, inducing euphoria.

Even euphoria can be frightening. One of our readers reports that she had occasionally experienced sexual highs without knowing how she achieved them. They sometimes grew so intense that they made her feel she was losing mental control, and she had consulted a doctor about them before she read *ESO* and found a context for her experiences. She wrote then to say she now understood and could reproduce the altered mental states of extended sexual arousal without feeling that she was "going crazy."

The altered states experienced in extended orgasm are apparently identical for men and women. As time slows and the body lets go, men and women both experience a wonderful combination of physical pleasure and dreamlike mentation, a continuous series of strong, hard, sharp, pleasurable sensations centered in the genital region and radiating throughout the rest of the body and a feeling of dreamy, half-conscious timelessness. This state of deep sexual arousal can last for surprisingly long periods of time, even an hour or more given a partner who's willing to provide the stimulation necessary to keep it going.

On the receiving end, you must be trusting enough of yourself and your partner to experience these increasing sensations of pleasure without fear of losing control. The man's trust must extend to his partner's ability to maintain him in that state of arousal without abruptly cresting him over into ejaculation before he's ready.

Women often react emotionally to their first experience of extending their orgasm. "My single orgasms are still very short and weak," one woman wrote to us after reading *ESO* and working on extending orgasm, "but if I continue making love, most of the time I can attain an elevated endorphin level. Along with this intense emotional and spiritual experience, my reaction is always to cry from joy, not hurt or pain. It is part of an intense experience and a feeling that all is right with myself and the world."

Women who have attended our seminars and achieved some level of extended orgasmic response are frequently moved to tears when they try to describe the intense emotional closeness they've shared with their partner for the first time.

Experiencing this state of ecstasy with a person you care about can erase for a time the sense of alienation that we all feel, the feeling of being completely isolated within ourselves. Every human being needs connection and closeness, not to the point of loss of identity, but enough to be convinced emotionally as well as rationally that we have a place and a role, that we love and are loved. The key to the intense *emotional* satisfaction of extended orgasm is that it creates that sense of wholeness without an accompanying loss of individuality or control.

The existential function of sex is to merge identities for a period of time. We believe that this merging, freeing the individual from isolation, is a basic human need.

The periodic anchoring that comes from connecting with another person in extended orgasm can have a beneficial effect that can sweep through your everyday life, strengthening relationships and enhancing your personal sense of well-being. Obviously, ecstasy, no matter how extended, can only be maintained through a small percentage of your waking hours. Nevertheless, the couples we train often report a sense of elation that warms them for days at a time.

VII
SAFER SEX

The wide-ranging exploration of sexual freedom that began in the 1960s has been checked to some degree by the emergence of two sexually transmitted viral diseases.

The first of these to appear was the herpes simplex virus. Though herpes had been known in its present forms for many centuries, it gained wide notoriety beginning in the early 1970s as a sexually transmitted disease. Herpes infection causes blister sores to appear periodically on the mouth or genital areas. While the symptoms of herpes infection are usually not considered major challenges to individual health, the fact that the disease is uncomfortable, incurable, and transmittable during partner sex when the virus is active has caused its sufferers serious relational problems. Many social commentators credited the herpes virus with dramatically slowing the sexual revolution.

AIDS

Since 1981, concern with herpes infection has been preempted by a much more serious sexually transmitted disease complex, AIDS. AIDS, or acquired immune deficiency syndrome, is a lethal disease of the immune system caused by an unusual disease agent, human immunodeficiency virus (HIV). People who succumb to AIDS die because their immune systems have broken down to such a degree that diseases that are usually not fatal, such as pneumonia, acquire lethal force.

HIV is transmitted when a transfer of body fluids, particularly blood or semen, occurs between two individuals, one of whom is already infected. In the United States, AIDS has infected primarily two population groups: homosexual and bisexual men and their partners, and users of illegal intravenous drugs. In Africa, where AIDS first appeared, the disease complex infects men and women in approximately equal numbers.

The reasons for this difference in incidence are not clear, since the possible modes of HIV transmission have not been determined unequivocally. Sexual and medical practices are different in Africa. Researchers think that HIV is transmitted in the United States primarily through the sharing of unsterilized hypodermic needles by users of illegal drugs and the practice of anal intercourse.

More than a million Americans are infected with HIV; of these, statistics indicate that 20 to 50 percent will develop AIDS within five years. Once AIDS symptoms appear, the disease is thought to be universally fatal. Despite a great deal of research, medicine has yet to find either a preventive agent or a cure for HIV infection. AIDS is an extremely dangerous and frightening disease. Given the African experience, heterosexuals can take little comfort from their relative exclusion to date from U.S. AIDS statistics. Doctors and public health officials are deeply concerned that AIDS may one day spread from its presently more limited population base to attack the population at large. If that transformation occurs, pessimistic scenarios envision an epidemic that would rival the medieval plagues. The degree of potential threat to the human species from AIDS has not yet fully revealed itself. However, with some sensible precautions, individuals can essentially protect themselves from the risk of AIDS. With the growing general awareness of these precautions, significant spread of the disease in the heterosexual population may be averted.

As reported in the *Journal of the American Medical Association*, the following are approximately the risks of contracting AIDS from a single act of sexual intercourse:

with an AIDS-test positive partner:
$$\text{no condom} \quad . \quad . \quad . \quad 1{:}500$$
$$\text{with a condom} \quad . \quad . \quad 1{:}5000$$

with an untested, high-risk group partner:
$$\text{no condom} \quad . \quad . \quad . \quad 1{:}1000$$
$$\text{with condom} \quad . \quad . \quad . \quad 1{:}10{,}000$$

with an untested non-high-risk group partner:
$$\text{no condom} \quad . \quad . \quad . \quad 1{:}5 \text{ million}$$
$$\text{with condom} \quad . \quad . \quad . \quad 1{:}50 \text{ million}$$

For comparison, the risk of death in an airplane crash on take-off or landing is $1{:}33{,}000$.

SAFER SEX

Couples who wish to begin a sexual relationship today confront worries that simply did not exist even ten years ago.

Sex continues alive and well, however. While AIDS remains a serious though statistically small threat in the heterosexual population, and may become more threatening in the future, its activity is presently restricted to a relatively limited portion of the general population. People in established relationships, especially those that have been sexually exclusive since at least the late 1970s, have little to worry about.

New would-be partners who are unsure of their AIDS status may choose to be tested for HIV infection. In the meantime, they may want to take precautions to protect themselves. These precautions collectively are popularly labeled "safe sex." Since risk is relative, we'd prefer to call them "safer sex." Most of the exercises described in this book are uniquely adaptable to safer sex, because the Ecstasy Program involves techniques for sexual pleasuring that do not depend on intercourse or spontaneity. The full pleasures of extended orgasm can be experienced even when using latex gloves, condoms, and other barriers to viral transmission.

Safer sex practices are recommended for those couples who have some reason to suspect that at least one partner has been or could have been exposed to HIV infection. Six months without sexual contact outside the relationship—some public health officials suggest a year—and with negative HIV tests at the beginning and end are considered moderately reliable measures of freedom from HIV infection. While couples wait to determine their AIDS status, they may choose to enjoy and practice the Ecstasy Program using a condom for intercourse and oral sex. Pleasuring and sexual knowledge and control are characteristics of both the Ecstasy Program and safer sex.

Two people considering beginning a sexual relationship today should understand that the best guarantee of their safety from HIV infection is mutual AIDS testing at the outset, before any sexual interaction has occurred, followed by six months of using only safer sex practices, followed by a confirming HIV test. If both tests are still HIV negative for both partners, then the probability is high that both people are not AIDS-infected. The six-month wait is recommended because six months may have to pass after infection before a test shows positive.

If the initial HIV test is negative for both partners, and neither has apparently been engaging in high-risk behavior in the past six months, they may feel relatively confident in engaging in "probably safe" practices. Negative tests again for both six months later would allow a couple options of fewer sexual practice restrictions. Alternatively, a couple starting a relationship may decide to have only a single HIV test after six months, while they engage in only "safest sex" practices for six months. These recommendations are only suggested guidelines. There is some recent indication that a small percentage of HIV infected carriers do not develop positive tests for up to three years.

We've begun seeing couples who are coming for AIDS testing together, without guilt. They do so as a sensible precaution, not from suspicion that either one is infected. Couples who care about each other and who wish to begin an intimate sexual relationship want to protect their partners as well as themselves. If it should happen that one partner turns up HIV positive, the couple has a serious problem. The couple may choose then to continue to practice safer sex. But even condoms cannot be considered absolutely safe and each encounter increases the odds of eventual condom breakage or slippage. Certain facts must be faced. In the end, HIV-positive people are probably going to have to confine their sexual relationships to each other or practice celibacy and self-stimulation. These limitations are hardly solutions. They're probably necessary accommodations until science finds means of prevention or cure.

EXTENDED ORGASMIC RESPONSE AND SAFER SEX

Many of the exercises in the Ecstasy Program emphasize manual stimulation. Manual stimulation alone by a knowledgeable partner can carry both men and women to extended orgasm. That distinction makes following a modified Ecstasy Program a highly desirable safer sex practice. Oral stimulation and intercourse can be omitted entirely from Ecstasy Program exercises if you choose. Thus the Ecstasy Program can provide wonderfully pleasurable techniques for couples who wish to practice safer sex but still want to experience higher levels of sexual response than they've ever experienced before. If they want to, they can work through the Ecstasy Program, without oral sex or intercourse, during the three- to six-month period when they're waiting out their voluntary quarantine before their first or second HIV test. If they test negative, they can then go back and incorporate the Oral Stimulation and Intercourse Exercises.

SAFER SEX CATEGORIES

The Institute for the Advanced Study of Sexuality promulgates three categories of sexual practices in the context of AIDS risk: safe, probably safe, and unsafe. Medical practitioners generally accept these categories as valid based on current information.

Sexual practices considered safe, or *very* low risk, are: social or dry kissing (kissing without the exchange of salivary fluids); hugging; body massage; nongenital petting; mutual manual stimulation of the genitals without anal contact; exhibitionism and voyeurism by consent; and the use of mechanical sex aids (such as vibrators and dildos), also by consent.

Considered probably safe are: vaginal and anal intercourse with the use of a condom and the spermicide nonoxynol-9; fellatio with a condom; oral-vaginal or oral-anal stimulation using a latex barrier such as a dental dam (so long as the skin is unbroken); and French kissing (tongue inserted) with the use of nonoxynol-9. Nonoxynol-9 is effective in destroying the viral agent HIV when used in intercourse with a condom. To make it effective in French kissing, it would have to be spread on the tongues and lips of both parties involved. That may be aesthetically unpleasant given the substance's medicinal taste. The HIV virus rarely appears in saliva. Nevertheless, French kissing can't be considered entirely safe.

Considered unsafe are: anal or vaginal intercourse without a condom; swallowing semen or accepting semen vaginally, orally, or anally. Manual anal contact without latex gloves is also considered unsafe because there's evidence that anal stimulation causes bleeding. If the manipulator has a break in his or her skin, blood could then be passed either way. A hangnail could be deadly.

CONDOMS

Lovers interested in practicing safer sex beyond manual stimulation should probably acquire a stock of two different kinds of condoms—dry for oral sex and lubricated with nonoxynol-9 for more assured protection during intercourse. Nonoxynol-9 has proven effective in destroying a wide spectrum of sexually-transmitted disease agents. A great many condoms available on the market today contain nonoxynol-9 as an ingredient of their lubricant. In the past this information has not always been clearly indicated on the label. With greater public concern about safer sexual practices, manufacturers have begun identifying nonoxynol-9 as an ingredient. Condoms with nonoxynol-9 may not contain a sufficient amount. As added protection we recommend that you purchase a spermicidal jelly or cream containing at least a 5 percent concentration of nonoxynol-9 and spread it generously on the outer surface of the condom-clad penis.

Some people are sensitive to nonoxynol-9, unfortunately, and develop a bright red inflammation of the penis or vulva after repeated use. If you experience such a reaction, you will need to use untreated condoms and exercise greater care during vaginal or anal penetration.

Condoms sometimes fail. They slip off or tear. A condom slips off because it hasn't been put on correctly, because sex has been particularly strenuous, or simply because of careless withdrawal. Withdrawal after intercourse with a condom should take place while the penis is still erect. The man reaches down and holds the condom in place while he's withdrawing.

Condoms don't commonly break because of manufacturing defects or even incorrect application. The commonest cause of breakage is corrosion from petrolatum, the ingredient in Vaseline. Petrolatum products should be avoided when using latex condoms, surgical gloves, dams, or diaphragms. The sexual lubricant we recommend, Albolene, also contains a small amount of petrolatum. It's safe for short periods of time, less than ten minutes of intercourse with any of the thicker latex condoms. For a listing of various manufacturers of condoms see the Sources section in the Appendix, page 407. In doing your own personal evaluations of different types, consider packaging accessibility, thickness, size, lubrication, design, color, cost, and any special features.

OTHER BARRIER MATERIALS

Wearing a latex glove on any hand that touches your partner's genitals can substantially reduce risk. Most dentists and ophthalmologists now wear gloves as a precaution against the transmission of disease. It's encouraging to note that none on record has contracted AIDS through patient contact. Latex gloves come in three sizes (small, medium, and large) and are available at many pharmacies. Using latex gloves may seem strange at first, but you'll probably find that you lose only a little sensitivity. Your partner may find additional pleasure in the subtly different sensations. Worrying about disease transmission can be a powerful inhibitor of sexual pleasure; using safer sex techniques can increase your feeling of security. Vinyl, "one size fits all" gloves may also be used, although they are made of heavier material and blunt sensitivity.

Anyone who has experienced dental surgery or root-canal work is probably familiar with the latex dam. It's a square of surgical latex stretched over the teeth in such a way that only the tooth being operated on is exposed. As an aid to safer sex, the thin latex square can be stretched over the opening to the anus or the vagina to serve as a barrier to viral transmission during oral stimulation much as a condom serves during fellatio. As with a condom, the latex dam to some degree reduces sensation. Many people find that latex dams are less acceptable for routine use than condoms or latex gloves. The Ecstasy Program can help overcome this obstacle to sexual pleasure by teaching you ways to work through your resistance and by improving your ability to concentrate on the stimulation you do receive. For men who wish to stimulate a partner orally who isn't documented to be AIDS-safe, a latex dam can offer a safer compromise. Alternatively, clear plastic food wraps can be used for cunnilingus.

You can add playing with latex as a component of foreplay during the initial encounter between you and your partner. Use your imagination to turn a necessity into an opportunity for pleasure. Blow up a dry condom and tie it off like a balloon, as most of us did on the sly when we were children. Rub the inflated condom over your partner's body. Use it to stimulate his/her nipples and genitals (use a separate condom for each person). It's an interesting sensation.

Play with a latex dam as you played with the condom before. Surgical gloves are hardly any hindrance to stimulation, and if you ever wanted to play doctor, now's your chance.

A significant sexual minority has always used latex materials and other rubber goods as adjuncts to stimulation. Such use may be fetishistic for some people, but it depends at least in part on sensual qualities inherent in the material—its similarity to skin. Not many people find sandpaper sensual. Couples who wish to practice safer sex have a new challenge today—to incorporate latex pleasurably into their sexual encounters.

SAFER SEX KITS

Safer sex kits are not generally available on the market. One is available from the Institute for the Study of Advanced Human Sexuality (see the Sources section of the Appendix, page 407), but you may easily obtain the components for such a kit at your drugstore. Made up from stock, your kit should include:

1. Two kinds of condoms, unlubricated and lubricated with nonoxynol-9.
2. A tube of spermicide containing nonoxynol-9.
3. Latex surgical gloves in two sizes—large for men, small for women.
4. A supply of latex dams.

Safer sex kits may eventually become standard equipment on dates. For now, we strongly advise you to be prepared.

LEARNING TO LOVE CONDOMS

To bring condom use into happy sexuality and intimacy, it's important to become comfortable with this sometimes intimidating stranger. Once you've accepted its importance as protection, you need to embrace it as an accessory to sexual enhancement. You need to decide to have fun with condoms. Remember, sex is fun no matter what you do.

Many women who arrived at sexual maturity after the development of birth control pills don't have much experience with condoms. Discovering their qualities can be fun. Even going into a drugstore and buying them can be a new and interesting experience for the uninitiated. They're much easier to buy now than they used to be. In most pharmacies they're not hidden behind the counter anymore; they're out on display in a variety of colors, textures, and shapes. Some have ribs and little bumps molded in to add to sensation. Some are lubricated, some are dry, some are treated with the spermicide nonoxynol-9.

Start by purchasing or collecting a variety of condoms. Be willing to spend five to fifteen dollars on a collection. Spread out a variety of condoms in their original packages within easy reach, then close your eyes, reach into the pile, and pick one. With your eyes still closed, practice quickly and gracefully opening the package. If you're single, you may want to try this exercise alone first. Among its other qualities, the type of condom you ultimately select for regular use should be one you can open easily with your hands or teeth. If you need any kind of sharp instrument to open the package, select another brand.

Before you roll a condom onto the penis, notice how it smells and tastes. Different condoms smell, taste, and feel differently. Be sure you handle, smell, and even lick the condom while still rolled. Evaluate it for bouquet the way you would a glass of wine.

Appearance. Condoms are produced in various colors. Most are transparent; others are milky white or yellow. Decide what color or appearance you like. Partners should make this decision together.

Lubrication. Lubricants are important to how a condom feels. Albolene Cream and Creme de Femme are oil-based lubricants that appear to be relatively safe for use with thicker-style latex condoms for brief periods —less than ten minutes. Lotions and creams are generally acceptable but some may also be oil-based; check ingredients. More specialized and longer-lasting products that can be used with condoms are listed in the Sources section of the Appendix.

For improved disease protection and for contraception, you may want to use a lubricant that contains nonoxynol-9. This spermicide is not an attractive taste to most people, and isn't likely to be acceptable for oral sex. The man should try applying it to his condom-covered erection so that doing so becomes a familiar experience and feeling. Enjoy the fun of applying it with stimulation supplied by the man himself or by his partner.

Nonoxynol-9 has been found to kill herpes simplex virus, genital herpes, and perhaps HIV, cytomegalovirus, hepatitis B virus, chlamydia, gonorrhea, and syphilis as well as sperm. Condoms alone are very good protection, since they help prevent viruses from entering the partner's body. Nonoxynol-9 is additional protection in case of condom breakage.

Texture. Some condoms are made up with textures: ribs, fine bumps, coarser bumps. Manufacturers claim in advertising that textures add to female pleasure. Most women don't notice any significant difference between condoms with or without these embellishments, but they may be fun for a change.

Tearing. Some people are inhibited from using a condom because of concerns about tearing. Condoms are surprisingly sturdy, particularly the thicker American brands. (Japanese brands are sometimes thinner and a little less sturdy.) We suggest you sacrifice several condoms to learn their tear strength. Go ahead and try to tear one. In fact, tear several. See what it takes to do so. Stretch one until it covers not only all four fingers, but your entire fist. Try putting one over your head. Clamp one around a faucet and fill it with water until it bursts. Fill one with a small amount of water, tie off the end, put the condom in your mouth, and chew on it. (It produces the same satisfying crackle and snap as chewing gum.) Some men brag about being "just too much man" for any condom to contain. Once they've seen a tiny latex tube stretched over a person's head, they may want to reconsider this boast. If you think that the intensity of your sexual activity is too great for condoms, you may need to reexamine your opinion after you've stretched, popped, and chewed a few.

Applying condoms. Many men learned how to put on condoms when they were adolescents, as part of their self-stimulation ritual. They used condoms as a way of disposing discreetly of their ejaculate. If you didn't discover condom use in this way, it's not too late to learn now.

With fantasy or friction, get yourself erect. Open the package. If the condom is dry, you may apply a small amount of lubricant to the end of your penis. Using a small amount of lubricant on the head of the penis adds to the male's sensitivity but may somewhat increase the possibility of the condom's unintentionally slipping off during intercourse. You may find your erection subsiding while you're distracted with putting on a condom but don't be concerned. Get yourself erect again.

Slowly roll the condom onto your penis shaft all the way to the base, leaving a small reservoir end at the tip if there isn't one in the condom. Enjoy the sensation of the condom sliding over your penis. Notice the pleasurable feelings and concentrate your attention on the arousal sensations that the condom provides.

For men without a foreskin, using a condom helps to duplicate to a degree the experience of having one. Try moving the condom at the penis head up and down. Rotate it back and forth from side to side between your thumb and forefinger at the glans. This stimulation can be highly arousing.

Use your condoms during self-stimulation. Wear one for the full time you're self-stimulating.

For women with or without partners, incorporate opening condoms and exploring and playing with them into your self-stimulation activity. Put one on your fingers and use it to touch yourself on your outer and inner lips, on your clitoris, and inside your vagina. It may be interesting to roll a condom over the head of your vibrator or dildo. Apply a condom over your fingers and suck on them. Try blowing one up, tying a knot at the end, and creating your own phallic toy. You may also enjoy learning to put a condom on your partner with your mouth, turning a responsibility into a game. Practice on your fingers first.

Couples can have fun exploring and playing with condoms together, laughing together. Remember, lovemaking is communication. One kind of communication is playing. Playing with condoms together can be a part of lovemaking.

CONDOM USE: A CHECKLIST

Some people find condoms easy to use. Others find them frustrating. Careful attention to handling them can maximize protection and increase your self-confidence. When condoms fail, they generally do so because of incorrect use. Proper usage will substantially increase effectiveness.

The basics of safer sex with condoms:

1. Always use condoms for vaginal or anal sex.
2. Always put on the condom *before* penetration.
3. Use only water-based lubricants.
4. Avoid use of oil-based lubricants such as mineral oil, cold cream, skin lotion, or petroleum jelly.

Steps in using a condom:

1. Select a brand that you have pretested for relative convenience of packaging and opening, for taste, texture, presence or absence of lubrication and nonoxynol-9 spermicide.
2. Add a small amount of lubrication to the head of the penis before putting on a condom to increase sensation without causing significant slippage.
3. Leave a little room at the head of the penis as you unroll the condom. Don't leave too much—air bubbles can cause breakage. Plain-end condoms should have half an inch of free space. Reservoir-end condoms have this space designed in.
4. Unroll the condom so that it covers the entire erect penis. If un-

circumcised, pull back the foreskin before rolling the condom on. Smooth the condom to eliminate any air bubbles. Add extra water-based lubricant on the outside of the condom before beginning intercourse. Insufficient lubrication can cause condoms to tear or pull off. If the condom begins to slip off, you can clamp it with your fingers at the base to hold it in place.

5. After intercourse, hold the base of the condom to avoid spillage, withdraw gently, discard the condom, and wash.
6. Communicate. Discussing using condoms with your partner can make it easier for both of you. Be honest about your feelings and needs.

When condoms break:

1. Stop what you're doing, withdraw, and examine the condom closely. If the man has not ejaculated or if the tear is near the base of the condom, there's little to worry about. Simply remove the torn remains, replace the condom with a new one, and continue. (Breakage during intercourse is why we recommend that the man try to break a condom deliberately during self-stimulation. He needs to learn to feel the difference between intercourse with and without.)
2. If the breakage occurs during or after intercourse with released semen, insert a generous amount of spermicidal foam or spermicidal jelly into the vagina (or anus, if intercourse was anal) to help destroy sperm or germs. Don't remove this spermicide for at least an hour.

With care and deliberate attention to detail, sex can be safer. The experience of practicing Ecstasy Program stimulation techniques adds to the intense physical pleasure and intimacy possible even through the protection of mechanical barriers.

VIII
THE ECSTASY PROGRAM

The Ecstasy Program is highly structured. There's a reason for that structure: it assures you and your partner that your training is thorough and it makes following the program easier. No matter how happy you are with your partner, each of you will experience resistance to changing your relationship. Some of that resistance will be unconscious. You'll be resisting without even knowing you're doing so. The structure we've built into the Ecstasy Program will help you overcome both conscious and unconscious resistance. We want you to succeed at improving intimacy and increasing the pleasure you experience and share.

For the same reason, we strongly advise you to make *no* modifications in the structure of the exercises. If you feel it's absolutely essential to modify any part of the exercises, please do so only with your partner's agreement, freely discussed and freely given. We recommend you write down any modifications you make. If writing down modifications feels too cumbersome, at least make deliberate verbal agreements and stick by them. Following the program will increase your chances of succeeding. If you do change the program and find that you are running into difficulties or not making apparent progress, it's possible that you may be missing important information or experiences. What's worked for several thousand other couples can work as well for you.

PROGRAM EVALUATION

Before beginning the Ecstasy Program, and again after you've completed it, we suggest that you and your partner each evaluate your relationship using the following outline as a guide.

EVALUATE YOUR SATISFACTION
WITH YOUR RELATIONSHIP

0 = poor   3 = good
1 = fair   4 = very good
2 = fairly good   5 = excellent

	Pre-Program		Post-Program	
	Date _____		Date _____	
	Man	Woman	Man	Woman
1. *Communication*				
Honesty of partner	____	____	____	____
Amount	____	____	____	____
Equality	____	____	____	____
Constructive vs. destructive	____	____	____	____
2. *Romance*				
Amount	____	____	____	____
Quality	____	____	____	____
Balance of who initiates	____	____	____	____
3. *Intimacy*				
Sharing feelings	____	____	____	____
Sharing thoughts	____	____	____	____
Sharing experiences	____	____	____	____
Conversation	____	____	____	____
Fun	____	____	____	____
4. *Sensuality*				
Affectionate touching	____	____	____	____
Foreplay	____	____	____	____
5. *Sexuality*				
Frequency	____	____	____	____
Time spent	____	____	____	____
Quality	____	____	____	____
Time in orgasm	____	____	____	____

6. *Overall relationship*
Friendship/caring _____ _____ _____ _____
Trust _____ _____ _____ _____
Love _____ _____ _____ _____
Relationship growth _____ _____ _____ _____

DECIDING PROGRAM SPEED

The Ecstasy Program is divided into twelve weeks of exercises, a rate of time commitment and emotional challenge that works well for most couples. Some couples with limited time together, difficulties in their relationship, or problems of sexual functioning may need to spend several weeks or more on each week's exercises. Some enthusiastic couples who currently enjoy frequent and satisfying sex and who can arrange to spend several additional hours of intimate time together each week may move through the program in less than twelve weeks. If you disagree about program rate and about when to move on to the next exercises, the partner who has the greater resistance to moving faster should prevail.

How long it will actually take you to complete each week's exercises will depend on a variety of factors: how much time you make available, your usual sexual frequency, how closely your levels of sexual desire match, how adequate your present communication patterns are, any problems you may have with sexual functioning, how well motivated you are, how much anger (hidden or overt) is present in your relationship, the quality of your past sexual interactions, and whether either partner feels coerced.

The key to your actual program speed is to continue to practice the current week assignments until you *both* agree you have done them satisfactorily. The Exercise Completion Agreement at the end of each week will assist you in making this judgment. Please discuss the agreement honestly and each sign it only if you have done the exercises as agreed. Take it seriously.

Week One lays the groundwork for all subsequent weeks. Doing the Communication Exercise and the Kissing Exercise satisfactorily are an essential foundation for practicing the attitude skills and building the trust with your partner that will allow you to progress through the rest of the program. Do not rush through Week One. Some couples need to take four weeks or more on the Week One exercises.

If you move on to subsequent weeks and find yourselves having continued difficulties completing one or more weeks, you should return to the last week you completed satisfactorily and do the exercises of that earlier week again, and also again sign the Exercise Completion Agreement. Then move ahead to the week you were unable to complete.

Some couples may wish to follow selected portions of the program. Virtually all couples, even those with problems, are likely to benefit by following Weeks One through Five, if they have the desire and reach agreement to do so. Feel free to spend as much time as you need to do each week's exercises.

Couples who discover that even the slowest of program speeds leads them into more serious arguments, disagreements, and hostility should consider discontinuing. First consult "Solving Problems," page 388, in the Appendix. If the advice and practice of the suggestions there don't help resolve the problem, refer to other self-help books for problem solving referred to in "Further Reading," page 405. One or both partners might consider seeking the services of a counselor or psychotherapist. If therapy or counseling helps to resolve some of the issues damaging your relationship, your time with the Ecstasy Program won't have been wasted. You may, after therapy, find that you can return to the program and follow it through to greater intimacy and pleasure after all.

STARTING THE PROGRAM

Most people don't read directions until something goes wrong (hence the well-known slogan "When all else fails, read directions"). We'd rather things went right rather than wrong for you. We've developed some guidelines to help make that happen. Read the directions, please.

Guidelines for Following the Ecstasy Program

1. At the beginning of each week, read through the entire week's discussion. Each of you should read each week's discussion separately. Don't ask your partner to do your reading for you.

2. Reread the exercise assignments. During this second reading, do a mental rehearsal. Visualize yourself following each assignment. In your mind's eye, *see* yourself performing each exercise step by step. At the same time, imagine what you will say to yourself at each step of the way. Think of positive statements to encourage yourself to succeed: "This feels good. I'm enjoying this. I'm looking forward to improvement. This is going to make things even better." Also imaginatively *feel* in your body the sense of what you expect to experience when you're doing each part of every exercise.

3. Decide who will be the initiator of each partner exercise for the entire week. The initiator is responsible for reminding his/her partner when it's time to do the exercise. He/she's responsible for getting his/her partner's agreement to proceed. If it isn't possible to do a particular exercise at the time previously agreed upon, or if it's jointly agreed not to do an exercise at a previously agreed time, the initiator takes responsibility for getting agreement on an alternate time and for recording that change in the Exercise Planning Agreement. The initiator prepares the setting for the exercise, delegating all or part of that responsibility to his/her partner only with his/her partner's express agreement. When you're ready to start an exercise, each partner should reread the exercise instructions. Alternatively, the initiator may read the relevant exercise instructions aloud. You may find it helpful to keep the book open to that section and placed within easy reach in case you need to consult it. The initiator keeps time and is responsible for arranging stopping times during the exercise.

4. Plan your solo assignments and exactly when you intend to do them. This planning is especially important for the longer exercises such as self-stimulation.

5. Execute an Exercise Planning Agreement. We'll print one at the beginning of each week of exercises. After you complete an exercise, the initiator should check it off on the agreement.

6. Instructions assume right-handedness. If you're left-handed, reverse the directions.

7. Part of the value of the Ecstasy Program comes from talking about the exercises you've done. After an interaction, lying in each other's arms may be one of the best ways to share. Talk about your feelings within a few minutes of the experience. Don't wait until later in the day or the next day when thoughts and feelings will be more distant. Discuss what felt good; what might have felt even better; what your highest level of sexual arousal was; what some of your distracting thoughts were while your partner was stimulating you or while you were stimulating him/her. Did you find yourself thinking that your partner might be getting tired or might end the interaction? Did you think, when your climb to arousal leveled off, that you might not be able to increase your arousal any more? Was your partner giving you enough stimulation or too little, at the right rate and pressure? How could stimulation have been improved? Did you feel you could trust your partner to keep you climbing reliably toward orgasm (if you're a woman) or to hold you at a high level just short of ejaculation (if you're a man)? If you were the giver, did you wonder or worry you were not arousing your partner well enough? That your partner might be impatient or bored? What did you learn from the exercise?

8. If you have difficulty completing any week's assignment, do *not* go on to the next week. Some couples need to spend two or three or even more weeks on a single week's assignment. Some weeks may challenge you more than others as you encounter resistances unique to your relationship. The important thing is to take as much time as you need to make agreements you actually keep.

Couples with extreme disparity of desire (he prefers lovemaking once a month, for example, while she prefers three times a week), or those who have fallen into habitually rare sexual interaction, or couples where great anger (which may be suppressed and not overt) diminishes the quality of lovemaking, may need six months or more to complete the Ecstasy Program. They may need to stay with Week One for four to six weeks.

We strongly urge you to follow the program sequence. Do not skip ahead. Do not change the structure. Our experience has been that when there is significant deviation from the program structure, important lessons are lost. If you don't find improvement occurring, it's quite possibly due to failing to follow the program as designed. Reread the instructions. Have your partner read them. Discuss them. Take the time for each other and for yourself. It's worth it. Whatever your rate of progress, enjoy your discovery of each other. We believe you'll be amazed by the new access of passion and intimacy you'll find. Good luck!

THE ECSTASY PROGRAM

WEEK ONE

SUMMARY OF EXERCISES

SOLO EXERCISES

1. 20–0 Countdown (3 minutes, 4 times per day).
2. Sex Muscle and Breathing (4 minutes, 2 times per day; may be combined with routine daily activities).

PARTNER EXERCISES

1. Discuss Resistances (5 times).
2. Execute Exercise Planning Agreement.
3. Communication (Appreciations and Resentments) (2 rounds each, 10 minutes per day, 5 times).
4. Kissing (15 minutes, 4 times = 1 hour per week).
5. Sign Exercise Completion Agreement (see end of Week One).
6. Any spontaneous, unstructured lovemaking you choose in addition to these exercises, throughout this and each subsequent week.

Week One introduces exercises of great importance to extending orgasmic response and to your relationship, but sexual intercourse isn't among them. We've reserved Week One for discussion and exploration, for getting to know yourself and your partner.

Your response to this statement may be, "But we already know each other. That's why we've agreed to follow the Ecstasy Program. Some of these exercises aren't necessary."

We're convinced that all these exercises are very necessary, and in the sequence designed. They'll give you more specific information about each other and your differences and preferences. They'll keep your learning and growing more parallel. We ask you not to skip an exercise even if, at times, you feel tempted to do so. The exercises in the Ecstasy Program are structured in a sequential, sensitive way to give you the maximum amount of comfort and growth in your partner interaction. In fact, intercourse doesn't enter the program as an exercise until Week Eight.

That reservation doesn't mean we expect you and your partner to abstain from intercourse for the next eight weeks. To the contrary, we hope you *will* continue to make love as often as you like in your usual and comfortable ways. The program is *additional* to your existing sexual relationship, not a substitute for it. That's what point 6 of the Summary of Exercises means. You can continue your usual and customary sexual pattern in addition to these assignments.

Remember, it's very important that you do not move on to next week's assignments until you and your partner both agree that you have completed each exercise of the current week's program in the manner assigned, however many weeks that may take you.

SOLO EXERCISES

EXERCISE ONE: 20–0 COUNTDOWN

Rationale

Sexual pleasure is an experience controlled partly by physical and partly by mental stimulation. The two systems of control overlap and to some extent duplicate each other. A man may have an erection, for example, while doing no more than thinking about a sexual situation. He may also have an erection while unconscious—on the operating table, for example, under anesthesia, when his genital area is being washed to prepare him for surgery. A woman may similarly feel the female equivalent of erection—vaginal lubrication and engorgement—while thinking sexual thoughts. She is equally capable of arousal under purely physical stimulation, such as when a partner gently stimulates her genitals while she's asleep and she lubricates without awakening.

Extending sexual response involves training both physical and mental control systems. For increasing mental control, the 20–0 Countdown is an extremely simple yet remarkably effective exercise. Mental control —learning to concentrate—by narrowing the focus of attention, more specifically to screen out unwanted thoughts, is important to helping to learn to experience extended orgasm. You do not have to be a victim of your destructive or counterproductive thoughts.

Our thoughts, a background of noise like static on the radio, constantly distract us. To see for yourself, close your eyes. Become aware of your breathing. Counting backward from 20, count your exhaled breaths silently to yourself. Whenever you're distracted by a thought, continue your countdown with the last number you remember. Try to notice how many times you're distracted. If you're like most of us, you didn't get very far down the list of numbers before a thought intervened. It probably took you several tries before you were able to count all the way down to 0. Most people are victims of their thoughts. A thought comes in and continues its development in your mind unless you have the skills to stop that thought and restructure it.

You're born with the ability to visualize. You can visualize many things simultaneously. Language doesn't work the same way. It's linear; you can only say one word to yourself at a time. Try to say yes and no to yourself simultaneously. You can't do it. You can say half of one word and half of another, but you can't say both at the same time. One way to block thoughts, then, is to repeat a word over and over to yourself. That's the basis for some traditional systems of meditation.

We counseled a stockbroker recently who had a problem achieving erection. Like many businessmen, he was a Type A personality—intense, driven, high-achieving, and impatient. We assigned him the 20–0 Countdown Exercise. He tried it. We asked him how far he got before his first distracting thought intruded. He grinned when he answered. "Twenty," he said.

Like our stockbroker, many people have trouble counting down past

19 or 18 before an intrusive thought appears. Such thoughts come in many forms. Physical needs intrude: "I have to go to the bathroom." "I'm hungry." "A beer would taste good about now." "My nose itches." Doubts intrude: "Why am I doing this?" "Will this really help?" Environmental distractions occur: "Is that dog ever going to stop barking?" "I think I hear the kids fighting." "Was that the door?" There seems to be a continual background of thinking going on just below consciousness; thoughts rise to the surface like bubbles. You may even find yourself thinking about the fact that you're not supposed to be thinking. The sheer quantity of thoughts that the mind manufactures every minute can be overwhelming. The mind doesn't like to be controlled. It likes to think whatever it chooses. The important point to remember, though, is that once any particular thought becomes conscious, your conscious mind can control or change it if you decide to do so.

The 20–0 Countdown Exercise is not only a valuable way of measuring the relative quiet (or noise) going on in your head. It's also a way to achieve a measure of control over that constant stream of thoughts. After a few weeks of practicing this exercise you should find that your concentration has improved significantly. The nice thing about the Countdown is that you can continually monitor your improvement.

The technical term for deliberately stopping thoughts and controlling the flow of conscious thought is "cognitive restructuring." Cognitive restructuring isn't mumbo jumbo. It's a commonplace of psychology, and it works. In some ways it's similar to the techniques used in some forms of Eastern meditation, and the goals are the same: control of the flow of thoughts passing through the conscious mind.

The 20–0 Countdown may be your first deliberate attempt to focus your concentration and take control of your thoughts. Doing this brief, deceptively simple exercise is a way to begin learning to relax. Relaxation is a key to improving your physical and emotional well-being. In sexual training we've found daily practice of the 20–0 Countdown invaluable for reducing the stress and distraction that interfere with intimacy and sexual pleasure.

The Exercise

Begin by making yourself comfortable. Sit in a comfortable chair with your back straight, your neck relaxed, and your chin resting on your chest or your head against a headrest. Position your feet flat on the floor.

Rest your hands comfortably on your thighs. Then close your eyes, clear your mind of intrusive thoughts, and become aware of your breathing. Focus your attention (concentrate) on the feeling of the cool air coming in through your nostrils and the warm air going out. Begin counting down silently from 20 to 0. Say the number to yourself. Count down one number at each exhalation, imagining the number being written on a blackboard. Keep repeating the same number silently to yourself over and over until the next exhalation, then change numbers.

If you find your attention diverted by a thought or a sound, remind yourself to return your attention to the number, repeating it and again visualizing it. If you have trouble visualizing the number, imagine writing it. Twenty, for example: imagine the 2 being written first and then the 0. Continue counting until you reach 0, then open your eyes.

Review when your attention was diverted. At what number did an intrusive thought appear? Keep track of how long you kept your attention focused on the Countdown before you were distracted by an intrusive thought. Your progress in concentration training can be measured in part by the gradual lowering of this number.

Do a Countdown *four times a day*. Do it before you get out of bed as your first waking act, at lunchtime, at the end of the workday, and last of all at night lying down before you go to sleep. This schedule will give you practice stopping thoughts during the active and less active parts of your day, preparing you to control your thoughts during your sexual interactions. Try in each case to find a quiet location where you won't be disturbed. The full exercise will take about three minutes each time you do it, for a total of twelve minutes a day, or about an hour and a half this week. In future weeks, beginning with Week Two, we'll ask you to do this exercise no less than twice a day every day. Four times a day is even better, not only for sexual training but also for general training in concentration. It's well worth the effort.

EXERCISE TWO: SEX MUSCLE AND BREATHING

Even knowledgeable men and women who may have heard of the great value of developing the special sex muscles usually have not worked to train them. For increased sexual pleasure, we strongly advise all our clients to develop their sexual muscles. In both males and females, these are called the *pubococcygeus*, or P.C., muscles. You may not know that you do, but you probably already use your P.C. muscles to increase your sexual arousal during self-stimulation and intercourse. The stronger your P.C. muscles, the more control you have over their action. The better exercised they are, the greater the flow of stimulating blood to the genitals. Weight lifters find pleasure in "pumping up" their muscles by exercising them at the beginning of a workout, causing them to enlarge and fill with blood. Working your P.C. muscles similarly adds pleasure during sexual stimulation.

P.C.-muscle exercises can be extremely helpful to increasing the intensity and length of orgasm for men and women alike.

Back in the late 1940s, a gynecologist named Dr. Arnold Kegel (pronounced *kay*-gull) developed a good, basic program of P.C.-muscle exercises to help women who have problems controlling their bladders. It's clear now that "Kegel exercises" also condition the P.C. for sexual arousal, and that they work equally as well for men as for women.

An *ESO* reader wrote us to report that she experienced painful cramps when she started Kegel exercises during her menstrual period. The cramps she experienced probably weren't menstrual pain but came from exercising untoned muscles. As the P.C. muscles gain tone, they'll stop cramping. There's a good chance that the discomfort of menstruation will lessen appreciably too.

Sex-muscle exercises help a man develop stronger erections. Learning to tighten, relax, and push out the P.C. muscle allows a man to control his sexual system the way he controls a car. *Tightening* is the accelerator, increasing arousal. Relaxing or *pushing out* is the brake—it can help prevent unplanned ejaculation.

The Exercise

Identifying a Woman's P.C. Muscle

Here's how a woman can identify her P.C. muscle:

The next time you go to the bathroom to urinate, starting with a full bladder, relax your legs and see if you can stop the flow of urine without moving them. The muscle you use to do that, the one that turns the flow on and off, is your P.C. muscle. If you don't find it the first time, don't give up. Try again the next time you have to urinate. If your sex muscles are already in reasonably good condition, you'll be able to stop the flow of urine quickly every second or two for three times or more. If you can't manage that many starts and stops easily, don't worry. You can increase strength and control with the exercises we'll be suggesting (you won't do those while urinating).

Identifying a Man's P.C. Muscle

Here is how a man can identify his P.C. muscle:

Try to stop the flow of urine during urination. The muscle you use to do that is your P.C. muscle. You may feel a tightening around your anus as well. You also use your P.C. to force out the last drops of urine.

The sex muscle exercises are a simple three-part process for men and women.

Sex-Muscle Exercises for Men and Women

Flutter Clenches. Clench and relax the P.C. repeatedly about once per second. Your anal muscles will be tightening and relaxing at the same time. Some people who are accustomed to checking their pulse find it convenient and interesting to adjust periodically the rhythm of the clenching to their heartbeat.

Flutter Push-outs. Bear down moderately, as if trying to expel the last drops of urine. Women may understand this as if pushing in labor. Then relax those muscles. Do this push-out-and-relax process repeatedly, about one per second. You may also feel the abdominal muscles tighten when you bear down, as well as the P.C. muscle. Certain of the anal muscles tend to open during each push-out. As with the clench contractions, some may prefer to match their push-out rhythm to their heartbeat.

Slow Clench/Inhales. Squeeze and clench the P.C. muscle as you did to stop the flow of urine. Clench firmly for a slow count as you breathe in. Hold your breath and your clench for a second or two. Then relax the P.C. muscle as you breathe out. Pause for a second before you begin your next inhale-clench. You'll be firmly contracting for the duration of your breath in and relaxing the same muscle for the duration of your breath out. The duration of your slow clench will vary depending upon your comfortable breathing rate. This time could range from two seconds to fifteen seconds.

You will also feel your anus tightening and relaxing. Allow yourself to breathe at a comfortable rate and depth. It's best not to push your breathing faster or slower than is comfortable. Deeper breaths, however, are generally more effective and relaxing than shallower ones.

If you've never done sex-muscle exercises before, you might begin training your P.C. muscle during Week One by doing ten flutter clenches, followed by ten flutter push-outs, and then ten slow clench/inhales. Doing the three types of sex muscle exercises in succession is one "set." Do one complete set at least two times every day.

Do as many repetitions of each exercise as you can without great effort. Initially, you may only be able to do a total of two or three minutes of exercises in each set. With daily practice, after a month or two, you may find your endurance and strength increasing to reach a goal of 300 total repetitions per day, divided into two sets of 150 repetitions. Alternatively, you can practice by allotting an amount of time, taking twenty minutes per set.

As you start your first week, however, you may find that ten repetitions are too many for you, that your beginning ability is closer to five. At the same time, some readers may already be doing fifty or more total repetitions in each set. To determine your starting number, we ask you to take a little test.

Right now, having finished reading the last paragraph, contract your P.C. muscle while breathing in, then relax it. Repeat. How many times can you repeat these contractions without getting tired, without straining too much? At a certain number you'll reach a point where continuing becomes more effort than you're willing to expend. Write down that number. It's a guideline to the number of flutters and slow clenches you can start with in each set in Week One.

So, if you found you were comfortable doing fifteen repetitions of the clench contraction, then fifteen becomes the number of repetitions of flutters and of slow clenches/inhales that you'll do four times a day in Week One. In later weeks, as your P.C. muscles strengthen, you'll increase that number in slow, steady increments. After a full program of training, you may find it comfortable to do a total of as many as 150 to 200 repetitions, possibly even more, per day, to maintain maximum sex-muscle tone.

Alternatively, you can measure your practice based on number of minutes—starting with two or three minutes and working up to twenty minutes twice per day.

You can do sex-muscle exercises almost anywhere—when you're driving, walking, watching TV, washing dishes, sitting at a desk, lying in bed. Sometimes we jokingly call Kegels the "I'm doing them now even as we speak" exercise.

When you start exercising, you may find that your P.C. muscle doesn't want to stay tightened during slow clenches. You may not be able to do flutters very quickly or evenly. That's because the muscle is weak. Control improves with practice.

To feel the contractions of her P.C. muscles and check on their increasing strength, a woman can insert one or two lubricated fingers into her vagina while exercising.

Holding an object in her vagina during the P.C. exercise can speed her progress toward strength and control. Other than fingers, a woman may use a penis-shaped vibrator, which may be purchased by mail order (see the Sources section in the Appendix), or a smooth, clean, phallic-shaped object such as a candle.

Remember to breathe naturally and evenly while you are doing sex-muscle exercises. Do your sets of contractions faithfully two times a day. They'll help you experience longer and stronger orgasms.

PARTNER EXERCISES

EXERCISE ONE: DISCUSS RESISTANCES

You've arranged a space of time away from distractions. The room is comfortable, the music pleasant, the telephone stilled. Both of you have read this book at least once through. You've discussed your hopes and your goals and decided that you want to follow the program. You want to improve communication, to create more romance, to find greater intimacy, to enjoy the ultimate sexual experience with each other. You've agreed that you will do all the exercises exactly as they're described. The book is open beside you and you're ready to begin.

Suddenly, your mind is crowded with intrusive thoughts. "I feel self-conscious." "I don't feel well." "Why should we have to follow a structure?" "He [she] will never know if I don't do my solo exercises." "Shouldn't all this happen naturally?" "I'm too tired." "Does he [she] really want to do this?" "I don't trust him [her]." "I ought to be doing my work." "Sex shouldn't be this deliberate—it's too mechanical." "We already communicate well." "I don't like this exercise; it seems silly." "I don't have time for this." "I don't have any resentments for the Communication Exercise." "It's too much work." "What good is the 20–0 Countdown? It's too simple." "I'm too angry with him [her]." "This is his [her] idea and he [she] is manipulating me."

One part of your mind seems to be saying, "I'd like to do this exercise." The other part is saying, "I don't want to do this exercise."

What's going on? Resistances are going on. You're facing a new and challenging experience. Your mind has found a space in which to rehearse its worries, fears, and preoccupations. In psychology, these intrusive thoughts are called "resistances." Once you've decided and agreed to do an exercise, do it even when you're distracted by last-minute reasons not to.

Resistances are mental conditions, conscious and unconscious, that determine what experiences we allow ourselves to have. They are the limits we set and rules that we follow. For instance: "Don't trust strangers," "Look before you leap," "Don't decide until you are sure," "Beware of free offers." Resistances in many areas are normal and essential to survival. You are aware of some of your everyday resistances. Others, probably the more emotionally entrenched, you're unaware of.

Sexual resistances include the attitudes, the rigidities, the rules, the fears, and the misinformation that define our ability to experience pleasure. Everyone has sexual resistances; if this weren't so, all of us might experience extending orgasm the very first time we were aroused.

The first step toward overcoming specific resistances is identifying them. The 20–0 Countdown allows your mind to quiet down sufficiently to be able to identify specific intrusive thoughts. Intrusive thoughts are the resistances that run counter to an intended action. Unless those particular resistant thoughts are identified and neutralized, they may lead to procrastination or inaction.

The steps to avoid the procrastination trap are:

1. Scan your thoughts for messages that may be opposed to the action you intend to do right now.
2. Simply continue to observe the message—the intrusive thought—without reacting to it or amplifying it. It should simply pass and

disappear within three to five seconds. Deliberately shifting your attention to another thought or to noticing a physical sensation such as breathing is another way to dispose of an intrusive thought.

3. Alternatively, you can form the intrusive thought into specific, concise words and neutralize it by changing the message. For example, you can change "I don't have time to do this exercise; I should be getting dinner ready," to "I agreed to have sex now. It'll be fun. We deserve to take more time for pleasure. Dinner can wait."

4. Write down your resistances or tell them to your partner. Telling your partner doesn't require a response. Once you've identified a resistance to yourself or aloud, it often loses some of its unconscious influence over you.

The resistances you're aware of you can identify easily. The ones that you're unaware of you'll have to discover as you go along. Sometimes intrusive resistances are continuous. At other times they occur intermittently for a few seconds, perhaps several times a minute.

Resistances are normal. Resistances are ways we define ourselves, but also ways we limit ourselves. They're the necessary friction of love. They arise in even deeply intimate relationships, framing sexual pleasure with necessary limits and rules—how frequently we make love, with whom, where, and how. When you've permitted yourself to have pleasure, unfortunately, they tend to get in the way. In the context of seeking to increase sexual pleasure, they're simply barriers that you can work through, every single time they arise.

Don't blame each other for resistances. If you do, you won't trust each other. If you don't trust each other, you can't fully let go to pleasure and to intimacy.

The Exercise

In the Discuss Resistances Exercise we ask you simply to take a moment with your partner each day before you begin each partner session throughout the program. Each of you briefly reports what's on your mind that might prevent you from following through with the specific exercise at hand, or might be distracting you from giving your partner your full attention or from taking pleasure yourself. Make a short written list if it helps. After you've both discussed your resistances, simply go ahead and do the exercises anyway, as you previously agreed and planned to do.

Some reasons for delay are legitimate, of course. Emergencies and surprises may intervene—a sick child, an unexpected visit, a flooded basement. You may renegotiate the time if absolutely necessary. At 1:00 you might reschedule your 1:30 appointment with your partner for 3:00. Make sure both of you agree on the new time.

When you do this exercise, it's important not to spend much time discussing the *content* of your resistances. Simply report them to your partner or write them out together. You're making yourself aware of them, not analyzing them. If you've provided the space of time you agreed in advance to provide for program work, the problems that have momentarily distracted you don't need to be solved now. Simply make a mental note to deal with them later. Then set the distracting problems aside and go ahead with the program exercises anyway. You shouldn't need much more than a minute to put resistances in their place.

EXERCISE TWO: EXERCISE PLANNING AGREEMENT

Rationale

This exercise helps you establish clear communication, keep agreements, and build trust. We've found that couples who skip this process each week are much less likely actually to do the exercises, even if they had intended to do them. Please take time to plan your pleasure times together.

The Exercise

Fill out the following Planning Agreement according to the guidelines we discussed in Chapter VIII, page 131.

EXERCISE PLANNING AGREEMENT/WEEK ONE

Communication Exercise

Initiator_____

Times Scheduled

Sunday	_____	_____
Monday	_____	_____
Tuesday	_____	_____
Wednesday	_____	_____
Thursday	_____	_____
Friday	_____	_____
Saturday	_____	_____

Kissing Exercise

Initiator_____

Times Scheduled

Sunday	_____
Monday	_____
Tuesday	_____
Wednesday	_____
Thursday	_____
Friday	_____
Saturday	_____

EXERCISE THREE: COMMUNICATION

Rationale

Read about the Communication Exercise in Chapter III, page 53. You may have decided to begin practicing it then. Whether you did or not, we'd like you to practice it this week and every week as part of the Ecstasy Program. It's probably the single most important exercise in this book. Let's review how the exercise works and what the ground rules are. These are the ground rules for the Communication Exercise:

1. Choose a *neutral* time to practice Appreciations and Resentments. Avoid the periods immediately before, during, or after other program exercises or around lovemaking.
2. Use a *neutral* tone of voice without judgment or sarcasm. Express your emotions in words, not in nuances.
3. Face each other. Avoid nonverbal signals ("body language"). Maintain eye contact.
4. Take turns initiating Appreciations and Resentments, your partner one day, you the next.
5. Follow the Appreciations and Resentments format strictly.
6. Start every round with an appreciation—a *positive* feeling or statement. Follow with a resentment—a *negative* feeling or statement.
7. Begin with current concerns—things that happened today, yesterday, or within the last week, month, or year. Or mention a general pattern, an overview of something you've observed in your partner repeatedly. Mention roughly when something occurred (last week, yesterday); what you observed and/or heard; your feelings about it. During the resentment statement, add how you would have preferred the situation to happen or what you would like to see different or changed in the future.
8. Use "I" statements rather than "you" statements. Make statements only; don't ask questions. Be brief and specific.
9. Avoid the words "always" and "never."
10. Apply the beltline rule: Don't hit below the belt. Some issues are inherently not resolvable and are therefore destructive to verbalize.
11. If you wish to discuss a particular appreciation or resentment, wait at least thirty minutes, ask your partner's permission, and respect absolutely his/her right to refuse.
12. Don't do a Resentment on the same topic or situation that your partner has just addressed. To do so would be to break rule 11. Responding immediately to a Resentment with your own Resentment is a covert way of defending yourself and could result in emotional escalation. Wait twenty-four hours before expressing a Resentment on an issue your partner has addressed.
13. Watch out for resistances to doing this exercise and discuss them.

In later weeks, you and your partner will be learning to incorporate Appreciations and Resentments spontaneously into your lives as communications to enhance your relationship's normal intimacy (if you haven't already done so). You'll also use the Communications Exercise more specifically for sexual communication.

But for now we would like you to agree to limit the exercise to everyday matters—your likes and dislikes and observations concerning each other outside the sexual sphere. Save your sexual Appreciations and Resentments for a later week.

To summarize (for Week One only): Do two complete rounds of Appreciations and Resentments per person per day. Take time at the beginning of the week to schedule a specific time of day for these important exercises. Avoid sexual topics. Alternate initiating the Communications Exercise daily.

THE SCRIPT

To review, the *basic communication process* is:

Appreciation:

You say: "[Your partner's name], there's something I'd like to tell you."

Your partner responds: "Okay, I'm listening."

You state an appreciation: what you saw or heard, when it happened, how you felt about it.

Your partner responds: "Thank you."

Resentment:

You say: "[Your partner's name], there's something I'd like to tell you."

Your partner responds: "Okay, I'm listening."

You state a resentment: when it happened, what you saw or heard, specifically how you felt about it, and what you would have preferred to have happened.

Your partner responds: "Thank you."

Remember, no discussion without permission. Wait thirty minutes before asking to discuss any Resentment.

EXERCISE FOUR: KISSING

Rationale

Kissing is reputed to be the world's most powerful aphrodisiac. Its reputation is deserved. The *Kamasutra*, the great Sanskrit love poem of ancient India, lists no fewer than eighteen different kinds of kisses, arranged according to their potential for arousal. Other Oriental love manuals classify different kisses by descriptive names: "tea blossom," for example, "rose hip," "summer squall."

Kissing is not simply one among many techniques of lovemaking. Kissing is a world in itself, a communication that simulates and mirrors the entire range of actions and experiences involved in intimate sexual expression. Not surprisingly, in Ecstasy Program training we spend a lot of time with the simple (and not so simple) kiss. Kissing is an excellent way of establishing emotional, physical, and mental connections with your partner.

Sadly, many couples have neglected the kiss as an instrument of communicating affection and arousal. "He doesn't like to kiss" is one of the more common complaints we hear from women in counseling. Women also frequently say, "He used to kiss more when we were dating. Now it's very brief at best. He just doesn't seem interested anymore." They sense that kissing is communication and feel unprepared for further intimacy without it. Kissing is a loving way to change the focus of your attention from other responsibilities to each other. It demonstrates caring and loving, which is a very helpful transition for lovemaking. It also helps eliminate intrusive thoughts.

At first, kissing as an exercise may seem silly. Partners who have been together for a long time will naturally resist being told how to kiss. Kissing is something most of us learned in junior high school. What could there possibly be to learn?

More than you might imagine. Doing the Kissing Exercise can deepen your physical and emotional understanding of each other and foster wonderful intimacy. Most people do not realize how important a communication a kiss is. A kiss isn't just two lips touching. There's a message behind that touch, complex and important. Whether you close your eyes when you kiss, or look at the person you love in intimate closeness, the kiss itself communicates what you're thinking and feeling to your partner. In the weeks to come you'll be setting aside the script. Then the Kissing Exercise will become more free form, though we'll still ask you to practice it as an exercise (hard work!) four times a week.

The Exercise

In Week One we ask you to practice the Kissing Exercise four times, fifteen minutes at a time, for a total of one hour. This week we'd like you to follow a script. Put this book near you when you begin and consult it as you go. Don't stop to look at your watch—approximate the time.

1. *A touch of romance.* Sit together comfortably on a couch, fully clothed, with the lights low, with music playing softly in the background.

2. *Say how you like it.* The man begins by telling his partner how he likes ideally to be kissed (without expecting that he will necessarily be kissed exactly that way) (thirty seconds).

3. *Show how you like it.* The woman then kisses the man the way *she herself* likes to be kissed, incorporating any of the man's earlier suggestions only if she wishes to do so (thirty–forty-five seconds).

4. *Puckering with a peck.* With soft and slightly puckered lips, she slowly and gently pecks around his lips from one side of his mouth to the other, circling or criss-crossing. Sometimes she may concentrate more on the top lip, sometimes on the bottom lip (thirty–forty-five seconds).

5. *Nibbling.* She then gently nibbles on his lips with her own, taking some of his lower lip between her lips, beginning at one side and moving to the other, then nibbling the top lip from one side to the other circling or criss crossing in the same way (thirty–forty-five seconds).

6. *Nibble and a peck, dry.* She next alternates pecking and nibbling (one minute).

7. *Nibble and a peck, moist.* The woman then moistens her lips and tongue and runs her tongue over her partner's lips, occasionally remoistening her lips while alternating this kiss with light, puckered kisses and nibbles (one minute).

8. *French and review.* She then begins to insert her tongue in his mouth intermittently, circling his tongue, alternating so-called French kissing with kisses from the previous steps—nibbling, puckered kisses, licking (one minute).

9. *Free theme.* Finally, the woman chooses whatever kisses she enjoys most, using the techniques we've described or others of her own devising, as she likes (one minute).

After the woman's part of the exercise is completed, you should reverse roles. Go through each of the kissing movements exactly as before, but the *woman* begins by telling her partner how *she* likes to be kissed. The man then kisses her as *he* likes to be kissed, incorporating his partner's wishes to the degree that he desires. The man then proceeds to the subsequent steps of the exercise.

When you've both taken turns, spend a few moments discussing what you liked most about the exercise, what you liked least, how you felt about doing it, and what you learned. Alternate who starts the Kissing Exercise.

EXERCISE FIVE: SIGN COMPLETION AGREEMENT

Rationale

Signing the Exercise Completion Agreements each week may seem unnecessary or even silly to some. Clients sometimes tell us, "We know what we've done, we don't have to bother with signatures." To the contrary, we've found that there's definite value to affirming your actions concretely, in writing. Written and signed agreements, whether between individuals or organizations, generally carry more authority than simple verbal agreements.

The Exercise

At the end of each week, we ask you to sit down with your partner in a quiet place and discuss your progress in the previous seven days. (Obviously, several of the exercises in the Ecstasy Program are done alone. These require honest self-evaluation.) As you talk, you and your partner can report frankly on your experiences with the 20–0 Countdown Exercise, for example, and the P.C. exercises. Also evaluate together your progress with Communication and Kissing—both are exercises, as we've discussed, that can bring up strong feelings of psychological resistance.

We designed Week One to assist you in making and keeping agreements, which builds trust. You should now have an idea of the kind of commitment you made when you and your partner decided to undertake the Ecstasy Program. Week One is a test of sorts to see if you're ready to keep further agreements in the weeks ahead.

For example, the kissing exercises are relatively easy to do. They don't require a major commitment of time. In later weeks, however, we'll ask you to schedule greater blocks of time for the program, moving from minutes a week to an hour and a half to two hours a week (which isn't *that* much time—most people spend more time than that every day watching television, and improving lovemaking can be a lot more fun than watching television). Similarly, we'll ask that you and your partner commit yourselves to explore each other sensually and emotionally. That commitment will require effort, trust, and determination.

EXERCISE COMPLETION AGREEMENT/ WEEK ONE

PARTNER EXERCISES   Initials

1. Discussed resistances prior to each exercise. _____ _____
2. Did Exercise Planning Agreement.   _____ _____
3. Did Appreciations and Resentments twice a
   day, 5 times.   _____ _____
4. Did Kissing Exercise 4 times.   _____ _____

SOLO EXERCISES

1. Did 20–0 Countdown 4 times every day.   _____ _____
2. Did Sex Muscle and Breathing Exercise twice
   a day.   _____ _____

I have accomplished the Solo Exercises described above. My partner and I have accomplished the Partner Exercises described above to our reasonable satisfaction. We also specifically reaffirm our agreement here to move on to follow the exercises of Week Two.

If there has been or will be any change in the program as assigned, we have both talked about those changes and agreed upon them together.

_____   _____
       Signature and Date   *Signature and Date*

WEEK TWO

SUMMARY OF EXERCISES

SOLO EXERCISES

1. 20–0 Countdown (2 minutes, 2 times per day, every day).
2. Sex Muscle and Breathing (increase number of repetitions of each exercise by 10 percent, 1 complete set of 3 exercises 2 times per day, every day).

PARTNER EXERCISES

1. Execute Exercise Planning Agreement.
2. Communication (Appreciations and Resentments) (2 rounds per day, planned, 5 times, plus unlimited spontaneous rounds as problems occur).
3. Kissing (without script) (15 minutes, 4 times).
4. Sensual Focus, Step I (nongenital, nonverbal; 20 minutes per person, 40 minutes total, 2 times).
5. Sign Exercise Completion Agreement.
6. Spontaneous lovemaking as desired.

SOLO EXERCISES

EXERCISE ONE: 20–0 COUNTDOWN

Do as in Week One. By now you may find yourself able to count down to lower numbers before experiencing intrusive thoughts. The Countdown Exercise may seem easier to begin and more pleasurable to accomplish as your interior monologue comes under increasingly conscious control. Remember, you're doing this exercise to learn improved control of your thoughts. Such control can allow you to focus your concentration more effectively on your sensual and sexual arousal. Doing a Countdown or even part of one when distracting thoughts interfere with sexual arousal can help you redirect your attention to your body.

The Exercise

Beginning with Week Two, you'll be doing one cycle of Countdowns at least twice a day. We recommend that those who wish to make the fastest progress in the program continue at four repetitions per day, this week and from now on.

At what number do you think you started to have distractions or intrusive thoughts? Generally, were you at number 18 or number 16 or where? After even a week or two, sometimes even a few days, your progress in counting down before a distraction interrupts may amaze you. It can be fun, and reinforcing, to share your progress with your partner. Here's a convenient chart to make that easier to do:

BEST COUNTDOWN NUMBER REACHED BEFORE DISTRACTION

	Man	Woman
Sunday	_____	_____
Monday	_____	_____

Tuesday   _____   _____
Wednesday _____   _____
Thursday   _____   _____
Friday   _____   _____
Saturday   _____   _____

EXERCISE TWO: SEX MUSCLE AND BREATHING

The Exercise

Continue as in Week One, but each of you increase the number of repetitions per exercise by 10 percent. Calculate that increase by multiplying your present number by .1, rounding up the answer, and adding it onto your present number (for example: $22 \times .1 = 2.2$; round 2.2 up to 3, add 3 to 22, and you have your new number of repetitions for this week, 25).

PARTNER EXERCISES

EXERCISE ONE: EXECUTE PLANNING AGREEMENT

Fill out the following Planning Agreement according to the guidelines we discussed in Chapter VIII, page 131.

EXERCISE PLANNING AGREEMENT/WEEK TWO

Communication Exercise

Initiator_____

Allow 8 minutes; 2 rounds per day planned; 5 times this week.

Times Scheduled

Sunday
Monday
Tuesday
Wednesday
Thursday
Friday
Saturday

Kissing Exercise (Without Script)

Initiator_____

Allow 15 minutes, 4 times this week.

Times Scheduled

Sunday
Monday
Tuesday
Wednesday
Thursday
Friday
Saturday

Sensual Focus Exercise

Initiator_____

Nongenital, nonverbal; allow 20 minutes per person, 40 minutes total, 2 times this week.

Times Scheduled

Sunday
Monday

Tuesday _____ _____
Wednesday _____ _____
Thursday _____ _____
Friday _____ _____
Saturday _____ _____

EXERCISE TWO: COMMUNICATION

The Exercise

As in Week One, continue to do planned Appreciations and Resentments, two rounds per day, for five days.

Don't be surprised if you don't want to do one or another of the assignments this week. You can expect resistances to appear as you work your way through the program. When a resistance does appear, you may find it helpful to state your resistance. Follow that statement with an affirmation of your intent to do the exercise anyway.

In addition to the planned Appreciations and Resentments this week, also do spontaneous Appreciations and Resentments whenever an occasion arises.

Spontaneous Appreciations and Resentments are different from their planned counterparts. They allow you to react to events as they happen. Thus, instead of storing up your appreciation or resentment, saving it for when you've agreed to do the exercise, you can clear the air immediately.

Spontaneous Appreciations and Resentments call for some creativity on the part of the initiator, since the rules still require you to begin with a positive statement even though a negative event may have set you off.

Here's an example of a spontaneous Appreciation and Resentment:

"Stuart, there's something I'd like to tell you."

"Okay, I'm listening."

"I was thinking tonight as I was waiting for you to come home how much I appreciate the hard work you do to give us a good income. It makes me feel good that you want to improve our life-style."

"Thank you."

"Stuart, there's something I'd like to tell you."

"Okay, I'm listening."

"I find I look forward to your getting home at around seven P.M. You arrived much later tonight. It's almost nine-fifteen now. I'm disappointed there's so little of the evening left. I feel unimportant, impatient, and lonesome waiting for you. What I'd like is for you to arrange to be home by seven at least three nights a week."

"Thank you."

All the rules for doing the Communication Exercise still apply when you're doing spontaneous Appreciations and Resentments except that either partner may begin a round at will, whenever he/she has something he/she thinks or feels and would like to express with the least possibility of misunderstanding or argument.

A word about the problem of finding a positive appreciation before you express a negative resentment: the best place to look is in the negative situation itself. Even if you don't immediately see anything positive in the situation, there's almost always something there of humor or compensating quality if you search. If you hate the inefficient way he/she squeezes toothpaste from the tube, it's also probably a small demonstration of the impulsive spirit you enjoy in him/her and find attractive. Hearing that positive appreciation may help him/her also hear your resentment.

EXERCISE THREE: KISSING

Rationale

How you kiss expresses to your partner something about how you feel about yourself and your partner in the areas of romance, intimacy, and sexuality.

You need to be consciously aware of the message you're communicating to your partner as you kiss him/her. Kissing is a way of communicating and the message you deliver can work for you or against you. Holding your message in mind as you kiss is a way of being deliberate. The script you're following determines who is giving and who is receiving. That leaves you responsible for the subtleties of timing and pressure, which determine the message you deliver to your partner. Like a snowflake, every kiss is different—and beautiful!

The Exercise

If you have any resistance to doing this exercise, briefly state what that is, affirm your commitment to what you are doing, and proceed.

Spend the same amount of time on the Kissing Exercise during Week Two as you did during Week One. This week, however, try to perform the exercise without referring to the script. Consult the script, of course, if you forget any part of the sequence (page 153). Take turns going first. By now you're beginning to know the script and to understand the concept of the Kissing Exercise. The concept, of course, is to begin winning your partner's trust by slowly and gently kissing him/her, then progress to more playful, provocative, and ultimately sexual kissing. Slowly prepare your partner for the sexual part of the kiss. Make your kissing smooth and flowing as you change rhythm and timing.

EXERCISE FOUR: SENSUAL FOCUS, STEP I

Rationale

Sensual Focus is light massage with ground rules. It's an excellent exercise in learning to feel pleasure over larger areas of your body, not specifically from genital stimulation. It's a simple way to relax, to move from distraction to intimacy with your partner, to pay attention to pleasure. It's always a good way to begin lovemaking.

Regular, daily hygiene is important to the Ecstasy Program. Before doing any planned exercise we strongly suggest that you bathe or shower. Hygiene is usually adequate if you showered or bathed earlier the same day. For your partner's optimum pleasure and for maximum self-confidence, you may want to consider bathing or showering together before doing the program's sexual-contact exercises. Bathing or showering together can be a pleasurable way to ease into intimacy.

Preferences about cleanliness vary among couples. Some people value hygiene more than others. It's important to ask—and respect—your partner's preferences.

The Exercise

Step I: Silent Touching (twenty minutes each partner)

In a warm, comfortable, private place, naked together, take twenty-minute turns touching and massaging each other. Use a light lotion-lubricant such as hand lotion or baby lotion. Or you may use an oil such as mineral oil. Several scented massage oils are available commercially; use them if they increase your pleasure. (You don't need a heavy lubricant such as Albolene for Sensual Focus.) You may want to light candles, dim lights, and arrange for soft music and wine or juice to enhance comfort and mood. You may want to cover the bed with an extra sheet that you can remove afterward. Here are the ground rules:

1. Start with the man giving and the woman receiving. The woman lies unclothed on the bed or floor on her stomach. She focuses her attention on her sensations or listens to music. No talking, please.

2. The man, unclothed, begins by touching and massaging the woman's extremities—hands and feet—working his way slowly toward the center of her body. Remember, avoid specific stimulation of breasts and genitals—at most, a casual touch in passing.

3. Working from her shoulders down her back, the man starts stroking her body lightly, increasing pressure as he goes. He may brush his tongue and lips anywhere on her body except breasts and genitals. The small of the back, the ears, the nape of the neck, may be particularly responsive to kissing. Sucking toes is sometimes surprisingly erotic. Soles of the feet often respond well to firmer pressure.

4. After about ten minutes, the man gently turns the woman over and repeats the process of touching, stroking, and lightly kissing, using his lips and tongue on the front of her body. He does *not* focus on breasts and genitals. He may lightly touch the breasts, but should totally avoid the genitals.

5. The woman takes as much pleasure from the man's stimulation as she can. She should be doing nothing but feeling as good as she will permit herself to feel. She keeps her hands to herself, resisting any temptation to touch her partner.

6. The man should try to experience the pleasure of caressing his partner and giving her pleasure. Her nonverbal sounds, the varied sensations of touching, stroking, and kneading that he feels through his hands and mouth, and the visual pleasure of looking at her body can be

highly arousing to him. The giver ideally derives as much enjoyment as the receiver.

7. When he's finished, the man gently drapes a towel over his partner's body and allows her to lie quietly for about three minutes. Then he can gently and tenderly kiss her (not a sexual kiss) and help her up.

8. Now reverse the above procedure, the woman giving the massage, the man relaxing and receiving without talking. The man should be lying on his stomach for the first ten minutes or so, then turn over for the second ten minutes. The woman should omit stimulating her partner's genitals. When finished, she should allow him about three minutes of quiet time with a towel over his body. Then she can gently and tenderly kiss him (not a sexual kiss) and help him up.

Take turns beginning the Sensual Focus Exercise, so that the balance of giving and receiving remains approximately equal. If you begin one session, your partner should begin the next.

EXERCISE FIVE: SIGN COMPLETION AGREEMENT

EXERCISE COMPLETION AGREEMENT/ WEEK TWO

PARTNER EXERCISES   Initials

1. Discussed resistances prior to each exercise. _____ _____
2. Did Exercise Planning Agreement. _____ _____
3. Did Appreciations and Resentments twice a
   day, 5 times. _____ _____
4. Did Kissing Exercise 4 times. _____ _____
5. Did Sensual Focus, Step I, twice. _____ _____

SOLO EXERCISES

1. Did 20–0 Countdown at least twice a day. _____ _____
2. Did Sex Muscle and Breathing Exercise twice
   a day. _____ _____

I have accomplished the Solo Exercises described above. My partner and I have accomplished the Partner Exercises described above to our reasonable satisfaction. We also specifically reaffirm our agreement here to move on to follow the exercises of Week Three.

If there has been or will be any change in the program as assigned, we have both talked about those changes and agreed upon them together.

_____   _____
    Signature and Date   *Signature and Date*

WEEK THREE

SUMMARY OF EXERCISES

SOLO EXERCISES

1. 20–0 Countdown (2 times per day, 5 days).
2. Sex Muscle and Breathing (increase number of repetitions of each exercise by 10 percent from Week Two, 1 complete set of 3 exercises twice a day).
3. Self-Stimulation (30 minutes, twice).

PARTNER EXERCISES

1. Execute Exercise Planning Agreement.
2. Communication (Appreciations and Resentments) (2 planned rounds per day; unlimited spontaneous).
3. Kissing (without script) (about 5 minutes, 3 times, at least 2 of those times not followed immediately by genital sex).
4. Sensual Focus, Step II (40 minutes; 20 minutes man giving, 20 minutes woman giving, twice).
5. Sign Exercise Completion Agreement.
6. Spontaneous lovemaking as desired.

SOLO EXERCISES

EXERCISE ONE: 20–0 COUNTDOWN

Rationale

By now you've done this exercise enough that you're probably noticing you have more control of your attention span in all areas, including perhaps sexuality. You're probably also noticing that you feel more relaxed after the Countdown cycle. At night, in bed, you may find you fall asleep more quickly and sleep more deeply after neutralizing your mind with the Countdown Exercise. Please continue to practice this exercise.

The skills that you're learning by doing the Countdown can be applied to help focus your attention on sensation during the Sensual Focus Exercises that you began in Week Two and will be continuing in Week Three. During the Sensual Focus Exercise, when you're receiving, you'll be telling yourself silently and specifically what's happening second by second and what you're feeling. "I'm feeling warm and tingly where she's touching my thigh. It feels good. It would feel good on my penis too." Deliberately verbalizing inner experience at the moment it's happening helps to keep out distracting thoughts. It's concentration training. We'll discuss it further in our instructions for the Sensual Focus Exercise.

The Exercise

Please continue to practice the 20–0 Countdown at least twice a day, five days a week.

After you've completed a Countdown, jot down the number you reached before you were distracted. Compare your numbers with Week Two. Any difference yet?

BEST COUNTDOWN NUMBER REACHED BEFORE DISTRACTION

	Man	Woman
Sunday		
Monday		
Tuesday		
Wednesday		
Thursday		
Friday		
Saturday		

EXERCISE TWO: SEX MUSCLE AND BREATHING

This week you'll be increasing your number of repetitions of each of the three exercises by another 10 percent. Continue in this and each subsequent week to practice two complete sets of exercises each day. You'll also be incorporating these exercises into your Self-Stimulation Exercise.

EXERCISE THREE: SELF-STIMULATION

Rationale

Practice with self-stimulation is a basic preparation for extending and intensifying orgasm. You may know self-stimulation by another name. The old medical term, derived from an obscure Latin word, is *masturbation.*

Self-stimulation doesn't cause insanity, warts, acne, blindness, criminality, homosexuality, ulcers, epilepsy, addiction, or hairy palms. The Victorians thought that female self-stimulation was a disease, one they sometimes "cured," horribly, by surgically removing the clitoris. Equally mistaken, the Victorians believed that each man had only a finite amount of semen and could "spend" himself to exhaustion and premature senility—a theory long since laid to rest. In fact, semen is a renewable resource. The more stimulation, the greater the number of ejaculations and the more total semen volume across a man's lifetime. The glands that contribute their fluids to the ejaculate, the prostate gland in particular, work much like the salivary glands. If no food is at hand, human beings produce less saliva. If no sexual stimulation is at hand, men produce less seminal fluid. It's true that the total number of sperm, present in the body at birth as germ cells, is finite. But sperm only accounts for about 2 percent of the ejaculate volume, and men start life with so many billions of sperm that they don't need to worry about running out.

In short, self-stimulation isn't bad for you and, in fact, can be good for you. Self-stimulation can help you learn how to achieve sexual arousal and—for men—ejaculatory control. It's a major sexual learning tool because it puts you completely in charge of your stimulation. You can find out what feels good without worrying about your partner at the same time.

Your partner can't possibly learn what touch and pressure you like if you don't know yourself. It's important for you to be a willing and helpful teacher, to teach your partner what pleases you. If you don't know what strokes, pressure, and rhythm stimulate you most effectively, you won't be able to assume that role. You'll be leaving your partner pretty much on his/her own, hoping he/she's doing it right, unsure and frustrated. Even if you have a good sexual relationship with a loving partner, you'll benefit from going back to basics, and so will he/she. Your purpose is to learn to give yourself pleasure or to review your skills. Then you'll know how to teach your partner. For additional discussion about the rationale for self-stimulation, see Chapter V, beginning on page 198.

What to Do if You Don't Want to Self-Stimulate

Some men and women feel strongly inhibited from self-stimulation because of religious training. If your personal beliefs or religious prohibitions are strong enough to prevent you from trying out the Self-Stimulation Exercises as described, do the following instead.

Self-Stimulation Exercise alternative. As a substitute during the assigned Self-Stimulation Exercises this week and during Weeks Four and Five, consider allowing your partner to stimulate you exactly as you direct, no more, no less. Tell him/her what you want him/her to do. Demonstrate with your hand. Then direct your partner's hand in the rhythm, with the pressure and to the areas you think will arouse you. If such stimulation produces no arousal after five or ten minutes, you can suggest another area of the penis or clitoris for stimulation and/or changes in pressure and rate. Continue to direct your partner by telling and showing him/her until you find the particular strokes, pressure, and patterns that work best. Your partner should try to follow your directions as carefully and accurately as he/she can. Allow twenty minutes per partner for this exercise.

The Exercise

Plan to set aside at least two thirty-minute periods during Week Three for self-stimulation. Tell your partner when these times are, but spend this time alone. Do this exercise at a different time from the Sensual Focus Exercise or any of the Partner Exercises.

Pamper yourself. Take a sensuous shower or bath and notice the pleasant feeling of warm water on your skin. Afterward, spend a few moments looking at your body and appreciating its good features. Be as positive and friendly with yourself as you try to be with your partner when you're creating a mood of romance.

Touch your body. Explore it for pleasure—kneading muscles, massaging scalp, caressing skin. Men especially may feel embarrassed caressing themselves. Do it anyway to learn what feels good, even if you think you already know. Many men are almost entirely focused on genital stimulation. They can increase their levels of pleasure enormously by widening their focus to include their entire bodies—scalp, head, face, neck, arms, hands, nipples, chest, back, belly, buttocks, thighs, calves, and feet.

At some point during this time of touching and self-exploration, move to a comfortable place where you can sit or lie down—on a chair or couch, on pillows on the floor, or in bed. When you've touched your body for pleasure for at least five minutes, start to explore your genitals. Even if you're familiar with self-stimulation, approach your genitals as if you're doing so for the first time. Don't fall immediately into a practiced pattern. Really *notice* what you're doing, what you're discovering, and how it feels.

After a while, add lubrication and notice the difference between dry stimulation and stimulation with a lubricant.

Now we'll discuss men and women separately, beginning with men. Both of you should read both discussions.

Self-Stimulation for Men: Rationale

The basic requirements for effective self-stimulation training are:

1. Ample time—at least thirty minutes.
2. Sex muscle strengthening and control.
3. Paying close attention to subtleties of sensation.
4. Learning and practicing a variety of strokes involving variations in rate, pressure, and area of contact.
5. Developing control to peak yourself repeatedly—approaching closely enough to ejaculation to experience intense peaks of pleasure— without cresting over into ejaculation.

The three basic skills of male sexuality are: (1) getting erect, (2) staying erect, and (3) ejaculation by choice. These are skills the Ecstasy Program is designed to develop and train. Self-stimulation is a basic exercise for all three skills. So is partner-assisted stimulation, which we'll introduce in Week Eight.

Each man needs to discover the simplest, most reliable way to get as fully erect as efficiently as possible. This process may occur easily in less than a minute, needing only light, slow stimulation, or it may require several minutes of intense stimulation and concentration. Manual methods predominate in self-stimulation. Lubrication is important to allow stimulation to continue for long periods of time and to simulate vaginal sensations. A vibrator may help, as may fantasy, eyes open or closed, and erotic media such as magazines or videos.

Staying erect, during self-stimulation as well as during lovemaking with your partner, is primarily a matter of working through the inevitable intrusive thoughts that come up. We've already discussed intrusive thoughts in the context of resistances to starting the Ecstasy Program exercises; we'll discuss resistances during sexual arousal and how to deal with them when we discuss the giver/receiver exercise in Week Nine (if you're curious, feel free to read that discussion now; it begins on page 261).

Focusing attention. To learn higher levels of awareness and control of sexual arousal, it's essential that you learn reliably to focus and maintain your attention, particularly on (1) selective physical sensations and (2) sexual thoughts. During self-stimulation, for example, focus your attention closely on the feelings your stimulating hand is producing. Appreciate every variety and sensation that comes from every single movement and touch. The more you notice the effect of the stimulating you're doing, the less energy you'll need to expend and the shorter the time you'll need to produce and maintain sexual arousal. Concentrate sufficiently on your pleasurable physical feelings so that you can efficiently dispose of intrusive thoughts as they occur. Work toward requiring no more than five seconds for letting go of a specific intrusive thought.

Self-Stimulation for Men: The Exercise

Begin by lubricating your penis. Now proceed to stimulate yourself to erection using whatever methods and aids work best for you. After you're erect, aim to keep your erection without ejaculation for at least fifteen minutes.

During this time, lubricate your scrotum and the area behind your scrotum—the perineum. Lightly caress your scrotum. With one or two fingers, locate and stimulate your external prostate spot. Alternate stimulation between all three major areas—penis, scrotum, and external prostate spot. During this fifteen minutes (or more), see if you can bring yourself at least six times to the crest of emission-phase orgasm, close to ejaculation. Stop your stroking or reduce speed and pressure each time you near the "point of no return" (ejaculatory inevitability). Ideally, as you become more aware of sensation and more in control, you'll be able to remain near emission-phase orgasm longer without cresting over into ejaculation. At first you may need sometimes to stop and start for several seconds or a minute to regain control. With practice, you'll learn to peak yourself multiple times by reducing the rate and pressure of your stimulation without actually stopping all motion. Your eventual goal in later sessions will be to peak yourself more than fifteen times in each session.

If at any time you slip over the crest by surprise and ejaculate, go ahead and enjoy the ejaculation. After the ejaculation, ask yourself what you learned from the pleasurable experience you just had that might help you in lasting longer next time. For example, did you let yourself get too close to the crest? Were you becoming impatient to ejaculate? Perhaps wanting to stop without acknowledging the fact? Or telling yourself that you were getting a little bored? Were you aware of a clenching of the anal muscles or P.C. muscles just prior to ejaculation?

If you're used to quick self-stimulation, you may find that sustaining an erection without ejaculation for fifteen minutes or more is difficult at first. You may want to start with the goal of maintaining your erection for fifteen minutes and practice peaking yourself only once or twice.

Then, at later sessions, add progressively more near-ejaculation peaks during the fifteen minutes.

Experiment with different kinds of strokes. Here are some to consider.

Types of Strokes

1. Most men stimulate themselves with a basic up and down stroke of one hand.
2. Some men stimulate themselves by rolling their penis in two hands.
3. Your hand can be turned thumb-up or thumb-down.
4. You can make a ring of your thumb and forefinger.
5. You can concentrate stimulation on the shaft or the glans.
6. You can use your index finger and/or third finger to lightly stimulate your sensitive frenulum area after erection.
7. You can use both hands and stroke from mid-shaft outward in opposite directions, toward the glans and toward the base.
8. You can press your penis against your belly and rub its underside with the flat of your palm.
9. You can switch hands, using your nondominant hand.

These are only a few of the many possible variations. Each time you stimulate yourself is a new experience, because you have added your previous experience to the total of what you know and feel. Your goal is not to ejaculate but to *feel more*—to enjoy the process. If you pay attention to the subtleties of your sensation, you won't be bored. Boredom is a form of resistance, a way of denying yourself more sexual pleasure.

When you've achieved hard erection and sustained it for at least five minutes, continue stroking your penis while stimulating your external prostate spot (see following) and controlling ejaculation with the scrotal pull technique (see following).

External prostate spot. External prostate stimulation is best pursued after you've been erect for at least several minutes. It involves pressing upward firmly with one or more fingers on the area of the perineum about halfway between the buried base of the penis and the anus. Press upward with your forefinger or a middle finger or both. Use your left hand while you continue to stimulate your penis with your right hand. Don't be afraid to try using very firm pressure. Try moving your fingers to slightly different areas and use varying pressure to find the most effective combinations.

If you find it awkward to stimulate your external prostate spot with your left hand (assuming you are right-handed and have been using your dominant hand to stimulate your penis), switch hands and stroke your penis with your left hand while you search out and rhythmically press your external prostate spot with your right.

It's usually better not to use this form of stimulation until you've been firmly erect for at least several minutes. Stimulating the external prostate area too soon sometimes feels uncomfortable. When you're near ejaculation, firm pressure in this area can help hold off the ejaculation reflex. Properly timed and placed, firm or rhythmic pressure can give you greater security in your gradual approach to the crest of emission-phase orgasm. You may not be familiar with the sensation. Explore it with an open mind.

Because this spot is located behind the testicles and the base of the penis, which is buried inside the body, pressing on it firmly pushes extra blood into your penis, which should then swell and pleasurably throb. Apply rapid rhythmic pressure.

If you wonder why pressure on this area is often pleasurable, remember that the emission stage of orgasm involves the production of fluid and contractions of the inner male glands, the chief of which is the prostate. Firm, rhythmic pressure on these areas mimics orgasmic contractions without necessarily triggering the ejaculatory reflex.*

If stimulating the external prostate area feels uncomfortable, reduce pressure and stimulate more lightly until you feel more arousal and feel more comfortable, or get yourself more aroused or stimulate yourself a longer time before starting external prostate stimulation.

Some men, though, never do find external prostate stimulation useful or enjoyable. If, after a fair trial, you find that happens to be true for you, don't worry. It doesn't necessarily limit your ability to enhance your orgasmic intensity.

Stop/Start Ejaculation Control Technique. When you find yourself approaching ejaculation, one good way to maintain control is to stop stroking for from five to thirty seconds. Stop stroking when you are three or more strokes from ejaculation. If you get closer than three strokes, you're likely to get too close and crest over into ejaculation.

Scrotal Pull Technique. Another way to assist with ejaculatory control is scrotal pulling. Pulling your testicles away from your body helps to prevent you from ejaculating. Try it.

---

* Recent research by Kevin McKenna of Northwestern University has demonstrated that stimulation of the deep urethral bulb area alone in male and female rats can trigger the orgasm reflex. This analogous anatomy corresponds to the prostate area in men and the Grafenberg area in women.

To apply the scrotal pull, grasp the scrotum between your testicles with the thumb and forefinger of your free hand. When you're near orgasm, pull firmly down. At other times, for stimulation, pull lightly in rhythm as you stroke. Become thoroughly familiar with the scrotal pull. You'll need to teach it to your partner later in the Ecstasy Program.

Another way to accomplish scrotal pulling is to make a ring with your left thumb and forefinger between your testicles and body and pull downward. (See illustration page 300 for a partner-assisted version of the scrotal pull.)

Aim to teach yourself to maintain hard, pleasurable erection with stimulation but without ejaculation for at least fifteen minutes. Once you can sustain arousal for fifteen minutes without ejaculating, you'll probably be able to sustain it for as much longer as you want. Fifteen minutes is also a necessary minimum to build up the muscular tension and vasocongestion that are essential for extending and intensifying orgasm.

If you usually use erotic media—magazines, books, videotapes—during self-stimulation, continue to do so now. If you've never done so, you may want to try, to see if they add to arousal.

Vibrators. A vibrator can be another good form of stimulation to add. It's especially effective for applying stimulation to the external prostate area. The small tip, on the type that has several interchangeable heads, is easiest to use for this purpose. See Sources, page 407, for more information.

You may not notice any improvement in your sexual experience the first time you add something new. You need time to become comfortable with new procedures, new sensations, and new props. If you find a vibrator disappointing the first time you use it, don't give it up. Try it again—try it several more times—experimenting with it at leisure before you pass judgment on its value.

Self-Stimulation for Women: Rationale

As a woman it can be helpful to realize first of all that self-stimulation can be useful. It's not a substitute but a supplement. It's healthy. It feels good. It allows you to learn how you like to be pleasured so that you can teach your partner. Best of all, it adds to your orgasmic capacity. The more frequently you experience orgasms, the easier they are to have and to have more of. (If you are preorgasmic—have never or only rarely experienced orgasm—it can be helpful to learn first to have orgasm reliably. See the Twelve-Step Training Program for Preorgasmic Women on page 396.)

Self-stimulation can also boost your level of libido. Often, if your level of desire is low, it can be increased by deliberately adding more frequent sex. You may resist adding such experiences with your partner for several reasons. One reason is that they're a significant commitment of time and energy. Another reason is that because your level of desire is lower than you would like or lower than your partner's, you may be less motivated to arrange deliberately to increase it.

We've found in counseling that the more often you have a pleasurable sexual experience, the more often you think about lovemaking and the more often you may be motivated to have further sexual experiences. That doesn't mean you'll become obsessive about sex. Natural personal and social controls always provide reassuring limits.

One way to increase sexual awareness and sexual thoughts is to self-stimulate to orgasm more frequently than you are presently doing. Self-stimulation isn't as deeply satisfying as sex with a loving partner, but it's a pleasant and efficient learning experience and it builds desire. It also adds to your knowledge of what stimulation you do and don't prefer. Even if your partner doesn't yet know how to stimulate you in the ways you prefer, he's going to learn by following the assignments in the Ecstasy Program. While he's learning, you can be increasing your level of desire with self-stimulation and discovering at the same time what you want to teach him.

Women have the potential to increase the perceived quality of their orgasm. Increased quality can be experienced in different ways at different times: as longer duration, as more or less intense, as squeeze contractions or push-outs. Deliberately practicing self-stimulation is one of the best ways to learn about possible variations in your orgasm.

Your goal for the Self-Stimulation Exercise is different from a man's. He's discovering what feels good. He's also learning to delay ejaculation—learning how to hold back. You're discovering what feels good, too, but your process of learning to experience better orgasms is learning how to let go more than holding back. If you already know how to have orgasm reliably with self-stimulation, you'll be learning to extend your capacity—to create a more intense orgasm, to make orgasm last longer, to have several orgasms in a row.

Self-Stimulation for Women: the Exercise

1. Touch your body for pleasure for several minutes. Lightly stroking your body will help put you in the mood and begin to sensitize your skin as a channel for pleasure.
2. Lubricate your genitals thoroughly.
3. Stimulate your clitoris. Use your dominant hand. Start with your index and middle fingers moving in a circular stroke on the top of your clitoris. Press your clitoris hard against the pubic bone, stroking it at about one to two cycles per second to bring more blood into the area. As blood fills the clitoris, you'll experience more sensation, just as a man does when his penis becomes erect. The clitoris is much more sensitive when it's engorged and erect. You can feel it standing up and out.
4. Once clitoral erection occurs, you can use lighter strokes, about one per second or slower, caressing the tip of the clitoris with two fingers or more. As the clitoris enlarges and fills with blood, both sides become more sensitive to touch.
5. Use a circular motion on the tip of the clitoris for several minutes and notice the effect on your sensation.
6. Try grasping the clitoris with your thumb and forefinger, rolling it between the two fingers rapidly and firmly.
7. Slide your forefinger and middle finger along each side of the clitoris—the shaft—up and down. Use your thumb simultaneously to press or retract the hood of the clitoris.
8. Alternate among strokes 5, 6, and 7.

Next, lubricate your outer and inner vaginal lips, the opening into your vagina, and even a little inside. Lubricate your perineum—the valley of skin between the lower margin of your labia and your anus. Remember that this is an experience for both your mind and your body: focus on sensation and feeling. You can use a mirror if you like, between your legs. Tell yourself, silently or aloud, how good it feels and how much you deserve this pleasure.

Feel free also to visualize and fantasize. Deliberately practicing fantasy can build excitement. Close your eyes and play with a fantasy or two. Start by talking to yourself, telling yourself where you are and with whom. This description will help you visualize. Try several different scenarios and decide which works most reliably for you. Enlist your mind to provide an exciting scenario while your hand almost automatically stimulates your genitals. Your thoughts can work with you or against you. (If deliberate sexual visualizations make you uncomfortable and reduce arousal, discontinue them until you feel they can add to your pleasure. If your belief system or emotions make your fantasies feel wrong or bad, don't force them. Fantasies are only one factor in creating sexual arousal.)

If you aren't used to self-stimulation, you may want to stimulate yourself for one or more sessions without trying to achieve orgasm. Later, when you feel you're ready, you can go all the way.

If you're used to self-stimulation with orgasm, you might spend some time exploring new strokes, touches, and pressures. Then go on through orgasm and see if you can give yourself more than one. It helps to learn how to stimulate yourself so you can teach your partner.

Vibrators. Many women today have taught themselves to have orgasm with a vibrator. Vibrators are helpful, especially in learning about orgasm for the first time and for efficiency. They often reduce time and effort necessary to reach orgasm, but you can ultimately get more pleasure without a vibrator, using your hands, than with one. Vibrators suitable for sexual stimulation have become widely available in department stores and large drugstores. For ordering by mail and for specialty types, see the Appendix under Sources.

If you only self-stimulate with a vibrator, begin this week teaching yourself to have orgasm with your hands. Use the vibrator to arouse yourself and to approach orgasm. Then put it down and use your fingers, as described in the exercises above, to crest yourself over into orgasm. Experiment with what pressure and strokes bring you to orgasm most effectively. If, after five or ten minutes, you find you haven't brought yourself to orgasm, use the vibrator to increase your stimulation level again closer to orgasm and then use your hands to crest over. You may repeat this process a number of times.

Don't be discouraged if you find that you're not able to bring yourself to orgasm in this way at first. It may take a number of practice sessions. Even when you're able to have orgasm using your hands, you may still want to use your vibrator at other times as a variation you enjoy.

For a discussion of advanced self-stimulation skills, turn to Chapter X. Some couples may wish to incorporate the individual, more extensive eight-week programs described there as a substitute for the Self-Stimulation I–III instructions in Weeks Three through Five.

PARTNER EXERCISES

EXERCISE ONE: EXECUTE PLANNING AGREEMENT

Fill out the following Planning Agreement according to the guidelines we discussed in Chapter VIII, page 131.

EXERCISE PLANNING AGREEMENT/WEEK THREE

Communication Exercise

Initiator_____

Allow 8 minutes; 2 rounds per day planned; 5 times this week.

Times Scheduled

Sunday   _____   _____
Monday   _____   _____
Tuesday   _____   _____
Wednesday   _____   _____
Thursday   _____   _____
Friday   _____   _____
Saturday   _____   _____

Kissing Exercise (Without Script)

Initiator_____

Allow 5 minutes, 3 times this week.

Times Scheduled

Sunday   _____
Monday   _____
Tuesday   _____

Wednesday _____
Thursday _____
Friday _____
Saturday _____

Sensual Focus Exercise

Initiator_____
Allow 20 minutes per person, 40 minutes total, 2 times this week.

Times Scheduled

Sunday _____
Monday _____
Tuesday _____
Wednesday _____
Thursday _____
Friday _____
Saturday _____

EXERCISE TWO: COMMUNICATION

During Week Three, as in Week Two, do two rounds of planned Appreciations and Resentments per day. Add spontaneous Appreciations and Resentments whenever you find you're uncomfortable about something your partner has recently said or done.

This week, work on discovering the positive in the negative in your spontaneous communication exercises. When your partner does something you disagree with, put yourself in his/her position and try to understand what his/her deliberate or productive reason might have been. Assume that your partner had some justification for his/her action and acknowledge what that was. Be generous rather than self-righteous. For example: "Mark, there's something I'd like to tell you."

"Okay, I'm listening."

"I really appreciate your willingness to drive on our weekend away. I feel grateful to you for taking that responsibility so that I can relax [expressing what you saw or heard, when it occurred, and how you feel about it]."

"Thank you."

"Mark, there's something I'd like to tell you."

"Okay, I'm listening."

"When you drive so much faster than the recommended speed limit around curves, I find myself becoming tight and tense and then I start to get angry with you, which is the opposite of our goal of a romantic weekend away [what you experienced, what you felt]. I'd really like you to slow down to no more than ten miles above the recommended speed limit around curves [what you would prefer to happen]."

"Thank you."

EXERCISE THREE: KISSING

The Exercise

Mention any resistances you have to doing this exercise and then go ahead and do it anyhow.

Do the Kissing Exercise without the script three times this week. You may abbreviate the exercise time to five minutes in this and subsequent weeks. The giver starts with what he/she has discovered his/her partner prefers. After at least one minute, the giver may smoothly shift to kissing the way he/she likes.

Each time you do this exercise, alternate who initiates.

Be sure at least twice that this exercise does *not* lead to a sexual interaction. During those two sessions, imagine that your only sexual interaction is through your lips. In your mind's eye, see two sensual lips communicating all the messages of caring and eroticism possible. Imagine you are only two lips on your partner's two lips and all sensation and feeling is in those lips.

EXERCISE FOUR: SENSUAL FOCUS, STEP II

Rationale

Many men and women hesitate to experiment sensually because they're afraid they'll do something wrong. This exercise helps break down some of that resistance.

The Exercise

Step II: Touching with Verbal Feedback (20 minutes per partner)

Step II continues where Step I of Week Two left off. The initiator, as previously agreed upon, confirms the planned time of the exercise with the partner and makes any advance preparations necessary to begin the exercise—window coverings, lighting, music, oil, extra sheet, children's needs, and so on. The initiator is timekeeper for beginning an exercise. The giver, however, has control of the timing once the exercise begins. A clock in view can help the giver to identify designated points of change in the exercise. During any exercise, whoever is the giver is in charge of time.

Repeat the same procedure as in the Sensual Focus I Exercise (page 163) with one significant change: the receiver now gives both verbal and nonverbal direction. The receiver describes what he/she is experiencing and says what he/she likes and dislikes. Dislikes need to be stated in a neutral and uncritical tone of voice. Please make it a habit to take turns starting the Sensual Focus Exercise. Avoid stimulation of nipples and genitals.

The giver locates pleasurable and sensitive areas and strokes, teases, and kneads them. Soles of the feet often respond well to stimulation with short, firm strokes of the thumb or forefinger. You can grasp a foot with your hand or hands and use your thumbs very effectively on the soles. Long strokes along the spine can be pleasurable. Light kissing, anywhere except the breasts or genitals, is allowed. For a pleasurable surprise, try sucking toes!

This week, see if you can discover some new aspect of your partner's preferences. The receiver may physically guide the hand of the giver to show how best to stroke or touch a particular area: to the thigh, for example, saying, "Please massage me here like this . . . that tickles a little . . . I'm getting a little bored with that . . . more with your palm . . . that feels nice." Or, "That feels nice, but a little more [or less] pressure would feel better." Allow yourself to sigh or moan with pleasure when the stroking feels good. Pleasure sounds act as a release and guide your partner.

Try spending a few minutes moving with exaggerated slowness, as if in slow motion.

You may continue to use a lotion or body oil for this exercise. A water-based lotion is fine.

Afterward, spend several minutes discussing the experience, talking together about what you learned and what you felt.

Men often complain that women don't give them enough feedback in this exercise. Without sounds or verbal directions they don't know if what they're doing feels good or bad. The same problem extends to sex, men tell us: they don't know if what they're doing feels good to the woman until she stops making love or has orgasm. Some women even have orgasm quietly enough to leave their men in doubt.

Women in turn complain that men often touch them, in this exercise and in lovemaking, in an aggressive, heavy-handed way that they don't at all enjoy. Too much pressure—too rapidly and too hard—is the commonest complaint we hear from women about men's touching. "He's too impatient. He expects me to respond right away." "It's too perfunctory. He's not sensitive enough to my feelings."

We counsel men to try much lighter pressure and slower, softer strokes. We counsel women to open up and express their feelings. They'll feel more if they do and direct their partners at the same time. To learn opening up to the sounds of lovemaking, see "Pleasure Sounds," p. 00.

Men often want more rather than less pressure from their partners. Their usually heavier musculature responds to such pressure pleasurably.

Should the receiver be concerned about the accuracy of the giver's timekeeping, the problem is best discussed at least ten minutes after the end of the exercise. We recommend conducting that discussion in the context of the communication structure. For example:

"Rosalyn, there's something I'd like to tell you."

"Okay, I'm listening."

"The Sensual Focus Exercise we did ten minutes ago was wonderful. I loved your light teasing."

"Thank you."

"Rosalyn, there's something I'd like to tell you."

"Okay, I'm listening."

"In that exercise, I felt as if you touched me a lot less than the twenty minutes we were supposed to do. If so, I'd prefer that you watch the time more accurately, as I try to do with you."

"Thank you."

"Paul, there's something I'd like to tell you."

"Okay, I'm listening."

"Your touching me all over this morning felt so sensitive and caring. I felt so good about you!"

"Thank you."

"Paul, there's something I'd like to tell you."

"Okay, I'm listening."

"The touching you did seemed to go on for more than twenty minutes, and at the end you were stimulating my genitals. That felt good, but it made me lose a little bit of confidence in whether you'll do what you agree to. I'd like you to watch the time more closely and to keep your agreements about following the exercise just as designed."

"Thank you."

EXERCISE FIVE: SIGN COMPLETION AGREEMENT

EXERCISE COMPLETION AGREEMENT/ WEEK THREE

PARTNER EXERCISES   Initials

1. Discussed resistances prior to each exercise.   _____ _____
2. Did Exercise Planning Agreement.   _____ _____
3. Did Appreciations and Resentments twice a
   day, 5 times.   _____ _____
4. Did Kissing Exercise 3 times.   _____ _____
5. Did Sensual Focus, Step II, twice   _____ _____

SOLO EXERCISES

1. Did 20–0 countdown at least twice a day.   _____ _____
2. Did Sex Muscle and Breathing Exercise twice
   a day.   _____ _____

I have accomplished the Solo Exercises described above. My partner and I have accomplished the Partner Exercises described above to our reasonable satisfaction. We also specifically reaffirm our agreement here to move on to follow the exercises of Week Four.

If there has been or will be any change in the program as assigned, we have both talked about those changes and agreed upon them together.

_____   _____
          Signature and Date   *Signature and Date*

WEEK FOUR

SUMMARY OF EXERCISES

SOLO EXERCISES

1. 20–0 Countdown (2 cycles, twice a day).
2. Sex Muscle and Breathing (increase number of repetitions by 10 percent from Week Three, twice a day).
3. Self-Stimulation II (combined with Sex Muscle and Breathing Exercise, external prostate stimulation, visualization, and fantasy) (15 minutes, 3 times).

PARTNER EXERCISES

1. Execute Exercise Planning Agreement.
2. Communication (Appreciations and Resentments) (2 planned rounds per day; 5 times unlimited spontaneous).
3. Kissing (without script) (about 5 minutes, 3 times).
4. Sensual Focus, Step III (30 minutes giving, 30 minutes receiving; twice).
5. Sign Exercise Completion Agreement.
6. Spontaneous lovemaking as desired.

SOLO EXERCISES

EXERCISE ONE: 20–0 COUNTDOWN

Rationale

As you continue this exercise, you'll probably notice you're able to focus your concentration more easily as you learn conscious control of your thoughts. This week you'll be practicing extending your focused attention time, preparing to increase your sexual attention span.

The Exercise

The two-cycle Countdown: Instead of one cycle counting from 20 to 0 and stopping, do two cycles, one right after the other. When you reach 0, begin counting backward from 20 to 0 again. Do this two times per day in place of your one-cycle Countdown. Observe and jot down the average low number you reach without distracting thought.

EXERCISE TWO: SEX MUSCLE AND BREATHING

Rationale

In addition to the 10 percent increase in the number of repetitions, this week you'll also be incorporating this exercise with self-stimulation (discussed below). Using the control you've learned over muscles and breathing, men can better regulate erection and ejaculation. Women can experience easier, stronger, and longer orgasms.

The Exercise

Men and women increase the number of repetitions by 10 percent.

EXERCISE THREE: SELF-STIMULATION II

Rationale

Fantasy is a good way to focus your attention on erotic feelings and sensations. Mental noise from thoughts and worries about other areas of your life, your mind dwelling on life's endless problems, can get in the way of pleasure. But two thoughts can't occupy the same mental space at the same time. If you create a fantasy scenario that's entertaining and exciting enough, you can push out and overwhelm the mental noise that's interfering with pleasure.

Doing your Sex Muscle and Breathing Exercise while you self-stimulate can be a useful combination for increasing sensitivity and control in men and enhancing arousal in women.

A reader of our earlier book, ESO, who was recovering from an inflammation of the prostate (prostatitis), wrote us worried that the extra stimulation of ESO training might cause a recurrence of his problem. He wondered if he should have more than one ejaculation a day. He also wondered if self-stimulation might actually strengthen his prostate.

In fact, frequent orgasm, with or without ejaculation, is an excellent preventive of prostate problems. The prostate is stressed when orgasm is avoided, not when it's only delayed. Peaking several times during extended self-stimulation exercises is good for the prostate so long as the experience culminates in orgasm. When men avoid orgasm entirely, the prostate can become swollen and boggy. Such men may develop a condition called "pelvic congestion syndrome." A similar condition can trouble women who have frequent sex but do not have orgasm. Vasocongestion (engorgement) is an important component of sexual arousal, but that congestion should be released. Orgasm in women and ejaculation or nonejaculatory orgasm from pressure on the external prostate spot in men are the mechanisms of that release.

Stimulating the prostate, both by ejaculation and by direct massage, is the best way to keep it healthy. We recommend such stimulation (via the external prostate spot) for enhanced pleasure. Stimulating the prostate is in fact what a physician does when he gives a patient with prostate problems a prostate massage. That medical procedure is usually uncomfortable because it's done when the man is not sexually aroused. Stimulation in the aroused state by a partner is easier, more pleasurable, and, in the end, probably more therapeutic, because in the absence of discomfort and with engorgement more stimulation is possible.

Men who have experienced the pain of prostatitis need not shy away from Ecstasy training. On the contrary, unless there is current active inflammation it will enhance the health of their prostate gland, not damage it. If in doubt, consult your physician.

The Exercise

Add one more session of self-stimulation this week for a total of three.

Men. Do your usual cycle of clenching, breathing in, relaxing the muscles, and exhaling. Now, however, do it while you're stimulating yourself. Focus your attention on genital sensations. Stimulate yourself intensely enough that you remain erect and gradually climb in sexual arousal. Notice the effect on your arousal when you clench and again when you relax. You'll probably discover that clenching helps to get you and keep you more firmly erect and takes you closer to orgasm. Relaxing and exhaling usually diffuse the arousal and help you to maintain control as you approach the emission-phase orgasmic crest.

When you have sustained a firm erection for several minutes, stimulate the external prostate spot with one or two fingers pressing up and in. Use your free hand. Continue stimulating your penis at the same time. Notice what happens to your level of arousal and the firmness of your erection.

Women. Do your usual clench, inhale, push-out, exhale exercises while you're stimulating yourself. Notice how this process usually results in additional engorgement and arousal. Notice the difference in sensation during clenches compared with push-outs. When your orgasm begins, do only push-outs but continue to breathe in and out. Holding your breath is a reflex tendency during orgasm that reduces sensation.

Men and women. A good time to explore visualization and fantasy, skills useful in lovemaking with partners as well, is during self-stimulation. We suggest you devote special attention this week to this aspect of arousal if you're comfortable with it. Follow the guidelines in our discussion of fantasy and visualization, beginning on page 94.

PARTNER EXERCISES

EXERCISE ONE: EXECUTE PLANNING AGREEMENT

Fill out the following Planning Agreement according to the guidelines we discussed in Chapter VIII, page 131.

EXERCISE PLANNING AGREEMENT/WEEK FOUR

Communication Exercise

Initiator_____

Allow 8 minutes; 2 rounds per day planned, 5 times unlimited spontaneous.

Times Scheduled

Sunday	_____	_____
Monday	_____	_____
Tuesday	_____	_____
Wednesday	_____	_____
Thursday	_____	_____
Friday	_____	_____
Saturday	_____	_____

Kissing Exercise (Without Script)

Initiator_____

Allow 5 minutes, 3 times this week.

Times Scheduled

Sunday	_____
Monday	_____

Tuesday _____
Wednesday _____
Thursday _____
Friday _____
Saturday _____

Sensual Focus Exercise

Initiator_____
Allow 30 minutes giving, 30 minutes receiving each for a total of 60 minutes, 2 times this week.

Times Scheduled

Sunday _____
Monday _____
Tuesday _____
Wednesday _____
Thursday _____
Friday _____
Saturday _____

EXERCISE TWO: COMMUNICATION

Continue doing both planned rounds and spontaneous rounds as they occur. By now, however, in the appreciation phase of your Communication Exercise, you should be looking for some positive aspect of the situation. Remember, you can potentially find a positive thought, experience, reason, advantage, or assumption in every negative experience. Assume your partner is doing, saying, acting as he/she is because he/she believes his/her behavior is correct, not because he/she is trying to make you suffer.

From now on instead of Appreciations being about subjects unrelated to Resentments, whenever possible, see if you can make your Appreciation have some connection with your Resentment.

EXERCISE THREE: KISSING

The Exercise

Take turns as giver and receiver. Switch back and forth several times over a period of about five minutes. Your aim is to make the switches smoothly, without banging heads or tongues and without any control or power struggle. When you're the giver, experiment sometimes with taking responsibility for the rhythm and motion of the kiss. Start out lightly and work toward the more intimate, internal erotic phase of the kiss. A kiss can be foreplay without any other bodily stimulation. See how smoothly you can flow between giving and receiving.

EXERCISE FOUR: SENSUAL FOCUS, STEP III

Rationale

This exercise allows you to put into practice what you have learned about your partner's response by stimulating him/her without verbal guidance. You will also be adding genital area stimulation and observing the effects of various kinds of touch. As the recipient, in turn, you will be concentrating on absorbing the maximum amount of sexual arousal you can allow yourself in the allotted time without the minor distraction of talking and without orgasm. The man will probably be relatively erect; the woman's clitoris will probably be erect and engorged.

Remember, suggested times are approximate. A visible clock may be helpful as a guide to the giver. Avoid being too rigid about assigned times, however.

Verbal silence allows both partners to concentrate more on the feeling of the experience. Pleasure sounds are permissible, of course.

The Exercise

Step III: Genital Arousal Without Verbal Feedback

Following the schedule given below, lovingly stroke and touch your partner's body from head to toe, then concentrate on stimulating the genitals for arousal. Be sure to use a recommended sexual lubricant, such as Albolene, on the genitals. Enjoy the experience *without* talking. Spend about equal time on each of the steps. You are not permitted to give your partner an orgasm or ejaculation.

Woman Giving, Man Receiving

1. Gently and lovingly stroke and touch your partner's body from head to toe. Don't concentrate too long on any one area. This general stimulation prepares your partner for more specific stimulation later. (3–5 minutes)

2. Stroke, tease, and massage his nipples. Circle around his nipples first several times without actually touching them. This builds sensitivity to touch in the area. It also creates anticipation of touch, which heightens arousal. Then brush his nipples lightly several times before proceeding to firmer squeezing and heavier pressure. Does he appear to enjoy this? Do his nipples engorge and become erect? Which appear to be the most arousing ways to stimulate them? (2 minutes)

3. Using one or two hands, touch, stimulate, stroke, and tease his pubic hair and inner thighs. (2 minutes)

4. Concentrate on stimulating his penis. Enjoy stroking the shaft, first with one hand, then with two. Assume any position that you find comfortable, then feel free to change positions whenever you find yourself getting tired. (5 minutes)

5. Move your attention to his testicles. Lightly stroke and fondle first one, then both. Explore the effect of gently tugging and stretching his scrotal sac (without including his testicles). Use your dominant hand to stimulate his scrotum and testicles, since they're the focus of your attention at this point. Continue stimulating his penis with your other hand. (2 minutes)

6. Lightly touch his perineum (the area between the scrotum and the anus). Stimulate and rhythmically pump the buried penile base by pressing on it. (2 minutes)

7. Locate the external prostate spot on the perineal area and stimulate it. With your forefinger or forefinger and middle finger together, push in and toward the base of the penis. Press at different points on the perineal area, noticing any changes in your partner's response. You may continue stroking his penis with your other hand in any way that you find comfortable. (2 minutes)

8. Experiment with the sensation of stimulating the outside of the anus. In response to loving, gentle stimulation, it may engorge and open up, relaxing, or it may clench and tighten, just like your vaginal lips and vaginal opening. A clenching reaction usually means that you're stimulating too intensely (even though the sensation may be pleasurable). The man should concentrate on relaxing his sex muscles as much as possible during anal stimulation. Your other hand continues to stimulate his penis. Remember to stop stimulation well short of ejaculation. (2 minutes)

9. The giver says aloud, "We've completed the exercise."

Man Giving, Woman Receiving

1. Lovingly stroke and touch your partner from head to toe without focusing long on any one area. (3–5 minutes)

2. Now concentrate on her breasts and nipples. The art of teasing requires building anticipation by gradually moving closer to the main target. It's a powerful method of arousal. Start by circling her breasts, making smaller and smaller concentric circles up to the breasts and finally lightly touching the nipples. Lightly roll her nipples between your thumbs and forefingers. You can use firmer pressure if she appears to enjoy it. You may focus on one breast and nipple at a time or both simultaneously. Does she appear to enjoy this stimulation? Do her nipples engorge and become erect? Which appear to be the most arousing ways to stimulate them? (3 minutes)

3. Using one or two hands, lightly touch, stimulate, stroke, and tease her pubic hair and inner thighs and the outer and inner lips of her vagina. Avoid touching her clitoris. Pull gently on her pubic hair. (2 minutes)

4. Using the lubricated index and middle fingers of your dominant hand, gently stimulate around the base of the clitoris without touching the shaft or the head itself. You can circle around first in one direction, then in another. Gently pull back the hood of the clitoris without actually touching the head. Notice any engorgement of the areas you're touching. (2 minutes)

5. Gently grasp the top and bottom of the clitoris with your thumb and forefinger. Your thumb may be positioned at the top and your forefinger at the bottom or the other way around. Roll her clitoris between your fingers at about one cycle per second. Use gentle pressure first, then firmer pressure, noticing the difference in your partner's engorgement and movements. You may notice her clitoris becoming firmer, harder,

and larger as it fills with blood and becomes engorged. Feel free to change your position as necessary to remain comfortable. If you do change position, try to do so while maintaining the same rhythm of stimulation, to avoid breaking into your partner's concentration.

6. Lightly stimulate the head and shaft of her clitoris with your forefinger and middle fingers together. Try a side stroke using the pads of your two fingers, then add your thumb at the hood of the clitoris and separate your forefinger and middle finger slightly, sweeping your forefinger up and down one side and your middle finger up and down the other. Notice if one side of the clitoris is more responsive than the other. Some investigators believe the left side is frequently more sensitive than the right side. (3 minutes)

7. Insert a forefinger and/or a middle finger into her vagina and slowly sweep the finger clockwise and counterclockwise, noticing areas of sensitivity and response (be sure your nails are short and smooth). Your other hand should provide gentle, continued clitoral stimulation. Your main area of attention should be inside the vagina. (2 minutes)

8. With a forefinger, stroke the lubricated external area around the anus lightly. When the anus relaxes, it's aroused and wants more stimulation. When the anus clenches tight, it's resisting and wants less stimulation. Notice if the area becomes more engorged. Your other hand can continue to stimulate your partner's clitoris. Try alternating between clitoral stimulation and light external anal touching. At times, stimulate both areas simultaneously. Stimulating the external anal area is best done lightly, with a playful, teasing touch, like a tickle. Do not later insert a finger that has been stimulating the anal area into the vagina. Stimulation of the anal area is optional; we suggest it only for couples who have discussed it in advance and agreed to doing so. (2 minutes)

9. Simultaneously stimulate two of the areas you've explored, one area with each hand: the anus and the vagina, for example, the clitoris and the anus, or the clitoris and the vagina. Use a light, teasing touch. (1 minute)

10. The giver says aloud, "We've completed the exercise."

Remember, *no orgasm* is permitted during this exercise. Talk about it only after you both have completed it. Then, if you wish, you may go on to orgasm outside the frame of the exercise.

EXERCISE FIVE: SIGN COMPLETION AGREEMENT

EXERCISE COMPLETION AGREEMENT/ WEEK FOUR

PARTNER EXERCISES   **Initials**

1. Discussed resistances prior to each exercise.   _____   _____
2. Did Exercise Planning Agreement.   _____   _____
3. Did Appreciations and Resentments twice a day; unlimited spontaneous.   _____   _____
4. Did Kissing Exercise 3 times.   _____   _____
5. Did Sensual Focus, Step III, twice.   _____   _____

SOLO EXERCISES

1. Did 20–0 Countdown at least twice a day.   _____   _____
2. Did Sex Muscle and Breathing Exercise twice a day.   _____   _____
3. Did Self-Stimulation 3 times.   _____   _____

I have accomplished the Solo Exercises described above. My partner and I have accomplished the Partner Exercises described above to our reasonable satisfaction. We also specifically reaffirm our agreement here to move on to follow the exercises of Week Five.

If there has been or will be any change in the program as assigned, we have both talked about those changes and agreed upon them together.

_____   _____

Signature and Date   *Signature and Date*

WEEK FIVE

SUMMARY OF EXERCISES

SOLO EXERCISES

1. 20–0 Countdown (2 times per day).
2. Sex Muscle and Breathing (increase number of repetitions by 10 percent from Week Four, twice a day).
3. Self-Stimulation III (20 minutes, twice).

PARTNER EXERCISES

1. Execute Exercise Planning Agreement.
2. Communication (Appreciations and Resentments) (2 planned rounds per day on sexual issues, 3 days; unlimited spontaneous).
3. Kissing (without script) (about 5 minutes, 3 times)
4. Sensual Focus, Step IV (2 times).
5. Sign Exercise Completion Agreement.
6. Spontaneous lovemaking as desired.

SOLO EXERCISES

EXERCISE ONE: 20–0 COUNTDOWN

The Exercise

Continue doing one- or two-cycle Countdowns from 20 to 0. Notice what number you're able to count down to fairly reliably. Compare that with the number you achieved in Week One.

EXERCISE TWO: SEX MUSCLE AND BREATHING

The Exercise

Continue practicing this exercise. Add 10 percent to the number of repetitions you do. You'll also be incorporating these repetitions into your self-stimulation exercises. Using the control you've learned over muscles and breathing will assist you to easier arousal and (in the man's case) better control of ejaculation.

EXERCISE THREE: SELF-STIMULATION III

Rationale

For men, self-stimulation combined with moving around and even standing or walking can help with learning to change positions during lovemaking without significantly losing arousal. Maintaining erection while making necessary changes in position can add to both partners' self-confidence.

The Exercise

Men. Get erect by stimulating yourself while slow-clenching as you breathe in and relaxing as you breathe out. After five or ten minutes of erection, stand up and move a few steps while continuing to self-stimulate. If your erection begins to subside, stop moving around the room, sit or kneel down, and rapidly add more firm pressure while stimulating yourself more intensely. With rapid stimulation and firm pressure, bring yourself to full erection again. After several minutes with relatively firm erection, resume walking around the room. Each time you find yourself losing your erection, stop your movements around the room and restimulate back to a firm erection. Determine whether your erection returns more easily by alternating sex muscle clenching and relaxing or by continuously clenching, as you stimulate your penis. Do this for at least twenty minutes on two separate occasions during the week. At the end of each session you may reward yourself with an ejaculation.

Women. Use or develop a fantasy that helps turn you on. Assume a position different from your usual position. For example, if you usually lie on your back when you stimulate yourself, move to your side. Take yourself up near orgasm at least six times, peaking without cresting over. Each time you peak yourself you may notice yourself becoming a little more aroused. This process of repeatedly peaking can result in your reaching significantly higher levels of arousal and more powerful orgasm. Finally, after twenty minutes, reward yourself with an orgasm. Count the number of contractions—including the subtle ones.

Note that repeated peaking, while useful to the woman for intensifying orgasm, is essential to the man who wishes both to intensify and extend his orgasm.

PARTNER EXERCISES

EXERCISE ONE: EXECUTE PLANNING AGREEMENT

Fill out the following Planning Agreement according to the guidelines we discussed in Chapter VIII, page 131.

EXERCISE PLANNING AGREEMENT/WEEK FIVE

Communication Exercise

Initiator_____

Allow 8 minutes; 2 rounds per day, planned on sexual issues; 3 days unlimited spontaneous.

Times Scheduled

Sunday	_____	_____
Monday	_____	_____
Tuesday	_____	_____
Wednesday	_____	_____
Thursday	_____	_____
Friday	_____	_____
Saturday	_____	_____

Kissing Exercise (Without Script)

Initiator_____

Allow 5 minutes, 3 times this week.

Times Scheduled

Sunday	_____
Monday	_____
Tuesday	_____
Wednesday	_____
Thursday	_____
Friday	_____
Saturday	_____

Sensual Focus Exercise

Initiator_____

Allow 1 hour, 2 times this week.

Times Scheduled

Sunday	_____
Monday	_____
Tuesday	_____
Wednesday	_____
Thursday	_____
Friday	_____
Saturday	_____

EXERCISE TWO: COMMUNICATION

Rationale

In previous weeks you've been free to roam in any areas of your experience with your partner for Appreciations and Resentments *except* the area of sex. During Week Five, use Appreciations and Resentments more specifically for sexual communication. Limit your comments to the broad area of physical intimacy.

This exercise can be particularly difficult for couples who in the past have found it safer to conceal their sexual feelings and attitudes from their partners. This concealment blocks greater intimacy. It's necessary, though, to tell your partner how you feel in an acceptable way, so that he/she will not become hurt, defensive, or angry.

For example, if you have a problem with your partner's hygiene, you may not have said anything about it because you feared hurting your partner's feelings or because you didn't feel comfortable bringing the matter up. Such concealment may have left you inhibited in lovemaking. Or you may have brought up your concern in a critical or sarcastic way. "Didn't your mother ever show you how to use a washcloth?" is a question likely to be met with counterattack.

A better approach might be to tell your partner your problem in the context of Appreciations and Resentments:

"Jim, there's something I'd like to tell you."

"Okay, I'm listening."

"When we make love in the day I notice you usually shower afterwards.

I appreciate your carefulness and sensitivity about others in making sure you're clean for the rest of the day or evening."

"Thank you."

"Jim there's something I'd like to tell you."

"Okay, I'm listening."

"Yesterday when we made love I was aware of a subtle odor from your body. It made me a little hesitant to let go and kiss you as freely as I wanted to. I've had that reaction at other times also. I'd feel more comfortable if you'd be willing sometimes to shower before we have sex, for my benefit. You can always shower afterwards, too."

"Thank you."

The Exercise

Two planned Appreciations and Resentments per day on matters related to romance, intimacy, and sex. Sexual Appreciations and Resentments should be planned rather than spontaneous. Doing them spontaneously during lovemaking may disrupt your sexual interaction. It's best not to schedule this exercise immediately before, during, or immediately after lovemaking. Choose a more neutral period of time.

Be aware that sexual communication is frequently loaded with emotion; feelings are easily hurt. Remember the ground rules of Appreciations and Resentments: neutral tone of voice, no discussion for at least thirty minutes and none without the consent of the partner delivering the resentment, no hitting below the belt. Take sexual Appreciations and Resentments for what they are: important communications that can help you improve your relationship.

EXERCISE THREE: KISSING

The Exercise

Do the Kissing Exercise described in Week Four (page 192) without a script, freely alternating between giving and receiving. Take three to five minutes. Observe your thoughts while kissing. If your thoughts are negative, distracting, or in some other way represent a resistance to the

Kissing process, switch your thoughts or attention—as you regularly do in the Countdown process. Also, you can review the discussion "Controlling Thought" page 98, Chapter V.

EXERCISE FOUR: SENSUAL FOCUS, STEP IV

Rationale

You and your partner communicate with each other in three main ways during sexual interactions: with words, with sounds, and with body movements. This week you'll be talking with each other, commenting on what you're doing, how you're feeling, and what you might prefer. It's important to learn how to say what you're feeling, especially what stimulation might be better, at the moment you become aware of it, rather than waiting until a loss of arousal becomes obvious even without words. Feelings and responses are always changing. People are frequently reluctant to say what they're feeling or how they think the stimulation they're getting could be improved. This exercise will help give you experience with the benefits of moment-to-moment communication.

There are several factors you need to be aware of in verbal communication during sex.

One is that the words and the tone of voice you use are important. In order not to hurt your partner's feelings, you need to speak in a relatively neutral tone of voice, choosing words that aren't loaded with criticism, sarcasm, anger, or impatience. A matter-of-fact or even an enthusiastic tone of voice is always best. Tell your partner what would feel even better rather than what he or she is doing wrong. Use sighs and moans and slightly tilt your pelvis toward or away from the stimulating hand to indicate you prefer more or less pressure.

Another is that any kind of talking distracts you to some degree from the pure experience of feeling. The benefits of constructive communication, however, outweigh the momentary loss of arousal. Deliberately switch attention to simple verbal comments, then quickly go back again to pleasurable physical sensations and positive mental self-talk and images. Communicating to learn what you and your partner like, even as your likes change from moment to moment, will give your sexual interactions a major boost.

The Exercise

Step IV: Genital Arousal with Verbal Feedback

Proceed exactly as you did in Week Four (page 192). This week, however, talk to each other during each part of the exercise.

Giver. Briefly tell your partner what he/she will be doing in each part of the exercise. This communication helps build anticipation: "I'm going to stroke your nipples." "I'm going to stimulate your external prostate area." The giver should also comment throughout the exercise on what he/she is noticing and enjoying. "I'm really enjoying watching your lips swell." "I love stroking your soft pubic hair."

Receiver. Say how you feel during the exercise. This communication should include helpful feedback, such as what doesn't feel pleasurable or could feel better: "I like your stroking my breasts. I'd prefer a little less pinching of my nipples." The receiver can also guide the giver's hand, directing changes in pressure, rate, and area of stimulation.

Partners can exchange dialogue. A man might say, "I'm really enjoying stroking your clitoris. I never noticed how expressive it is." His partner might acknowledge this pleasure: "I like what you're doing; I'm glad you enjoy it." A woman might also remark, "I can't tell exactly what you're doing, but it feels good." The man might then explain where he's stimulating and how.

After about twenty minutes, reverse roles.

The giver should declare that the exercise is concluded.

Be sure you come to explicit verbal agreement after this exercise before you have intercourse or some other sexual connection.

EXERCISE FIVE: SIGN COMPLETION AGREEMENT

EXERCISE COMPLETION AGREEMENT/ WEEK FIVE

PARTNER EXERCISES

Initials

1. Discussed resistances prior to each exercise.
2. Did Exercise Planning Agreement.
3. Did Appreciations and Resentments on sexual issues twice a day, 3 times.
4. Did Kissing Exercise 3 times.
5. Did Sensual Focus, Step IV, twice.

SOLO EXERCISES

1. Did 20–0 Countdown at least twice a day.
2. Did Sex Muscle and Breathing Exercise twice a day.
3. Did Self-Stimulation twice.

I have accomplished the Solo Exercises described above. My partner and I have accomplished the Partner Exercises described above to our reasonable satisfaction. We also specifically reaffirm our agreement here to follow the exercises of Week Six.

If there has been or will be any change in the program as assigned, we have both talked about those changes and agreed upon them together.

_____   _____
Signature and Date   *Signature and Date*

WEEK SIX

SUMMARY OF EXERCISES

SOLO EXERCISES

1. 20–0 Countdown (2 times a day).
2. Sex Muscle and Breathing (increase number of repetitions by 10 percent from Week Five, twice a day).

PARTNER EXERCISES

1. Execute Exercise Planning Agreement.
2. Communication (Appreciations and Resentments) (2 planned sexual subjects per day, 3 times; unlimited spontaneous).
3. Sexual Exploration (incorporating Kissing Exercise) (20 minutes giving, 20 minutes receiving, once).
4. Simultaneous Partner Stimulation (30 minutes, 3 times)
5. Sign Exercise Completion Agreement.
6. Spontaneous lovemaking as desired.

SOLO EXERCISES

EXERCISE ONE: 20–0 COUNTDOWN

We suggest that you continue doing this exercise twice a day throughout this week and each of the remaining weeks of the Ecstasy Program. We hope that by now this simple, brief exercise will have become a matter of habit and that you will no longer need specific reminding. We also hope that you will have noticed that your ability to concentrate is improving as measured by your more frequently reaching lower numbers before you become distracted, or even reaching all the way to 0 without any distractions intruding. If this exercise has worked for you, you'll have noticed that your mental focus during sexual activities and perhaps in other areas of your life as well has improved.

EXERCISE TWO: SEX MUSCLE AND BREATHING

If, by this week, you're able to do a set of 75 flutter clenches, 75 flutter push-outs, and 50 slow inhale/clenches at a time, that's a good level of conditioning regardless of age. You can feel satisfied doing this number twice a day for the remainder of the program. If you aren't up to this number yet, we suggest that you continue to increase the number of repetitions week by week until you are.

PARTNER EXERCISES

EXERCISE ONE: EXECUTE PLANNING AGREEMENT

Fill out the following Planning Agreement according to the guidelines we discussed in Chapter VIII, page 131.

EXERCISE PLANNING AGREEMENT/WEEK SIX

Communication Exercise

Initiator_____

Allow 8 minutes; 2 rounds per day planned, 3 times; unlimited spontaneous.

Times Scheduled

Sunday	_____	_____
Monday	_____	_____
Tuesday	_____	_____
Wednesday	_____	_____
Thursday	_____	_____
Friday	_____	_____
Saturday	_____	_____

Sexual Exploration

Allow 40 minutes, once this week.

Times Scheduled

Sunday	_____
Monday	_____
Tuesday	_____
Wednesday	_____

Thursday _____
Friday _____
Saturday _____

Simultaneous Partner Stimulation

Initiator_____
Allow 30 minutes, 3 times this week.

Times Scheduled

Sunday _____
Monday _____
Tuesday _____
Wednesday _____
Thursday _____
Friday _____
Saturday _____

EXERCISE TWO: COMMUNICATION

Rationale

Many couples find that they develop resistances to doing the Communication Exercise. It's work to think of Appreciations and Resentments. Sometimes it's scary to risk telling your partner how you feel. You have to think and plan in advance, you have to create a time and place that's absolutely private, it's more fun to have sex than to talk about it, and you can't do sexual Appreciations and Resentments immediately before, during, or immediately after sex.

With all those problems, why bother? Doing Appreciations and Resentments is a little like brushing your teeth. It takes a little time and it's sometimes inconvenient, but if you don't do it, you're likely to develop bad breath in the short run and lose your teeth to gum disease in the long run. Similarly, if you don't communicate with each other day by day, keeping your lines of communication fresh, you may become offensive to your partner.

By now it's very likely that you've found doing Appreciations and Resentments helpful. Think of the times you were able to express some difficult feelings that you used to hold in. Think of the times when saying something in the structure of the Communication Exercise forestalled an argument. Preventing one major argument may have as much value in limiting pain as having orgasm does in creating pleasure. Using the Appreciations and Resentments process regularly will help reduce your overall level of emotional pain, the pain that's an inevitable part of all human relationships.

The Exercise

Do planned sexual Appreciations and Resentments three times this week. Do spontaneous Appreciations and Resentments on nonsexual issues whenever feelings arise. That may be several times a day or several times a week.

EXERCISE THREE: SEXUAL EXPLORATION

Rationale

The purpose of this exercise is to teach you and your partner how you prefer to name the parts of your genitals and the subtleties of how you like to have specific areas touched. It will give you practice in telling your partner your reactions directly and with minimal distraction from the pleasure of the entire experience. This exercise is similar in some respects to the Sensual Focus Exercise, Step IV, which you practiced in Week Five. Sexual Exploration is not necessarily sensuous or romantic, nor is it likely to be unusually sexually arousing. It's more analytical. Unlike Sensual Focus, Step IV, you'll both be communicating your experience back and forth to each other out loud. The exercise is also specifically localized in the genitals and doesn't include stimulation of any other part of the body. It's an exercise in each of you discovering information about your partner's reaction to your stimulating various parts of the genitals—information for your future use.

Please don't skip through this exercise, thinking that you're familiar enough already with sexual anatomy or sexual terms. In the Sexual Exploration Exercise you'll be fine-tuning your sensitivity to your partner's sexual nerve centers. You'll also learn to communicate more accurately with each other.

You'll have a chance to learn what words you prefer used to describe your genitals. Shared information is important in this regard. The words you use for sex, words that perhaps turn you on, may be the very words that turn your partner off. If you use the formal terms, "penis," "vagina," "labia majora," and so on, your partner may find them cold and clinical. If you use the colloquial slang terms, your partner may find them disrespectful or offensive. There's no right or wrong here, only the necessity of agreement based on good communications skills and compromise. Prior to arousal, a four-letter word may be inappropriate. But during more passionate times, such as during intercourse or orgasm, such words may be acceptable or even desirable. You'll be finding out what words and what times to use them excite your partner and what other words and times turn him/her off.

You may feel embarrassed or inhibited if you've never exposed your genitals to your partner in this open way before. Looking at, discussing, and touching your genitals are very private matters, even for couples who've been together for years. Sexual Exploration is an exercise in trust as well as in teaching. It may help you to teach and show this private area of your body and mind to the person whom you trust the most. You may be uncomfortable at first. Once you've shared with your partner, you'll ultimately feel more relaxed and intimate. Sharing sometimes takes courage. Remember, "courage" means that in spite of fear or embarrassment, you're taking an action of sharing and trusting.

Intimacy is a physical but also a spiritual experience. The genitals are the most private and personal area of the body. Sharing that privacy with your partner is a gift that breaks down emotional as well as physical barriers. Most men are interested and curious about women's genitals; most women are interested and curious about men's. It's important not to exclude your partner from this intimacy.

Finally, the Sexual Exploration Exercise will, perhaps, allow you to become more knowledgeable about describing the various parts of your own and your partner's genitals. You may also become more responsive to the subtle ways in which your partner prefers you to stimulate his/her genitals.

Please do this exercise at least once, even if you think you have done something similar or if it seems elementary. Everyone, including sexually experienced couples who have been together for a long time, can benefit from practicing this exercise once in a while. Physical responses change and so do psychological needs. It's a way of staying in touch.

The Exercise

Begin by doing the brief form of the Kissing Exercise for three to five minutes. The giver starts with what he/she has discovered his/her partner prefers. After at least one minute, the giver smoothly shifts to kissing the way he/she likes. Then reverse the roles—giver becomes receiver.

Woman Exploring Man

1. Both of you should be positioned in bed, with enough light to see by. Have a hand mirror and lubrication available. The man sits with his legs spread with knees slightly bent, reclining at about a 45-degree angle with his back supported by one or more pillows. He holds the hand mirror to conveniently view his genitals.

2. Position yourself comfortably between your partner's spread legs. You may sit with pillows supporting your back as you face his genitals, with his legs resting over your thighs. Or you may lie on your stomach, leaning on your elbows facing his genitals. It's important that you be comfortable.

3. Touch and identify the visible, external parts of your partner's genitals (see illustration on page 66). This examination should include the penis, urinary opening, glans, coronal ridge, frenulum, raphe (seam) on the shaft of the penis, base of penis in front, base of penis in back (penis root), scrotum, testicles, external prostate spot, anal opening, and pubic hair. You may find you're more comfortable with anatomic terms or perhaps simpler descriptive terms. You may have a favorite name for certain parts. After you've described and identified a particular part of your partner's anatomy, ask him if he prefers any other term for that area. Find out if his preference changes depending upon his level of arousal. His preferences are for your information only. You don't have to comply with his preferences and change your terminology. If you wish to, you can make mental notes to discuss this question with him later, perhaps in an Appreciations and Resentments process.

4. Lightly brush your partner's pubic hair above the penis on the lower

abdomen, barely brushing, for thirty seconds or more. Describe to him exactly what you're doing. Then ask him how it feels. For instance, "My hand is lightly brushing your pubic hair above your penis. How does it feel?" To which your partner might reply, "That feels tingly . . . also kind of tantalizing." Lightly pull on a few strands of his pubic hair near the base of the shaft of the penis. Describe what you're doing and where you're touching and then request feedback from your partner.

5. Now move your attention to the penis shaft, using your index finger to stroke lightly from the base along the underside of the shaft to just under the coronal ridge at the frenulum. Trace the raphe along the underside center of the shaft, moving up and down five to ten times, saying aloud what you're doing and asking your partner how it feels. Your partner should reply briefly, emphasizing the positive, pleasurable aspect of the experience. Now stroke up and down with your forefinger on the underside of the penis. Do that for five to ten strokes lightly, and then repeat the process using firmer pressure. Then do about ten rapid strokes, two or three times faster than your previous slower speed. Tell your partner exactly what you're doing and where and then ask for his reactions. He should mention what part of the stimulation was most pleasurable, as well as any moments of possible discomfort. You have the opportunity to learn the amount of pressure and speed and location of stimulation that the penis responds best to in the soft state and, if there happens to be an erection, in a firmer state.

6. Run your index finger lightly around the entire coronal ridge, circling around and around one way, then another, for at least ten complete circles. Describe to your partner what you're doing and then ask him how it feels. Circle the coronal ridge more rapidly ten or twenty times and ask your partner for feedback. In men who haven't been circumcised, this area is covered by a tube of skin, the foreskin. You should slide back the foreskin to expose the penis head. Holding the foreskin down with your left hand, you can use your right hand to stimulate the head of the penis in circular motions, as described above. Say what you're doing and then ask your partner for a brief description of his sensations. For instance, you might say, "I'm now lightly touching the head of your penis. How does it feel? I'm changing the stroke now and applying more pressure. How does that feel?"

7. Focus on the most sensitive sexual spot on the male body—the frenulum. In terms of sensitivity, this pea-sized spot is equivalent to the tip of the clitoris. Like the clitoris, it's most sensitive when erect. Rapid light stimulation with a forefinger, focused on this tiny area alone, can

result in erection and ejaculation without any additional stimulation. Spend several minutes stimulating the frenulum. Imagine it's your clitoris. Describe to your partner what you're doing. Ask him how it feels. As men get older, mental and visual stimulation become less effective and they require more direct physical stimulation. Learning to stimulate the frenulum effectively gives a woman more control over the firmness and duration of erection.

8. Using a light, feathery touch, circle around and stroke the scrotal sac. Say what you're doing. Ask your partner how it feels. Caress his scrotum and cup his testicles. Stroke with one or more fingers the skin behind the scrotal sac. Press upward with your forefinger on the external prostate spot, gently at first, then more firmly. Stimulation of this area is usually most pleasurable and most effective in helping to control sexual arousal when the penis has been fully erect for several minutes. The man's penis may not be fully erect during this exercise.

9. Place your forefinger over the opening of the anus. Ask your partner to do some repetitions of the Sex Muscle and Breathing Exercise. Keeping your finger lightly over the opening, lightly stroke the outside anal area as he does twenty or so flutter contractions and then ten or so squeeze/inhale/relax/exhale clenches. Describe to him exactly what you're doing and how you're stimulating his anal opening. Then ask him what sensations he's experiencing. Is it hard for him to keep his attention on doing the sequences of flutters and slow clenches? Observe for your information if there's any movement in the scrotal sac during the exercises, or any change in penis engorgement.

10. Now apply lubrication to both your hands. Beginning with step 3, above, go back with your lubricated hands and repeat the series of strokes and stimulation pattern described above. If your partner chooses, he can give feedback this time using a sequential numerical rating scale from -10 through 0 to $+10$, where 0 is neutral, and numbers on the plus side indicate levels of pleasure (with $+10$ the greatest) and numbers on the minus side indicate levels of discomfort or pain (with -10 the greatest).

11. When you're ready to stop, tell your partner that you're stopping. It's important for this and every other partner exercise in the Ecstasy Program that you define the end of the exercise structure by telling your partner you're stopping. Take a minimum of fifteen minutes for completing steps 1 through 10.

Man Exploring Woman

1. The woman sits, preferably on a bed, with her legs separated and slightly bent, lying back at about a 45-degree angle, perhaps propped up with pillows, with a hand mirror available with which to observe her genital area.

2. You, the man, position yourself between your partner's spread legs. You might be sitting with her legs draped over your thighs or you might be lying on your stomach, leaning on your elbows facing her genitals. It's important for both partners to be comfortable.

3. Touch and identify the visible, external parts of your partner's genitals (see illustration on page 62). This examination should include the pubic hair, the pubic bone, the major and minor labia, the clitoral shaft, hood, and glans, the urinary opening, the vaginal opening, the perineum, and the anal opening. You may find you're more comfortable with anatomic terms or perhaps simpler descriptive terms. You may have a favorite name for certain parts. After you've described and identified a particular part of your partner's anatomy, ask her if she prefers any other term for that area. Find out if her preference changes depending upon her level of arousal. Her preferences are for your information only. You don't have to comply with her preferences and change your terminology. If you wish to, you can make mental notes to discuss this question with her later, perhaps in an Appreciations and Resentments process.

4. Using the broad surface of your hand, lightly brush and stroke your partner's pubic hair.

5. Move your stroking now to the outer lips (*labia majora*) and with your index and middle fingers, lightly stroke just one side, asking your partner how it feels. Then stroke the other side, telling your partner what you're doing and asking how it feels. Separate your fingers slightly, and simultaneously stroke both sides of the outer lips lightly. Repeat this stroking again with more pressure, describing your action and asking your partner how it feels. Increase the speed and continue stroking the outer lips, asking for feedback.

6. Move your lubricated index finger to the inner lips (*labia minora*), stroking one and then the other. Do at least thirty circles, subtly varying rate and pressure. Try a few strokes gently grasping the inner lips between your thumb and index finger. Describe exactly what you're doing and ask your partner how it feels.

7. With your index finger, trace circles around the base of the clitoris

without actually touching the shaft or hood. Do at least thirty circles, varying the rate from one-half to three cycles per second. Tell your partner what you're doing and ask her how it feels.

8. Touch the clitoris lightly with your index finger, tapping the head of the clitoris slowly and lightly at first, then with more pressure, then tapping more rapidly. Do at least thirty taps. Tell your partner what you're doing and ask her how it feels.

9. Trace your lubricated index finger lightly around the hood of your partner's clitoris, describing to her what you're doing and asking her how it feels. Continue with heavier pressure and more speed, moving the clitoral hood side to side and up and down. Gently pull back the hood of the clitoris with the thumb of your other hand and make very small circles with your index finger on the now-exposed upper tip of the clitoris. Do at least eighty stroke cycles, varying stroke rate from one-half to three cycles per second. Approximately every ten cycles, change pressure and rate of your strokes. Tell your partner what you're doing and ask her how it feels.

10. Insert your well-lubricated index finger into your partner's vagina up to the second knuckle. Rotate your finger around, pressing on the vaginal walls and stroking various points at varying depths. Use an average stroke rate of one cycle per second. Describe what you're doing in terms of the positions of your hand relative to imagining the vaginal opening as the face of a clock, with noon up toward the clitoris and six o'clock down toward the buttocks. Slowly sweep around the interior of the vagina with one finger, using increasingly more pressure. Tell your partner what you're doing and ask her if any particular location or pressure feels better than another.

11. With inserted finger or fingers, ask your partner to do a few sex-muscle clenches. Notice the sensations of pressure around your inserted fingers at the entrance of the vagina. Then ask your partner to do several push-out contractions (bearing down). Your finger will probably feel pressure and perhaps feel as if it's being expelled. Ask your partner to describe her sensations.

12. Remove your fingers from the vaginal opening. Lightly touch the ridge around the anal opening with a lubricated finger. Circle around and across the anal opening in a gentle, teasing motion. Ask your partner to do several quick flutter-clenches as you lightly stroke this area. Then ask her to do five or ten slow inhale clenches while you continue lightly to touch the anal area. Ask for her reactions.

13. Discuss with your partner what you and she enjoyed and learned, what may have felt uncomfortable or embarrassing, and what may have been pleasantly surprising.

EXERCISE FOUR: SIMULTANEOUS PARTNER STIMULATION

Rationale

An important skill the Ecstasy Program is designed to develop is mental flexibility, including trading roles easily with your partner. "Giving," as we use the term here, means becoming the designated driver for a period of time. When, with your partner's agreement, you assume this active role, you take a greater degree of control. You assume responsibility for guiding your mutual experience. You learn to direct your attention more to your partner's responses than your own, actively giving your partner your attention.

"Receiving," in turn, means learning to direct your attention more to your own feelings, thoughts, and physical responses than to your partner's. The receiver trusts the giving partner and surrenders a degree of control for a time, by mutual agreement.

This ability to focus your attention selectively on yourself or your partner is one of the secrets of learning to extend your orgasmic response.

When you and your partner stimulate each other simultaneously, as you'll be doing in this exercise, you'll be dividing your attention to some degree and diluting this focus.

Nevertheless, simultaneous and equal stimulation has the quality of immediate balance and obvious fairness. Simultaneous stimulation may be a pleasurable way to initiate a sexual interaction. It allows both of you to switch attention at the same time away from the analytical mode that characterizes our thinking most of the time to the more intuitive sexual mode. For most couples in well-established relationships, how easily both partners can switch to erotic feeling at more or less the same time partly determines how often they have sex and how intense the sexual experience is.

After beginning erotic play with simultaneous stimulation, you can switch effectively to taking turns as giver and receiver. Later in the Ecstasy Program, we'll be suggesting that you begin your sexual interaction with Simultaneous Partner Stimulation and then move into sequential giving and receiving.

The Exercise

Both partners lie on their sides, resting on an elbow, facing each other's genitals. Both partners use lubrication. With one hand, the woman stimulates the man's penis shaft and glans. With her other hand she's free to stimulate the scrotum and external prostate area. The man stimulates the woman's clitoris with one hand and the vaginal opening with the fingers of his other hand.

Stimulate each other simultaneously for at least thirty minutes. While you're doing so, talk to each other about your feelings and reactions. Tell your partner what feels good and what doesn't and what you'd like done differently. Start positively: "That's great." Then perhaps suggest a modification: "A little faster and lighter now—yes, that's better."

If one of you becomes even slightly bored or loses excitement, say so, along with a suggestion for changing the manner of stimulation. Your partner can suggest ways you can redirect your attention to increasing pleasure and can alter the stimulation you're getting.

If either of you wishes, you're free to provide oral stimulation in addition to, or instead of, manual stimulation. Keep it brief for now. Oral stimulation limits talk. Do this exercise at least three times this week. You'll find it useful as a prelude to further lovemaking.

MUTUAL SIMULTANEOUS STIMULATION
(COMMUNICATION POSITION)

The man and woman both lie on their sides resting on an elbow facing their partner's genitals. Full manual (or oral) stimulation is possible. This position allows teaching one's partner and learning from one's partner at the same time. The couple alternates between verbal and nonverbal communication, noticing the differences. A good initial position, creating sexual arousal and interest in both partners and establishing equality in the relationship. Easy transition to one of the giver-receiver positions.

EXERCISE FIVE: SIGN COMPLETION AGREEMENT

EXERCISE COMPLETION AGREEMENT/ WEEK SIX

PARTNER EXERCISES   **Initials**

1. Discussed resistances prior to each exercise.   _____   _____
2. Did Exercise Planning Agreement.   _____   _____
3. Did sexual Appreciations and Resentments
   twice a day, 3 times.   _____   _____
4. Did Sexual Exploration once.   _____   _____
5. Did Simultaneous Partner Stimulation 3 times.   _____   _____

SOLO EXERCISES

1. Did 20–0 Countdown at least twice a day.   _____   _____
2. Did Sex Muscle and Breathing Exercise twice
   a day.   _____   _____

I have accomplished the Solo Exercises described above. My partner and I have accomplished the Partner Exercises described above to our reasonable satisfaction. We also specifically reaffirm our agreement here to follow the exercises of Week Seven.

If there has been or will be any change in the program as assigned, we have both talked about those changes and agreed upon them together.

_____   _____
Signature and Date   *Signature and Date*

WEEK SEVEN

SUMMARY OF EXERCISES

SOLO EXERCISES

1. 20–0 Countdown (1 cycle daily).
2. Sex Muscle and Breathing (combined this week with Self-Stimulation).
3. Self-Stimulation IV: Advanced (30 minutes, 2 times)

PARTNER EXERCISES

1. Execute Exercise Planning Agreement.
2. Communication (Appreciations and Resentments) (2 planned sexual subjects per day, 2 times; unlimited spontaneous).
3. Soft-Penis Intercourse (20 minutes, 3 times).
4. Sexual Requests (planned, 2 requests each; may be incorporated with spontaneous lovemaking).
5. Sign Exercise Completion Agreement.
6. Spontaneous lovemaking as desired.

SOLO EXERCISES

EXERCISE ONE: 20–0 COUNTDOWN

Skills you're acquiring by regularly practicing the 20–0 Countdown are probably helping you now to focus your attention more efficiently on sexual sensations during your lovemaking and to move quickly past intrusive thoughts. Continue to practice at least one cycle of Countdowns per day.

EXERCISE TWO: SEX MUSCLE AND BREATHING

Regular muscle development and breathing training should be intensifying sensitivity in your genitals. Increasingly, you'll be combining the skills you've been learning by this exercise with self- and partner-stimulation skills. This week, we'll ask you to incorporate aspects of this exercise into the Advanced Self-Stimulation Exercise that follows below.

EXERCISE THREE: SELF-STIMULATION IV: ADVANCED

Rationale

Both men and women can learn to increase the intensity and duration of orgasm with self-stimulation. That experience is not only intensely pleasurable in itself; it also prepares you for the more intense and potentially longer orgasms possible with a partner.

You can begin exploring the possibility of extending your orgasmic response with self-stimulation this week. First review our discussion of extended orgasm (Chapter VI) to be sure you understand the direction you're aiming for. Then simply adapt our directions to self-stimulation, making yourself your own partner.

The Exercise

Advanced Self-Stimulation for Women

Women don't need to worry about delaying orgasm, of course; their aim can be to improve the ease, intensity, number, and duration of their orgasms. Breathing, bearing down, pushing out, and pressing the clitoris against the pubic bone without moving your hands or body during orgasm can extend orgasmic contractions by a minute or more. The main problem women will face in learning to extend orgasm is mental resistances; to deal with those, review our discussion of that problem beginning on page 98. This is where the skills you've learned doing 20–0 Countdowns come in; the better you are at concentration, the more success you'll have with directing your thoughts where you want them and countering intrusive thoughts.

Often one area of the clitoris is somewhat more sensitive and responsive than another. Discover if this is true for you by first stimulating one side, pausing for a few seconds to allow arousal to drop a bit, and then stimulating the other side with the same number of strokes and approximately the same pressure and in the same location. For instance, stimulate the right side of the shaft of your clitoris with your right forefinger, up and down at about one stroke per second for thirty seconds, then pause for ten or fifteen seconds and stimulate the other side of the clitoris with the same finger at the same rate and same pressure for thirty strokes. Notice which type of stimulation felt better. If you aren't sure, repeat the process several times.

Hold the shaft of your clitoris between your index and middle fingers and rub up and down and from side to side at about one stroke per second. Vary the rate and pressure of this up-and-down movement, noticing what effect it has on your arousal. You need to become an expert on the subtlety and great variety of methods of stroking and stimulating your clitoris.

Now try using a circular motion on your clitoris, applying firm pressure with your index and middle fingers over the entire clitoral area as if you're massaging a muscle under the skin. Circle one way, clockwise, and then the opposite way. Start with a rate of about one cycle per second for at least fifteen seconds, and then change direction. Experiment with faster and slower stroking. You may want to increase the rate of your stroking to two or possibly three strokes per second. It's possible to move your hand very rapidly for short distances. Often the alternation of very fast with very slow and very firm with very light strokes, both in predictable and in teasing, unpredictable patterns, can be an effective way of rapidly increasing your arousal levels.

Try another method. Place two or three fingers over your clitoral area and vibrate your hand as fast as you can, as if you were duplicating a vibrator at slow speed for a short period of time. Also try brushing your fingers rapidly side to side across your clitoris. Remember that the more effectively you can learn to stimulate yourself, the better able you will be to teach a partner to do the same. The more you understand the subtleties of stroking and the variety of methods, the better able you will be to train a man to do the same or even better. Men are likely to be more receptive to learning how to stimulate you if you can analyze some of the basic components, such as the different types of clitoral strokes, and break down the learning process into separate steps. After some practice, the separate steps can be combined into a smooth, flowing, spontaneous process and you both benefit.

Be sure to experiment with fantasy. Many women require more mental stimulation than men (hence their need for romance and foreplay). Be a scriptwriter. Create a sexual scenario in words and pictures. Try several different fantasies as you stimulate yourself with predictable, steady rhythm. As your mental story increases in excitement, speed up your stimulation to match it. Stretch out your fantasy to allow sexual tension to build. Avoid culminating your fantasy too quickly. Physical stimulation should keep pace with your mental images, steadily increasing muscle tension in the genital region.

Practice a complete set of your three sex muscle/breathing exercises at the same time you stimulate your clitoris. Use a relatively steady clitoral stroke pattern to allow you to observe the effects of repetitively contracting and relaxing, pushing out separately and also in synchrony with breathing.

After about thirty minutes of stimulating yourself in this way, reward yourself with an orgasm. Deliberately try to stretch it out in time and intensity. You don't have to leave better orgasms to chance. Stop moving your hand as you slide down the other side of orgasm, cup your hand and press it firmly against your clitoris and pubic bone. Remember to breathe and do deliberate push-outs. Eventually, as your knowledge of this process improves, you'll be able to teach and guide your partner to providing the most effective strokes, pressure, and timing, while you supply the fantasy.

Advanced Self-Stimulation for Men

A man's object can be to see how close he can come to ejaculation without actually doing so and how long he can stay at this level. You've been working toward that goal anyway during self-stimulation exercises these past weeks. The only difference now is focusing more closely on staying at the edge of ejaculation, pursuing maximum sensation. You'll need to pay attention to ejaculatory control techniques, particularly push-outs and the scrotal pull.

Extending orgasmic response by self-stimulation requires you to become both giver and receiver simultaneously. That means dropping into a meditative state such as you may have learned to experience doing the 20–0 Countdown, when the room dims and you're entirely focused on pleasure, pulling yourself back up into awareness enough to allow conscious effort to exert ejaculatory control, then dropping down again. Eventually such alternations become largely automatic, emission-stage orgasm stabilizes and opens out, and you can continue in a state of high, pleasurable arousal for long periods of time.

Men may want to pursue the following advanced exercises that add to pleasure and to ejaculatory control:

Erection exercises. Sit on the edge of a chair with your legs spread apart. While you are fully erect, contract the muscles that make your penis throb—that is, that make it get fuller. Locate the muscles that make your penis move up and down, side to side, and back and forth.

Practice moving your penis in these different directions. Practice with your knees together. Practice while squatting and while lying on your back. You've already begun exercising the muscles involved in making your penis move. They're the P.C. muscles, the abdominal muscles, the buttocks, and the thighs. Notice the effects that contracting single sets and combinations of these muscles have on your penis's movement and on your sensations of pleasure.

Practicing these exercises will increase the strength and hardness of your erection. You can develop further strength by hanging a wet washcloth or towel on your erect penis and lifting it by repeating a number of flutter clenches. Start with a small face towel and work up to larger, heavier bath towels.

These exercises not only develop extra muscle strength but also increase the supply of blood to your genitals.

Repeated ejaculation. Stimulate yourself without ejaculation for thirty minutes. Reward yourself with ejaculation. Keep stimulating yourself throughout the entire time of your ejaculation. Even after your contractions stop, continue stimulating your penis. Keep your full mental attention focused on the sensation you're feeling. Experiment with methods of stimulating yourself to keep the sensation of ejaculatory contraction going longer. When you think the contractions may be dying out, go *all out* to bring them back, increasing speed, pressure—go for it! Instead of becoming soft, your penis may remain relatively hard. As you continue stimulating, you may gradually become more erect, though perhaps not as firm as the first time. You may need to increase the amount of stimulation significantly the second time. If your penis is extremely sensitive to touch after your ejaculation, use the lightest stroking and touching possible for a number of seconds, gradually increasing the pressure and speed as the extreme sensitivity diminishes.

Continue to stimulate yourself for at least another ten minutes. You may experience another ejaculation, with the volume of your ejaculate somewhat reduced. Each time you approach ejaculation, instead of distracting yourself by thinking of other things, pay attention to your penis and to the sensations in your testicles, your perineal and anal areas, and internally.

Seminal fluid retention. This exercise is a variation of the repeated-ejaculation exercise. Stimulate yourself without ejaculation for thirty minutes, then increase stimulation. When you feel yourself just beginning to ejaculate, stop stimulating. Take your hands away from your penis, hold your breath for a few moments, and contract your P.C. muscles and your other sexual muscles as tightly as you can. Your goal is completely to stop the ejaculatory fluid from squirting out. If you have trained your P.C. and other sexual muscles, you'll discover that you can retain some or most of your ejaculate. Surprisingly, though, your orgasm will continue and may even feel stronger.

After your contractions have ceased, resume stimulating yourself. Your erection will probably have decreased somewhat. Continue stimulating yourself, and your arousal will return to a high level. Since you have retained some of your semen, you may not have to wait as long as usual before you can have another ejaculation. You may find you can ejaculate again within several minutes. When you do arrive again at the point of ejaculatory inevitability, contract your sex muscles again. Your second orgasm can be as strong as or stronger than your first.

Notice the amount of fluid you produce in each modified ejaculation. Count the number of internal contractions you experience each time. Compare the number of contractions in your usual orgasm with the number of contractions you experience during these modified procedures.

This skill at self-stimulation can enable you to develop the same multiple-ejaculation pattern with your partner. Such ability is aided significantly by her knowledge, willingness, and technical ability. Next week, in Week Eight, you'll be talking to her, showing her and encouraging her to participate with you as your assistant. You may then be able to use your additional erection and ejaculatory time to include intercourse for her additional benefit and potential enjoyment. Even men over sixty can learn to experience a second ejaculation with these techniques, although greater persistence and attention may be necessary.

As you strengthen your sexual muscles and develop control, you may be able to enjoy two or three separate and distinct ejaculatory orgasms during a single session of self-stimulating. Since you reestablish muscular and vascular tension almost immediately after each modified ejaculation, the cumulative effect is additive: each ejaculation may feel as strong as or a little stronger than the one before, even though the fluid output will likely be less or even "dry," and there may be fewer contractions. You certainly don't have to try for three, by the way. Whenever you think you're ready for the final big ejaculation, simply let go and enjoy it without holding back any semen.

Stretching ejaculatory orgasm. You've practiced your sex-muscle exercises long enough to be ready to begin stretching your ejaculations.

Notice how many contractions you feel during a usual ejaculation—normally between three and twelve. Once your muscles are toned, you may be able at least to double that number and to reverse their order of intensity. Instead of the strongest contractions coming at the beginning, you can learn to space them further apart and to save the best for the end.

Begin as you began the two preceding exercises with thirty minutes of stimulation. This time, however, as you approach ejaculation, tighten your muscles as you did to hold your ejaculate in, but instead of completely stopping all stimulation, continue stimulating your penis very slowly throughout ejaculation, pushing the sensation on and on, stretching it out for as long as you can sustain it. Just before contractions begin, press in firmly with a finger of your free hand on the external prostate spot. Focus your entire attention on the subtleties of your internal contractions and supply the necessary stimulation to your penis to keep those throbs of pleasure going on and on. You may be surprised at how long you can stimulate these sensations to continue.

Creating distractions and interruptions. It's inevitable that you'll encounter distractions in the course of lovemaking. Men have a particular problem maintaining sensation and especially erection in the midst of such distractions. This simple exercise, done sometime before ejaculation, prepares you for that challenge.

Stimulate yourself while you're doing something else—reading a newspaper, watching television, listening to music. You may not be highly aroused, but you can learn to maintain a basic level of arousal even doing two things at once. You'll recover from distractions more quickly with this training.

Walkabout. Men often lose erections when they're shifting positions, particularly when they move from oral and manual lovemaking to intercourse, or when changing locations, such as from couch to bed. Stimulation briefly stops and moving around is distracting. To learn confidence in your ability to return to erection after changing position, sometime before ejaculation move around while self-stimulating. Walk. Stop. Shift from the bed to the floor or to a chair. Or stand and continue to stimulate yourself with your eyes closed, creating a sexual fantasy or focusing on sensation and feeling. If you're uncomfortable standing, kneel. Teach yourself to maintain erection during movement and to return to arousal after distraction. Distractions are inevitable. If a telephone call interrupts lovemaking, laugh about it to yourself afterward and count it as another chance to practice returning to erection.

PARTNER EXERCISES

EXERCISE ONE: EXECUTE PLANNING AGREEMENT

Fill out the following Planning Agreement according to the guidelines we discussed in Chapter VIII, page 131.

EXERCISE PLANNING AGREEMENT/WEEK SEVEN

Communication Exercise

Initiator_____

Allow 8 minutes; 2 rounds per day planned on sexual issues, 2 times; unlimited spontaneous.

Times Scheduled

Sunday	_____	_____
Monday	_____	_____
Tuesday	_____	_____
Wednesday	_____	_____
Thursday	_____	_____
Friday	_____	_____
Saturday	_____	_____

Soft-Penis Intercourse

Allow 20 minutes, 3 times.

Times Scheduled

Sunday	_____
Monday	_____
Tuesday	_____

Wednesday _____
Thursday _____
Friday _____
Saturday _____

Sexual Requests

Initiator_____
Two times, as agreed upon in advance; see discussion below.

Times Scheduled

Sunday _____
Monday _____
Tuesday _____
Wednesday _____
Thursday _____
Friday _____
Saturday _____

EXERCISE TWO: COMMUNICATION

Continue practicing planned Appreciations and Resentments on sexual subjects twice this week. Also continue to use spontaneous Appreciations and Resentments as necessary to encourage communication and clear the air of problems.

EXERCISE THREE: SOFT-PENIS INTERCOURSE

Rationale

Soft-Penis Intercourse can be a pleasurable way to begin genital stimulation after foreplay if the man is not yet erect. It establishes sexual intimacy without rushing sexual performance. It's also useful and pleasurable after ejaculation to coax another possible erection or to prolong intimacy. Virtually every couple will benefit from practicing it.

The Exercise

We suggest you begin this exercise with the now-familiar Kissing process. One of you functions as the giver for a couple of minutes, then you wordlessly switch roles so that the giver becomes the receiver for a couple more minutes.

The woman then lies on her back with her right leg tented over the man's hips. The man lies at a 45-degree angle to her body on his left side, facing her. He holds his penis in his right hand and rubs the glans up, down, and around the woman's clitoris. Both areas, penis and vulva, should be well lubricated.

The man concentrates on stimulating particularly the sensitive frenulum area of his glans, focusing his attention on the pleasurable sensations he receives from rubbing it against his partner's genitals. The woman allows herself to enjoy the clitoral stimulation she's receiving without thinking ahead to what she hopes or anticipates should happen—to her arousal or to his.

Part of the time, if she wishes, the woman can take the penis in her hand and rub the glans against her clitoris. Soft-penis intercourse can be passed back and forth in this way. Both of you can look at each other silently. You can sigh. You can perform this exercise with your eyes closed. Or you can talk about what feels good to you or how you feel good about each other (but don't initiate any negative discussion at this time).

If you, the man, start this exercise with an erection, rest your penis without movement against your partner's clitoris until erection lessens or move it so that the shaft more than the glans is touching your partner's clitoris and labia. If you find it "hard to stay soft" and your erection remains even after ten or fifteen minutes of the lightest possible stimulation, announce to your partner that you are interrupting the exercise and then go ahead and ejaculate any way you wish. As soon as you have ejaculated, switch back to the soft-penis position and proceed with the exercise. It should be much easier for you to follow the instructions after you've had an ejaculation.

If you happen to develop an erection during this exercise, don't be concerned. Slow your stimulation, reducing rate and pressure. After at least five minutes of stimulation with your penis relatively soft, you may partly insert yourself—no more than one inch—into your partner's vagina. If you do partly insert yourself, continue to use your right hand to move your penis from inside the vagina to outside, up and around the clitoris—in, out, around and around. This will probably be arousing to your partner.

Experiment with your thoughts. Close your eyes as you focus on what you're feeling and visualize the immediate present moment in time. Imagine seeing through the zoom lens of a camera. Visualize the larger picture of both your full bodies moving together. Now zoom in to just the penis and clitoris moving, touching, and feeling. Notice the differences when you shift your frame of reference from large to small and detailed.

After five minutes or more of partial insertion and clitoral teasing, if you have less than a full erection, you may gradually increase penetration while decreasing clitoral stimulation. Don't introduce hard thrusting, only gentle, slow transition from clitoral stimulation to vaginal penetration. After twenty minutes, you may announce the conclusion of the exercise and then proceed to lovemaking in any way that you and your partner wish.

Do this exercise at least three times during Week Seven for at least twenty minutes each session (including Kissing). Please do this exercise even if you or your partner resists doing it, even if it seems silly or sounds boring. It won't be when you do it. Don't expect an erection. Soft-Penis Intercourse is a training exercise. Boxers jump rope for training to develop their reflexes, stamina, and concentration, not because they expect to jump rope in the ring.

EXERCISE FOUR: SEXUAL REQUESTS

Rationale

People have preferences for what they enjoy—which particular foods, what programs on TV, which piece of music—and these preferences usually vary from hour to hour, day to day, and month to month. There's no way that any other person can reliably guess what your choice might be at any particular time. You probably don't hesitate to ask your partner if he/she would be willing to make your favorite dinner tomorrow or go to the movies with you. When it comes to sex, though, many people are reluctant to ask their partners for something at all out of their regular routine. They generally hesitate because they're afraid of being refused or even of causing their partners offense.

The Sexual Requests Exercise is an opportunity to practice asking your partner to consider a specific sexual request. We identify two types of requests: familiar and novel. Familiar requests are for activities you've shared before which you expect your partner to be quite comfortable doing, for example, using a prop such as lingerie, watching an erotic video, or making love in a nonroutine place, such as on the couch. Novel requests are those which you've rarely or never incorporated into your lovemaking before and which you're unsure how your partner will react to. These might include a request for oral sex or anal stimulation, renting an erotic video if you've never done so, or simply an unusual time such as when you arrive home in the evening and before dinner.

Some thought may need to go into making a novel request. Don't suggest activities that you are fairly certain your partner will find unacceptable, or that may make your partner very anxious or create performance pressure.

The Exercise

This exercise can be incorporated as part of any spontaneous lovemaking. Since Week Seven has relatively less total assigned, structured partner exercise time than the previous five weeks of the Ecstasy Program, you may have more opportunity or interest in an additional one or more spontaneous unassigned sexual interactions.

Alternatively, Sexual Requests can be a planned, scheduled exercise.

Either way, each of you should make a request to the other at least twice this week. Requests may be made in advance of lovemaking or immediately before a sexual encounter. Select a time to make your request when you can have your partner's relaxed attention—not when he/she is distracted.

The structure is:

"I have a [novel or familiar] sexual request. Would you like to hear it?"

The other partner may answer, "No." If he/she wishes, he/she can give a reason. He/she should state when he/she may be available for such a request at another time.

Or the partner may answer, "Yes," in which case the initiating partner states the request as specifically as possible, and if appropriate, the amount of time to be allotted, and then asks, "Is that agreeable with you?"

The partner receiving the request then answers, "Yes" or "Yes, with this modification" or "No" with an explanation if he/she wishes to explain.

Requests may be brief and familiar ("I'd like you to turn off the TV, turn down the lights, and light a candle") or they may be novel and require more time ("I'd like you to stimulate me all over with a feather and then rub me from head to toe with massage oil") or they may be familiar and more extensive ("I'd like you to stimulate me with a vibrator and then with your hands and mouth until I come").

The tone of voice of your request is important. If you sound demanding or annoyed, your partner may be less willing to agree or do so reluctantly. Being enthusiastic or at least matter-of-fact works best. You may find it useful first to bring up the content of a proposed novel request about which you are uncertain of your partners's approval in one of your planned sexual Appreciations and Resentments processes. This can help to prepare your partner for your later sexual request.

Even when this exercise is not specifically assigned in the weekly plan, in future weeks we suggest you incorporate it into your spontaneous, unassigned lovemaking.

EXERCISE FIVE: SIGN COMPLETION AGREEMENT

EXERCISE COMPLETION AGREEMENT/ WEEK SEVEN

PARTNER EXERCISES   Initials

1. Discussed resistances prior to each exercise. _____ _____
2. Did Exercise Planning Agreement.   _____ _____
3. Did sexual Appreciations and Resentments
   twice.   _____ _____
4. Did Soft Penis Intercourse 3 times.   _____ _____
5. Did Sexual Requests at least twice each.   _____ _____

SOLO EXERCISES

1. Did 20–0 Countdown at least twice a day.   _____ _____
2. Did Sex Muscle and Breathing Exercise com-
   bined with Self-Stimulation.   _____ _____
3. Did Advanced Self-Stimulation twice.   _____ _____

I have accomplished the Solo Exercises described above. My partner and I have accomplished the Partner Exercises described above to our reasonable satisfaction. We also specifically reaffirm our agreement here to follow the exercises of Week Eight.

If there has been or will be any change in the program as assigned, we have both talked about those changes and agreed upon them together.

_____   _____
Signature and Date   *Signature and Date*

WEEK EIGHT

SUMMARY OF EXERCISES

SOLO EXERCISES

1. 20–0 Countdown (1 cycle twice a day).
2. Sex Muscle and Breathing (daily).

PARTNER EXERCISES

1. Execute Exercise Planning Agreement.
2. Communication (Appreciations and Resentments) (2 rounds sexual, 2 times; unlimited spontaneous).
3. Genital Hygiene.
4. Partner-Assisted Stimulation (30 minutes each partner, 1 hour total, 2 times; optional oral stimulation; proceed to Intercourse).
5. Intercourse I (minimum 15 minutes, 2 times).
6. Sign Exercise Completion Agreement.
7. Spontaneous lovemaking as desired.

SOLO EXERCISES

EXERCISE ONE: 20–0 COUNTDOWN

Notice your ability to focus your attention without as many intrusive thoughts. At what number are you distracted? You might be amazed when you compare your progress with the first weeks of the Ecstasy Program. Continue to apply to your sexual experiences what you are learning from the regular practice of the 20–0 Countdown, stopping thoughts and redirecting your internal monologue.

EXERCISE TWO: SEX MUSCLE AND BREATHING

Continue to do as many repetitions as you feel comfortable with, one or two times a day. A total of 200–300 combined repetitions of the 3 exercises per day is a reasonable daily goal. We won't specifically assign Sex Muscle and Breathing exercises from here on. We recommend, though, that you continue to do this exercise at least once a day.

PARTNER EXERCISES

EXERCISE ONE: EXECUTE PLANNING AGREEMENT

Fill out the following Planning Agreement according to the guidelines we discussed in Chapter VIII, page 131.

EXERCISE PLANNING AGREEMENT/WEEK EIGHT

Communication Exercise

Initiator_____

Plan 2 rounds of sexual Appreciations and Resentments 2 times this week; unlimited spontaneous.

Times Scheduled

Sunday	_____	_____
Monday	_____	_____
Tuesday	_____	_____
Wednesday	_____	_____
Thursday	_____	_____
Friday	_____	_____
Saturday	_____	_____

Partner-Assisted Stimulation Plus Intercourse

Allow 1 hour and 15 minutes, 2 times this week.

Times Scheduled

Sunday	_____
Monday	_____
Tuesday	_____
Wednesday	_____
Thursday	_____
Friday	_____
Saturday	_____

EXERCISE TWO: COMMUNICATION

By now you and your partner are spontaneously using Appreciations and Resentments as a form of communication whenever you're together. From this point on, only sexual Appreciations and Resentments should be planned for at the beginning of the week. You may practice nonsexual Appreciations and Resentments as they come up, without limit.

In Week Eight, practice two rounds of sexual Appreciations and Resentments two times during the week.

EXERCISE THREE: GENITAL HYGIENE

Rationale

Concerns about cleanliness are frequently the reason partners resist performing oral sex. Surprisingly, this is often true even when the partner desiring oral stimulation believes him/herself to be relatively attentive to cleanliness. A soap-and-water washing just prior to oral sex reduces such concern. When the giver does the washing, he/she may find his/her resistance eliminated or significantly reduced. (We discuss cleanliness in more detail in Chapter IV, beginning on page 75.)

Before proceeding with the Oral-Stimulation option in the next exercise, Partner-Assisted Stimulation, we suggest you arrange the pleasure of washing your partner's genitals.

The Exercise

You can accomplish this exercise in the shower or bath or simply with soap and a washcloth. What's important is that each of you take turns washing the other, concentrating on the genitals. A few extra pats, rubs, or strokes can add extra pleasure to the cleaning process.

Men: Be sure to retract the hood of the clitoris gently and clean any material—discharge, lint—that may have been lost in the folds.

Women: If your partner is uncircumcised, gently pull back the hood of the penis (the prepuce) and wash carefully around the glans.

EXERCISE FOUR: PARTNER-ASSISTED STIMULATION

Rationale

In this exercise, first you watch your partner self-stimulate, then assist him/her in his/her self-stimulation, and finally take over the process for him/her.

We sometimes call the Partner-Assisted Stimulation Exercise "Mirroring," because this exercise asks you to mimic what you've seen your partner do until you can stimulate him/her as effectively as he/she can stimulate him/herself. Let your partner be the judge of your sensitivity and effectiveness. Learning these important skills with your partner's participation and guidance and to your partner's satisfaction may take only one session or five or ten. Budget at least one hour for Partner-Assisted Stimulation during Week Eight in two separate sessions. Your partner gives verbal and nonverbal instructions, guiding your hands whenever necessary. Remember, your partner is the expert, you are the student.

Watching each other self-stimulate is an excellent way to learn how your partner likes to be pleasured. You may find this exercise unusually fascinating at first because of the prohibitions our society places on self-stimulation. You may never have seen your partner "making love" to him/herself before. You may well be letting each other in on private, vulnerable secrets. It's especially pleasurable for a man to watch a woman charging herself with sexual energy to the point of orgasm. Women similarly find this often-hidden area of their partner's life a pleasurable secret to unlock.

Both men and women also sometimes experience feelings of being left out during this exercise. They may feel that their partners have no need for them, that they have become self-contained. They may feel that their own skills, their experience, their intimate commitment are unnecessary. In short, they may feel rejected.

Reassure each other. You know, and your partner knows, that the experience of pleasuring with a partner is completely different from the experience of self-pleasuring. Each may complement the other.

You may find that you have special resistances about stimulating yourself in front of your partner. If so, you may need to spend extra time discussing them before you begin. Prohibitions against self-stimulation learned in childhood can be very strong, and even if they were eventually overcome when self-stimulating alone, such resistances may reappear in force when you stimulate in front of your partner.

Many people encounter resistances connected to past or present religious prohibitions. You must finally decide if any form of sexual pleasuring violates your faith, and, if so, whether or not you want to accept that prohibition and the limitation on pleasure it enforces.

Unfortunately, some men and women who learned religious prohibitions as children find themselves inhibited as adults. They find they've emotionally generalized specific rules until all of sexuality is permeated with a sense of sin, even sexuality permitted within the context of their faith and even, in some cases, after they've given that faith up.

If you discover more specific and limited religious-based resistances, the techniques for overcoming resistances we discussed earlier (see pages 98–102 and 145–48) should work for you.

Resistance to self-stimulation in particular can be a religion-based anxiety. Besides the relaxation techniques built into the Ecstasy Program, the best way we know to work through the resistance is to realize that you aren't learning self-stimulation only for yourself. You're learning it to improve your relationship with your partner, to improve your ability to give and receive pleasure, to add to intimacy and commitment. In any religion, intention is crucial in judging behavior. The intention of the self-stimulation exercises here, which serve for learning and as a kind of extended foreplay, is to strengthen your bond of love with your partner.

An exercise that can help you work through self-consciousness about self-stimulation is making your partner your self-stimulation assistant. Men and women both need to make sure that their partners are learning to be the best assistants that they can help them become. You need to give good verbal and nonverbal instructions, guiding your partner's hand precisely, whenever and wherever necessary. Remember, you're the expert where your own stimulation is concerned; your partner is the student.

The Exercise

Your partner may ask questions but should not touch you. Decide from what vantage point, near or far, you would like your partner to observe you. Take turns. Alternate who goes first. Talk about your experiences afterward. Remember, your partner is the expert, you are the student. You and your partner should alternate initiating this exercise.

To begin the exercise, each of you stimulates yourself simultaneously in front of your partner for five minutes or more (be sure to use plenty of lubricant). The man can peak himself several times using his favorite techniques but should not ejaculate. The woman uses her preferred strokes and may peak herself, but she should not let herself go through with orgasm.

Let yourself really go—to show your partner what you have learned from the self-stimulation practices described in earlier weeks.

The man then stops self-stimulating to watch his partner while she continues her self-stimulation for five minutes longer. The man then begins to help the woman with her stimulation, trying to copy as closely as possible the process that he has observed. He tries to imitate her technique, emphasizing clitoral stimulation. She may continue her stroking while he places his hand or fingers over hers or under hers, letting her lead while he follows, as in dancing. She gives both verbal and nonverbal direction. She lets him assume more control as he learns to reproduce her optimum pattern. After five or ten minutes, she withdraws her hand from her clitoral area and allows him to take over. She is free to use her hands to stimulate other areas of her genitals, her breasts, or any area she wishes. Whenever her partner's stimulation pattern is less than optimum, she resumes directly helping him with her hands, and/ or with verbal direction. After at least twenty minutes the man may take her through orgasm.

(For more training in this process of alternating following and leading, refer to and practice the exercise "Dancing Hands," page 77, Chapter IV.)

The man then becomes the receiver and starts to stimulate himself, in his usual manner, while his partner observes without touching. After about five minutes, she joins his stimulation process, trying to reproduce as closely as possible the process she saw him doing. He can place her hand(s) where he would like, and tell her and show her exactly what to do. When her stimulation is good enough, he can let her take over, while he stimulates himself on other areas of his genitals or body. Whenever her stroking process results in climbing arousal less effective than he is able to do himself, or she is taking him excessively rapidly or closely to the point of no return, he guides her hand subtly or directly. The man practices sex-muscle squeezes, push-outs, and breathing techniques and notices what effects these maneuvers have on his level of arousal— how close they bring him to ejaculation and how successfully they hold him there. The woman practices being very aware of his communication of ejaculatory proximity. Are his hands moving toward your hands to stop you or push you away? If the sounds he may be making signal you to slow down, do so immediately. Be aware of his pelvis. Is it moving toward your hand, indicating desire for more stimulation, or is it pulling subtly away, indicating that you should reduce or stop stimulation on the head or shaft of the penis?

The woman should practice the scrotal pull technique as she peaks her partner at least six times, for a total time of about twenty minutes. It's important that the woman take up a comfortable position, anchoring her arm, to provide the optimum manual stimulation. Her elbow can rest on his thigh or on the bed to help her provide the stroke rate and the pressure necessary with a minimum of fatigue.

Proceed now to oral stimulation. If oral stimulation isn't a usual part of your sexual routine, you may omit it here and skip ahead to Intercourse, Partner Exercise Five.

Optional Oral Stimulation: Rationale

Oral stimulation in this and later exercises is for couples who are already comfortable with this form of activity, or who wish to experiment with adding it to their repertoire. If you and/or your partner are not comfortable with oral stimulation, but want to learn more about it, please read our discussions of the subject on pages 276, 325, and in the Appendix under "Solving Problems" (page 388).

We strongly recommend that you both learn to like oral lovemaking and to perform it skillfully. Women tend to resist oral sex—giving *and* receiving—more than men. Some feel it's "dirty." Some don't like the idea of their partners ejaculating in their mouth. Some object to semen's texture. Others, when they think about receiving oral stimulation, worry about their own hygiene and possible odors. These are really conditioning problems and can be dealt with by practicing deconditioning, as we discuss on page 404–5 in the section "Fellatio" in the Appendix.

Most men like, even crave, oral stimulation. They consider it the height of eroticism. It proves to them that their partners love their genitals, something many men doubt. It's intensely stimulating, psychologically as well as physically. It's also intensely intimate, the more so because it carries with it, even today, a heavy freight of stigma. Women who choose to limit such potential pleasure and intimacy are choosing to limit their relationship with their partners. More men seek out prostitutes for oral sex than for any other single reason. Right or wrong, what they miss at home they sometimes look for elsewhere.

Oral lovemaking, we believe, is an important addition to sexual pleasure for men and women both. We suggest that couples push through their resistances and learn and practice this intensely pleasurable art.

Optional Oral Stimulation: The Exercise

If both you and your partner have previously included oral sexual activities in your routine sexual interaction, then the initiator may request his partner to stimulate his/her genitals orally during the Partner-Assisted Stimulation Exercise. The initiator can guide the partner's head with his/her hands to indicate more or less pressure and give simple, encouraging instructions: "That's it." "Maybe a little harder." "Try a little lighter." "That's good." "How about a little higher up." The initiator is free to use his/her hands on his/her own genitals while the partner is giving oral stimulation.

The woman may peak her partner several times but should not allow him to ejaculate. After five to ten minutes, proceed now to Intercourse, Partner Exercise Five.

EXERCISE FIVE: INTERCOURSE I

Rationale

During Week Eight, for the first time in the Ecstasy Program, we add intercourse to your set of exercises. You've undoubtedly continued to enjoy intercourse as part of your informal lovemaking, but by now you've also learned how much pleasure is available sexually even without that intimate culmination. We hope the lesson isn't lost that intercourse is only one aspect of sexual pleasuring, a part of the whole. All the sense organs, the surface of the skin and the brain—the entire body—participate in sexual pleasure.

But the symbolic and actual importance of intercourse in joining two human beings together, emotionally as well as physically, cannot be overstated. Part of your sexual well-being comes from sharing the intimacy of physical connection with your partner.

Performing a number of complex actions need not detract from the experience. All activities that require skill—skiing, tennis, dancing—require a subtle variety of skills. Intercourse is a skill as well as an intimacy and a pleasure.

Couples usually fall into a predictable pattern of intercourse. Your partner has a pretty good idea of what pattern and rhythm of stimulation you're likely to follow. While following familiar patterns may feel comfortable, some variation and teasing in rhythm, stroke, depth, and angle of penetration can create surprise and anticipation and build arousal. Slow stroking and only partial penetration for a minute or two, for example, including occasionally rubbing the head of the penis on the clitoris, can be an excellent prelude to gradually moving toward deeper, faster stroking. The benefit is likely to be double, since slower, teasing penetration also allows the man to build arousal and maintain control.

Men often resist this gradual, teasing approach to intercourse until they discover its benefits.

Caress each other with your hands and your mouths. Now is an especially good time to apply the kissing skills you've been practicing all these weeks.

Since intercourse requires the man's active participation, controlling ejaculation becomes particularly important for extending the sexual encounter.

Paying close attention to breathing is one method that helps, as do contracting and relaxing the sex muscles.

The man should seek out the patterns that help him control ejaculation when he's thrusting. He'll probably feel less in control during intercourse than he did during self-stimulation or when his partner stimulated him. He needs to pay more attention to other controls. He should ask himself if his sex muscles are tensing or relaxed and pushed out. Is he breathing in a regular pattern, and if so, what is that pattern? Combining the patterns of breathing and sex-muscle contractions can give him great control over his level of sexual arousal. Here are some possible combinations and their effects on climbing or leveling of arousal:

1. For moderate to rapid climbing arousal: continuous clench contraction, regular breathing rhythm.
2. For slow climbing: alternating clench/inhale with muscle relaxation/exhale.
3. For most rapid climbing: continuous clench contraction, inhaling and holding breath for thirty seconds or less.
4. For a quick switch from climbing to leveling: push out and exhale.

5. For maintaining level of arousal: sex muscles relaxed, regular breathing.

The patterns the man combines in intercourse can become relaxing and meditative: thrust, contract, *inhale*; withdraw, relax, *exhale*. Keeping his mind occupied with this pleasurable, repeatable process can also help the man avoid distracting thoughts. It's an effective physical and mental discipline.

The skills you've been practicing in the 20–0 Countdown will be practical in enhancing intercourse. Just as you focused on numbers in counting, returning to a number each and every time you were distracted, so also you can focus on a single sensation. Pick out a desirable image and focus on it in your mind's eye. Return to this image every time your mind wanders. Tell yourself exactly what you're paying attention to. Direct your attention to the muscle tension you're experiencing in your genital region. What exactly are you feeling that could leave you vulnerable?

Close your eyes and picture your firm, erect penis in your partner's vagina. Tell yourself, "My penis is tingling and hard. Her vagina is hot and responsive. I'm keeping my sex muscles clenched even when I'm tempted to relax them." You may experience many distracting thoughts, just as you do when you're practicing the 20–0 Countdown. Don't be discouraged. Each time, change each distracting thought to the image you're keeping in your mind. Limit your attention to a specific image or picture of exactly what you are doing or feeling at the particular moment, as you simultaneously describe to yourself the details of what's occurring. Rather than an image, you may prefer to concentrate your attention on feelings in your body. Describe sensations in your genitals or feel the air going in and out of your nose, mouth, and lungs or the tight clenching or relaxing of your sex muscles. Be determined about switching away from any and every distracting thought just as you do when you practice your breathing countdown.

Every man needs to find the pattern that works best for him. When he feels that he is approaching ejaculation, he needs to manipulate the rate, depth, and angle of thrusting. A general rule is to stop climbing to higher levels of arousal when he's within three seconds or three strokes of ejaculation. This is a point that every man *must* learn accurately for himself. That's what the self-stimulation exercises are for. Men should not rely on their partners to control their ejaculatory urge during intercourse. The habit of ejaculating within only a couple of minutes after starting intercourse is hard for many men to break. Even if a man knows he can last longer, he's often so focused on ejaculation that he doesn't bother to do so. "It feels too good" and "I can't help it" are frequent rationalizations.

Men who have the best control in intercourse usually report that they make many small, subtle adjustments in their thrusting pattern—a slight change in the angle of the pelvis, a subtle decrease in rate, a slight decrease in penetration. These are the subtleties that create the "art" of intercourse. The man needs to pay close attention to his thoughts and his physiological reactions as well as to those of his partner. Many men find such a challenge exciting, like the challenge of driving a fine sports car.

As part of controlling the urge to ejaculate, the man needs to learn as well how to stop his partner's pelvic movements completely. The woman may be so focused on her own pleasure, moving and thrusting to increase her own arousal, that she simply isn't aware of her partner's need to slow down or stop stimulation in order to retard ejaculation. For his part, if his partner is highly aroused as measured by her pelvic thrusting, he may feel that he shouldn't stop, forgoing the possibility of longer-term pleasure for both of them (which requires an erect penis for intercourse) in the interest of her immediate satisfaction.

Instead, the man should stop moving his pelvis when he feels he's within three strokes of ejaculation. As a clear signal to his partner, he may need to hold her hips assertively and physically stop her motion. If she continues moving, he may need to be even more assertive and restrain her further. It's better if he accomplishes this end wordlessly, letting the restraint itself communicate his reasons, but if restraint alone doesn't work, he can say, "Please stop," to emphasize his intent. It's the man's responsibility to control his ejaculation, even if that means temporarily restraining his partner. The man may also pull out of his partner's vagina, if necessary, if he finds he has climbed too close to the point of no return.

A majority of men, we've discovered, have never seriously considered stopping their partners' thrusting movements. They're afraid their partners will be annoyed, or they may feel ego gratification at finding their partners swept away by their rush to ejaculation.

Annoyance may be a possibility if the woman isn't near or actually experiencing orgasm. What should the man do? Ideally, he should stimulate his partner to orgasm before intercourse begins. A woman who has an orgasm by oral or manual means before intercourse is likely to be more receptive to being temporarily restrained in her movements during intercourse. In fact, she's likely to find the slow deliberateness of stopping and starting to be stimulating and arousing. She'll probably feel less urgently driven toward orgasm if she's already had at least one orgasm before intercourse and therefore less driven to encourage rapid, hard thrusting. Her vagina, engorged and sensitized by her previous orgasm, will be more sensitive to smaller, subtler movements.

Alternatively, the man can use his hand, or possibly a vibrator, to stimulate his partner toward orgasm during the periods when he needs to stop moving in order to control his urge to ejaculate. Even if his partner doesn't usually experience orgasm with intercourse, clitoral stimulation as an interlude during intercourse will probably help her sustain her interest.

Imaginative men and women in every country and of every age have invented hundreds of different positions for lovemaking. We won't even attempt to list them all. We do want to mention a few, to point out their advantages for control. Then you can have the pleasure together of assessing the others on your own.

Some positions allow the man easier control over movement and therefore over the amount of stimulation he's receiving. Others allow the woman better control over her movement and her stimulation. Yet others make it possible for a couple to pass control back and forth, or to control movement mutually and more equally.

Male-Control Positions

The "missionary" position—the woman on her back, the man on top between her legs—tends to be a male-control position (see illustration, page 250). The man is giver, the woman receiver. The man thrusts and the woman's movement is restricted. Yet it's a good position, which is why so many people use it. It allows couples to look at each other, enjoying the nuances of facial expression, to kiss and caress and hold each other intimately. During orgasm in this position the woman may apply additional pressure against her clitoris by pressing her heels against the lower part of the man's buttocks, forcing his pubic area closer and lifting it upward.

The woman can encourage deeper penetration in this position by drawing her knees higher and locking her feet behind the man's back rather than behind his buttocks.

For deepest penetration, the woman can move her knees closer to her chest and place her ankles over the man's shoulders on either side of his neck. The man can move to a more kneeling position rather than simply extending his legs behind him.

Although this position offers the man good control of thrusting and penetration, it requires relatively more sex-muscle tension, which encourages quicker arousal and ejaculation. So it's less desirable for delaying and extending male orgasm.

Female-Control Positions

A corresponding position where the woman is more in control locates the man lying on his back, legs extended straight and together, the woman lying on top of him with her legs extended on the outside of his legs, supporting herself on her elbows or hands or resting her hands on her partner's chest (see illustration, page 251). An easy way to move to this position is simply to roll over from the basic man-on-top position. In this and other female-above positions, the woman can move more easily while the man's movements tend to be restricted.

Although penetration isn't especially deep, this position does allow the woman considerable freedom to determine the depth of penetration. She can also thrust her hips forward and pull them back, taking the vagina through a short arc and creating highly pleasurable variations in the angle of the penis as it travels back and forth. This movement can be accomplished with a minimum of effort. There's relatively little clitoral and G-spot stimulation in this position, however.

Much more effective for clitoral and G-spot stimulation is the woman kneeling astride the man. The man may influence movement to a degree by bending his legs up against the woman's buttocks, but she has primary control. In this position, the woman can easily direct her partner's penis to stimulate her inner trigger areas. She can also angle her pelvis forward and back to rub her clitoris directly against the base of her partner's penis. She can move her torso down onto his head and chest or up and back toward his knees. She's free to stimulate the base of his penis, scrotum, and external prostate spot by reaching behind herself with one hand.

Many men resist these female-control positions. They falsely equate female control with emotional domination. In fact, the female-astride position is a good one from which to learn and practice ejaculatory control. It allows him to relax his sex muscles and focus on his internal sensations. If a man wishes to become a skillful lover, it's important for him to allow and encourage his partner to be on top when she desires and to allow her to initiate movements while he relaxes. There's no

INTERCOURSE POSITION: MAN ABOVE (MISSIONARY) POSITION

The most traditional and widely used position.

Male has good thrusting, leverage, and control of movement. The addition of a pillow under the woman allows relatively deep penetration.

Easy eye contact, caressing and kissing possible.

If the woman's feet are placed against the bed (rather than raised up as illustrated), she can elevate her hips and participate more actively in thrusting. Penetration depth is also decreased.

Disadvantages: Man needs to support himself on his elbows or arms, leading to earlier fatigue. Woman has relatively less control over directing and guiding movement. Her legs may become fatigued.

For longer intercourse, move to another position after several minutes, depending upon comfort level. Natural progression to the scissors position.

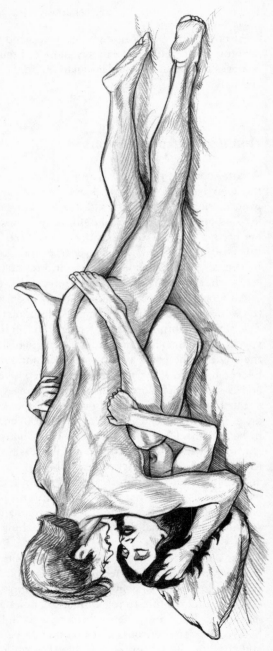

250

INTERCOURSE POSITION: WOMAN ABOVE

In this position the woman can control thrusting and penetration depth. She is free to move her torso from leaning forward, as illustrated, to sitting upright, or leaning back, resting on her outstretched arms. At least four distinct types of motion are possible. She can use her legs for heavy thrusting up and down. For less exertion, she can slide her pelvis forward and back, or tilt it forward and back. She can also rotate her pelvis left and right. The woman's range of movement allows for optimal internal stimulation of the inner trigger area (G spot) and can produce unique sensations for the man.

Further advantages are intimacy of face-to-face contact and ability to kiss. If the woman sits upright, the man can caress her clitoris.

Disadvantages: Heavy thrusting may tire the woman's thighs. The man is pinned down and has less freedom of movement. Slowing or stopping her thrusting to control his ejaculation is more difficult.

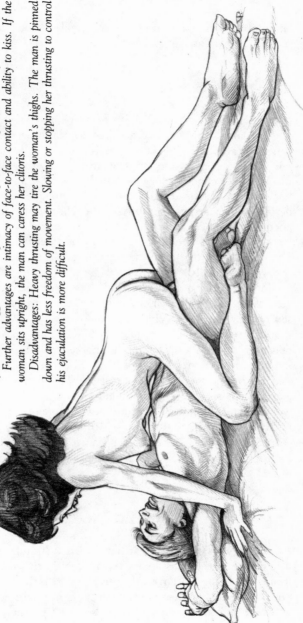

251

"natural" position for intercourse. Female-above positions are just as natural as male-above positions.

Rear-Entry Positions

In the rear-entry positions, both partners are positioned on their knees with the man behind the woman (see illustration, page 253). The woman can easily alter the angle of her pelvis to change the angle of penetration. For medium penetration, she can rest on her extended hands. There's much deeper penetration when she bends more at the waist, resting on her elbows. Her head may be up or lowered, resting on the bed if she desires. The man may grasp her hips. He may bend at the waist, supporting himself on both his arms or on one arm, with the other arm on her hips. He has free access to stimulating her breasts.

Alternatively, the man may stand against the edge of the bed while the woman kneels.

Many experienced couples find these rear-entry positions to be the best of all. They allow mutual and equal control over stimulation. Insertion is potentially very deep, including pressure against the G-spot that can result in intense stimulation. The man may thrust; the woman may sway forward and back on her hands and knees or her forearms and knees; they both may move together. The man can relax his sex muscles and let his partner control thrusting. The man's penis can easily be angled to press against and stimulate the woman's inner trigger area. The woman can tilt her pelvis forward or back, bouncing the male's swinging testicles against her clitoris as he's thrusting, stimulating it.

Intercourse follows the Partner-Assisted Stimulation Exercise in Week Eight. In effect, you and your partner will be flowing from one to the other.

The Exercise

At the conclusion of the Partner-Assisted Stimulation Exercise, begin intercourse in the "missionary" position with the man on top (continue to use ample lubrication). After five minutes, the man shifts his weight onto his right shoulder, the woman slides her right leg between his legs, and both of you continue in this "scissors" position. See page 282 for instructions and illustrations.

INTERCOURSE POSITION: REAR ENTRY

Relatively mutual control. Woman can tilt or rotate her pelvis for maximum stimulation of internal trigger area (G spot). The clitoris is accessible to either partner for additional stimulation. Deep penetration is possible. With the man's hands on his partner's hips he can control her thrusting movements to delay ejaculation. This position allows heavy thrusting. Additional control of the angle of entry is possible when the woman raises her torso by resting on her elbows or hands.

Disadvantages: Penetration may be uncomfortably deep. There is lack of face-to-face intimacy and caressing.

The scissors position is often the most comfortable for both partners when intercourse is extended. The missionary position may be tiring for the man because he has to support his body on his elbows or arms. Even supported, his weight can be a burden on his partner and pinning her down. She can't move freely. The same problems occur in reverse when the woman is on top.

In the scissors position, both partners are more balanced. The woman can use her legs to anchor her thrusting, and man and woman both have greater freedom to move their pelvic areas as they wish. Facing each other, they can kiss and caress. The woman can reach around and stimulate her partner's scrotum and external prostate spot. Since they don't have to support the weight of each other's body, they can go on in this position for a long time if they wish. (The scissors is also an excellent position for pregnant women, for older people, and for anyone convalescing after surgery or illness.)

Your objective for intercourse is to maintain with your genitals and your bodies the high level of arousal to which you previously stimulated each other during manual and oral stimulation. Take turns focusing attention on each other as you move together, trading off giving and receiving. Search out the rhythms and the stroking that bring each of you higher levels of arousal.

After about five minutes in the scissors position, move to the rear-entry position for about five minutes, then conclude by taking each other to a peak of orgasm. Do this by increasing the depth and speeding up the rate of your thrusting. Should you require harder stimulation (heavy thrusting), you may move to the missionary position, or use the female-above position. When you choose to have an orgasm and ejaculate, please remember to vocalize your pleasure during your finale; it can give you an extra boost. As the man starts to ejaculate, the woman should bear down and push out with her sex muscles.

After ejaculation, the man continues his thrusting movements even as his penis softens. Engorgement of the woman's genitals magnifies her perception of size. Even a partially erect penis will feel much larger than its actual dimensions during her orgasm and afterwards, if there is effective stimulation, as during intercourse. Simply arrange to keep the softened penis inside the vagina during these continued thrusting motions. The woman's engorgement creates more voluptuous pleasure on his soft organ.

If Erection Wanes

If the male loses his erection during any phase of intercourse (such as during insertion or while changing positions), do the following: If his erection flags during insertion, the man (or the woman if the position is female-above) can modify his rate of thrusting or angle of penetration. He should focus increased attention on appreciating every subtle sensation coming from his penis. If thrusting has been very rapid, slow it down. If thrusting has been slow, speed it up to a comfortable, maximum rate, maintaining insertion as well as possible. The man should clench his sex muscles strongly and continuously, and hold his breath in for as long as is comfortable.

Should the penis slip out of the vagina, or if the erection is not reestablished within a couple of minutes, then the man can resume self-stimulation, assisted by his partner, until erection is reestablished. Then resume intercourse as before.

Repeat these processes each time the man experiences reduced erection during the intercourse and all subsequent exercises. They're important for increasing the man's sexual self-confidence and reducing any concerns the woman might have about herself or her partner. They're enjoyable, pleasurable processes that reduce anxiety about performance and assure the couple of an opportunity for intercourse and each partner of an opportunity for orgasm.

If loss of erection during intercourse is a recurrent problem, consult the section "Erection Insecurity," page 390, in the Appendix.

If the man has any difficulty achieving ejaculation during the Intercourse Exercise, or if he experiences repeated loss of erection, he should resume self-stimulation with his partner's assistance until ejaculation is achieved.

Some men lose their erection in the missionary position. There are two suggested methods of proceeding: use a pillow under your partner's buttocks to raise the vaginal opening for easier access; or have the woman push out upon penetration. This widens the external opening of the vagina, allowing for easier entry.

EXERCISE SIX: SIGN COMPLETION AGREEMENT

EXERCISE COMPLETION AGREEMENT/ WEEK EIGHT

PARTNER EXERCISES   **Initials**

1. Discussed resistances prior to each exercise.   _____ _____
2. Did Exercise Planning Agreement.   _____ _____
3. Did sexual Appreciations and Resentments
   twice a day, 2 times.   _____ _____
4. Did Genital Hygiene Exercise.   _____ _____
5. Did Partner-Assisted Stimulation twice.   _____ _____
6. Did Intercourse twice.   _____ _____

SOLO EXERCISES

1. Did 20–0 Countdown at least twice a day.   _____ _____
2. Did Sex Muscle and Breathing Exercise daily.   _____ _____

I have accomplished the Solo Exercises described above. My partner and I have accomplished the Partner Exercises described above to our reasonable satisfaction. We also specifically reaffirm our agreement here to follow the exercises of Week Nine.

If there has been or will be any change in the program as assigned, we have both talked about those changes and agreed upon them together.

_____   _____
Signature and Date   *Signature and Date*

WEEK NINE

SUMMARY OF EXERCISES

PARTNER EXERCISES

1. Execute Exercise Planning Agreement.
2. Communication (Appreciations and Resentments) (2 planned rounds on sexual issues, 2 times; unlimited spontaneous on nonsexual issues).
3. Genital Hygiene (1 to 3 minutes).
4. Learning to Extend Orgasmic Response I (man giving, woman receiving, 30 minutes; woman giving, man receiving, 30 minutes; 2 times).
5. Intercourse II (15 minutes), following Exercise Four.
6. Sign Exercise Completion Agreement.
7. Spontaneous lovemaking as desired.

EXERCISE ONE: EXECUTE PLANNING AGREEMENT

Fill out the following Planning Agreement according to the guidelines we discussed in Chapter VIII, page 131.

EXERCISE PLANNING AGREEMENT/WEEK NINE

Communication Exercise

Initiator_____

Plan 2 rounds of sexual Appreciations and Resentments 2 times this week; unlimited spontaneous.

Times Scheduled

Sunday	_____	_____
Monday	_____	_____
Tuesday	_____	_____
Wednesday	_____	_____
Thursday	_____	_____
Friday	_____	_____
Saturday	_____	_____

Learning to Extend Orgasmic Response I

Allow 1 hour and 15 minutes, 2 times this week.

Times Scheduled

Sunday	_____
Monday	_____
Tuesday	_____
Wednesday	_____
Thursday	_____
Friday	_____
Saturday	_____

EXERCISE TWO: COMMUNICATION

Do two planned rounds on sexual issues two times this week. As we have instructed since Week Four, for the Appreciation, search for a positive aspect within each negative experience. For example:

"Jerry, there's something I'd like to tell you."

"Okay, I'm listening."

[What you observed, how you felt] "When you close the bedroom door before we have sex, I feel pleased you're concerned to protect our privacy."

"Thank you."

"Jerry, there's something I'd like to tell you."

[What you observed, how you felt, and what you would prefer to have happened.] "When you close the bedroom door but don't lock it, I still feel somewhat vulnerable to one of the children coming in. I'd feel less inhibited if you'd remember to lock it every single time."

"Thank you."

Remember, talking about your sexual experiences, feelings, and preferences in a safe situation that is not likely to escalate, expressed in a structure least likely to cause offense, is a valuable way to improve your relationship. We encourage you to continue this exercise on a regular daily basis. It can be the most helpful way to assist with problems in all areas of your relationship, including intimacy and sex. It's a tool that can lead to compromise and resolution in a fair and honorable manner.

EXERCISE THREE: GENITAL HYGIENE

Rationale

Just as you made a point last week of washing each other's genitals, we'd like you from now on to continue to pay attention to hygiene before proceeding to the sexual interactions we'll be assigning. One or both of you may have higher standards of cleanliness for oral stimulation than for manual stimulation and intercourse. It's not uncommon for this difference to be an issue which neither partner has raised or discussed. A good, safe policy for any man and woman who wish to engage in oral sex from time to time is routinely to wash their genitals shortly before lovemaking. Even a once-a-day bath or shower may be insufficient to satisfy a partner's expectations and preferences.

The Exercise

Using soap and water, simultaneously or separately wash, rinse, and dry your partner's genitals. Enjoy the process for its sensual pleasure. Alternatively, you may prefer to shower together or separately before the sexual exercises that follow.

EXERCISE FOUR: LEARNING TO EXTEND ORGASMIC RESPONSE I

Rationale

Taking turns pleasuring each other is vital to extending orgasmic intensity and duration. It allows the partner being pleasured to let go of outward attention and concentrate as fully as possible on his/her own sensation and feelings. The receiver needs to be completely free of concern about what to do next, what comes next, how the other person feels. The giver takes charge and remains in control. The man needs to allow his partner to take responsibility for ejaculatory control when he's receiving her stimulation. That's why trust is crucial to success.

The Learning to Extend Orgasmic Response Exercise allows you to practice these skills. Agree on who will first be giver and who will first be receiver: who will give pleasure first and who will receive. We advise couples learning to extend orgasm to begin with the man giving and the woman receiving. If a man has an ejaculatory orgasm, he's not as likely to give his partner his full attention afterward. A woman is less likely to lose sexual interest in her partner after her own orgasm. If, taking her pleasure first, she has an orgasm, that only adds to her experience; it's less likely to end it. A woman also needs to feel cared for. She may not trust her partner to give her the pleasure she requires. Once her partner has pleasured her to orgasm, she will trust him more and thus more easily let go of resistance. It's a wise man who takes care of his partner first. Her enthusiasm to stimulate him when his turn comes will be his delightful reward.

Later, when you've both gained more confidence and perhaps each learned how to extend your orgasm, you can vary the sequence. While you're learning, we suggest women first. It works better that way.

Each partner gives his/her total attention to stimulating the other for at least thirty minutes. A key to learning to extend your orgasm is for giver and receiver both to give their full attention to the pleasuring of the receiver. When two people concentrate their full attention on creating maximum pleasure in one of them at a time, the results are additive and can be surprisingly powerful. Two attentions focused on one person is more effective than two attentions divided between two. You achieve balance in this arrangement by taking turns receiving.

Remember, as you read the description of the exercises, stop periodically and picture in detail the process described. Imagine you and your partner in the position described, doing each element and stroke. This mental rehearsal, done in real time, slow motion, and fast forward play, will enhance your learning and make each exercise more effective.

The Exercise: Man Giving, Woman Receiving

Spend several minutes in affectionate foreplay—including kissing, hugging, or nongenital touching. The woman lies comfortably on her back, either flat or leaning against pillows at up to a 45-degree angle. The man positions himself kneeling at her side with his knees at the level of her hip (see illustration, page 262). This position gives the man easy access with both hands to his partner's genitals and allows him (if he wishes) to lean forward to provide oral stimulation. Alternative positions you may move to or begin with include kneeling between your partner's separated legs or leaning at right angles to her pelvic area with one elbow between her legs and the other arm resting lightly on her abdomen (see illustration, page 263).

Apply lubrication such as Albolene to clitoris, vaginal lips, and internal vaginal area. After several minutes of light, gentle teasing of the area around the clitoris to build anticipation, begin to focus stimulation directly on the clitoris. As you've learned from your previous experience and your partner's instruction, stimulate the clitoris directly (see illustrations, pages 265–66). The thumb of your other hand can rhythmically pull back and manipulate the clitoral hood. That thumb can also keep the hood retracted, at the same time anchoring the clitoral base. It may be helpful to think of the clitoris as a penis, oriented upside down, and to think of the hood as the penis foreskin. With the fingers of your dominant hand, stimulate the sides and the tip of the clitoris. One finger can provide stimulation by circling the sides and lower part of the clitoris

MAN STIMULATING WOMAN
KNEELING AT PARTNER'S SIDE

Good initial short-term position. Promotes alertness and concentrated attention on the partner, including intimate eye contact. Easy access to genitals with both hands. The stroke illustrated is the "Basic (Two-Fingered) Manual Stroke." (See illustration page 265, for detail.)

Comfortable transition possible, while continuing stimulation, to other longer-term, more relaxed positions:

a. Man extending legs behind him, leaning over on his elbows between her legs, facing her genitals.

b. Man lying back on his left elbow at her side. (See illustration, page 263.)

MAN STIMULATING WOMAN
LYING BACK ON HIS ELBOW AT HER SIDE

Comfortable, long-term stimulation position. There is visual intimacy of eye contact and easy manual access with both the man's hands to the woman's genitals. Basic (Two-Fingered) Manual Stroke is shown. (See illustration page 265 for detail.)

If fatigue occurs after a period of time, there is easy transition to another position, such as between her legs on his elbows with his legs extended behind him.

263

and exposed tip. At the same time, your thumb can gently stimulate the tip of the clitoris while your forefinger and middle finger sweep up and down the sides.

Remember that the clitoris corresponds to the head of the penis but is much more condensed. If you find the right area and apply optimal pressure and stroke at the right rate, only a small part of the clitoris needs to be stimulated for maximum effect. Spend fifteen minutes on direct clitoral stimulation, repeatedly taking your partner to a peak of arousal just short of orgasm and then reducing stimulation to drop her arousal slightly. Doing this peaking at least six times will help build her engorgement and help produce a longer, stronger orgasm when you maintain your stimulation consistently enough to allow her to crest over into orgasm. (This peaking process is exactly analogous to the peaking that the woman does to the man to maintain erection and ejaculation control as well as to build his orgasmic intensity.)

During this period of receiving stimulation, the woman should focus as consistently as she can on the pleasurable sensations she's experiencing and on fantasy. When she begins her orgasm, she should voluntarily and deliberately push out (bear down) rather than contracting her sex muscles, which may be her usual habit. She needs also to remember to breathe in and out rather than holding her breath, which also may be a habit. She allows the feeling of the orgasm to spread and take over

---

BASIC (TWO-FINGERED) MANUAL STROKE

Generally the simplest, most efficient stroke for producing climbing arousal, from initial genital stimulation through Phase I: Extended Orgasmic Response.

The clitoris is rolled between the thumb and index finger of the right hand. Movement can be circular or up and down.

Initially, the inserted finger of the left hand is relatively motionless; its function is sensing the onset of squeeze contractions. When squeeze contractions begin, the inserted finger can stimulate the inner trigger area (G spot).

When there are push-out contractions (Extended Orgasmic Response, Phase I), reversing hand positions may be advisable with finger(s) of the right hand inserted in vagina for more effective internal stimulation, and left hand providing periodic clitoral stimulation, if desired.

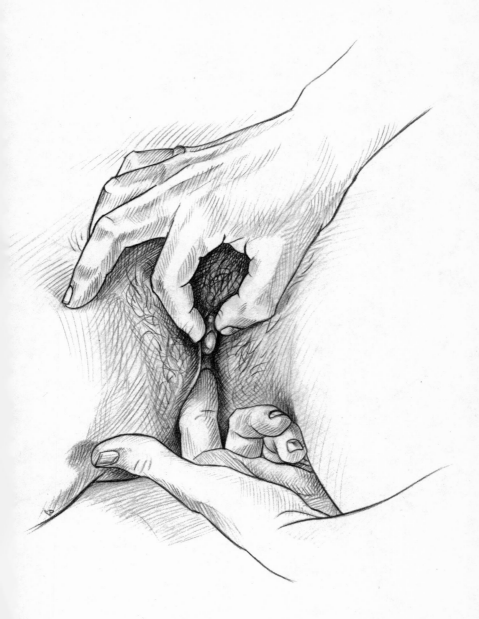

265

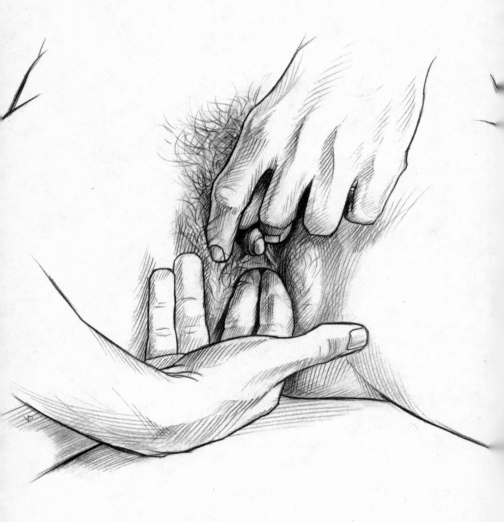

266

her whole body. If you notice that she's not remembering to breathe, you can gently remind her. "Breathe . . . that's it . . . again . . . good."

When the woman begins to have her orgasm, you can slip one or two fingers of your dominant hand partway inside her vagina with the pads of the fingers facing upward. Your other hand remains resting on the clitoris without stimulating it at this point, when it's probably too sensitive to accept any direct stimulation. You'll probably feel squeeze contractions (tightening of the vaginal opening) around your fingers. When you feel your partner beginning to experience squeeze contractions, her clitoris will probably become too sensitive for continued direct stimulation. So switch stimulation to the inner trigger areas of the vagina. Remember to apply gentle pressure and regular rhythmic stimulation (about once per second) to the G-spot area. As long as you sense that your partner is increasing her arousal level by this type of stimulation, you should continue. If you sense that her arousal is decreasing, if she's subtly pulling her pelvis away, if she's communicating any verbal or nonverbal messages that the internal stimulation is uncomfortable, you should stop internal stimulation and switch your attention back to stimulating the clitoris lightly with your other hand.

Like the penis, the clitoris usually has a refractory period after orgasm starts, during which time any but the lightest stimulation is uncomfortable. This period may vary from a half minute to several minutes or even longer. You'll need to discover your partner's particular characteristic in this matter.

While you're stimulating her clitoris with your left hand, keep the

---

(THREE-FINGERED) THUMB ANCHOR STROKE

A variant of the Basic (Two-Fingered) Manual Stroke shown on page 265. The thumb controls the hood, the top of the shaft, and tip of the clitoris. The forefinger and middle finger stimulate the sides of the clitoris. Together the three fingers can completely encircle and intensely stimulate the clitoral area.

This stroke, particularly in the early stages of arousal, can promote rapid clitoral engorgement. When a moderate level of arousal is achieved, the man may switch to the Basic (Two-Fingered) Manual Stroke.

fingers of your right hand inserted in her vagina to sense any internal squeeze contractions or push-outs. If light clitoral stimulation results in squeeze contractions, you can stop clitoral stimulation and resume vaginal stimulation with your fingers in the G-spot area. Continuing to use both hands, alternate between inner stimulation and clitoral stimulation to find the best and most effective pattern and rhythm. Spend at least ten minutes after the beginning of your partner's orgasm following this pattern of alternating internal and clitoral stimulations.

The woman continues to focus her attention on the pleasurable feelings she's having and imagines them spreading throughout her entire body. She practices deliberate push-outs if automatic push-out contractions don't occur, and she continues to remember to inhale/exhale. Even if no further contractions follow her initial orgasm, this period of internal stimulation is likely to be very pleasurable.

Oral-Stimulation Exercise (5 to 10 minutes)

Adding oral stimulation after about fifteen minutes of manual stimulation is a potentially effective way to increase response.

Men who wish to add oral stimulation will need to modify their positions. From a kneeling position on either side, or between the woman's legs, you'll need to bend forward. If you are lying propped up on an elbow, you'll need simply to move your head a short distance to her genitals.

You can use the tip of the tongue or the flat surface of the tongue to stroke the clitoris orally. You can suck it with your lips. Use regular rhythm, a baseline average of one stroke or suck per second with periodic teasing, faster alternating with slower. Use light, gentle pressure, alternating with brief periods of firmer strokes or suction. Use your tongue and lips to sense clitoral engorgement and modify your stroke type, rate, and intensity accordingly. If engorgement is increasing, continue exactly what you're doing. If, after a minute or so of a particular stroke pattern, there's little or no increase in engorgement, alter your pattern.

Peak your partner near orgasm several times. Then encourage her to have an orgasm by increasing speed and pressure of stimulation. You can also tell her directly, "Okay, I'd like you to let yourself have orgasm now."

The Exercise: Woman Giving, Man Receiving

This exercise may follow the man-giving, woman-receiving exercise directly, the two partners reversing roles, or it may be done at a separate scheduled time.

The man lies back, either flat on a comfortable surface or partially inclined against pillows. The woman positions herself between her partner's separated legs. You may kneel, sit back on your haunches, or sit with your partner's thighs draped over yours. Alternatively, you may kneel or sit back at his left side at the level of his pelvis.

Apply lubrication to your partner's penis, scrotum, and perineal area and stimulate him manually to produce a full erection as you've learned to do in previous weeks (see illustrations, pages 270–72).

Stroke Types

1. The basic stroke finds your dominant hand encasing the shaft of the penis, thumb side up, and moving up and down from the bottom of the shaft to the head with equal pressure during the entire length of the stroke. When your dominant hand becomes fatigued, switch to your nondominant (usually left) hand and use the same stroke. Should this arm tire, you can again switch hands, use your mouth, and/or anchor your elbow using the longer arm muscle groups rather than your biceps.

2. A good variation is the milking stroke. It's similar to the basic stroke, but you reverse your hand on your partner's penis so that the thumb side is down, wrap your thumb around the shaft directly below the lip of the head, and stimulate the head by squeezing and moving your whole hand up and down on it. The advantage of this stroke is that it provides direct stimulation of the most sensitive part of the penis, the frenulum, with the strong and versatile pad of the thumb. When stimulation becomes too intense, and for teasing variety, you can move your whole hand down onto the shaft away from the head. This variation also provides a resting state if your hand gets tired.

3. A third variation is the finger-ringing stroke, with your thumb and third finger ringing the penis, stimulating shaft or head or, most intensely, working back and forth across the lip of the penis glans. Your thumb may be in an upright position or, with your hand rotated 180 degrees, down toward the body as in the milking stroke above but with the third, fourth, and fifth fingers lifted away.

WOMAN STIMULATING MAN
KNEELING BETWEEN PARTNER'S LEGS

Suggested for beginning or early stage of stimulation. Good for the woman's alertness and focus of attention to create and maintain erection. Easy access to male genital area with both hands. Oral stimulation may be added by bending over. Intimate eye contact possible.

Disadvantage: Requires relatively more physical energy to support her body in an upright position.

The man, when stimulating his partner, may equally well utilize this position.

270

WOMAN STIMULATING MAN
BETWEEN HIS LEGS, LEANING ON HER ELBOW

One hand stimulates the penis; the other hand is available for stimulating the scrotum, base of the penis, and external prostate spot.

If the woman's neck tires, she can lower her head to rest on the man's thigh while she continues stimulation. If one hand tires, she can easily shift to the opposite elbow. Shifting to oral stimulation is also easy in this position.

271

272

4. A fourth stroking variant is the double-ring stretch stroke. In this stroke, you place the thumb and forefinger or the thumb and third finger or your nondominant hand tip-to-tip at the base of your partner's penis to form a ring and form an identical ring with your dominant hand at the head of the penis. Then you move one ring up and down on the upper part of the penis, while you move the other ring up and down on the lower part of the penis. Stimulation is most intense when your hands are moving in opposite directions. For variety, you may twist one hand one way and the other hand the other way, then reverse the direction of the twist.

5. A fifth variant is to use the pad of your index finger to stimulate the sensitive frenulum. Even very light, slow stimulation of this area can provide surprisingly effective arousal. Experiment with somewhat firmer pressure and rapid, tiny strokes. Your thumb on the opposite side on the head of the penis stroking the coronal ridge adds further arousal. Stimulating the frenulum is much like stimulating the most sensitive part of your clitoris, so you may need to apply only the slowest, lightest movement and pressure to produce rapid arousal. We advise all women to become skilled at stimulating the frenulum.

Stroke Rates and Rhythms

Essential elements for controlling male arousal are rate of stimulation, rhythm, and amount of pressure. A good, basic stimulation rate on the

---

WOMAN STIMULATING MAN
SIDE BY SIDE

A pillow supports the woman's head, allowing her to relax in a fetal-like position, free from exertion. Excellent position for long-term stimulation. Easily adaptable for oral stimulation. She can lock her elbows at her waist and stimulate the shaft and base of the penis with her hands while applying oral stimulation to the penis head. Gently rocking herself back and forth can then provide almost effortless stimulation for an extended period.

head and shaft of the penis is 1 to 2 strokes per second, which translates to 60 to 120 strokes per minute. Very rapid stimulation is 3 to 4 strokes per second, which translates to 180 to 240 strokes per minute. Women often aren't familiar with these faster rates, although they're quite common as part of a man's routine self-stimulation pattern. You may need some practice in achieving and maintaining the more rapid rates. To produce the more rapid stroke rates requires that you rest your elbow comfortably on a surface such as the bed, or a pillow, so that the motion comes from moving your forearm, rather than your upper arm or shoulder. If you move your shoulder extensively, you'll probably tire more quickly. You can switch back and forth, change muscle groups, anchor the elbow and lower arm, switch arms, and repeat.

Stroke *rhythm* refers to the *pattern of changes* in stroke rate. A good baseline rhythm is to change stroking rate every ten to twenty seconds. That would mean, for example, maintaining a consistent rate of about one stroke per second for fifteen seconds, then changing to three strokes per second for ten seconds, then reverting back to one stroke per second for fifteen seconds.

As your partner achieves more arousal, stay with the shaft and occasionally incorporate stimulation of the head for two to five strokes, then go back to stimulating the shaft alone. Be aware of muscle tension increasing in the man's stomach, thighs, and rising scrotum. As muscle tension begins to be apparent, go back to stimulating the shaft only. When the signs of tension subside, incorporate more stimulation of the penis head. As more arousal occurs, provide fewer strokes to the head and more strokes to the shaft.

Many variations and rhythms are possible, of course. You might enjoy imagining yourself to be a musician playing the instrument of your partner's penis. The combination of predictable rhythm and unpredictable rhythmic surprise can be a powerful factor in a man's arousal and your control. Have fun experimenting with variations in rhythm, observing which kinds of rhythmic patterns seem to be the most effective for your partner.

Variations in pressure of the hands on the penis are yet another important element in arousal. Alternating firm pressure for a number of strokes with soft, light touching can help level arousal or create more rapid arousal, building your partner's appetite for still more stimulation.

How you use stroke type, rate, rhythm, and pressure can supply you and your partner with unlimited creative possibilities.

You should spend approximately fifteen minutes in this exercise on variations of manual stroking on your partner's penis. Your goal is to know more about how his penis responds than he does.

Move your attention next to the part of the penis buried inside of the body. Press the deep penis base with the tips of the middle and index fingers of one hand while simultaneously stroking the shaft of the penis with the other. After about five minutes of rhythmic pressure on the buried penile base while continuing to stroke the penis, you can move your attention still further back to the external prostate spot. Again use one or two fingers to press firmly up and slightly forward behind the buried penile base and in front of the anal area. (If you have long nails, you may use a bent second joint of the index or middle finger.) Your other hand continues to stroke the penis.

Peak your partner at least six times. How high is a peak? It's the level of arousal that would result in ejaculation within about three seconds if stimulation continued unchanged. Recognizing a partner's peak requires sensitivity and quick reflexes. When you sense that your partner is peaking, you need to stop all stimulation immediately. In Week Ten, we'll detail other ejaculation-stopping methods—the squeeze technique, the scrotal pull, and the external-prostate-spot press. Your partner should help control his urge to ejaculate when he's at a peak with sex-muscle push out or relaxation, deep breathing, especially exhaling, verbal signals such as a crescendo of moans, by saying "Stop!" or by his covering your hands with his to stop or slow down the motion.

Your partner can add to his arousal and aid you in knowing how near he is to ejaculation by making pleasure sounds. It helps if he can give you some advance warning, verbal or nonverbal, when he's nearing a peak. Tapping you in a way you've both agreed on in advance is a signal, or simply saying, "I'm close, go slow," may be all the information you need. Without this feedback, you may feel like you're driving a car with your eyes closed. In this case the man needs to be the navigator while the woman drives.

After a period of about thirty minutes during which you peak your partner at least six times and preferably more, both of you should proceed to the Intercourse Exercise, which follows. Alternatively, after about fifteen minutes of manual stimulation, and before intercourse, you can add oral stimulation.

Optional Oral Stimulation: Rationale

Orally stimulating a man can add a great deal of pleasure to his sexual experience. It's an important, though not an essential, element in training him to extend his orgasmic response, for these reasons:

1. It can provide sensations that can't be duplicated by any form of manual or vaginal stimulation.
2. It gives the woman the most direct feedback about the effects of her stimulation on the man's response.
3. It provides a further avenue of stimulation in addition to a woman's two hands.

Effective oral stimulation requires you to focus your attention in a consistently deliberate manner. You may want to close your eyes to allow yourself to concentrate on the specific moment-by-moment experience of what you're doing and experiencing with your tongue, lips, and mouth. With your attention focused on what you're feeling at each moment, you'll have considerably more control over your partner's arousal level. You'll probably notice that when you have distracting, nonsexual thoughts, your partner's arousal level will decrease or he may crest over into unintended ejaculation. When you can keep your attention on your immediately pleasurable feelings with few distracting thoughts, your partner will notice and his penis will respond positively. Such focus will allow your partner to gain trust in your ability to give him your undivided attention. That trust enables him to relax and feel even more, becoming progressively more excited without ejaculating.

If you choose, you can experiment with your thoughts to discover the pleasure and control you can gain by giving your partner the concentration of both your physical stimulation and mental attention.

It's worthwhile for you to experiment with focusing your mind in different ways and observing the effect on your partner's arousal and response. For example, you can try having sexual fantasies for several minutes while you're stimulating your partner orally and manually and notice how he responds. Then you can deliberately switch to nonsexual thoughts for several minutes and observe the effect. Then you can focus on the pleasure you're feeling and your partner's response to what you're doing, which gives you instantaneous feedback about the effectiveness of the stimulation you're supplying. One of the great advantages of oral stimulation is that it gives you the potential power to influence your partner's thoughts, his mental attention. By concentrating on his penis, you can pull his mental focus away from distractions and rivet his mind to the immediate pleasure that you're creating for him. This is a position of control. The more specific your thoughts on a sexual experience, the more he will respond to your attention. That's likely to make him enthusiastically grateful and appreciative, which can immediately add to your own pleasurable experience as well.

Optional Oral Stimulation: the Exercise

Women: After about fifteen minutes manually stimulating the penis as described earlier in this exercise, shift yourself into a position where you can comfortably stimulate your partner's penis orally. You may arrange yourself on your knees and bend over, or rest on your elbows between your partner's legs. It's better not to adopt the "69" position, which invites your partner to stimulate you at the same time you're stimulating him and therefore could be distracting.

The tongue and lips are best for oral stimulation. Despite the common words for this sexual activity, there's very little blowing or sucking in oral sex. Nor should you use your teeth. The tongue stimulating the frenulum can be especially effective.

We suggest alternating oral with manual stimulation. Emphasize oral stimulation when your hands become tired. Emphasize manual stimulation when your jaw becomes tired. Both kinds of stimulation together can be especially effective. Lightly stimulate the head of the penis with your tongue and lips while stimulating the penile shaft and scrotal area with your hands.

Stimulate your partner to at least six peaks using a combination of manual and oral stimulation. Stop within three seconds of ejaculation each time. After about ten or fifteen minutes, move on to the Intercourse Exercise, page 278.

If either of you has any reservations about orally stimulating your partner, please consult the discussion "Learning Oral Lovemaking," page 402, in the Appendix.

EXERCISE FIVE: INTERCOURSE II

Rationale

Intercourse is the ultimate expression of both your individual sexuality and your interaction as a couple. It's also the most vulnerable part of your sexual relationship. You need to be patient and not let yourself be discouraged if you're not experiencing what either you or your partner thinks you should be experiencing. You're both practicing timing and pacing as well as trust. Your attention to and awareness of your own and your partner's experience are important.

You're both moving together toward experiencing more feeling and sensation without ending intercourse prematurely. This expansion of feeling gives you more time to evaluate what feels good and what feels better and more control in achieving it. We can't tell you what feels better for you, but we can give you exercises to assist you in making that decision for yourselves. Keep in mind, however, that some couples are satisfied with sexual interaction patterns that may not include intercourse.

A basic guideline for the man is to learn to maintain at least a three-fourths firm erection with a substantial level of confidence for ten minutes or more after insertion for intercourse. At this level of functioning, it's likely that the woman will be able to realize her potential ability to improve her responsiveness in intercourse.

Each couple needs to determine the most reliable and pleasurable methods which result in the man's gaining at least a serviceable erection. We suggest you vary intercourse positions from time to time, to determine which positions work best for you.

A man's skill at delaying his ejaculation and then ejaculating when he chooses significantly increases his potential enjoyment of intercourse. Free from moment-to-moment anxiety about the reliability of his erection or the imminence of ejaculation, he and his partner may find they can experience the feeling of dancing in intercourse.

In this exercise we're going to ask you to use three basic positions to elicit information for yourself and from your partner about what feels good and what might feel relatively better, as well as about any discomfort. We'll also discuss possible alternative movements that might alleviate the discomfort.

This week, we'd like you to incorporate the scissors position into the Intercourse Exercise to evaluate its usefulness. This position is one of relative equality between man and woman. It's particularly good for longer periods of intercourse and for extending orgasmic response during intercourse. Both partners have approximately equal freedom of pelvic movement and a relatively low level of physical burden of body support and movement. The scissors position isn't necessarily the best for ejaculation or rapid movement, though, since the man has relatively limited thrusting ability. We suggest you move into a rear-entry position for more vigorous thrusting and ejaculation.

There are three possible combinations of pelvic motion during intercourse:

1. The man moving (giving), the woman motionless (receiving)
2. The woman moving (giving), the man motionless (receiving)
3. Simultaneous movement by both partners. They may be moving toward each other or away. Simultaneous movement requires more practice than separate movement. It's much like dancing. While men are more traditionally assigned to lead in dancing, and women to follow, good dancers trade off as movement and mood require; there's an understood simultaneity. Skillful intercourse is similar, except that both partners have to allow for the man's special need to avoid ejaculation.

The Exercise

Man-Above Position (Missionary Position)

From the previous exercise where the woman has been stimulating the man manually and/or orally, move into the missionary position for approximately five minutes. The woman can place her hands under her hips crisscrossed under the coccyx (the center of the buttocks at the base of the spine), palms down on the bed, backs of the hands resting against her body. In this position she can push her hips up with the backs of her hands. She can use her hands and fingers to stimulate the base of the penis and the scrotum. If the man should slip out, she can easily reinsert him. Alternatively, the woman can use a pillow under her hips. Experiment with the comfort and effect of small, medium, and large pillow sizes. Her legs are separated outside of his, or crossed at the ankles over his thighs or above his waist. Deepest penetration occurs if she raises her hips more and brings her knees toward her chest.

The man lies between his partner's spread legs, resting the bulk of his weight on his outstretched arms, or on his elbows and forearms. His legs are slightly bent to achieve greater leverage. This is the most commonly used arrangement for this position. (See illustration, page 250.) Alternatively, the man may position his legs outside the woman's, which gives somewhat increased vaginal tightness but reduces penetration depth and leverage for thrusting.

You'll be moving into this position from the woman-giving and man-receiving position of Exercise Four, above. Should there be any loss of erection in the changeover, the man can stimulate himself back to erection with his partner's assistance. Or she can stimulate him directly to help him regain his erection.

The man uses slow thrusting strokes in this intercourse position. The woman ideally keeps pace with her partner, thrusting back against his lead. The man starts with about one stroke per second and may decrease speed to one stroke every three to four seconds depending on his arousal level. He becomes increasingly aware of the buildup of muscle tension in his stomach and thighs, and particularly any subtle contractions of the anal muscles and prostate. The closer he gets to ejaculation, the slower he thrusts.

The woman should be sure to slow down with her partner when he does and match his pace. If she doesn't, her thrusting is likely to crest him into ejaculation. The man can restrain his partner's pelvic movement, if necessary, by placing one hand on her hips or by pressing the weight of his hips against hers. At this point both of you want to extend stimulation, not end it. Allow the man to lead; the woman follows. She can have the lead later. The man establishes a stroke rate and varies depth and angle of penetration to maintain his erection and experience multiple peaks. Evaluate your experience in this position for subtle changes that can improve your feelings and for how much control you have over your erection and peaking.

When a man in this position of control is secure in his ability to peak himself reliably without ejaculation, he can then determine and practice the optimum thrusting pattern for his partner's arousal. One highly effective pattern is a series of slow, partial, shallow penetration strokes interspersed either randomly or predictably with several deep, hard strokes in succession.

Scissors Position

Now move into the scissors position, with the man rolling onto his right shoulder and the woman rolling with him to a modified left-side position facing him. She inserts her right leg between his legs and over his left leg. (See illustration, page 282.)

Notice the advantages and limitations of this position. It's excellent and physically comfortable for long-term intercourse, provides face-to-face equality of movement for both partners, allows moderately deep penetration, and permits easy access by the female to the penis base, scrotum, external prostate, and anal area. It's relatively less effective for G-spot stimulation and leveraged thrusting.

Practice alternating control of thrusting movements. If you are correctly positioned, each partner will be able to move his/her pelvis freely and comfortably. If not, make some additional adjustments. Thrust more slowly, more shallowly, and more softly for thirty seconds to one minute, then experience the man incorporating slow sex-muscle clenches, on inhalation, alternating with relaxing the sex muscles on exhalation to allow him to move closer to ejaculation. Remember, when practicing peaking, the male should not get closer than three seconds or three strokes to ejaculation. Spend about five minutes in this position.

Rear-Entry Position

Move from the scissors position to the rear-entry position as smoothly and as comfortably as you can. (See illustration, page 253.) If there's any loss of erection during the switch, the man stimulates himself back to erection, possibly with his partner's manual and/or oral assistance. Spend about five minutes in this position. You may move to rapid strokes in this position, as long as the male retains control of his ejaculation. Neither of you is leading now. You both can move as rapidly as you choose and thrust as hard as you choose. If you still feel uncomfortable with the rear-entry position, use, instead, a female-above position, or return to the man-above position as a substitute.

Experiment with your legs. First try the woman's legs between the man's, his thighs spread as he kneels behind her. Alternatively, the woman can spread her legs with the man kneeling, thighs together, between her spread knees and legs, holding her hips for support and assistance with control over thrusting. Couples usually find the woman with her legs

282

spread and the man kneeling between them is the most comfortable. An exception is couples with a significant discrepancy in height, in which case the taller person with legs spread has the ability to compensate for the height difference with less or more spread.

When you're ready to conclude, speed up the motion. The man can experiment with the experience of trying to hold in his semen when he ejaculates, as he practiced in the Advanced Self-Stimulation Exercise of Week Seven. Practicing this process regularly may allow the man to have a second ejaculation more easily should he and his partner wish to try to do so.

During the man's maximal thrusting, the woman pushes out her sex muscles, angles her pelvis for the maximum amount of feeling, and breathes slowly and deeply to allow herself the most pleasure possible.

Further considerations for improving intercourse:

When a woman who is not usually orgasmic during intercourse experiences intercourse, she will probably find it pleasurable, but she may also not find it interesting enough to continue for longer than about ten minutes. Without having orgasm during intercourse, she has little incentive to continue if she feels she's running out of energy or time. That's

---

INTERCOURSE POSITION:
SCISSORS POSITION

Excellent longer-term position. Enter from the man-above (missionary) position, with man rolling onto his right side, woman rolling slightly onto her left shoulder and side and placing her right leg between his legs. Both partners position hips for relatively equal freedom of movement. Woman can gain additional thrusting force by pushing her right foot against the bed for leverage. Woman's right hand is free to hold the man's buttocks for guidance and leverage, to caress the scrotum (including Scrotal Pull), or to stimulate the base of the penis and external prostate area. There is the intimacy of face-to-face and extensive body contact.

Disadvantage: Relatively less hip thrusting distance and force possible.

when she's likely to speed up her thrusting to stimulate her partner to ejaculate.

She can assist her approach to orgasm during intercourse by practicing internal squeeze contractions, particularly the slow-clench type (not push-out contractions, which are more useful for helping to intensify and extend orgasm). Her partner can stimulate her clitoris manually while they're having intercourse in the rear-entry position. She can stimulate herself manually or with a vibrator. Or man and woman together can organize some combination of these additional sources of stimulation.

The woman's deliberate internal squeeze contractions can help the man as well. He's stimulated by her internal movements, but not as intensely as he is from pelvic thrusting. This continuing but low-level stimulation may allow him to approach the emission phase more closely while remaining in control of ejaculation. This slower climb toward his ejaculation makes him more sensitive to pleasure because he has more time to study and experience the subtleties of his own arousal. The goal is for him to climb slowly to ejaculation using minimum physical move-ment. His attention is focused entirely on the intensely pleasurable sen-sation he is experiencing from her internal movements. As the man gets closer to ejaculation, he feels a greater level and intensity of arousal. The longer he experiences that feeling, the more he is able to control the speed of his arousal. More subtle and slow movements may be suf-ficient to take him steadily to higher levels of arousal without ejaculation. His partner will be considerably more sensitive to his level of arousal if she is experiencing orgasm or has had an orgasm in the previous several minutes.

When a woman has had an orgasm prior to or during intercourse, her vagina becomes more engorged and sensitive. This change helps her to pace her partner's sexual climbing and produces a more pleasurable en-vironment for the penis. The most desirable situation is when the woman is able to have extended orgasm during intercourse.

The woman in orgasm, because of her greater sensitivity to the man's communications through his penis, is able to assume some responsibility for initiating or stopping pelvic movements, based on his level of arousal. If the woman experiences orgasm during intercourse for more than a minute or so, the man may need little or no pelvic thrusting. Her au-tomatic contractions, combining both push-out and squeeze type, may provide all the stimulation he needs along the entire length of his penis. He can experience relatively slow, steady climbing towards emission-phase orgasm by enjoying the exquisite, relatively predictable rhythms and pressure of her spontaneous, continuous internal contractions, occurring without conscious effort. Without pelvic movements, he may occasionally brake his arousal simply by relaxing or pushing out his genital muscles.

EXERCISE SIX: SIGN COMPLETION AGREEMENT

EXERCISE COMPLETION AGREEMENT/ WEEK NINE

PARTNER EXERCISES   Initials

1. Discussed resistances prior to each exercise.   _____ _____
2. Did Exercise Planning Agreement.   _____ _____
3. Did Communication Exercise on sexual is-
   sues twice per day; 2 days; unlimited spontaneous.   _____ _____
4. Did Genital Hygiene.   _____ _____
5. Did Learning to Extend Orgasmic Response
   twice.   _____ _____
6. Did Intercourse twice.   _____ _____

SOLO EXERCISES

1. Did 20–0 Countdown at least twice a day.   _____ _____
2. Did Sex Muscle and Breathing Exercise daily.   _____ _____

I have accomplished the Solo Exercises described above. My partner and I have accomplished the Partner Exercises described above to our reasonable satisfaction. We also specifically reaffirm our agreement here to follow the exercises of Week Ten.

If there has been or will be any change in the program as assigned, we have both talked about those changes and agreed upon them together.

_____   _____
   Signature and Date   *Signature and Date*

WEEK TEN

SUMMARY OF EXERCISES

PARTNER EXERCISES

1. Execute Exercise Planning Agreement.
2. Communication (Appreciations and Resentments) (2 planned rounds on sexual issues, 2 times; unlimited spontaneous).
3. Learning to Extend Orgasmic Response II (man giving, woman receiving, 30 minutes; woman giving, man receiving, 30 minutes; total time 1 hour, 2 times).
4. Intercourse III (15 minutes), following Exercise Three.
5. Brief Sexual Interaction (10 to 15 minutes, 2 times).
6. Sign Exercise Completion Agreement.
7. Spontaneous lovemaking as desired.

EXERCISE ONE: EXECUTE PLANNING AGREEMENT

Fill out the following Planning Agreement according to the guidelines we discussed in Chapter VIII, page 131.

EXERCISE PLANNING AGREEMENT/WEEK TEN

Communication Exercise

Initiator_____

Plan 2 rounds of sexual Appreciations and Resentments 2 times this week; unlimited spontaneous.

Times Scheduled

Sunday	_____	_____
Monday	_____	_____
Tuesday	_____	_____
Wednesday	_____	_____
Thursday	_____	_____
Friday	_____	_____
Saturday	_____	_____

Learning to Extend Orgasmic Response

Initiator_____

Allow 1 hour and 15 minutes, 2 times this week.

Times Scheduled

Sunday	_____
Monday	_____
Tuesday	_____
Wednesday	_____
Thursday	_____
Friday	_____
Saturday	_____

Brief Sexual Interaction

Initiator_____

Allow 10–15 minutes, 2 times this week.

Times Scheduled

Sunday	_____
Monday	_____

Tuesday   _____
Wednesday   _____
Thursday   _____
Friday   _____
Saturday   _____

EXERCISE TWO: COMMUNICATION

By now we expect you'll have recognized the value of sharing feelings that you used to hold inside or use destructively. You may be discovering that you and your partner both greatly value hearing appreciations, however modest they may be and despite past assumptions that your partner already knows how you feel. You may also be feeling relieved of a burden as you convert hurt feelings and feelings of annoyance into words. Expressing your feelings, you may have found, means not storing them up in a negative file until they burst forth in argument. This file needs regular purging.

EXERCISE THREE: LEARNING TO EXTEND ORGASMIC RESPONSE II

Extending Female Orgasmic Response

The designated initiator for the week establishes the starting time and arranges the environment. The partners start the exercise by initiating a period of mental and physical foreplay. They ensure that there's at least a brief period of light, intimate, pleasant conversation before moving to physical foreplay. The woman finds a comfortable position lying on her back. She props her head on a pillow if she likes. She separates her legs. She can flex them, knees raised, or extend them. Comfort with access is the key.

The following instructions will be addressed to the man, but the woman should read them and understand them as well.

The man may kneel, sit cross-legged, lie on his stomach, lie beside his partner or between her legs, arranging himself so that he can see and easily touch his partner's genitals. Make yourself comfortable and use your hands as they work best for you. It's important for you to take responsibility for changing your position to maintain your own comfort as you stimulate your partner throughout this exercise.

Now gently apply sexual lubricant—warming it first in your hand—to your partner's entire genital area: major labia, minor labia, the clitoris and its structures, the opening of the vagina, a little way into the vagina itself, and down along the perineum.

Too much lubricant is better than too little. Be generous. Even though a petroleum-based lubricant such as Albolene is nonabsorbent, some of the lubricant you apply will evaporate. Reapply when necessary. Without adequate lubrication, extended stimulation can cause reddening and discomfort. Remember that a woman's genital lubrication comes from the inner walls of her vagina. The clitoris (like the penis) produces no natural lubricant of its own.

Begin now lightly stimulating your partner's external genitals—the pubic hair, the major labia. Lightly brushing the pubic hair, gently pulling it, creates arousal because all the structures in the area are connected. What you're doing is a version of foreplay, gradually approaching the sensitive areas enclosed within the major and minor labia. Just as you did in the Sensual Focus Exercises, you're following the principle of general stimulation before localized stimulation. This practice builds anticipation, sexual desire. It also assists your partner with focusing more on her genitals. When women pleasure themselves, they usually do the same thing, caressing the overall genital area before concentrating on the clitoris.

In a sense, you're teasing. Teasing creates arousal. Circle the clitoris, slowly closing in. Press lightly with the palm of your hand or several fingers together on the major labia and the pubic hair. Then, over a period of a minute or two, gradually make teasing circles closer to the clitoris, brushing the clitoris sometimes as your hand circles. Make the circles small, the size of a quarter, around the clitoris.

When you approach the clitoris itself, touch it only lightly at first. All the nerve endings found in the much larger penis are concentrated into the clitoris's small area. It's extremely sensitive.

Every woman's preference for clitoral stimulation is unique. Some women like a very light touch. Some prefer the clitoral shaft stroked rather than the glans. Others don't want the clitoris touched directly at all. Often the clitoris is more responsive on the left side, sometimes on the right. You need to get to know your partner's clitoris well. You and your partner's clitoris need to become intimate friends.

You began that friendship with the Sensory Focus and Sexual Exploration Exercises. You observed the clitoris change shape, color, and position with sexual arousal. Now you need to extend your knowledge by giving your partner's clitoris your close, full attention. Your goal at this point is to stimulate your partner to orgasm with your hand. No single stroke will work reliably for all women. You'll have to proceed by trial and error. Your partner showed you what felt good to her during the Sensory Focus and Sexual Exploration Exercises.

Many women complain that their men don't experiment enough with different kinds of strokes. Or that the experimenting happens too fast, that the man is too impatient, moving from one stroke to another before the woman has had time to relax with it and see how it feels, that he uses too much pressure.

To find a stroke that your partner likes, try different areas of the clitoris and different pressures on it. Change strokes only gradually and watch your partner's response. If her clitoris becomes more engorged and erect and she's moving her pelvis toward your hand, you're doing fine. A good way to approach the clitoris is with the thumb and forefinger. Your thumb at the base of the clitoris—toward the stomach—anchors it. Your forefinger strokes it at the tip. Stroke one side for a while, the tip, the other side. The motion can be up, down, or circling and your thumb can rock. Or roll the clitoris lightly between forefinger and thumb. (See illustration on page 265.) Try these variations; you can make up others as you go.

Your basic stroke should be slow and steady, about one cycle per second.

Women clients often tell us that their partners aren't consistent with stimulation. Find a consistent pattern and keep it up for several minutes at a time without change, except the changes we mention below.

Watch your partner's reaction. If a stroke is working, it arouses her. You see the arousal. Her genital area swells, adding fullness to the major and minor labia. Her clitoris enlarges and moves downward and inward. The clitoral glans engorges much as the glans of the penis does with erection. The vaginal area and the clitoris darken from the added flow of blood.

Your partner can guide you by making sounds. If what you're doing feels right, she can moan, hum, sigh with pleasure. These communications tell you to continue exactly what you're doing. Vocalizing during lovemaking is arousing in itself. It also lets you know that arousal is happening. Talking at this point is distracting; that's why we've encouraged you during the Ecstasy Program to learn nonverbal vocalizing. If you need to review that skill, see the discussion "Pleasure Sounds," beginning on page 73.

Your partner can also guide you by moving her pelvis toward your hand or away. This movement is partly involuntary. If your stroking is arousing her, if she's climbing toward orgasm, she'll press her genitals into your hand because she's reaching for more stimulation. If the stimulation is ineffective or uncomfortable, or if she's resisting, she'll move her genitals away. These movements are subtle. You need to pay attention and look for them. They may amount to shifts of only a quarter of an inch or so, against your hand or away.

Watch as well for larger signs of arousal, especially muscle tension. Pelvic-muscle tension and general body-muscle tension are signs of sexual arousal. So are sighs, panting, jerky movements, sweating, facial grimaces, curling of the toes and feet.

If your partner moves away even slightly from your hand, you need to back off. That doesn't mean lifting your hand completely away. It means letting up a little on pressure, slightly slowing your stroke, or moving your fingers to a slightly different area of her clitoris. The clitoris is small. Your changes in response to your partner's signals need to be small too.

A teasing cycle builds arousal. When you've found a basic stroke that your partner likes, use it for about ten strokes and then relax to a resting stroke—lighter pressure or a slower rate such as one back-and-forth or up-and-down stroke per two seconds. Or move off the clitoris and stimulate the area immediately around it for a stroke or two. That increases sexual tension. Your partner will signal her arousal by moving her genitals toward your hand, asking for the stimulating stroke again. Ten stimulating (climbing) strokes to one or two resting strokes is a good pattern to follow. It's not the only pattern. Six to one may be better, or three to one, or fifteen to one. Experiment and see.

You can stimulate your partner to extremely high levels of arousal with only your thumb and forefinger. For a variation, you can add the middle finger, so that you have three fingers cradling the clitoris. (See illustration on page 266.) Your thumb continues to anchor the clitoris from above; your forefinger and the middle finger then stroke the sides of the clitoris and its base. The point is to find the best way to build arousal to higher and higher levels, always backing off when the climbing stops.

At any time during this initial stimulation, after at least five minutes of clitoral stimulation, you can insert one or two lubricated fingers of your other hand into your partner's vagina. That hand won't be especially active yet. It's there to give you information about the degree of your partner's arousal, especially her degree of engorgement and any first signs of sex-muscle contractions around your fingers that may herald the approach of orgasmic squeeze contractions. Your forefinger (and, optionally, your middle finger) needs to be comfortably inserted about an inch into your partner's vagina by the time she begins orgasm.

We encourage adding oral stimulation to the clitoris at this point, alternating with manual stimulation. Try circling the area of the clitoris with the tongue for a number of strokes in a teasing fashion, then centering lightly on stimulating the tip of the clitoris itself for a number of strokes. Some men think that women prefer oral stimulation of the vaginal area. However, women generally prefer oral stimulation of the clitoris itself. After several minutes of oral stimulation and teasing of the clitoral area, return to manually stimulating the clitoris as described above.

Eventually—building arousal, working through resistances, climbing and leveling and climbing—your partner will probably begin regular one-second contractions of the outer vagina. At that time she should bear down and push out voluntarily and deliberately while making sure she doesn't hold her breath but continues to breathe. At that point, *switch your attention to her vagina.* She may want you to continue clitoral stroking during these first contractions. If she does, then you should do so, but you'll probably need to lighten your touch. Any but the lightest stimulation will probably be uncomfortable. You may need now to simply rest your hand lightly and without motion on the clitoris. Pay attention to your partner's pelvis. If it's moving toward the hand touching the clitoris, clitoral stimulation is probably okay. If it's moving away, avoid any clitoral stimulation for the moment.

Continue vaginal stimulation through these first orgasmic contractions and after they taper off. You can move your finger(s) in and out of your partner's vagina in a motion imitating the thrusting of a penis, or sweep them around the vaginal barrel. But the most effective stimulation is likely to be rhythmic stroking with one or two fingers of the inner trigger areas you've previously identified, usually the front wall of the vagina in the center, the twelve o'clock position.

By stimulating your partner's vagina when her orgasm begins, you may cause a sharp increase even then in her arousal. You may notice her back arching more and she may be vocalizing louder. If you directly stimulate her inner trigger areas much before orgasm, she may find it uncomfortable. But once orgasm begins, inner stimulation is arousing rather than uncomfortable. The trigger areas can then take hard pressure, while the clitoris, which was stimulated before by regular stroking, now responds to more than the very lightest touch with something like pain. You've probably noticed a similar sensation. Most men find touching the glans penis uncomfortable immediately after ejaculation. So we advise you to stimulate your partner's vagina rather than her clitoris at this volatile time.

When you switch attention to your partner's vagina while she's having orgasmic contractions, you continue to supply her with a high level of stimulation. Whether you're moving your fingers in and out of her vagina or stroking her inner trigger areas with your index or middle finger, continue the regular, once-per-second rhythm you established when you stroked her clitoris earlier, continuing to build on that ten-to-one (or six-to-one, whatever worked best) cycle, increasing and decreasing pressure.

This internal stimulation can eventually create a deeper, rhythmic, push-out contraction which feels different from the squeeze contractions of the outer part of the vagina. This is the beginning phase of Extended Orgasmic Response (Stage III orgasm), characterized by spontaneous vaginal push-outs of the deep pelvic musculature, including the muscles of the uterus. These deeper, rhythmic push-out contractions are longer and experienced as more pleasurable. Compared with the voluntary muscular push-outs that the woman has been practicing regularly, these push-outs are automatic, involuntary, feel like they involve more muscles, and are distinctly more pleasurable. They represent the physical basis for extending female orgasm. The rhythmic push-out contractions in this Stage III of extended orgasm are longer in duration than the squeeze contractions of stage I orgasmic response. Push-out contractions typically last from one to ten seconds. After several minutes of push-out contractions, their duration tends to increase. In the second phase of the extended orgasmic response, each push-out may last thirty seconds or longer.

In the usual Stage I squeeze-contraction orgasm, the vagina responds by "tenting"—by enlarging at the back and pulling up into the body. To a finger fully inserted into the vagina, that response feels like a loosening and a pulling away. (See the female anatomy illustration on page 62.)

With the beginning of the extended orgasmic response, your partner's vagina will respond to your stimulating finger by *pushing against it—pushing out*, as if the uterus were pushing toward the opening of the vagina and closing the vaginal space.

When you feel the vagina pushing outward, your partner is likely to be beginning a deep pelvic orgasmic push-out that may herald the beginning of the first phase of the extended orgasmic response.

When you feel your partner's vagina drawing back—pulling away—and also detect muscular squeezing at the entrance of the vagina, her orgasm is probably leveling off rather than climbing. You should lighten the pressure you're applying inside the vagina and slow your stroke. Soon your partner will begin to want more stimulation again. Add pressure then and speed up your stroking of the inner trigger area. Your partner will probably begin to push out against your fingers again. That indicates you're supplying the right amount of stimulation to the inner trigger area. You can continue at that level. Or you can increase the pressure and rate to bring on more climbing. When there are push-outs against your fingers, it can also be effective to switch from stroking the inner trigger area to applying continuous pressure to it. That pressure can prolong push-out time. Continue the kind of stimulation that best works to produce continuous waves of push-out responses.

Two factors determine the intensity and frequency of your partner's push-outs: the rate, pressure, and location of your stimulating inner finger or fingers; and your partner's skill at letting go of her mental resistances to climbing continuously toward more pleasure. During *leveling* periods of extended orgasm (Phase I), the woman will usually be more quiet, her body less active and her pelvic contractions of the squeeze type.

When your partner's climbing stops—when her push-outs cease—you should once again immediately shift your attention from the inner trigger area and focus more on the clitoris. Within a few seconds you may feel stronger squeeze contractions or push-outs. That's your signal to redirect your stimulation to the vaginal trigger areas. If your pattern of rhythmic stimulation is optimal, the periods of time during which there are no push-outs will be brief—approximately one to five seconds. Your partner's experience of continuous push-outs will be longer—in the range of ten to thirty seconds.

As you continue this pattern for ten minutes or more, you'll find that the brief leveling periods occur less and less frequently and your partner has push-outs more and more of the time. When the leveling periods disappear, and there are simultaneous squeeze contractions of the external vaginal area and sustained deep push-outs, she will have entered the second phase of extended orgasmic response, which we also refer to as ESO.

During the woman's extended orgasm, the man will be more in control of the stimulation than she. She will have some control of her movements, moving toward the stimulation or away, and of her breathing, but her attention will be and should be devoted exclusively to her own inner experience.

Much more than before, in earlier stages of arousal and orgasm, she'll be lost in feeling and will be doing very little thinking. She'll be reacting rather than controlling. The man will be in charge of supplying the right stimulation. As he learns what he's doing, he'll become progressively more effective. As long as he doesn't do anything to cause her discomfort, the woman will let him—and should let him—control. When the stimulation is right, she won't move toward him or away. Pleasurably immobilized, she's in a continuous climbing phase, experiencing increasing pleasure on a mental level, an alteration in consciousness. She is entirely receptive and has little awareness of her physical responses. Observing those allows her partner to help maintain her in this ecstatic state. One characteristic of this state that may seem surprising is that her heart rate and blood pressure are at relatively relaxed levels.

Communication can continue during extended response just as it did before—with body movements, with the man's careful reading of the woman's responses, with vocalizing. The woman's body movements and vocalizing are likely to be much more obvious now, because she's experiencing much higher levels of arousal. Moaning, eyes rolling back, jaw dropped with mouth open, rhythmic motions of her arms and legs, tossing her head, curling her toes and feet, arching her back, panting, all are signs the man may observe in the climbing stage as extended orgasm continues. *The main sign that should guide his stimulation is the vagina pushing outward against his fingers.*

When either partner wishes to conclude, the man increases rate and pressure of stimulation to create the most intense response, the climax, which results in maximum vaginal push-out strength. This is an altered state of pleasurable mental experience so intense that each time it occurs it always seems to be a nearly unbelievable surprise.

At the conclusion of the climax, the man stops stimulation, positions the palm of one hand over his partner's vaginal and clitoral area, and presses lightly to moderately for a minute or two. His other hand and arm may rest on her pelvic area and abdomen with light-to-moderate pressure. This pressure allows his partner to come down more smoothly from her altered physical and mental state. The man can then hold her for another minute or two or even lie quietly on top of her (supporting his weight on his elbows), which can create reassuring feelings of comfort and security.

Extending Male Orgasmic Response

Following the previous exercise, you may want to proceed immediately to changing places and switching roles. Or you may want to take a brief break for refreshments, to use the bathroom, or simply to rest.

When you're ready, come back to your intimate setting and enjoy once again a time of pleasant foreplay, talking tenderly, kissing, and caressing. The man finds a comfortable position lying on his back. He props his head on a pillow if he likes. He separates his legs. He can flex them, knees raised, or extend them. Comfort with access is the key.

Many men resist being pleasured. They're used to giving pleasure. They need to learn to be totally receptive—to accept lying back and relaxing and letting someone pleasure them. That means not paying attention to their partners' arousal. The man's only responsibility in the receiving position is to feel as good as possible for himself, not to concern himself with how his partner is doing or feeling. Achieving this condition often takes deliberate intention and practice, since men more often evaluate the quality of their sexual experience by the response they can create in their partners rather than appreciating their own reactions. For themselves, men tend to be satisfied with simply having an ejaculation. Many of the exercises you've done in previous weeks had acceptance of pleasuring as one of their collateral purposes.

A man's goal at this point is to be totally receptive, like a sponge, to see how much pleasure he can absorb. Men need to learn that sex doesn't always have to be a performance (so do women, if they're used to thinking of their partners as performers). Men who feel uncomfortable lying back and taking should remember that they've just given their partners an intense time of energetic attention and pleasure. They've done their duty. It's fair and reasonable that they should have pleasure in return.

The highest levels of pleasure possible with extended orgasmic response can be achieved only with a partner's stimulation. They can't be achieved if the man is actively controlling his responses. They can be achieved only by giving up control. Difficulty with giving up control is a resistance, to be dealt with like any other resistance.

External Prostate Stimulation

The role of the prostate gland in male sexual response has largely been ignored. Most men and their partners don't realize that stimulating this organ can add significantly to sexual arousal. You've already done some exploration of the external prostate spot. We'll discuss prostate stimulation in more detail in this exercise. Here we'd just like to review why that stimulation is important.

Stimulating a man's prostate is similar in some ways to stimulating a woman's inner trigger areas. Stimulating the prostate along with stimulating the penis can potentially produce a deeper, more powerful, longer orgasm. Prolonged stimulation results in greater semen volume, and semen volume is one factor in a man's sense of the intensity of his orgasm. For many men, alternately or simultaneously stroking the penis and the prostate area can also produce higher levels of stimulation and arousal. That's very much like the pattern of stimulation we described for women that involved alternately or simultaneously stimulating the clitoris and the vagina.

In the exercise which follows, you'll be stimulating the external prostate spot. Some more adventurous couples may wish to experiment with internal prostate stimulation, an option described in Week Twelve.

The man reclines with his legs partly separated, knees flexed. He may lie flat or with his torso propped at a comfortable angle.

The woman has several options for positioning herself during this part of the exercise:

1. She can sit between her partner's legs, facing him, with his thighs resting over hers.
2. She can kneel between his legs.
3. She can move from the kneeling position to sitting on her side leaning on one elbow, one of his legs between hers.
4. She can lie between his legs, resting her head on one of his thighs.
5. She can kneel or sit to one side at his pelvic level.
6. She can lie on her stomach perpendicular to him so that the two people make a "T," with her head and hands at the level of his genitals.
7. She can lie at his side, head supported on a pillow at pelvic level.

Positions 4, 5, 6, and 7 are the most convenient for adding oral stimulation. All of the positions we list allow the woman free access to the man's genitals with both her hands. These are good, basic starting positions. From them both partners can move easily into variations.

It's important that the woman be comfortable. Otherwise, she won't be able to give her partner her fullest attention. She should feel free to shift position when she begins to feel uncomfortable—to bend her legs more or less, to prop an elbow, to add or subtract a pillow. Altering positions also results in a momentary change in the stimulation pattern and may help the man maintain ejaculatory control. Moving around is part of your sexual dance together. The woman should try to continue genital stimulation even while she's moving to another position to reduce the distraction.

Once both partners are comfortably positioned, the woman proceeds to stimulate the man to erection as she has learned to do in previous exercises. At any point after five to ten minutes of stimulation, if he is not erect, he can assist with self-stimulation to get erect as you've practiced in the Partner-Assisted Stimulation Exercises of Week Eight.

Be sure to apply lubrication. The penis should be lubricated thoroughly as well as the scrotum, the perineum, and, optionally, the anus. The woman should lubricate both her hands. Too much lubricant is better than too little. The preejaculatory fluid that men produce is insufficient for lubrication.

The woman begins now to stroke her partner's penis, remembering what she learned from him in past exercises about the strokes he prefers. The basic manual stroke finds her dominant hand circling the glans of the penis with the thumb emphasizing the coronal ridge. Strong pressure and a rapid stroke are often best at the beginning. The woman should let her partner's penis be her guide. If it's hardening and stiffening, she's doing fine. Remember, the glans is like the clitoris. Most of the nerve endings in the penis are concentrated there. It's a small area but very sensitive.

STIMULATING BASE OF PENIS AND EXTERNAL PROSTATE AREA

Advised for use only after achieving full, firm erection for several minutes. Use the pads of the index and middle finger (or knuckle of index finger) behind the scrotum in an up-and-down or side-to-side motion. This external pressure conveniently stimulates the internal Cowper's and prostate glands. Such stimulation helps the man shift attention to deep internal sensations, thereby diffusing ejaculatory urgency while continuing to increase arousal. The woman's other hand (or mouth) stimulates the shaft and head of the penis, including the very sensitive frenulum.

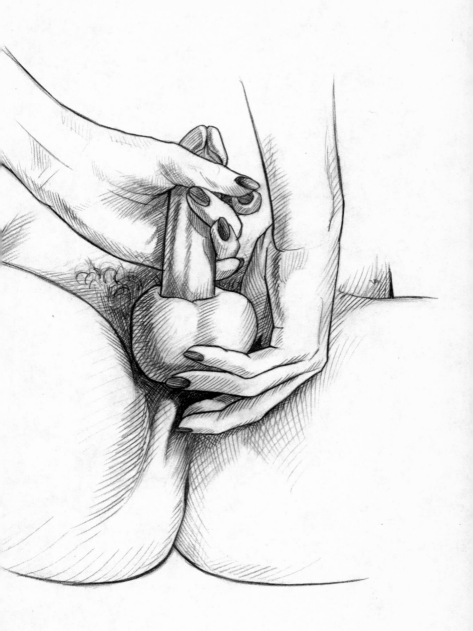

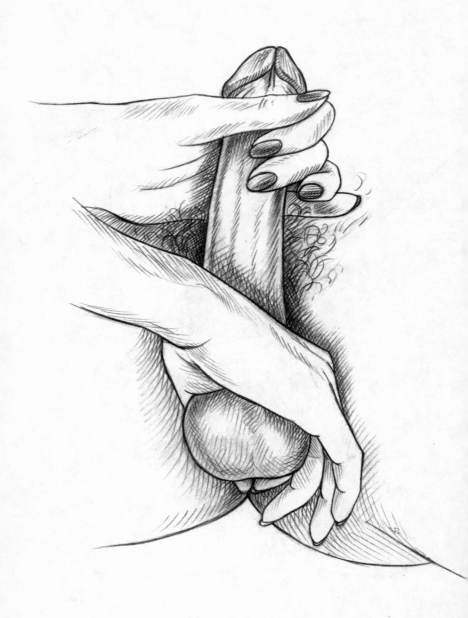

When the man has arrived at full, hard erection and remained that way with the woman's stimulation for at least fifteen minutes, she can begin to stimulate his scrotum and external prostate spot (see illustration, page 299). Pressure on the external prostate spot usually isn't comfortable until a man is fully erect and his scrotum is elevated and hard. Then stimulation can create additional arousal.

The woman can add further to her partner's pleasure by caressing his scrotal and external prostate areas in several ways.

She can use the scrotal pull technique (making a ring of her fingers between the testicles and the base of the penis or grasping the scrotum between the testicles), pulling lightly in rhythm as she strokes her partner's penis (see illustration, page 300). While she's applying scrotal traction she can lightly tease the penis by tickling the glans with a circle of fingers. She's pulling on her partner's scrotum partly in order to stop him from ejaculating, so she needs to lighten stroking his penis. Teasing the glans can add to arousal even while she's holding her partner back from cresting to ejaculation.

Another way to caress her partner is by applying pressure with one or two fingers or knuckles to his external prostate spot while continuing to stimulate the shaft of the penis with the other hand. Steady pressure feels good. It can allow increased arousal and simultaneously help retard ejaculation. So does stroking pressure in rhythm with stroking his penis. How hard she should press depends on how aroused he is. The more aroused, the more pressure is comfortable. She should watch her partner's

---

SCROTAL PULL

The scrotum is ringed with index finger and thumb touching each other above the testicles. Advised for use only after achieving a full, firm erection.

For increasing arousal: Slow, steady pressure downward, preferably with left hand, while continuing to stimulate the head of the penis manually or orally. Primary attention with pads of fingers or tip of the tongue focused on the frenulum. The sensitive frenulum is like the tip of the clitoris.

For ejaculation control: Quick, firm, brief pull down on the scrotum can decrease the urge to ejaculate. The other hand (or the mouth) should slow or stop stimulating the penis during the pull.

response. If she's applying too much pressure, he'll pull away. If he wants more, he'll move toward her. Many men complain that their partners are *too* gentle when handling their penis. The testicles require more care. The woman shouldn't be afraid to experiment.

A third caress we call the "prostate squeeze." The woman can do it two different ways. She can either press the forefinger of her dominant hand into her partner's external prostate spot, with the thumb of the same hand hooked around the base of his penis pressing against the pubic bone. Alternatively, she can reverse the position of the digits, anchor her forefinger around the base of the penis against the pubic bone, and push in on the external prostate spot with her thumb. One method works better for some people, the other for others. If the woman's prostate-pushing index finger needs more support, she can back it up with her middle finger, pushing her middle finger against her index finger. Either way, she should stroke her partner's penis with her other hand at the same time. The more pressure on the external prostate spot and the faster the stroking, the faster the climb to arousal.

With continued, climbing stimulation, the man will approach ejaculation. The point now is to avoid ejaculation, not to encourage it. Otherwise, his orgasm will end until he can return through the refractory period to arousal.

At first, just as before in the Ecstasy Program exercises, both the man and the woman will have to pay close attention to controlling the man's urge to ejaculate. When the woman brings him up to the high level of arousal near ejaculation (peak), he'll feel on the edge of going over. She has to be very careful then, watching his signs of arousal and stopping or lightening and changing stimulation when he gets too close. She should watch for his hands moving toward his genitals to push her away and listen for changes in his sounds. Jerky movements of his body, fluttering hands, testicle elevation, grimaces, are all signs of approaching ejaculation. Ideally, she should not let him get closer than about three seconds of reaching the point of no return.

The woman has several means of control whereby to reduce the man's arousal. One is the scrotal pull. A second is pressure on the external prostate spot, which distracts him. A third is squeezing firmly at the base of the penis with the forefinger in front and the thumb in back. A fourth is simply stopping stimulation. A fifth is the squeeze technique on the head of the penis. She can alternate from one control method to another. If she is not paying close attention, it may be necessary for the woman to take her hands away entirely. She should stop stroking and simply pause, hands on or off, until the man's arousal decreases slightly, which may take only a few seconds or as much as a minute. Then she can begin stimulating him again cautiously.

During this week and in the weeks to come, the woman should try all these control techniques, alternate them, and see which combinations work best.

The man, for his part, is also paying attention to control. He pulls away from the woman's stroking. He shifts mental attention to focus more closely on his sensation and uses sex-muscle exercises to help with control.

There'll be slips along the way. It's like learning how to ski or roller-skate—you may fall a lot at first. If he ejaculates early, the man can enjoy his orgasm by relaxing and letting go. Then both partners should discuss the experience to find out why it happened and to plan for more effective control. The primary responsibility for control at this point is the woman's. If the ejaculation happens earlier than expected, alternatively you may experiment with extending and intensifying it. This process will be described shortly.

Just as women do, men contract their pelvic muscles to build arousal. When the man feels ejaculation approaching, one way he can regain control and momentarily stop the climb to ejaculation is by exhaling and relaxing or pushing out his pelvic muscles—bearing down. This process is like straining to move his bowels. Then it's up to the woman to reduce the stimulation momentarily until her partner regains arousal control.

Some men find that deliberate, slow, deep breathing or, contrarily, faster panting helps control ejaculation. They may combine deliberate, slow breathing with bearing down, or sometimes deliberate, slow breathing with clenching.

Pressing the tip of the tongue against the roof of the mouth can sometimes help retard ejaculation. A few men discover this effect on their own. It's also mentioned in ancient Tantric literature. This technique probably affects the bracing of the jaw, which is surprisingly important in the alignment of the whole body. Misalignment of the jaw can cause a variety of physical disturbances, the most frequently reported of which is headaches. But whatever the physiological reasons, pressing the tongue against the hard palate is a possible aid in ejaculatory control.

Each man must determine for himself the most effective combination of control techniques that works for him.

Having regained control while the woman reduced stimulation, the man can now maintain control as she begins stroking again by again contracting his sex muscles. It's a question of shifting attention. Anything that shifts the man's attention will momentarily level off his increasing arousal. However, persistent distraction for more than a brief number of seconds or distraction to nonsexual areas actually reduces a man's control by decreasing his awareness of the level of his sensations. The old myth about controlling ejaculation by thinking about emptying the garbage or reciting the Gettysburg Address is actually countereffective.

Control becomes a matter of teamwork: the woman senses the man's level of arousal and changes rhythm and stroke to help him with control; at the same time, he responds with sex-muscle contractions for increasing stimulation or relaxes the sex muscles for decreasing arousal.

If he is becoming more and more aroused—climbing—his legs will usually flex more as his body reaches for stimulation. When he wants to level or come down to avoid ejaculating, he will usually extend his legs and pull away. The woman must learn to read these motions accurately, and stop or change her stimulation pattern when she judges he is no closer than three to five seconds or three strokes from the point of no return. As if she were driving a racing car, she wants to get close to the red line on the tachometer but not into the red zone. She wants the pot to boil, but not to boil over.

The man may indicate by his arousal that he wants to ejaculate quickly. He shouldn't be encouraged. To learn through these exercises about the much greater amount of pleasure possible by extending his emission-stage orgasm, he needs to delay ejaculation. His partner must be strong and help him resist his impulse to ejaculate. If she gives in too soon and stimulates him to ejaculation, she'll be robbing him of greater pleasure, and he may feel responsible for failing to control himself. The more non-ejaculatory peaks he experiences, the greater his total amount of pleasure.

During Weeks Ten through Twelve, the woman's goal is to take her partner to a peak of arousal close to ejaculation at least fifteen times, on the average, during a thirty-minute session. As she and her partner learn control, he'll stay at higher and higher levels between peaks. Eventually there won't be much decline between peaks and she will be supplying only very light, subtle changes in pressure and rhythm.

After a while, as the man works through his resistances, and as man and woman both learn the teamwork of ejaculatory control, she'll find it easier and easier to stimulate him to very high levels of arousal. He'll find it easier and easier to stay there.

The maximum stimulation potential the woman possesses is simultaneously (1) stimulating the head and coronal ridge of the penis with her mouth, (2) alternating stimulation of the penis shaft base and scrotum with one hand, and (3) stimulating the buried penile shaft and/or external prostate spot with her other hand. Women with long nails may need to use a bent knuckle on the external prostate spot or trim the nails of the right forefinger and third finger.

Extended Orgasmic Response

The intensely pleasurable state close to ejaculation becomes more stable with experience and extends in time, as we saw in the graph of the male response (see illustration, page 110). This is the beginning (Phase I) of the Extended Orgasmic Response. This response is characterized by the blending of multiple, nonejaculatory peaks, where each peak is virtually indistinguishable from the previous one. The man's penis may secrete clear fluid intermittently. His penis will be hard and engorged and usually won't soften unless the woman completely stops stimulation. The woman becomes the driver, controlling his level of arousal and maintaining him just this side of ejaculation. The man becomes the passenger, along for the ride—he's giving up control to her, totally. In the first phase of Extended Orgasmic Response, he may show the same signs of extreme arousal that the woman displayed—thrusting, straining, moaning, panting, sweating, jerking his arms and legs. His heart rate and blood pressure are higher. He's testing her sensitivity to his level of arousal and his feelings. He's learning that her goal is not to push him over that point of no return, but instead to extend his pleasure by closely observing him as she continues to stimulate him and not allowing him to get too close to the point of no return.

Phase I, Extended Orgasmic Response, may last from one to fifteen minutes or more. How long depends on (a) the woman's ability to provide a continuous and reliable pattern of stimulation that is not so intense as to crest him into ejaculation and (b) the man's ability to discover how to allow himself increasing levels of arousal without ejaculation.

In the beginning of practicing the Extended Orgasmic Response Exercises, if the man can simply allow himself to experience ten to twenty nonejaculatory peaks, he and his partner may be doing very well. With regular practice, these peaks may become more frequent and more closely spaced, resulting in the experience of Phase I, Extended Orgasmic Response. When that happens, the man has gained some skill at controlling his ejaculation by alternating sex-muscle contraction and relaxation and by guiding his partner's stimulation. About half the time during emission-phase orgasm, his sex muscles, including the external anal sphincter, are relaxed. The woman provides a stimulation pattern which produces as many peaks as possible. She should ignore his pleas for going to ejaculation.

After several minutes, if he's able to slide into the second phase of the Extended Orgasmic Response, he'll become more stabilized. The jerking, straining, rhythmic movements and panting stop. His sounds diminish or cease as he experiences quieter ecstasy. Blood pressure and heart rate actually drop moderately from their higher levels in Phase I, Extended Orgasmic Response. His pelvic muscles relax, his external anal sphincter relaxes and remains open without the periodic tensing characteristic in Phase I. He feels a powerful sensation opening up his entire pelvic region. The man isn't intimidated by the nearness of the point of ejaculatory inevitability. He's achieved a feeling of awareness and control over it, relaxing with its impending approach in the multiple peaking process. There's no concern about cresting over into ejaculation. This is a state of pleasurable immobilization. In this second phase of Extended Orgasmic Response, control of ejaculation becomes more automatic on the man's part. It proceeds without effort or anxiety and the man feels as if he's entered an altered state of consciousness. Time slows and the world feels completely perfect. This condition can last as long as he and his partner wish to continue, until either one or the other, or both (which is ideal), decide to conclude. This Phase II, Extended Orgasmic Response, may last several minutes or even half an hour or more, for those dedicated couples who practice together extensively.

In this state, his penis may become so sensitized that a light touch, a teasing tickle, even simply blowing warm air on it or applying cool lubricant to it and letting the lubricant melt, give intense pleasure.

When we discussed giving the woman pleasure, we said it was important for the man not to vary his stroking too much—some teasing, but not a lot of variation. The opposite is true for men. Steady, unvarying stroking will usually either reduce arousal or carry the man straight to ejaculation. Because extending his orgasmic response requires control, he needs lots of variety. Changing strokes prevents ejaculation. The woman may want to supply a steady, stimulating stroke when the man is climbing to greater arousal. But she will need to change the stroking when he's close. She is creating increasingly greater arousal by peaking him as many times as possible.

She'll find it will be necessary to change positions and switch hands for her own comfort. That requirement has the added value of distracting the man, which can give him more control.

After about thirty minutes (or more if she wishes) of her full attention on manually or orally stimulating the man for his maximum pleasure, the woman says aloud that it's time to switch to the next part of the exercise, intercourse.

What to do if the man ejaculates early. It's quite possible that the man will ejaculate before either of you intends. This response is an expected part of the learning process. Don't worry. You can simply relax and enjoy it and review what happened to help you next time. Alternatively, you can experiment with intensifying the feeling and making the ejaculation last as long as possible. Once the man knows he's crested over and is feeling full ejaculatory inevitability, he can tell his partner so that she can intensify the stimulation. He can extend the ejaculation in time and amplify its intensity by reclenching his sex muscles, trying to hold in the ejaculate. The woman can place firm pressure with her forefinger at the base of the penis, clamping off the urethra to help with fluid retention. This safe procedure can intensify the ejaculatory experience and can make a second ejaculation easier. Alternatively, rather than squeezing the base of the urethra, she can stimulate the external prostate spot, which will generally add to the ejaculatory pleasure, since the prostate gland contracts during ejaculation.

The woman continues stimulating the penis and external prostate spot or applies pressure to the base of the penis on the urethra during the ejaculation. Rather than stopping at the conclusion, the woman can continue stimulation to experiment with the possibility of helping maintain her partner's erection and arousal level. Since the penis may be extremely sensitive immediately after ejaculation, she may need to lighten her stimulation for a number of seconds, then increase speed and pressure to rebuild sensation quickly. The man needs to focus his full attention on staying erect or regaining his erection if it has diminished, just as he has done in earlier exercises.

If the woman keeps stimulating after ejaculation appears to be over, she may be able to extend her partner's ejaculatory orgasm by half a dozen contractions or more. She'll be *lightly* caressing his penis and pushing and milking the external prostate spot. Part of the man's pleasure during ejaculation comes from the sensation of fluid pushing up from the base of the penis. By pushing on the external prostate spot, the woman can mimic that good feeling. Then the pulsing of the deeper pelvic muscles can continue for several pleasurable minutes.

Continue this process for five to ten minutes. If an erection is maintained or reestablished, then proceed directly to intercourse, as described next. If not, use all the information you have learned the next time you do this exercise.

EXERCISE FOUR: INTERCOURSE III

The man will probably have a relatively strong erection from the stimulation the woman has been giving him, assuming he hasn't ejaculated, and the couple shifts into an intercourse position directly.

The Exercise

Begin with a man-above position. Because of the extended stimulation and multiple near-ejaculatory peaks the man has been experiencing, he'll probably have greater control than usual over his ejaculation timing during intercourse. Take five to ten minutes to enjoy the freedom of various rates, rhythms, and angles of thrust.

Then switch to another position which gives the woman more control: woman-above, rear-entry, or scissors. (See illustrations, pages 251, 253 and 282.) It's possible that women who have previously developed the ability at times to have orgasm with intercourse may be able to experience orgasm during this phase of the exercise, particularly in the woman-above or rear-entry position. After five to ten minutes, conclude with a finale, thrusting as hard and as rapidly as you feel comfortable with, ending with ejaculation. Men, make pleasure sounds as you ejaculate. Then embrace each other and talk about your experience together.

EXERCISE FIVE: BRIEF SEXUAL INTERACTION

Rationale

This exercise is an opportunity to learn to focus your attention for efficient sexual experience.

Many couples report that one partner or the other is dissatisfied with how often or how quickly they make love. Often the man wants to make love more often while the woman wants to spend more time during less frequent sexual interactions. Ecstasy Program training satisfies both of these concerns. Following Program exercises, you've experienced several more lengthy sexual interactions together each week. Now it's time to discover and practice the pleasures and possibilities of briefer sex.

For men. During this exercise you'll be practicing the skills you've learned in earlier exercises of stimulating yourself quickly and efficiently to erection. You'll also apply the skills you've learned to assist your partner in having an orgasm. The Countdown Exercises you've been doing will help you to direct your attention away from distracting thoughts such as time pressure or worries about performance: "Will I get erect?" "Can I stay erect long enough?" "Can I last long enough?" "Can I ejaculate quickly enough?" "Will I be able to give her an orgasm?" Each and every time you find yourself thinking about anything other than the physical pleasure you're experiencing or your partner's response and what you can do to increase it even further, you'll be letting go of such distractions by refocusing on your experience of the exact present moment.

The Sex Muscle and Breathing Exercise has helped you to get erect and stay erect more easily. The Self-Stimulation Exercises have helped you to become more comfortable and efficient about getting erect and ejaculating at will. They'll be especially useful here.

Closely focusing your attention on your partner's response, as you learned to do in extending orgasmic response, allows you to help her respond rapidly to the stimulation you'll be supplying.

For women. In this exercise you'll be allowing yourself to have an orgasm ideally with five or ten minutes of direct genital stimulation. To do so, you may need to apply the skill of focusing your attention that you've learned practicing the 20–0 Countdown to direct your attention to sexual feelings. Each time distracting thoughts or negative resistances cross your mind, direct your attention away from those competing thoughts to your immediate physical experience and to positive self-talk. Use the skills you've learned practicing the Sex Muscle and Breathing Exercise —the clenching process in particular—to assist in your most rapid arousal while your partner is stimulating you manually and/or orally.

The Exercise

After you complete the twelve-week Ecstasy Program we'll be suggesting that you arrange one or two longer sessions of lovemaking each week, usually on weekends, and two or more brief sexual interactions per week, usually on weekdays. This exercise will begin to give you the practice and skills for doing so.

Mutual Stimulation, Emphasizing Female Response

The woman lies back, legs slightly separated, either flat on her back or propped up at an angle. The man positions himself in one of the following positions:

1. Side by side: he lies alongside her, heads at about the same level, with his right hand reaching down to her genitals. Kissing is possible and convenient.
2. Kneeling: he kneels on either her right or left side at the level of her pelvis.
3. Inverted side by side: he rests on his side with his head toward her pelvic area and her head toward his.

The man stimulates the woman using his hands and/or mouth. Be sure to use lubrication. He focuses on the clitoris, concentrating his attention sufficiently to allow her to have an orgasm.

The woman may stimulate the man's genitals manually, giving him attention to the degree she finds such stimulation adding to her own arousal. If stimulating his genitals distracts from her own arousal, she should reduce or stop such stimulation. A compromise may be for her to merely hold or touch his genitals while he's stimulating her. Ideally, she should allow herself to have an orgasm within five to ten minutes.

Intercourse

If the man has a more or less firm erection after stimulating his partner to orgasm, he can shift directly to intercourse. Use any intercourse position that you've both found to be comfortable and effective.

If the man has a less than serviceable erection, he should stimulate himself to as full an erection as possible as quickly as he can. He needs to focus his full attention on genital sensations, clenching his sex muscles, perhaps holding his breath for thirty seconds or so, using his most effective stroke at maximum speed, and perhaps closing his eyes. The woman may assist and stimulate her partner if he wishes and if doing so doesn't distract her from the pleasurable aftereffects of her orgasm and the anticipation of imminent intercourse. Alternatively, she may stimulate herself to maintain her own arousal level during the time the man is getting himself erect.

Still another possibility, if the man has a less than full erection, is for the woman to devote her full attention to stimulating him to gain an erection, using her hands and, if she wishes, her mouth.

When the man is relatively erect, he and his partner assume their preferred intercourse position.

Particularly recommended for efficiency and effect is the rear-entry position. In this position the woman is on her knees, leaning on her elbows. The man is kneeling between her legs with his hands on her hips for support and control. This position provides equal potential movement for both partners and allows particularly effective stimulation of the inner trigger area.

The man can proceed with vigorous, rapid thrusting and ejaculate as quickly as he wishes after insertion. If his partner has learned to have a rapid orgasmic response (see Week Eleven, page 315) with intercourse, the man might delay his ejaculation until she has an orgasm.

Total suggested intercourse time—five minutes or less.

EXERCISE SIX: SIGN COMPLETION AGREEMENT

EXERCISE COMPLETION AGREEMENT/ WEEK TEN

PARTNER EXERCISES   Initials

1. Discussed resistances prior to each exercise.   _____ _____
2. Did Exercise Planning Agreement.   _____ _____
3. Did sexual Appreciations and Resentments
   twice per day—2 times.   _____ _____
4. Did Learning to Extend Orgasmic Response
   with Intercourse, twice.   _____ _____
5. Did Brief Sexual Interaction twice.   _____ _____

SOLO EXERCISES

1. Did 20–0 Countdown at least twice a day.   _____ _____
2. Did Sex Muscle and Breathing Exercise daily.   _____ _____

I have accomplished the Solo Exercises described above. My partner and I have accomplished the Partner Exercises described above to our reasonable satisfaction. We also specifically reaffirm our agreement here to follow the exercises of Week Eleven.

If there has been or will be any change in the program as assigned, we have both talked about those changes and agreed upon them together.

_____   _____
Signature and Date   *Signature and Date*

WEEK ELEVEN

SUMMARY OF EXERCISES

PARTNER EXERCISES

1. Execute Exercise Planning Agreement.
2. Communication (Appreciations and Resentments) (2 planned rounds on sexual issues, 2 times; unlimited spontaneous).
3. Learning to Extend Orgasmic Response III (man giving, woman receiving, 30 minutes; woman giving, man receiving, 30 minutes; total time 1 hour, 2 times).
4. Intercourse (15–30 minutes or more), following Exercise Three.
5. Brief Sexual Interaction (10–15 minutes, 2 times).
6. Sign Exercise Completion Agreement.
7. Spontaneous lovemaking as desired.

EXERCISE ONE: EXECUTE PLANNING AGREEMENT

Fill out the following Planning Agreement according to the guidelines we discussed in Chapter VIII, page 131.

EXERCISE PLANNING AGREEMENT/WEEK ELEVEN

Communication Exercise

Initiator_____
Plan 2 rounds of sexual Appreciations and Resentments 2 times this week; unlimited spontaneous.

Times Scheduled

Sunday _____ _____
Monday _____ _____
Tuesday _____ _____
Wednesday _____ _____
Thursday _____ _____
Friday _____ _____
Saturday _____ _____

Learning to Extend Orgasmic Response

Allow 1 hour and 15–30 minutes, 2 times this week.

Times Scheduled

Sunday _____
Monday _____
Tuesday _____
Wednesday _____
Thursday _____
Friday _____
Saturday _____

Brief Sexual Interaction

Initiator_____
Allow 10–15 minutes, 2 times this week.

Times Scheduled

Sunday _____
Monday _____

Tuesday   _____
Wednesday   _____
Thursday   _____
Friday   _____
Saturday   _____

EXERCISE THREE: LEARNING TO EXTEND ORGASMIC RESPONSE III

Rationale

This week will refine skills and add oral stimulation exercises.

We included a basic discussion of the full range of extended orgasm in Week Ten so that you could see extended orgasmic response as a whole. It's unlikely that you moved beyond Phase I of extended orgasmic response in your first week of deliberate practice. Refer to our Week Ten discussion (which begins on page 288) and continue incorporating and practicing during Week Eleven.

Male stimulation is often misunderstood and more often neglected. As you advance in learning to extend orgasm, you'll want to explore it in more detail.

When a woman is stimulating a man, she pays close attention at all times to his nearness to ejaculation. The man trusts her ability to keep him sexually at the highly pleasurable crest of emission-stage orgasm without shifting him to the subtle further point of ejaculation. When he can trust her to do so, he can allow the sensations he's feeling to flood his consciousness and can feel more and more pleasure without the burden of ejaculation anxiety. Trust comes when the man has trained his partner to stimulate him better than he can stimulate himself.

The man's goal when stimulating his partner is to take his time with stimulating, watching, feeling, and listening. His objective is to know more about how his partner likes to be stimulated than she herself does. He learns to anticipate her needs by paying attention and pacing himself sensitively and steadily both orally and manually. We have added oral stimulation to this exercise because it can add significant arousal and intimacy to your interactions.

Oral Stimulation: Rationale

The lips and tongue are richly endowed with closely spaced nerve endings. That design makes them more sensitive than the hand or the vagina to receiving and sorting information. Such sensitivity offers significant advantages in detecting changes and responses in your partner's genitals. In addition, the moisture, warmth, and almost infinite range of pressures and movements of the mouth and tongue can stimulate your partner sexually with degrees of subtlety that no other source of stimulation can match.

Oral-stimulation techniques aren't something partners know instinctively. They have to be learned. There's no natural innate ability to guide you in giving your partner maximum pleasure orally. Oral stimulation allows the giving partner to learn the receiving partner's sexual responses better than any other form of interaction.

Oral stimulation is very commonly practiced among younger couples today. Older couples may have some resistance to this sexual practice. Whatever your reluctance may be, we hope you'll be willing to suspend your judgment for a week or two and give this potentially exquisitely pleasurable form of sexual interaction several trials.

Oral stimulation involves the acceptance and approval of your partner's genitals, which may be the opposite of what you were taught as a child. Assuming careful hygiene, "down there" isn't necessarily "dirty," a place where you "mustn't touch." Oral stimulation is a reliable way to restore a full erection. A woman doesn't have to cover the entire head and shaft of her partner's penis with her mouth. Covering the head of the penis with her mouth and stimulating the shaft with her lubricated hands is sufficient if she varies the stimulation for a stroke or two every minute or so, by taking the entire head into her mouth and as much of the shaft as she's comfortable including. With continued, regular strokes in all of the man's genital areas, he soon won't be paying specific attention to exactly what and where the woman is stroking. The entire genital area will be engorged and highly enough aroused that all the various sources of stimulation will blend together. Become aware of the very sensitive, delicate tissue of the penis or clitoris and how satinlike and smooth it feels to the tongue and mouth.

We encourage oral stimulation. Even if you have strong resistances, you can choose to overcome them by practicing slowly to learn to trust your partner, dealing deliberately with your hygiene requirements, and slowly desensitizing yourself to the process. Some women who are reluctant to practice oral sex find that covering the penis with an unlubricated condom helps them feel secure against the possibility of having to deal with oral ejaculation. With experience, they may eventually find the condom unnecessary. Other women learn to trust their partners to give them sufficient advance warning of impending ejaculation to avoid having to deal with oral ejaculation until they're more comfortable with the prospect. The more control of his ejaculatory response the male develops, the more confidence and trust the woman gains that he won't inadvertently ejaculate in her mouth.

Women and men who have deep, religiously based resistance or strongly held negative feelings about oral stimulation should simply substitute manual stimulation in this exercise. You can still accomplish extending orgasm with manual stimulation by doing the prescribed exercises sensitively and consistently. For more assistance, consult "Learning Oral Lovemaking," page 402, in the Appendix.

Before proceeding with oral stimulation, please give attention to your own and your partner's genital hygiene. Either shower or bathe, together or separately, or wash each other's genitals. Remember, although the major purpose of this process is your partner's psychological comfort, the bathing or washing is a ritual that in itself can be pleasurable.

When receiving oral stimulation, a woman generally feels more comfortable if the man has shaved recently. A beard or a mustache isn't usually objectionable at such times, but the roughness of recent hair growth often is. Your partner will appreciate your taking care of this matter.

Man Stimulating Woman: The Exercise

The woman assumes a reclining position and the man adopts a position at her side, kneeling, sitting, or lying at pelvic level, or he may kneel or lie between her separated legs.

Men, stroke and appreciate your partner's body for about three to five minutes anywhere you wish except her genitals. Then apply a lubricant to your hands and her genital area. In the same way you did in Week Ten, lightly tease the area around the clitoris for a minute or two to build anticipation. Then apply direct stimulation to the clitoris with your right hand, using the basic two-fingered, up-down stroke with thumb at the top of the clitoris and clitoris base and the forefinger at the lower side of the clitoris. Roll the clitoris between thumb and forefinger and the base at a rate of approximately once per second, gradually building arousal. (See illustration, page 265.)

Adding oral stimulation. After about five minutes of direct manual stimulation, change your position to allow you to stimulate your partner's genitals orally. If you were sitting, you'll need either to kneel or to lie on your stomach. We suggest that you start by kneeling between your partner's legs, then bend down toward her genitals. This position allows you to concentrate more directly on your partner and her responses without the possible distraction of her stimulating you.

Just as you gradually approached the clitoris manually, so now you should gradually approach the clitoris orally, pulling on pubic hairs with your lips, blowing warm air, nuzzling the clitoris with your nose. These teasings make for a slow, sensitive approach.

The tongue has several different ways of stimulating the genitals. It has a pointed tip and a broader flat surface. The tip can provide more focused stimulation; the broader flat surface can provide licking sensations. The lips can suck at the same time that the tongue is moving. Using the teeth carefully for very gentle biting is also possible. Women generally like a lighter touch than men. Oral stimulation involves less pressure than manual stimulation, so women are usually less concerned that their partners might stimulate them too forcefully.

The basic stroke pattern we suggest is gentle licking with the broad surface of your tongue in an up-down motion from the base of the clitoris to the tip at about one stroke per second. Which direction you'll stroke through depends on whether your head is aligned in the same direction as your partner's or reversed. This basic up-down motion can be varied with side-to-side movement with the flat of the tongue across the tip of the clitoris.

The same motion is effectively performed by the very tip of the tongue. The tip can move from the base of the clitoris up to the clitoral tip and then to the hood of the clitoris or the top of the clitoris under the hood. A variation is using the tip of the tongue to move the tip of the clitoris from side to side. Another pleasurable variant is tapping the tip of the tongue on the tip of the clitoris at about one tap or more per second. The tip of the tongue can also move in a rapid, vibratory stroke, vibrating up and down and side to side as rapidly as possible, creating the sensations of a warm, moist, low-speed vibrator.

We suggest you experiment with the effects of these various strokes.

Apply each stroke separately for about a minute and notice the effects. Then try combining up-and-down and side-to-side strokes, which produces a rolling, undulating motion of the clitoris. You'll be able to observe and feel changes in clitoral engorgement quickly, easily, and directly. This feedback will guide you in learning the most effective stroke pressures, rates, and locations.

You should also experiment with applying the tip of your tongue to different locations on the shaft of the clitoris to determine areas of sensitivity. Sometimes extremely small areas of the clitoral shaft can be surprisingly responsive to small oscillations. When you find an effective stroke, location, or pattern, stay with it until it appears to lose some effectiveness or until your partner appears to be ready to crest into orgasm. Avoid allowing her to begin an orgasm until you've stimulated her orally for at least twenty minutes. The longer and more frequently you build her arousal to a peak and then slow down or stop and resume again a few seconds later, the greater the probability of more intense and longer orgasmic contractions.

Add sucking motions with the lips for an exciting variation. Experiment with gentle suction and stronger suction. Women usually prefer a lighter touch than men expect. Brief periods of firm suction, however, interspersed with longer periods of lighter suction can be an excellent teasing means of arousal.

Optionally, try inserting the tongue into the vagina as deep as you can, moving it in and out in simulated intercourse. You can accomplish this stimulation most easily and effectively when you're approaching your partner from her underside with your head between her thighs. Although oral stimulation of inner and outer lips is usually less arousing than on the clitoris, it is nevertheless useful to explore your partner's response.

You'll probably discover that your level of mental attention can increase or reduce the effectiveness of the oral stimulation you're delivering. The more you direct your mind to observe and experience and enjoy the moment-to-moment effect of your stroking, the more effective you'll probably find your stimulation to be. When your mind wanders with distracting thoughts or negative mental thoughts, your partner's arousal level is likely to decline or not increase as rapidly.

Your partner can assist you in learning to stimulate her orally by making louder or softer pleasure sounds depending upon her level of arousal. Brief, constructive verbal feedback can also be useful. Men need to remember to put their egos aside in learning to stimulate their partners. It's impossible for you to know as much as your partner knows about what pleases her without considerable instruction and practice. It's her body; they're her nerve endings and she's the ultimate expert.

After at least twenty minutes of manual and oral stimulation, you can increase the rate and intensity of your stimulation to allow your partner to have an orgasm. As she begins the automatic squeeze contractions, you can insert a finger into her vaginal opening to provide internal stimulation as you learned to do in earlier exercises. During the squeeze contractions and immediately after, you'll need to lighten your clitoral stimulation. You can then focus your concentration on internal stimulation, with an inserted finger or two, to allow your partner's orgasm to continue and perhaps develop into a push-out orgasmic response. Your partner assists herself by deliberately pushing out, breathing, and focusing her full attention on sensations. If the woman is having push-out contractions, she allows that process to occur as long as possible.

When the woman has had a fully satisfying orgasm, the two of you can then reverse roles.

Woman Stimulating the Man: The Exercise

A man's erection may wax and wane at first until the woman has sustained him in full erection for enough time, perhaps fifteen minutes, to make a consistent mental impression of sustained stimulation and pleasure relatively free of distracting nonsexual thoughts. These variations in erection strength aren't a problem. They simply indicate that one or both partners aren't concentrating their full attention consistently enough.

Remember that the woman is in charge when she's stimulating her partner. She's responsible for developing a rhythm and keeping count. Just as she needs regularity in stimulation and stroking, so does the man, with a little teasing interspersed. Building to the first peak, her stroking should be regular, rapid, and intense. Once the man is at his first peak, close to ejaculation, she needs to vary her stroking and to decrease its intensity to keep him there. The woman varies stroking rhythms and rates in stimulating his penis. It's helpful to count the strokes (silently!). The woman alternates stroking the penis shaft and head of the penis.

Here's a suggested stroking pattern:

1. Just prior to the first peak, the woman alternates rapid stroking of the shaft, including the head, for fifteen full strokes, then switches to stimulating only the shaft, stopping just below the coronal ridge, for fifteen rapid strokes. She then does fifteen rapid strokes including the head, switching back and forth, fifteen strokes on the shaft, then fifteen full strokes including the head.

2. As the man becomes still more aroused and closer to ejaculation, change to twenty strokes to the shaft alternating with ten full strokes incorporating the head as well.

3. As arousal increases still further, go to thirty strokes to the shaft excluding the head and five full strokes including the head.

4. As the man gets closer to ejaculation, or the woman has peaked him one or more times already, use still fewer strokes that incorporate the head of the penis and use slower strokes on the shaft.

5. Utilize the scrotal-pull method, ringing the scrotum or incorporating stimulation of the external prostate with the left hand as the right hand stimulates the penis shaft slowly at a ratio of about thirty strokes to the shaft and one or two including the head. Two strokes, one after the other, to the head of the penis, can be used if the man is able to accept this level of stimulation without ejaculation.

If ejaculation seems to be too close to avoid, heavy pressure on the external prostate spot, or doing a quick, firm scrotal pull, a strong frenulum squeeze, or strong pressure on the base of the penis in front of the testicles, may stop it. In extremity, a vigorous slap on the buttocks may also help prevent ejaculation. Note that performing any of these maneuvers to prevent ejaculation may also help to build further arousal at the same time.

The woman gives her partner her full attention when she's stimulating him. Her mind as well as her hands need to be on his penis.

Women, here's where the lessons of thought control you've learned doing the 20–0 Countdown can assist you. You don't have to be the victim of your thoughts. You know you can deliberately shift your thoughts from other, intrusive, nonsexual thoughts to the responsibility at hand, narrating in silent internal dialogue the story of what you're doing at that moment and the pleasure you're taking from it and the positive results you expect your actions to produce.

If you're planning next week's menu while stimulating your partner, you'll unknowingly communicate that inattention to him. He'll sense your distraction and become distracted himself (this point applies equally to men stimulating women).

Women, and men as well, sometimes go on automatic pilot. Their hands are moving up and down, but their minds are elsewhere. They need to pull their concentration back to what they're doing. Your partner has learned to trust you to focus exclusively on his arousal and not on your own feelings and thoughts. One good way you can do so is to communicate silently to yourself: describe in detail what you're doing, tell yourself how good it feels, and fantasize about what power pleasurably stimulating your partner gives you. Such thoughts can help you pay attention. They'll translate into actions and your partner will pick them up and respond.

It can require physical stamina to stimulate a man to extended orgasm and maintain him in that state. The woman must make up her mind that she's going to stimulate him for as long as it takes. If he's having difficulty maintaining an erection, she may speed up her stroking and include the head of the penis in all her strokes. Her goal at this point is to stimulate him enough to bypass his resistance. She may want to look on the goal as a challenge. It can be an enjoyable position of control.

Perseverance is important. The woman can decide that no matter how her partner resists, no matter what his negative thoughts are, she's going to see him through.

Once the man is aroused and fully erect, variety is extremely important in keeping him aroused without ejaculation. If a woman has been stimulating her partner for five minutes using one particular stroke and he's not climbing in arousal, she should switch to another stroke. If he's erect, add stimulation of the scrotum, the testicles, the buried base of the penis, the external prostate spot. If he's not erect, use oral stimulation as described later in this exercise. If stimulation has been heavy and fast, switch to the barest tickle or the lightest stroking. The idea is to disorient the man enough to distract him from his mental resistances. Work with his mind.

If the couple reaches an impasse, then the man should take over. The woman may lightly touch or caress the scrotum while the man stimulates himself to erection. This allows the woman to participate in the process and gives her the added security of knowing and feeling inclusion. That's one value of the exercises you've practiced. You've learned reliable self-stimulation and you've learned not to feel self-conscious when self-stimulating in each other's presence and with the partner's assistance.

The woman shouldn't feel she's failed if a man's resistances have overwhelmed her stimulation. The man's self-stimulation at this point is an addition, a help when she's run out of ideas, a chance for her to rest. Maybe her timing was off, maybe she tired early. Perhaps he had worries or problems on his mind. She can take over again when his erection returns.

Some women resent male self-stimulation during sex. They need to understand that although men enjoy self-stimulating, they prefer to be stimulated by their partners. When a woman learns through the Ecstasy Program that she can stimulate her partner as well as he can stimulate himself, she can resolve that resentment.

We find that when the woman is fully attentive to arousing her partner, her concentration usually leads to maximum erection. If other thoughts intrude, her partner can lose erection fullness. It's interesting how closely the woman's attention and the man's responses are linked!

The woman can deliberately create positive thoughts that focus her attention on her partner's penis: how good it feels in her hand, how good it looks, how warm, how exciting, how wonderful is her ability to create an erection. She can visualize the penis getting harder and fuller. She can silently recite positive statements: "When my attention is focused, my timing and pressure are perfect." "I like stimulating my partner's penis." "I share this pleasure with love." When intrusive thoughts appear, these positive statements can block them out.

Paying attention to sounds can help. The lubricant you're using makes a slippery sound that can serve as a focus, adding hearing to sight and touch.

For monitoring the man's arousal, as well as for stimulating him, particularly after he's been kept in full erection for ten minutes or more, the woman can place one finger on his anus. This arrangement alerts her to the status of his sex muscles. When his sex muscles are relaxed, his anus will be relaxed. When he's contracting, the anus will register the change. The anus isn't the only monitoring point, but it's one that couples often overlook.

Like the external prostate spot, the scrotum, and the buried penile base, the anus is an erotically sensitive area once there's engorgement. That filling of genital tissue with blood may require anywhere from five to fifteen minutes of stimulation. Stimulation usually moves in progression from the head of the penis to the shaft to the base, then to the scrotum, to the perineum, to the external prostate spot, and finally to the anus.

A woman may use a finger or (if she has long fingernails) a knuckle to stimulate the anus. With finger stimulation she can encourage her partner to alternate his contracting and relaxing. If she wants him to switch from contracting to relaxing, she can give him extra stimulation by pressing and stroking his anus. A finger doesn't necessarily have to be inserted. The man may contract against the stimulation or consciously relax. If the woman continues stimulating the shaft and head of the man's penis lightly while she stimulates his anus, she can exert a great deal of control over his state of sexual tension. Many couples don't take advantage of this added avenue to stimulation, control, and monitoring.

Many women find a man's testicles intimidating. They require care, and women should take instruction from their partners in how best to stimulate them. After a period of arousal and engorgement they can usually be stimulated more vigorously. Most men, once erect, find oral stimulation of their testicles, licking the scrotum and taking one testicle at a time into the mouth, highly arousing. The hand works equally well. Lubrication is important; the scrotum is just as sensitive as the penile shaft.

Refining the Woman's Control

The woman's main technique is observation. She learns to detect the signs of muscular contraction of the man's thigh muscles and to observe and feel the throbbing pulsations in the penis that occur just prior to ejaculation. Other signs of the man's peaking are:

1. Muscular tension evident in the thighs and the stomach; the woman should watch for sometimes subtle, sometimes more obvious contractions of thigh and abdominal muscles.
2. Scrotum elevating. This change may be a modest quarter of an inch or a more apparent half an inch of elevation. The scrotum becomes firm, tight, and high rather than hanging and loose.
3. Knees closing. This movement may be subtle and involuntary or it may be more obvious and deliberate.
4. Pelvis moving away from the woman's stimulating hand or mouth. Again, such motion may be subtle or may be obvious.
5. Hands moving toward his genitals to move her hands or her head away. They may never arrive, only signaling the man's need for less stimulation to retard ejaculation.
6. Increasing volume or urgency of his sounds. A man who has learned to communicate with love sounds will be sighing and moaning with stimulation anyway; as he approaches the ejaculatory point of no

return he'll get louder. The register of his voice is likely also to change, becoming deeper and more guttural with increasing intensity.

It's the woman's responsibility when she's stimulating her partner—when she's giving and he's receiving—to keep him as fully erect and aroused as possible without ejaculating. But he can assist her by using his own control mechanisms and by communicating his state of arousal. He can alternate contracting and relaxing his sex muscles. He can combine contracting with breathing in and relaxing with breathing out or continuously contract or relax while breathing in and out.

Love sounds can be extremely helpful, both to add to his own arousal and to communicate that arousal to his partner. Changes in pitch and volume—which come naturally with increasing and decreasing pleasure if you've learned to vocalize comfortably during lovemaking—can guide his partner with remarkable precision.

If a man's partner misjudges his signs of arousal and brings him too close—less than three seconds—to ejaculation, he should simply tell her, "Stop!" That request should signal the woman to stop all stimulation *immediately*. If she fails to do so because she's concentrating so intensely on stimulation, the man should repeat his request and also use his hands to stop or control her stimulation.

When, after reducing or stopping stimulation, the woman detects that the man's arousal has declined to at least fifteen to thirty seconds away from ejaculation, she can resume more intense stimulation. Stimulating the head of his penis if his erection diminishes will restore it to its full erection most rapidly.

If the man signals in any way that he wants his partner to decrease stimulation, she should move immediately to do so. But having done so, she should quickly return to stimulating him to multiple peaks without ejaculation. Alternating fast and slow stroking is very effective.

Adding Oral Stimulation

The man lies flat on his back or propped reclining. Women, position yourself kneeling between your partner's legs. Caress as much of his entire penis in your mouth as comfort allows, creating suction as you move your head up and down. Apply pressure at the same time at the base of the shaft with your hand next to the pubic bone. A fairly tight ring of your circled fingers can help block the outflow of blood from the penis, a restraint that assists in the rapid development of erection. The best way to arrange this restriction is to circle the shaft at its base with the index finger and thumb.

Once your partner has become fully erect, you can emphasize covering the head of the penis and part of the shaft with your mouth and then moving your neck up and down to stimulate as much of his penis as you comfortably can. When your neck becomes tired or your jaws fatigued, you'll want to change stimulation by using your tongue on the most sensitive area of the penis, the coronal ridge, especially the frenulum. Apply the tip of your tongue up and down in very small oscillating motions and simultaneously use a lubricated hand or fingers to stimulate the shaft of the penis. Your other hand can caress the testicles and the external prostate spot.

You'll be more aware when your partner is reaching a peak, close to ejaculation, if you position one hand intermittently on his belly. The long muscles there, the *rectus abdomini*, will be contracting if he's close to ejaculation. His pelvis will probably be pulling away from your mouth. You can apply a scrotal pull at that point to control his tendency to ejaculate and you can stop moving your head, neck, and tongue.

Another way of compensating for any fatigue you might experience in your neck or jaws is to rest your head on your partner's thigh or have him shift to a side position that allows you to support your head on a pillow facing his genitals. His penis will be at mouth level then and your body curled in a semifetal position. This position is excellent for conserving energy and still allowing you great freedom to stimulate the entire penis with little neck movement necessary. You can focus your attention with your tongue on the tiny frenulum of your partner's penis, using your hands to caress his scrotum and external prostate area or to tease the anal area. This kind of stimulation requires you to expend very little energy. If your partner begins to lose his erection, speed up manual stimulation or apply more suction with your mouth, at the same time moving your head up and down, taking as much of the penis as possible into your mouth. You may wish to change back periodically to a kneeling position. Such position changes help to break through your partner's resistances. They can help you narrow your focus and clear away distracting thoughts.

Another variation involves positioning your hands under your partner's buttocks with index fingers pressing against the spine at the level of the coccyx (tailbone). This pressure pleasurably stimulates the sacral nerve that runs just below the surface of the back.

Your thoughts at these times are important to the quality of the stimulation. You should notice when your thoughts start to wander and observe the change, probably toward subtle reduction, in your partner's arousal level. Help prevent distractions by self-talk that identifies the experience that you're having at every moment, the pleasure that you're getting, and the satisfaction that comes from having pleasurable control over your partner's response.

The real challenge of this exercise is to experiment with your partner's reaction by focusing your attention closely and consistently on his response to your oral stimulation. You may discover that you have the equivalent of a direct line to his mind and can control the general direction of his thoughts. You can help divert his attention away from distractions, concerns, and worries to the most positive thoughts about you and his relationship with you. We suggest that each woman experiment with this exercise.

Use your developing skill at oral stimulation to peak your partner as many times as you can. After a period of passively receiving multiple peaks from your stimulation, he may be experiencing the first phase of extended orgasmic response. You can help identify this stage by placing a finger on the anal sphincter. It should be relatively relaxed and open periodically, about half the time. When a man is in this initial phase of extended orgasmic response, peaking him becomes progressively easier. Less intense stimulation is usually required and you will be needing less frequent use of stop-start, squeeze, and scrotal-pull control methods. More subtle variations in stimulation will be sufficient to create each peak.

When he's in the range of fifteen minutes or more of Phase I extended orgasmic response, the man may become aware of profound alteration in his physical and mental experience. Trusting his partner, knowing she's paying close attention to his pleasure and isn't bored or tired, knowing she'll keep him climbing without cresting over into ejaculation, he's able to relax his pelvic muscles and give up conscious control. The intense, euphoric, altered consciousness he may then move into may be Phase II of the extended orgasmic response. In this state, which may last from several minutes to thirty minutes or even more, he feels pleasurably, physically and mentally, immobilized. When one or both partners wish to conclude, they may move as smoothly as possible to the Intercourse Exercise, which begins with the "laptop" position described in the next section (page 328). To boost her arousal in preparation for intercourse in the laptop position, the man may take several minutes to kneel between her legs and restimulate her with his hands or mouth.

Multiple Ejaculations

Alternatively, the man may ejaculate, deliberately or inadvertently. If the man does ejaculate, however, it isn't necessary for the woman to cease stimulating him. It appears reasonably possible for a motivated man of almost any age to have two ejaculations on the same erection. Some men learn to have three or even more ejaculations in close succession. Most men don't pursue more than one ejaculation per session of love-making because they or their partners may not know or believe it's possible for them. They can demonstrate it for themselves in self-stimulation. With increasing confidence, they may find it's possible with a partner.

Problems of circulation, diabetes, alcoholism, hormone imbalance, and a variety of medications can interfere with increasing the number of ejaculations without a long refractory period between them. But even with some physical detriments to functioning, including age factors, it is worthwhile for every interested man to investigate his potential ability to experience multiple ejaculations.

Practicing increasing the number of ejaculations can facilitate learning extended orgasm. Subsequent ejaculations after the first will likely find the man with a somewhat firm erection and he will produce less semen. Eventually he'll produce no semen at all. Orgasm is defined by contractions, not by expulsion of fluid, and there can be equally pleasurable contractions without ejaculation of semen. A teenage boy's first orgasms are usually dry, yet they're often an orgasmic experience more memorable than later orgasms with expulsion of fluid.

Men who have learned to or are practicing having multiple ejaculations can move into intercourse as described next.

EXERCISE FOUR: INTERCOURSE

The Laptop Position

The man kneels back on his calves (sits back on his haunches); the woman sits on the man's pelvis (lap), her legs extended behind him, supporting herself by leaning back on her extended arms, which are extended beneath her at shoulder level, elbows locked. (See illustration, page 329.) The woman uses her arms as a pivot to rock her body forward

INTERCOURSE POSITION:
LAPTOP POSITION

A good position when the woman is highly aroused and near to or into orgasm. Man can provide moderately heavy thrusting. Woman can thrust her pelvis forward and back by rocking her torso from her extended arms. She can also sit more upright on his lap to change the angle of entry and rotate her pelvis in a circular or undulating motion. Face-to-face intimacy, allowing kissing and hugging and providing relatively mutual control. Easy transition from or to the man-above (missionary) position.

Disadvantages: This is often a short-term position. The woman's arms and man's back and thighs may tire.

329

and back easily, as if swinging. This arrangement permits her to thrust her pelvis with minimum effort, rocking her entire body forward and back with little muscle movement necessary. She's also able to angle her pelvis forward and back to control the angle of entry and to obtain additional internal stimulation.

This position is particularly easy for couples to adopt where the man has been kneeling between the woman's legs, providing her with manual or oral stimulation. From there, the woman merely needs to slide forward a short distance up onto the man's lap and insert the man's penis. The man need not have a full erection for penetration.

Additional advantages include good stimulation of the G-spot trigger area; easy movement from this position into the missionary position—the man merely needs to lean forward and rest on his elbows or hands above his partner; and easy control for the woman of her thrusting—abandonment with little conscious effort.

We suggest using this position for three to five minutes and then moving smoothly into the missionary position. A variation is for the woman to sit on his lap, resting on her knees with her feet behind her rather than her feet behind him. This provides deeper penetration and may be more comfortable as there is less weight on the woman's hands.

If a couple finds adopting these positions difficult for any reason, simply omit using them and proceed directly into the missionary position.

The Three Basic Intercourse Positions

Now move into any one of the three basic intercourse positions of your choice—missionary, female-above, or rear-entry. In whatever position you choose, the woman pushes out and continues to breathe deliberately if she is not experiencing the continuous push-out contractions of extended orgasm. Remain in whatever position you've chosen for at least three to five minutes. You may choose to shift to another one of the basic positions as well. We suggest taking a total of at least fifteen minutes for intercourse, depending upon your desire and energy level in each position.

When you're in a face-to-face position such as man-above or woman-above, take a minute or two to make eye contact. Each of you keep your eyes open and look silently into the other's eyes as you move in rhythm. These moments of unspoken communication can be the most pleasurable times that couples experience together. They can compensate for untold hours and days, even months and years, of life's inevitable struggles, disappointments, and pain. It takes a surprisingly brief time of shared, ecstatic experience, periodically renewed, to strengthen and enlarge your relationship and give intimate meaning to your lives.

If, when you make this eye contact during intercourse, you find yourself thinking uncomfortable thoughts, feeling embarrassed or self-conscious, deliberately change the content of your thoughts. Recall the beginning of your sexual relationship, when you looked into your partner's eyes with joy and approval and anticipation of the future you would share. Use the same mental process that you used in the 20–0 Countdown to change your immediate negative thoughts to positive, pleasurable thoughts. Tell yourself in vivid detail how you would like to experience this particular moment. It may help briefly to close your eyes and recall past feelings of appreciation, affection, intimacy, and oneness that you would like to feel again now.

When you are ready to conclude, the woman goes to her maximum peak. If she is in an active position, such as the laptop, woman-above, or woman-superior, she can initiate this conclusion. If the man is in the man-above position, then he may initiate the finale. Do this by increasing the depth and speeding up the rate of thrusting. At this point the man may choose to ejaculate. Both of you should remember to vocalize your pleasure during your finale. It will give you an extra boost. The woman bears down (pushes out) and continues to breathe as her partner is thrusting. With your whole attention on your physical sensations, see if you can let go a little more than usual to stretch out your orgasm and increase its intensity.

Couples often find themselves routinely making love in the same position week after week. That's fine as long as it's a deliberate choice among other positions, communicated and agreed upon. But choosing other positions for lovemaking can be useful, and arousing, from time to time, to see what new pleasures you can find in them. You don't necessarily need a book. You can make up your own. Fantasize about what you might like, then discuss your ideas with your partner and experiment. Don't be concerned if unfamiliar positions seem a little awkward at first. It's often fun simply to experiment now and then.

Extended orgasm by intercourse is the ultimate in intimacy as well as in pleasure. You may well feel closer to each other than you have ever felt before: eyes looking lovingly into eyes, mouths and tongues teasing, bodies locked together and thrusting, both of you moaning. As you learn to trust each other to sustain and to share this level of sensation, you can make it continue for as long as you both want. It is heaven on earth, and not many people find it for the first time without tears of joy.

If a man loses his erection at any time during intercourse, whether before insertion, after a minute or two, or after several minutes, neither of you need be concerned. The man simply needs to stimulate himself with his partner's assistance (as in the Partner-Assisted Stimulation Exercise of Week Eight). The man should direct his mental focus to the sensations in his genitals as he stimulates his penis rapidly and intensely while directing his partner to stimulate his other genital areas. In a short time, he'll probably be erect enough again for insertion. The couple may resume the same position they were in when there was loss of erection, or assume a different position. Couples usually discover positions that they find comfortable and reliable. If you've been making love in some other position and the man has lost his erection several times, we suggest that you assume a preferred position to conclude intercourse.

EXERCISE FIVE: BRIEF SEXUAL INTERACTION

Rationale

Sex would rarely happen if you waited until the perfect moment when you and your partner both felt sexual simultaneously. The "rapid orgasmic response," which women who regularly experience extended orgasm often find they can learn to have, can help to compensate for their partners' greater ease of arousal.

It's important even in a busy life to connect sexually and regularly with your partner. Getting into the mood to do so seems to be easier for men than for women, but women benefit just as much as men once they've done so. A woman may feel sexual inertia because she isn't having sexual thoughts or feelings at some particular moment. Men are often quickly aroused. Even their morning erections from bladder pressure and dreaming stimulate arousal.

A woman can deliberately arouse herself by using the same attention control methods she's been practicing in the Countdown Exercise. While her partner is stimulating her and she him, she can close her eyes and concentrate on picturing exactly what's happening at the moment. If she visualizes her own genitals and what they look and feel like as they become engorged, she can encourage that engorgement much as the man does to achieve erection. Once engorgement occurs, inertia disappears and she's on the road to orgasm. Many women choose to wait for spontaneous thoughts to occur. Unfortunately, such thoughts often occur when their partners aren't present.

It's necessary to be deliberate to maintain a well-balanced sexual relationship. If you agree to take ten to fifteen minutes in the morning, when time presses, and stick to that agreement, you may be very pleasantly surprised at the intimate feelings and the sense of connection with your partner that you'll enjoy throughout the day.

Women who regularly practice extended orgasm often discover the ability to have a "rapid orgasmic response" with intercourse. Orgasm occurs with only a brief period of intercourse, in noticeably less time than the woman usually requires. When the practice of extended orgasmic response is a regular part of a couple's repertoire, natural lubrication and rapid orgasmic response may occur within a minute of penetration and thrusting.

Women who don't always naturally lubricate quickly should use a lubricant to facilitate rapid orgasm. The rear-entry position works particularly well. The woman *pushes out*, opening the vagina to the penis and allowing her to accept penetration and find it immediately arousing. Rapid orgasmic response turns the "quickie" from what may be experienced as an insult into a pleasure. The memory of recent extended orgasmic response allows a woman to reproduce that push-out type of orgasmic response with minimal foreplay.

With rapid orgasmic response, the man needs relatively little attention on delaying his ejaculation. He may be able to thrust as hard or as rapidly as he wishes. Because his partner requires somewhat less vaginal stimulation for her orgasm, even a less than fully hard erection may be sufficient.

The Exercise

Mutual stimulation. The couple assumes a comfortable position in a side-by-side (their heads at the same level) or inverted side-to-side position (heads directed toward the partner's genitals). (See illustration, page 219.) The man arouses the woman with manual and/or oral stimulation; at the same time the woman stimulates the man manually and/or orally. The man stimulates his partner to orgasm. The woman has her predominant attention on her own experience. She may stimulate the man sufficiently for him to have an erection but not to the point of ejaculation. If the man isn't serviceably erect by the time the woman has had an orgasm, he stimulates himself with his partner's participation to a relatively full erection as efficiently and as rapidly as he can. Spend two to five minutes on this part of the exercise.

Switch to intercourse. Assume the rear-entry position. The woman separates her legs to allow her partner to kneel between them. If her legs are somewhat shorter than his, she'll need to keep her legs more together. If his legs are considerably longer, he may prefer to straddle outside of her legs. The rear-entry position is especially well suited to the rapid orgasmic response because it allows some clitoral stimulation when the woman tilts her pelvis and also provides excellent inner-trigger-area stimulation. The woman continues deliberately to push out, arch her back, and exhale. She shouldn't hold her breath. The man grips her hips with his hands for support and forcibly pulls her hips as he moves forward, increasing the intensity of his thrusting. This exercise is brief—one to three minutes of thrusting—so the man can thrust hard, and with abandon, ejaculating virtually as quickly as he wishes.

EXERCISE SIX: SIGN COMPLETION AGREEMENT

EXERCISE COMPLETION AGREEMENT/ WEEK ELEVEN

PARTNER EXERCISES   Initials

1. Discussed resistances prior to each exercise.   _____ _____
2. Did Exercise Planning Agreement.   _____ _____
3. Did sexual Appreciations and Resentments
   twice a day, 2 times.   _____ _____
4. Did Learning to Extend Orgasmic Response,
   with Intercourse, twice.   _____ _____
5. Did Brief Sexual Interaction twice.   _____ _____

SOLO EXERCISES

1. Did 20–0 Countdown at least twice a day.   _____ _____
2. Did Sex Muscle and Breathing Exercise daily.   _____ _____

I have accomplished the Solo Exercises described above. My partner and I have accomplished the Partner Exercises described above to our reasonable satisfaction. We also specifically reaffirm our agreement here to follow the exercises of Week Twelve.

If there has been or will be any change in the program as assigned, we have both talked about those changes and agreed upon them together.

_____   _____
        Signature and Date   *Signature and Date*

WEEK TWELVE

SUMMARY OF EXERCISES

PARTNER EXERCISES

1. Execute Exercise Planning Agreement.
2. Communication (Appreciations and Resentments) (2 planned rounds on sexual issues, 2 times; unlimited spontaneous).
3. Learning to Extend Orgasmic Response IV ($1\frac{1}{2}$ to 2 hours, 2 times).
4. Intercourse.
5. Sign Exercise Completion Agreement.
6. Spontaneous lovemaking as desired.

EXERCISE ONE: EXECUTE PLANNING AGREEMENT

Fill out the following Planning Agreement according to the guidelines we discussed in Chapter VIII, page 131.

EXERCISE PLANNING AGREEMENT/WEEK TWELVE

Communication Exercise

Initiator_____

Plan 2 rounds of sexual Appreciations and Resentments 2 times this week; unlimited spontaneous.

Times Scheduled

Sunday	_____	_____
Monday	_____	_____
Tuesday	_____	_____
Wednesday	_____	_____
Thursday	_____	_____
Friday	_____	_____
Saturday	_____	_____

Learning to Extend Orgasmic Response

Allow 1½ to 2 hours, 2 times this week.

Times Scheduled

Sunday	_____
Monday	_____
Tuesday	_____
Wednesday	_____
Thursday	_____
Friday	_____
Saturday	_____

In Week Twelve you complete the structured Ecstasy Program for couples. We designed it to be a beginning, though, not an end. We'll discuss in the next chapter how to weave what you've learned into the fabric of your everyday life. For now, continue to plan your week of exercises together and enjoy them. You've achieved a high level of skill. We hope you've also achieved a high level of pleasure. If you've come this far, we're sure you have.

EXERCISE THREE: LEARNING TO EXTEND ORGASMIC RESPONSE IV

Rationale

By now we hope you're experiencing longer and stronger orgasms than when you started the Ecstasy Program. Let's review some of the characteristics of extended orgasmic response. For both men and women there are physical components and psychological (mental) components.

Physically, for women, the muscular tension throughout the body that occurs in the buildup toward and during the beginning of orgasm is released. Muscles become and remain relaxed from head to foot. Eyes are generally closed, although they may be opened. At times, heart rate, blood pressure, and breathing are slowed to near normal, nonelevated levels. The woman may be able to converse while in this state, although she generally isn't inclined to do so. There may be slow, rhythmic movements of the arms, legs, and body during Phase I of extended orgasmic response as the waves of pelvic contractions expand to include the upper and lower body.

The woman experiences push-out pelvic muscular responses which originate deep within her pelvic area. These feel like an opening up, bearing down, pressing outward. At first, in Phase I, these push-outs alternate with squeeze-type contractions. In the later Phase II, push-out contractions combine with squeeze-type. This blending of squeezes and push-outs provides spontaneous, continuous rhythmic undulation of the vaginal walls, resulting in stimulation along the entire length of the inserted penis. Little movement is required by either partner.

For men, the buildup of muscular tension throughout the body that is usually released by the climax of ejaculation is released without the ejaculatory climax. There's a switch from the experience of pelvic muscular contractions and tightness to a relaxation of the sex muscles, an opening, a bearing down. The anal sphincter relaxes. The man has no concerns about the imminence of ejaculation. He knows that he could ejaculate if he chose, but has no sense of urgency to do so. His eyes are generally closed, although he may choose to open them for brief periods. Heart rate and blood pressure are near normal levels. The body is relaxed.

For both men and women, there's a sense that each moment feels perfect. There's complete relief from worry, anxiety, guilt, obligation, and doubt. The experience is one that rarely occurs in day-to-day life. Analytical thinking fades. There's profound relaxation with no sense of boredom. You appreciate every moment. Time seems suspended. Thoughts which drift by are positive, even thoughts on subjects that normally would be distressing. Creative thoughts and solutions tend to occur. There's a feeling of confidence in yourself, a sense of tranquillity. There's a change in consciousness which feels like an alteration of brain chemistry (in effect it probably is). There's a deep, fundamental appreciation of one's partner, who's making this experience possible, who cares enough to put so much concentrated, sustained attention on your pleasure. There's a sense of being merged with your partner and integrated with life.

This is ecstasy.

The Exercise

Man Giving, Woman Receiving

The woman assumes a position on her back, completely or partly reclining. The man assumes the same position he used in earlier exercises, between his partner's legs, kneeling or resting on his elbows, or on her left or right side, kneeling or propping himself on his elbows.

Men: Proceed with increasingly direct stimulation to the clitoral area. Using the techniques that you've learned and practiced in previous weeks, stimulate the clitoris directly with finger stroking and then add oral stimulation. The focus of this week's exercise is to locate and stimulate the most sensitive area of the clitoris. With your finger, you'll want to apply extremely short strokes up and down or side to side, movements of perhaps a third of an inch or less. With your tongue, you'll find the tip most effective in locating the smallest area of sensitivity. Small movements back and forth and up and down, or vibrating, will probably be most effective. Take your partner to repeated peaks, just short of orgasmic contractions. When she reaches a peak, pause for five to thirty seconds, then resume stimulating her just as you were before. Don't allow yourself to be swayed by your partner's urging or pleas to crest her to the beginning of orgasm until you've peaked her at least fifteen times.

When you're ready, continue the stimulation or increase its intensity to push her into the beginning of her orgasm. You then switch attention to her inner trigger area and stimulate her internally in the ways you've learned are most effective. Use a pattern of internal stimulation with one or two fingers to encourage maximum push-out vaginal response alternating with light clitoral stimulation when push-out response diminishes or is absent.

The woman becomes aware during this time of sexual thoughts that occur in concert with paced physical stimulation to the clitoris and internal trigger areas. Her fantasies can build initially from relatively slow, provocative teasing or romantic thoughts to more directly sexual images, as her partner provides consistent stimulation. The script in the fantasy scenarios ideally moves at a similar rate and has some match to the physical arousal she is experiencing.

Devote a total of at least thirty minutes with your full attention on stimulating your partner to maximum response.

Woman Giving, Man Receiving

The man assumes his customary position lying on his back or partly reclined. The woman assumes the position between his legs or on either his right or left side that allows her easy two-handed stimulation of his genitals.

Women: Stimulate your partner to full erection manually. The focus of this week's exercise is to develop your skill at stimulating the most sensitive area on the head of the penis, the frenulum. Use the pad of your forefinger or the pad of your thumb to provide a variety of stroking motions, light to heavy. Experiment with the type of stroke and motion that appears to produce the maximum response. Experiment with the smallest oscillation of your finger. How slow a motion is possible? How light a motion?

Switch to oral stimulation. Make sure you're in a comfortable position. Using your tongue, particularly the tip, focus on the target spot of the frenulum and apply the precise rate and pressure that appears to produce the greatest arousal.

Devote a full thirty minutes (more if you wish) to peaking your partner repeatedly, using the most focused stimulation you can devise. You may use your hands to add to his arousal by stimulating the shaft, base, scrotum, and perineal area.

Put it all together now. With maximum mental attention and physical sensitivity, the woman draws her partner to pre-ejaculatory peaks again and again. Each peak climbs a little higher than the previous one, and a little bit closer in time. The man is confident that his partner is giving him her full attention and feels a growing sexual energy defusing throughout his body.

It's time now either to take a detour to add internal prostate stimulation, or to move directly into intercourse.

Internal prostate stimulation (optional). Adding internal prostate stimulation can produce a significant "turbo boost" of arousal for some men. When skillfully combined with manual stimulation of the penis shaft and oral stimulation of the penis head, internal prostate stimulation creates what some have called the ultimate physical pleasure.

Recognize that some men will be uncomfortable with any form of anal insertion. Others may find that pressure on the prostate area feels uncomfortable. This discomfort is much like the initial response of women to inner-trigger-area stimulation. The key to overcoming this resistance is to make sure that insertion takes place and internal prostate pressure is applied only when your partner has been fully engorged and has sustained a hard erection for a long enough period of time. Then follow a very slow, gradual approach to direct prostate stimulation. Some men associate internal anal stimulation negatively with homosexuality; others may simply find the physical stimulation too uncomfortable. Some women may consider this form of activity to be unacceptable to them.

Talk about this exercise with your partner. It's optional; do it only if you both want to.

The exercise. As preparation, the man has recently evacuated his bowel and careful cleansed his anal area. When the man has been fully erect for ten to fifteen minutes, the woman uses a well-lubricated finger with a short nail to stimulate the anal area lightly. If she prefers, she may wear a latex or vinyl glove, also lubricated, which can be disposed of at the end of the exercise (if you aren't using a glove, remember to avoid later inserting this finger into your vagina without washing it first). Women, you can use a tickling approach, gently stimulating with a circular motion, much as you would use to stimulate your clitoris. Observe your partner's response. As the anus relaxes and dilates, which may take a number of minutes, slowly insert your right index finger into the opening, pointing it toward the pubic bone—not straight into the body but curved somewhat forward. The prostate gland is approximately one and one-half inches inside the opening and can be located with a moderately firm pressure toward the man's front. It's walnut-sized, somewhat bumpy, and quite firm compared to the surrounding soft tissue of the rectum. When you've located it, you can apply rhythmic massaging pressure to it. Additionally, you can press the pad of the thumb of same hand up into the external prostate spot, in which case your index finger and thumb will now have the prostate gland more or less surrounded front and back. Using a pincerlike squeezing or milking stroke between thumb and index finger can produce very effective stimulation of this gland.

With your other hand, continue to stimulate the shaft of the penis. Adding stimulation to the head of the penis increases arousal still further. Providing oral stimulation at the same time may provide the woman the greatest possible control of her partner's arousal and can potentially produce the maximum sexual stimulation possible for a man.

Peak your partner several times, but try to avoid ejaculation, since you'll be proceeding next to intercourse. Let your partner's verbal and nonverbal responses guide you to effective stroke pressure, location, and rhythm.

EXERCISE FOUR: INTERCOURSE

Rationale

Extending the orgasmic response is easiest to learn during manual and/ or oral stimulation when partners adopt roles as giver and receiver. This week, though, you'll be experimenting with extending your orgasmic response during intercourse. Although it's potentially easier for women, men can also learn to do so.

For a man to have the possibility of extending his orgasmic response in intercourse, the woman usually needs to be experiencing the vaginal push-outs and squeeze contractions of continuous orgasmic response herself. Only at such a time is she likely to have sufficient sensitivity to provide the subtle variations in stimulation to the penis and to have sufficient patience to allow the man to extend his orgasm. Recognize that experiencing extended orgasmic response by both partners during intercourse is a challenge that relatively few couples, even those who are adventurous and dedicated practitioners, will achieve. We discuss it here so that you will know that it's possible.

The Exercise

Move directly from the woman-giving, man-receiving position of the previous exercise to your initial intercourse position with as little pause as possible. Adopt a position that you've found to be the most comfortable and advantageous in producing the most effective stimulation for the woman (discuss in advance which this will be). Take as much time as necessary, using the most effective stroke, rate, and pattern to allow the woman to experience an orgasm. The man should not allow himself to ejaculate. If the woman doesn't generally have an orgasm by intercourse alone in any position, we suggest that you conclude after about ten minutes of intercourse by moving to ejaculation with intercourse, thrusting as vigorously as you're comfortable with. If orgasm is a usual part of intercourse, continue in your preferred position until the woman begins to have an orgasm. We suggest you then change to the scissors position.

Usually the man will have been peaked a number of times by now. At this stage he'll probably require only fairly slow, subtle movements to bring him to further peaks. If the woman is having push-out vaginal responses by penis thrusting, she probably won't require a great deal of stimulation to sustain her push-outs. She probably feels quite satisfied and feels she has the choice of either concluding the sexual interaction or continuing. In choosing to continue, she's able to modulate her movements to provide the man with enough stimulation to bring him to repeated additional peaks, but without the self-focused drive that is often characteristic of the woman's push to reach the beginning of orgasm. In other words, she's able to give the man enough of her attention to continue to peak him, bringing him increasingly close to extended emission-phase orgasm, while continuing her own continuous push-out orgasmic response.

The scissors position is well suited to allowing the man to increase or decrease his level of stimulation with minimal effort in order to assist his moving over into the extended orgasmic phase.

This balance takes considerable skill and practice to achieve, so don't be in any way discouraged if you find that you're not experiencing a simultaneous extended orgasmic process, even at this late phase of the Ecstasy Program. But don't give up or become discouraged. If you're committed to improving your communication within your sexual relationship and your relationship as a whole, this experience may well be possible at a later time in your relationship. Don't give up; have fun, and keep practicing! With experience, lovemaking with extended orgasm becomes like dancing, two people moving together without having to think about the steps, sensitive to the music, the rhythms, and their pleasure in each other. We set no time limits on this part of the exercise—you're on your own.

EXERCISE FIVE: SIGN COMPLETION AGREEMENT

EXERCISE COMPLETION AGREEMENT/ WEEK TWELVE

PARTNER EXERCISES   **Initials**

1. Discussed resistances prior to each exercise.   _____ _____
2. Did Exercise Planning Agreement.   _____ _____
3. Did sexual Appreciations and Resentments
   twice.   _____ _____
4. Did Learning to Extend Orgasmic Response,
   with Intercourse, twice.   _____ _____

SOLO EXERCISES

1. Did 20–0 Countdown at least twice a day.   _____ _____
2. Did Sex Muscle and Breathing Exercise daily.   _____ _____

I have accomplished the Solo Exercises described above. My partner and I have accomplished the Partner Exercises described above to our reasonable satisfaction.

If there has been or will be any change in the program as assigned, we have both talked about those changes and agreed upon them together.

_____   _____
Signature and Date   *Signature and Date*

IX

BEYOND ECSTASY

We hope you've learned a good deal about your partner, yourself, and your relationship by following the Ecstasy Program. If these changes are to become permanent and your relationship is to continue to grow, you will need to incorporate some ongoing agreements into your daily life.

Relationships that aren't growing and evolving are usually deteriorating. It's essential that you develop reliable ways to deal with life's inevitable pressures and demands. Couples who have regular, frequent, and mutually satisfying sexual interactions find they have more enthusiasm and energy in other areas of their lives as well. They appear to enjoy improved physical health, greater creativity, and general life satisfaction. Men may notice a direct correlation between the irritation, impatience, and discontent of their partners and a lack of regular, satisfying sexual interactions. The woman, whose testosterone level is considerably lower than a man's, experiences a slow buildup of unreleased sexual tension that she or her partner may not consciously notice. A satisfying sexual interaction fulfills a woman's symbolic needs for her partner's undivided positive attention. On the other hand, for a man, whose testosterone level is fifteen times higher or more, the buildup of sexual tension is more obvious and conscious and can usually be quickly and more directly released by partner stimulation, self-stimulation, or nocturnal emission.

Each time you successfully deal with your separate needs and problems as a couple, your relationship gains strength. You develop trust, self-confidence, and mutual confidence in your ability to deal with future problems as well.

As you did during the Ecstasy Program, we recommend that you establish an important safety net of deliberateness to allow you to enjoy in turn the fun and freedom of spontaneity. You'll need deliberate agreements to ensure healthy, satisfying interactions even if other parts of your life become excessively demanding, pressured, or complicated.

We understand that being deliberate, making agreements, adhering to a structure, and keeping a schedule may be disciplines which you resist and would prefer to put off. They're essential, however, to protect your relationship from deterioration. Planting the seeds of deliberateness allows the flowering of spontaneity.

Remember, the more you're both happy and satisfied with your lives and relationship at any time, the less need you have for structure and the more spontaneity is possible.

We hope you've learned much more than you knew before about processes that work well for you and your partner as a result of following the Ecstasy Program. We hope you've also learned what doesn't work well for you. If you have, you'll be able to discuss more openly, logically, objectively, and unemotionally the roles you play as giver and receiver. It's useful to agree, and continuously reaffirm, who initiates and who is responsible at defined times in the areas of affection, intimacy, romance, and sexuality. It's best to share the role of initiator equally over the long haul rather than allow either partner to dominate.

We suggest that you regularly practice spontaneous Appreciations and Resentments whenever problems or differences come up in your day-to-day living. Also continue two complete rounds of planned Appreciations and Resentments, one during the week (perhaps in the evening) and one on the weekend. Following this structure reliably can be like having a therapist in your relationship.

The Communication Exercise offers a safe haven from which to communicate to your partner your problems, feelings, or concerns without escalating the discussion into an argument. Taking the time to put your feelings into words can allow your partner to hear your message without feeling he/she is being lectured to, yelled at, or simply ignored, helping to prevent the discussion from deteriorating into argument. It also protects you from becoming self-righteous.

We also strongly recommend that you both decide, deliberately, how frequently each week you want to interact sexually. Then compromise fairly on a schedule that is somewhere between your different preferences and follow it faithfully in letter and spirit.

Based on our experiences of personally counseling several thousand couples, we suggest that you consider interacting sexually a minimum of two times a week, ideally four. This number includes one or two longer interactions of one to one and a half hours' duration on your days off together to incorporate time for romance, affection, sensuality, and sexuality, and one or two fifteen-minute brief sexual interactions. If your agreed frequency involves making love two or three times a week, we suggest one longer session and one or two brief sexual interactions. If you make love four times a week, we recommend two longer and two shorter sessions.

A structure for these longer interactions might be:

1. Man is giver; woman is receiver. Man stimulates woman to orgasm (if she is orgasmic) for twenty to thirty minutes or more. Man uses any combination of manual or oral techniques he wishes, creatively and spontaneously, to bring his partner maximum pleasure.
2. Woman is giver; man is receiver. Woman stimulates the man for twenty to thirty minutes or more. Woman uses any combination of manual and oral techniques she wishes that bring her partner maximum pleasure. Unless the man is easily multi-ejaculatory, this process will probably not include ejaculation if the couple proceeds to intercourse.
3. Intercourse for five minutes or more.

The other two weekly interactions might be briefer. These are more convenient on workdays, when time is limited—before going to work or in the evening. Because there's less time during the week to redirect thoughts from outside matters to sensuality, thought control and thought changing are important. This is especially true for women, who are often less practiced than men at quick sexual focus. A woman should tell herself to change her thoughts away from worries and concerns and put aside resistances by deliberately focusing on sexual thoughts or fantasy.

A sequence for a twelve- to fifteen-minute brief sexual interaction might be:

1. Woman is giver, stimulating the man to erection but not ejaculation (five minutes). Simultaneous, mutual stimulation is an alternative.
2. Man is giver, woman receiver. He stimulates her manually and/or orally to orgasm (five minutes). Woman may have an orgasm with manual or oral stimulation or couple may switch to intercourse when her orgasm is near.
3. When the man inserts his penis, the woman can voluntarily push out and bear down to assist herself with orgasm. Manual as well as penile stimulation during intercourse may be used if desired (two

to five minutes). If the woman generally doesn't have orgasm with intercourse, she may wish to have her orgasm before intercourse, when her partner is stimulating her. Sometimes the woman can feel more intensity more quickly in the woman-above or rear-entry position, since she can tilt her pelvis for maximum inner-trigger-area stimulation in those positions.

Enjoy spontaneous interactions as well—as often as you both wish.

We recommend that couples work out an agreement and a schedule that allow these one or two extended and one or two briefer interactions every week, with an explicit understanding that there may be weeks when unusual circumstances allow fewer interactions or more interactions.

We strongly recommend making an agreement to have a minimum of two interactions except for those occasional times when severe pressures such as illness or crisis interfere, when you may want to agree temporarily to reduce frequency further. When you change a sexual frequency you've previously agreed on, please acknowledge that fact and talk about the change. Please keep your time agreements as well.

Elderly couples, or couples where one or both partners have a debilitating illness, may prefer a lesser frequency, perhaps one or two times per week. Discuss scheduling and come to clear agreement. Time is likely to be less pressing for couples in these circumstances, so each of these interactions can be more extended—lasting for an hour or more. These longer interactions allow for the more leisurely buildup of stimulation.

If both you and your partner are fortunate enough to be relatively unpressured by time schedules and both have the desire to do so, we enthusiastically recommend one or more sexual interactions per day.

One reason relationships gradually deteriorate is that partners allow themselves to focus more on other interests—jobs, raising children, housekeeping, television, sports, or exercise—than on each other. That's why it's important to plan regular overnights away from home without children or friends, the two of you alone as you probably were at the beginning of your courtship. We suggest you plan such a romantic escape at least once every three months. Once a month would be even better. Budget at least twenty-four hours, perhaps from a Saturday afternoon to a Sunday afternoon. You'll need at least that much time to slow down and focus exclusively on each other.

BUSINESS MEETINGS

We discussed business meetings in Chapter Three, beginning on page 41. They're extremely important to maintaining the quality of a relationship. We recommend holding one at least once a month. Agree who will initiate arranging them and preparing a brief agenda. Alternate being the initiator. Meet privately, without children, and at a time when you can devote at least thirty minutes to an hour to discussion. If you get into difficulty during the meeting, use the spontaneous Communication Exercise process to assist. Review those guidelines on page 53.

EVALUATING THE PROGRESS OF YOUR RELATIONSHIP

As therapists we've guided thousands of couples to enhanced sexual relationships with the Ecstasy Program. We've seen the degrees of enhancement people actually experience. One way to decide how far you've come, compared to where you started, is to complete the form "Evaluate Your Satisfaction with Your Relationship," which we reproduced on page 129. Fill it out separately and discuss your responses with each other. Compare it with your initial evaluation. It seems to us that whatever improvement you've made should be cause for celebration. You've succeeded if any part of your sexual and emotional relationship is better.

You've succeeded if you've completed the Ecstasy Program to your own satisfaction. If you are having more romance, if you take more time for sex or have learned to be more deliberate about arranging sexual time, if you've changed your sexual pattern for the better in any way, you've succeeded. If a woman was nonorgasmic when she began and she's now able to have orgasms in certain circumstances, or if she was averaging one orgasm per sexual encounter and now sometimes has two, these are big improvements. If a man experienced only ejaculatory orgasm before and now has learned to enjoy more extended emission-phase orgasm, he's likely to be happy with the change. If your orgasms formerly lasted ten seconds and they're now averaging fifteen seconds, that's 50 percent more pleasure than you enjoyed before. If a man enjoys staying erect longer or finds he has more control over his ejaculation or timing, he's expanded his sexual options. If a couple has found they can talk more openly about their feelings without necessarily escalating into arguments, if a couple has discovered the additional freedom of deliberately planning sexual encounters, the program has been a success. If both partners are enjoying extended orgasm regularly, that's an ultimate benefit of the Ecstasy Program.

ECSTASY, HEALTH, AND AGING

The beneficial health effects of regular exercise are well documented. Exercise restores the balanced functioning of many different bodily systems. Regular sexual interaction, especially incorporating extended orgasmic response, appears to be at least as effective in improving and maintaining general health as regular exercise. That shouldn't be surprising, since the sexual response system is linked to many different bodily systems, including the nervous system, the circulatory system, the musculature, the system of hormone production, and the gastrointestinal system. Sexual responsiveness is an intrinsically natural, healthy function. Extended orgasmic response in particular reaches into the depths of emotional life as exercise alone can never do. That gives it far more influence on health and happiness. Regular sexual interaction is the safest, the most powerful, and certainly the most pleasurable preventive medicine we know.

Age is no barrier to sex, nor to extended sexual response. None of us uses more than a small fraction of his sexual potential. By learning to use more, men and women of any age can increase their response, often beyond the levels they achieved when they were younger.

One of the most charming letters we received after we published ESO came from a man in his seventies who extolled the virtues of extended sexual response. He and "the wife" already knew most of the techniques we described, he claimed, but they were happy to hear about prostate stimulation. He passed along an experience we hadn't mentioned. There were few pleasures as great, he informed us, as the pleasure his wife gave him stimulating him orally after she removed her false teeth!

We've seen many couples and individuals who have increased their sexual abilities to high levels, more than compensating for their natural decline with aging. The sex-muscle exercises are crucial to that increase.

The first and most important requirement is giving sex time and priority in your life.

The best guarantee of a good sex life in your later years is making sure you have a good sex life in your earlier years. But even if your sexual activities have been limited, you can usually improve significantly by following the Ecstasy Program. Every activity and exercise we've discussed here should be available to you regardless of your age. It's good for your health. It's good for life.

CONTINUING ECSTASY PROGRAM TRAINING

If you and your partner would like to continue Ecstasy Program training, either because you haven't achieved what you consider to be a desirable level of sexual experience or because you enjoy and have benefited from the structured approach to lovemaking, you can go back to Week One of the Ecstasy Program and work forward again, repeating the exercises thereafter as often as feels comfortable. Or you may prefer to start at one of the later, more advanced weeks such as Week Seven and proceed sequentially. Alternatively, you may decide to selectively repeat certain weeks or specific exercises, following them thereafter again as often as you wish or feel the need.

Don't forget the possible usefulness of repeating one or more of the exercises described prior to the structured Program Weeks, in Chapter III, IV, and V, such as "Sharing Sexual Information," page 35; "Identifying Priorities," page 37; "Sex by Request," page 39; "The Business of Love," page 41; "The Dumping Exercise," page 59; "Loving Eyes," "Dancing Hands," page 77; "Conversation Time," page 93.

For some couples the Ecstasy Program will take longer than for others. That difference is entirely normal and expected. Your capacity to assimilate the training depends on many factors, including your relative sexual knowledge and experience at the outset, time, stress, and desire levels. What's important is committing yourself to the program. Keeping track of your progress can help provide incentive to follow the program as it's designed.

MAINTAINING SKILLS

To maintain skill at extending orgasmic response after you've completed the Ecstasy Program, continue to plan at least two and preferably four sessions of lovemaking per week. We suggest that you structure one of these sessions informally on the Week Eleven exercises, another on the Week Twelve exercises. The third can be ad lib—freestyle, any way you choose and you both enjoy. Generally, since the exercise-based sessions may take longer, we suggest that you schedule them over the weekend. The freestyle encounter may be a shorter interaction; you'll probably be able to fit it in during the week. This maintenance process can continue indefinitely.

We wish you a happy and healthy intimate relationship. Other than the relationship you have with your inner self, we feel the quality of your intimacy with your "significant other" is most important in determining the quality of your life.

X

SINGLES

If you're single, you're a member of a substantial minority—more than 64 million over the age of eighteen in the United States. Sex is the magnetic force that first attracts singles together for relationships.

If you are single with a regular sex partner, you can follow the standard twelve-week Ecstasy Program. If you live together or can see each other sexually at least three times per week, this program structure should work nicely for you.

If you see each other sexually twice a week or less, you'll probably need to extend the twelve-week program.

You will, of course, need your partner's explicit agreement to participate in the program. Be aware that you're agreeing to work together on a three-to-six-month project. That's a commitment, even if it's not engraved in stone.

Do an Exercise Planning Agreement for each week of assignments. And an Exercise Completion Agreement. You may need approximately two weeks to complete each week of program exercises.

Those singles with partners who wish to practice safer sex may want to modify the Twelve-Week Program to omit the oral sex and intercourse exercises. Couples are frequently surprised at the variety and intensity of sexual arousal and orgasmic experience possible with manual stimulation only. Lust, passion, and ecstacy involve communication, trust, and emotional freedom with a partner. Intercourse is not required.

If you don't currently have a sex partner, we suggest that you still read through the entire book, including the twelve weeks of the Ecstasy Program, so that you know what the full program involves.

Men and women of any age or level of sexual experience can learn to improve their sexual skills and extend and enhance their orgasms. Although extended orgasmic response, defined as orgasm with continuous contractions lasting more than a minute, is more challenging to learn without a dedicated partner, solo singles can usually learn to extend their orgasm time using self-stimulation techniques, doubling or tripling it and increasing its intensity.

SELF-STIMULATION

Rationale

Improving self-stimulation skills and experience will almost certainly improve your sexual responsiveness when you have sex with a partner.

We assume that you already enjoy self-stimulation from time to time and that you don't feel a great deal of guilt about doing so. You've recognized that you're not going to become mentally ill or go blind from pleasuring yourself (unless, as the doctor cautioned in the old joke, you do it while staring into the sun!).

Almost all men and a great majority of women self-stimulate at some stage in their lives. Many practice self-stimulation from adolescence even into their nineties. Some people self-stimulate mostly or only when a partner is unavailable. Others include self-stimulation with other sexual activities. Frequencies vary enormously. Some self-stimulate only rarely. Others do so once or more a day. All medical evidence points to self-stimulation's absolute safety. We and many other experts contend that regular practice of self-stimulation can help maintain or improve mental and physical health.

Despite this information, some people feel so negative about self-stimulation that they are unable to practice it even in private and alone. If your feelings about self-stimulation are so strong that you are depriving yourself of this healthful learning experience and wish to change your viewpoint, you may benefit from a brief course of sexual therapy with a counselor. Ask your physician to refer you, or call your local mental health association for a recommendation.

Self-stimulation, like any other human activity, improves with practice. People generally do activities most frequently that they do well, and therefore tend to get better at them. If you have only one or two orgasms in a week, they're likely to be pleasant, but somewhat routine and unremarkable. If, on the other hand, you have one or two orgasms a day, the muscles you use for sexual arousal have a good workout and grow stronger. Perhaps even more significantly, you train your mind to focus on sensations and increased pleasure. That concentration often carries over to reinforce sexual experiences for several days afterward.

A century ago, a Victorian theory of sexual economics, unsupported by any evidence, argued that human beings are allotted only a limited amount of vitality, which needs to be budgeted and conserved. Ejaculation was labeled "spending," as if one's savings were being spent. Semen in this antiquated theory was claimed to be the most important of a man's "vital fluids" and men were enjoined not to "waste" their seed.

Self-stimulation might be considered excessive if it occupies your time to the exclusion of socially responsible activities such as job, child care or establishing and maintaining an intimate relationship. Such a judgment could apply equally to eating, reading, jogging, or watching soap operas on television. In our experience and in the reports of sexual therapy professionals, problems of obsessive or excessive self-stimulation are rare. If you're considering increasing your self-stimulation time and skills by following the Ecstasy Program, you don't need to worry that you'll become addicted to self-stimulation. At its best, it's not as potentially ecstatic as sex with a partner. Improving your self-stimulation skills isn't going to supplant lovemaking.

As a matter of fact, even people with partners will benefit from this program. The advanced self-stimulation program we'll be outlining here will provide an excellent foundation for the best possible sexual experiences with a partner. (Since the self-stimulation program for singles is more extensive than the four-week program described for couples, some individual partners who are following the Ecstasy Program for couples may want to substitute the singles protocol instead. Beginning on Week Three of the Ecstasy Program, substitute each week of the singles program and follow the singles program to the end.)

We encourage anyone who decides he or she doesn't wish to follow the Ecstasy Program, or whose partner doesn't agree to do so, to follow the singles program.

THE ECSTASY PROGRAM FOR MEN WITHOUT PARTNERS

Men who ejaculate more quickly than they or their partners would prefer will probably learn from self-stimulation how to achieve better control over timing. Men who have difficulty becoming erect will also find that diligently practicing the singles program will probably make erection easier to accomplish and sustain. Finally, following self-stimulation exercises here may allow you to intensify and perhaps extend your orgasm.

As you've learned from reading previous sections of this book, orgasm and ejaculation have been shown to be distinct processes which usually occur more or less simultaneously but can be trained to occur separately. The key to separating these reflex responses is developing the sexual muscles and learning conscious control. Doing so requires strengthening the muscles with exercise, slowing down your self-stimulation rate, and learning to pay closer attention to subtle variations in sensation.

The sensation of fluid moving through the penile urethra at ejaculation adds to the experience of orgasm. But this feeling, though pleasurable, isn't necessarily the most intense sensation involved in the male orgasm. If you faithfully follow the program that we're about to outline, you can learn how to have longer and stronger orgasms without the movement of semen through the urethra. The feelings you'll have in delaying this fluid movement can be even more pleasurable than the sensations of expelling the fluid, and the choice of when to ejaculate will be yours.

You can decide, based on your preference, if you want to work toward having a longer orgasm before you ejaculate. Or you may wish to experience ejaculatory orgasm quickly and vigorously just as you probably do now.

ADVANCED SELF-STIMULATION SKILLS FOR MEN

We discussed basic self-stimulation skills in Week Three of the Ecstasy Program, beginning on page 168. You may want to turn back to that section for review. Here we'll briefly list important skills and techniques we will be suggesting you incorporate before moving on to a week-by-week program. A similar program for women follows the men's program, beginning on page 372.

Lubrication

Since self-stimulation is inherently completely safe in terms of disease transmission or impregnation, rubber products are not necessary (except that you may want to practice for partner sex by incorporating rubber products occasionally into your self-stimulation exercises). You can use any type of lubrication that you wish, including petroleum-based products. We recommend Albolene Unscented Liquefying Cleanser as a sexual lubricant. Albolene is one of the longest-lasting, most comfortable, reasonably priced lubricants available.

Stimulation Methods

1. Stimulating the head of the penis rapidly (up to three strokes per second) with the hand
2. Stimulating the shaft of the penis rapidly (up to three strokes per second) with the hand
3. Stimulating the head and shaft of the penis slowly (one-half to one stroke per second) with the hand
4. Stroking the scrotum and the perineal area behind the scrotum
5. Pressing and pumping the penis base, behind the scrotum, with the hand
6. Stimulating the external prostate spot. Firm, rhythmic pressure on the external prostate spot while sustaining erection can assist with extending emission-phase orgasm.
7. Stroking the anal area
8. Using a vibrator
9. Using graphic materials: photographs, video tapes, erotic reading
10. Using fantasy and visualization for arousal and to assist in transferring self-stimulation skills to partner sex
11. Using a condom to provide alternative sensations and to train for using a condom with partner sex

Methods of Controlling Arousal and Ejaculation

20–0 Countdown. See our discussion of this useful mental concentration technique beginning on page 138.

Sex Muscle Exercises. We strongly advise all our clients to develop their sexual muscles. We discuss how to identify them, and how to exercise them beginning on page 141.

Deep Breathing. Many people hold their breath during orgasm. Conversely, deliberate deep breathing helps to delay ejaculation by diffusing the arousal feelings throughout the body.

Pressure on the External Prostate Spot. The prostate gland contracts during the emission phase of orgasm when it secretes fluid. Prostate fluid enters the urethra at the base of the penis. Firm upward pressure at the base of the penis with the index and/or third finger can help control the ejaculation reflex. When a man has been fully engorged and erect for at least several minutes, such pressure is often felt subjectively as highly pleasurable. Since it's a different form of stimulation, however, such pressure usually distracts from and does not contribute toward the reflex to ejaculate. Regular, firm rhythmic stimulation of the external prostate spot after several minutes of full engorgement will often increase arousal and help extend emission-phase orgasm. (See Stimulation Methods, above.)

Scrotal Pull. Pulling your scrotum away from your body can help to prevent ejaculation. To apply the scrotal pull, grasp your scrotum between the testicles with the thumb and forefinger of your left hand (or make a ring with your thumb and forefinger between your testicles and body). When you're near orgasm, pull firmly and steadily down on the scrotum. At other times, for stimulation, pull lightly in rhythm as you stroke your penis. Become thoroughly familiar with the scrotal pull. Then you'll be prepared when you have an opportunity to teach it to a partner.

Squeeze Technique. This technique of ejaculation control has long been used by therapists. Place your first two fingers on the underside of your penis just below the head. Clamp your thumb on the other side. Then give a firm, strong squeeze. When squeezed with a full erection, the penis may expand a little, lose some firmness, or go completely limp. Whichever happens is fine. Continue firm pressure for a few seconds and then restart stimulation. Use the squeeze technique as often as necessary to help prevent ejaculation. As you gain confidence you'll be able to get closer to ejaculatory inevitability before you squeeze.

Testicle Elevation. We said earlier that the scrotum usually contracts up against the body just prior to and during ejaculation, and that ejaculation can be delayed by limiting this elevation. Cocking a pistol is a good analogy. The pistol won't go off unless the hammer is pulled back. If you can learn how to raise and lower your scrotum voluntarily, you can gain control over this important automatic function. That control may also help increase your erection strength and degree of arousal.

Deliberately elevating the scrotum may seem difficult at first. It takes time to learn to identify the specific muscles involved. Initially, you'll tighten all the lower abdominal muscles to raise your scrotum. Later, with practice, you'll be able to raise it using only the appropriate pelvic muscles without tensing the abdominal muscles at all. It's also difficult at first to feel the scrotum moving up and down. Use a mirror to help you see what's happening. Even better, ring your scrotum above your testicles with thumb and middle finger and gently pull down. Then you'll be able to feel a slight movement of your testicles when you correctly contract and relax the internal muscles that control elevation.

Once you locate the right muscles, practice raising and lowering your scrotum at first just a few times in succession, increasing until you can do so up to one hundred times in succession. Practice this exercise either sitting at the edge of a chair or standing with your feet spaced about eighteen inches apart. Elevate your scrotum both with and without an erection, while you are stimulating yourself, and, if and when you have one, while you are being stimulated by your partner.

Relaxing Pelvic Muscles. During sexual arousal and orgasm, there's usually a tendency to tighten muscles in the pelvic area, including the buttocks, the thigh muscles, the muscles around the anus, and also the P.C. muscles. By noticing this tendency to contract and countering it by consciously relaxing the muscles, you can gain some additional measure of control over the urge to ejaculate.

WEEK-BY-WEEK ASSIGNMENTS FOR MEN

Week One

Monitoring and Tracking Your Sexual Response

During the first week we'd like you simply to observe and time certain aspects of your sexual response. If you want to control and enhance response, it's useful to measure it first. To learn any skill it's essential to get feedback about how you're doing. With that information, you can correct and make changes. It will also motivate you to improve.

Follow this procedure on three separate occasions during the week:

Arrange your environment as you usually do when you self-stimulate. Whatever time and pattern you usually follow in self-stimulating, continue to use it during this first week. But observe the timing of what you do. Arrange to have a clock or your watch in easy view and keep a notepad and pen or pencil handy.

Stimulate yourself in your usual and customary manner. At this time, don't try anything that isn't part of your usual routine.

Observe and record the following on the "Pre-program" lines:

MONITORING YOUR SEXUAL RESPONSE: MAN

	Day 1		Day 2		Day 3	
	Pre-program	*Post-program*	*Pre-program*	*Post-program*	*Pre-program*	*Post-program*
Minutes to achieve full erection						
Minutes of sustained erection						
Seconds between emission-phase orgasm and point of no return						
Number of seconds of ejaculation						
Number of ejaculatory contractions						
Total minutes spent in self-stimulation						

When noting contractions, count them all, not only those associated with fluid expulsion.

If you normally stimulate yourself to another ejaculation, record the same information for the second session.

You will be recording the same information again after you complete the program, in the "post-program" column.

Week Two

1. 20–0 Countdown Exercise (twice per day). (To review this exercise, see page 138.)

2. Sex Muscle and Breathing Exercise. (To review this exercise, see page 141.) Suggested starting numbers: 30 flutter-squeeze contractions at 1 per second; 30 flutter push-outs; 10 slow clench inhale/relax exhales as you inhale; relax the sex muscles as you exhale. Do 2 sets of these per day.

3. Self-Stimulation (30 minutes minimum, 3 times this week). Arrange a private time and place where you won't be interrupted. Pay attention to lighting, room temperature, music that you enjoy.

Undressed, lie down on your back, preferably on a bed, and make yourself comfortable. Relax. Allow your knees to bend and separate. Slowly and gently stroke your inner thighs, then up your torso to your nipples (50 percent of men enjoy nipple stimulation). Caress your penis and scrotum.

Stroke your penis from head to base with gentle, slow, light stroking. Use moderate pressure equivalent to that of vaginal pressure. Since you're training yourself for intercourse, generally avoid hard pressure. Duplicate a level of pressure approximating the feeling of the vagina around your penis.

Continue your slow, up-and-down stroking until you achieve full erection. If you don't achieve full erection in about five to ten minutes, increase the rate of stimulation, concentrating on the head of your penis. Do whatever is necessary—physical stimulation or mental focus—to get fully erect. Most men can get themselves erect if they're aggressive enough and sufficiently determined to do so. If you have continued difficulty doing so, consult the section entitled "Male Problems" in the Appendix beginning on page 390. You can usually achieve maximum stimulation at a rate of three or four strokes per second concentrated on the head of the penis.

Once you get a full erection, slow down your stroke rate. Maintain your erection for a full twenty minutes. Its fullness and firmness may wax and wane. When you feel yourself close to ejaculation, use the stop-start or squeeze technique to reduce arousal. Alternate use of the stop-start or squeeze technique with changing the tension of your P.C. muscles. If your P.C. muscles are contracted and tight, quickly relax them or push out. You'll notice a drop in your arousal. Alternatively, if you're aware as you near ejaculation that your P.C. muscles are relaxed, a quick, hard, firm contraction may help block further arousal. Use the stop-start or squeeze technique or the change in P.C.-muscle tension whenever you get near ejaculation. Continue slow, regular stimulation of your penis while you're performing the stop-start or squeeze or the P.C.-muscle change. Don't be concerned if your erection decreases. Use the scrotal pull technique to help control the ejaculatory urge.

After thirty minutes of stimulation, allow yourself to ejaculate. At the same time, practice trying to hold in the ejaculate by clenching your P.C. muscles as tightly as you can while holding your breath. Count the number of expulsion contractions and record that number on the chart. Observe the amount of ejaculate and the force with which it is expelled. Does the amount seem to be more, the same as, or less than usual? Is the distance of expulsion more, the same as, or less than usual?

Week Three

1. 20–0 Countdown Exercise (2 times per day).

2. Sex Muscle and Breathing Exercise. Increase the number of sets by 10 percent from last week. This means that if you started at the basic 30 repetitions last week, this week do 35 flutter contractions at 1 per second; do 11 slow clench inhale/relax exhales. Do 2 sets of these groups every day.

3. Exploring your genitals. Even though you've carried your genitals around with you all your life, it's possible that you've never really examined them slowly and carefully. Doing so now will be a distinct help in improving your sexual response. Closely examine your penis and testicles while they're in an unaroused and relaxed state. Cup your testicles in your hand, lifting them and weighing them to see if you can feel the cords connecting them to your penis. Notice the smooth texture of your scrotum and the feeling of the skin of your penis. Touch the entire area lightly with your fingertips. Pull, squeeze, stroke, massage your genitals lightly and then more heavily, using quick strokes and then slow strokes. Notice what feels good. Pay close attention to all that you feel. This

attention may result in erection or it may not. Erection isn't important up to this point.

Now stimulate your penis slowly to erection. Observe the changes that take place as your penis becomes erect. Cup your testicles again in your hand. Are they bigger than before? Notice the texture of the scrotal skin and how it thickens and puckers. Is it more sensitive to touch than before? Tickle the surface lightly to see if your testicles react.

Keep yourself stimulated to full erection. Use fantasy, thinking sexual thoughts, remembering an earlier sexual encounter or imagining a new one. Use erotic photographs or sexual reading material if you wish. Do whatever is necessary to keep yourself erect. Remember, it's up to you to keep yourself erect.

Now explore your pelvic area again, with your mind as well as with your eyes and hands. Then close your eyes and take inventory entirely by touch. Focus on the sensation. Explore each area in turn, including around your anus. Keep a full erection by providing enough stimulation to your penis, but don't let yourself ejaculate.

Keeping yourself erect, change positions and observe what happens to your penis and to your testicles. Stand up and observe yourself; lie down on your back; kneel on all fours; lie on your stomach; pull your knees under you so your buttocks are up in the air. Observe and feel your genitals.

If you start to lose your erection, stop looking at yourself, close your eyes, and picture your penis becoming hard and erect. In whatever position you find yourself, stimulate your penis with your hand intensely enough to get erect again.

Get in your most comfortable long-term position. This may be lying on your back, sitting, or kneeling. Add a lubricant. Notice how it changes your sensation. If you're uncircumcised, you may not have been using lubrication in the past as a matter of habit. If you're circumcised, it's likely that you've used lubrication in the past. Choose a stroke that stimulates the head and shaft of your penis sufficiently to maintain a full erection, but not so much that you approach ejaculation. If you do get closer than you intend, use the squeeze technique or the scrotal pull and quickly relax your P.C. muscles. After a total of about thirty minutes of erection, deliberately allow yourself gently to crest into ejaculation.

Continue to stimulate your penis as you pay close attention to each moment and each contraction. Count the number of seconds of these highly pleasurable sensations. Stretch out the time in your mind, imagining the experience will continue as long as you want.

Clench your P.C. muscles as tightly as you can, trying to hold in the fluid. Of course, some fluid will come out. The more often you practice doing this exercise and the more faithfully you practice doing the P.C.-muscle exercises daily, the more you may be able to hold in increasing amounts of ejaculate. Retaining ejaculate in this way is an entirely safe process and will allow you to increase the possibility of having a second ejaculatory orgasm soon after the first.

Week Four

1. 20–0 Countdown Exercise (2 times per day).

2. Sex Muscle and Breathing Exercise. Increase the repetitions of flutters and of slow clenches with breathing each by 10 percent. Do 2 sets of these groups per day.

3. Self-Stimulation (30 minutes minimum, 3 times this week). Stimulate yourself to erection as quickly as you can. Use lubrication; use a rapid stroke concentrating on the head of your penis. Notice how long it takes for you to get a full erection.

Observe the effect of consciously relaxing your P.C. muscles while you slowly stroke both the head and shaft of your penis. Find a regular stroke, rhythm, and rate and allow your sexual muscles to relax completely. Observe what you feel and what happens to your erection.

Tighten your P.C. muscles while you continue the same rate of stimulation. What happens now to the level of your arousal and to the hardness of your erection? Does your arousal increase, remain the same, or decrease?

Now increase the rate and intensity of your stimulation. Practice keeping your sex muscles clenched continuously as you breathe in and out. Observe what happens to your level of arousal and to your erection. Does your arousal increase? Does your erection get harder and firmer?

Observe what happens when you keep your P.C. muscles relaxed as you continue regular stimulation on the penis head and shaft. Does your arousal increase or decrease; does your erection increase or decrease? Take yourself to a peak near ejaculation several times.

With a firm erection, try stimulating your external prostate spot with one or two fingers pressing firmly up and in. Use your free hand. If you're right-handed, continue stimulation of your penis with your right hand and press up on your internal prostate spot with your left hand. Notice what happens to your level of arousal and the firmness of your erection. Peak yourself several times.

Using the stop-start method of ejaculation control, bring yourself to a peak, near the point of ejaculatory inevitability, stop all stimulation for a few seconds, then resume stimulation. Repeat this stopping and starting several times.

Using the frenulum-squeeze method of ejaculation control: Stimulate yourself to a peak and give a good hard squeeze with your index and middle finger to the frenulum area on the head of the penis. Squeeze this area very firmly whenever you feel that you are getting within three strokes of the point of reaching ejaculatory inevitability. When you can go for fifteen minutes or more fully erect while continuously stimulating your penis head and shaft, then you can allow yourself to approach even more closely than three strokes to the point of ejaculatory inevitability.

Extending Emission Point. Practice allowing yourself to approach closer to that point of no return before you stop or do a frenulum squeeze. You may find that you wait too long, perhaps only by half a second or so. Your goal is to stop yourself from ejaculating, but not from experiencing an orgasm. With practice, and probably not the first few times, nor this week, it's possible to get the timing right so that you slip into the point of no return but do not ejaculate as quickly afterward. If the emission "point" becomes extended to a minute or more rather than the usual several seconds, it can be termed an emission phase of orgasmic response. Notice and observe this timing.

When you do ejaculate, practice, this week, stopping all stimulation while you strongly clench your P.C. muscles trying to hold in the fluid. Count the number of contractions that you experience and make a note of it.

Second-Ejaculation Exercise. This week, after you've begun having your ejaculation contractions, start to stimulate your penis again before the last contraction dies down. Keep your attention fully focused on the experience of the contractions. If you find yourself thinking, "This is the end, I'm through, I've had enough stimulation, I've had my orgasm and that's the end," tell yourself instead, "Let's see if I can have another orgasm."

With your attention focused on the sensation of your internal contractions, find the rate, pressure, and stimulation of your penis that keep those contractions going. It may be that your penis is sensitive and responds best to slow, gentle, continued stroking. It may be that you need more intense, vigorous stimulation, especially at the head of the penis, to overcome a natural tendency to have a refractory period. Keep the stimulation at an intense level to stretch the number of contractions as long as possible. You may be surprised to discover that you can have more contractions than you expected. If you keep the stimulation vigorous enough and keep your attention focused on the pleasurable feelings, you'll probably find that you can have a second ejaculation. This second ejaculation may not happen the first or second time you try it. If you're sufficiently determined, it's quite possible that you'll find you can have a second ejaculatory experience, particularly if you've held in fluid from the first ejaculation.

Know that a second ejaculation is possible and allow yourself to be patient and determined. It may take a number of weeks of practice.

Week Five

1. 20–0 Countdown Exercise (2 times per day).

2. Sex Muscle and Breathing Exercise. Increase number of repetitions by another 10 percent.

3. Self-Stimulation (30 minutes minimum, 3 times this week). This week incorporates the Walkabout Exercise, which is designed to help you learn to maintain and also to reestablish your erection while you're moving from one position to another, as in intercourse. It can help increase your erection self-confidence.

Slowly stimulate yourself to erection using lubrication and fantasy or visual material if those are helpful to you. Once you get erect, practice alternating erection control with your mind and your hand. Your hand will want to speed up, because the stimulation feels better the closer you get to ejaculation. Use the ability of your mind to focus your attention to put on the brakes; use your sex muscles, relaxing and pushing out, to help. To speed up, increase the rate and pressure of the stimulation your hand is supplying and add in sexual fantasy.

Create "coasting" times when you're neither climbing nor dropping in arousal by reducing these forms of stimulation. During these coasting times, pay close attention to the subtle changes in your sex-muscle activity, your breathing, how close you are to ejaculation. Seek to establish a comfortable stimulation pattern that allows you to experience multiple peaks confidently without ejaculation, at the same time maintaining a relatively reliable erection with a minimum of effort. Try to get to and remain in this balanced, low-effort state for at least fifteen minutes.

Walkabout Exercise. After about fifteen minutes, stand up and continue to self-stimulate. Continuing to self-stimulate, take a few steps. If your arousal level starts to decrease or you start to lose your erection, stop where you are, sit down or kneel, and stimulate the head of your penis rapidly and intensely while imagining a stimulating fantasy or referring to your visual materials. Once you return to firm, secure erection, start to walk around again. Practice moving around within the same room, sitting in a different chair, kneeling on the floor, turning on the TV, changing a cassette, radio station, or record, and walking into the bathroom or into another room if privacy permits. If your erection starts to decrease again, follow the same procedure, rapidly restimulating yourself to regain it.

Now stop all stimulation and start walking around, or doing another activity, deliberately allowing your erection to subside. When it does, return to a comfortable self-stimulation position and resume stimulation of the head and shaft of your penis, adding lubrication if necessary, to get yourself erect again. Deliberately hold your P.C. muscles clenched as you stimulate yourself. When you have reestablished erection, move around, lose, and redevelop your erection again, at least three times.

Assuming a comfortable self-stimulation position, eyes open or closed (whichever is better for concentrating), peak yourself several times.

Then as gradually as you can, over a period of two or three minutes, increase your arousal level to crest yourself gently into emission phase. Keep your sex muscles relaxed by concentrating your attention on relaxing and opening your anal sphincter. Sometimes it's helpful to place your left hand over the outside of the anal opening for extra feedback to your brain about whether your sex muscles are starting to clench as you use your right hand to stimulate yourself into emission-phase contractions. Keep your sex muscles relaxed, with your anal area open, throughout your emission.

When your ejaculation starts, try to keep your sex muscles relaxed the entire time. That may require some extra concentration, since the reflex is usually to clench. But it may give you a different experience and is a part of training to extend the number and time of expulsion contractions.

Week Six

1. 20–0 Countdown Exercise (2 times per day).

2. Sex Muscle and Breathing Exercise. Increase repetitions by 10 percent. Do inhale/slow clenches. Do 2 sets of these groups each day.

3. Self-Stimulation (minimum 30 minutes, 3 times this week).

Stimulate yourself to erection. This week we suggest obtaining and using a plug-in vibrator of the hand-held, two-speed massager type, which are readily available in department stores and many larger drugstores. They may also be obtained by mail order. (Consult the Sources section in the Appendix.)

Use the vibrator to keep yourself fully erect, stopping stimulation at least five seconds before the onset of ejaculation. It may take some practice getting used to this novel form of stimulation. Experiment with the high and low speeds. Hold the vibrator relatively steady. Continuously hold a clench contraction and notice the effect on your level of arousal. Then, while continuing to keep vibrator intensity constant, relax your sex muscles. Repeat this alternating clench-and-relax process several times in a ten-minute period. Compare and note in your mind your rate of climbing, erection firmness, and level of arousal with clenching versus relaxing your sex muscles. Notice also the difference when you push out or bear down while you stimulate your erect penis with the vibrator.

Change the location of stimulation with the vibrator to the perineal area. That is, direct the vibrator to the base of the penis behind the testicles while you stimulate the shaft and head of the penis with your free hand. If you're using a vibrator with interchangeable heads, you'll probably want to use the knob-shaped head rather than the dish-shaped head. Use a lubricant. Close your eyes, focus your attention on your sexual feelings, and breathe slowly and deeply for several consecutive minutes. Then deliberately hold your breath for a number of seconds and compare your relative level of arousal.

Turn off your vibrator and continue stimulating the shaft and head of your penis with a lubricated hand. Continuing that stimulation, apply pumping pressure with your free hand to the base of the penis, regularly and rhythmically pressing and stroking blood from the base of the penis into the shaft. Observe the feeling of increased fullness, pressure, and hardness of your penis as you do so. Very slowly and gradually sneak up to the point of ejaculatory inevitability. Take at least five minutes carefully, gradually edging toward this point. Try to keep your P.C. muscles relaxed and open.

Now apply the squeeze technique to the head of the penis. Apply the squeeze just half a second prior to the moment you anticipate will be the point of no return. If you get your timing precisely correct, you may be able to have a dry ejaculation. That is to say, you have the experience of starting and entering the ejaculation phase of orgasm, but with relatively little fluid expelled. This helps improve your chances of experiencing more than one ejaculation with a minimum refractory period.

At the time that you slip into the ejaculation phase, deliberately relax your P.C. muscles, breathe rhythmically in and out, and bear down on your P.C. muscles to observe the experience. Notice the difference between deliberately holding in, squeezing, and contracting your P.C. muscles, compared to relaxing, opening up, pushing out, and bearing down on your P.C.'s. Count and record the number of contractions.

Before the last contraction fades, resume more active stimulation. Notice what kind of stimulation appears to work best to stretch out the number of contractions. Increase the rate and pressure of your stimulation to see if you can have another ejaculation. In our experience, a surprising number of men, even older men, can in fact eventually learn to do so, if they're sufficiently motivated and if they practice.

A man who knows he has the ability, if he wants to use it, to have a second ejaculation, is more confident and secure in his sexual interactions. Partners of men who develop this skill are usually appreciative, since the man has the potential for a second round of intercourse.

If you find that you're not able to have a second ejaculation, don't be concerned. Most men are quite content with one at a time.

Week Seven

1. 20–0 Countdown Exercise (2 times per day).

2. Sex Muscle and Breathing Exercise. Increase repetitions by 10 percent. Do 2 sets each day.

3. Erection Exercises. (30 minutes, 3 times this week).

Get yourself reasonably erect. Then, by alternately relaxing and contracting your P.C. muscles, notice which muscles make the penis throb. Observe which muscles and what kind of contractions make the penis move up and down and side to side. It's easiest to observe and practice this exercise sitting on the edge of a chair with your legs spread at about 90 degrees. Also practice while sitting with your knees closer together, and while kneeling, standing, and lying on your back.

When you've established a moderate degree of control, you can try adding some weight to the penis to give the supporting muscles greater work. A progression from dry washcloth to squeezed wet washcloth, to a dry handtowel, then eventually a wet handtowel, are easy ways to drape the penis with increasing resistive weight. Or a smooth bathrobe waist belt tied to the end of the erect penis can serve to suspend suitable objects, such as a small and then larger cushion. Move on to a heavier weight when your erection can lift the weight easily doing your usual number of flutter contractions. You will thus have some measure of your erection strength as it increases. As these supporting muscles get stronger, your erection will get firmer. The firmness results partly from strengthening the muscles at the base of the penis and the supporting muscles and partly from the additional blood supply that these exercises stimulate.

After practicing these penis-movement exercises, practice slow stimulation. Stimulate the penis shaft slowly and subtly. Stroke your testicles and practice light, gentle (teasing) stimulation of your lubricated anal area. This gradual, slow stimulation from front to back allows time for the slow buildup of muscle tension and vascular congestion, which are the prerequisites for exceptionally long and strong orgasms.

Whenever you feel close to the point of no return, stop stimulating until the feeling of urgency passes. Then bring yourself slowly back to the same high level, backing off and restimulating yourself as necessary.

After a full thirty minutes of slow stimulation, reward yourself with an ejaculation while continuing the same slow stimulation. Try to hold in the ejaculate. Your sex muscles will probably be stronger by now and you may be able to retain more of the fluid. The more you retain, the shorter may be your refractory period, and the more likely you'll be to have a second orgasm if you continue stimulation.

Continue the stimulation and see if you can maintain your erection as fully as possible for another few minutes before allowing yourself to have a second ejaculation. Try to stretch that ejaculation as long as possible. Notice how many seconds it seems to last and try to hold it in by strong contractions of your P.C. muscles and holding your breath. Some men may even learn to have a third ejaculation.

As a dedicated advanced sexual self-investigator, discover for yourself what your abilities and limits are, based on your interest, time, and general physical condition.

Week Eight and Beyond

You have now learned the basic elements of advanced sexual self-investigation. We strongly recommend you continue this regular practice. In subsequent weeks, while you are self-stimulating and enjoying remaining fully erect for a half hour at a time, practice closing your eyes and fantasizing sexual experiences with a partner.

Imagine in detail a desired sexual encounter with a partner, starting at the beginning with a kiss and progressing through fondling one another, undressing, caressing your partner's body while she fondles you, touching her breasts, moving your hands to her pubic area, imagining her stroking and sucking on your penis, playing with her buttocks. Enjoy imagining the smell of her freshly washed hair, rubbing your penis on her vaginal lips, inserting your penis in her vagina, and sinking all the way deep into her, pounding, thrusting, feeling her having an orgasm, moving her hips against you, her vagina squeezing you firmly.

Stretch out this fantasy process with self-stimulation over five, ten, fifteen minutes. If you find yourself ejaculating more quickly than you expect, practice rerunning this fantasy and stimulating yourself more slowly. You can also practice doing a squeeze on your penis head, contracting or pushing out your P.C. muscles, breathing, stimulating your external prostate spot, applying a scrotal pull. These control techniques can enable you to extend your time in intercourse when you have sex with a real partner.

For men who have a problem with getting erections, we suggest that you practice rapid self-stimulation. This exercise involves getting yourself erect and stimulating yourself to ejaculation as quickly as possible. Notice how long you take to do so. When you can stimulate yourself to erection and ejaculation in several minutes or less, you'll have gained an important measure of self-confidence.

Learning how to extend your orgasm time as well as how to shorten arousal to orgasm helps you gain control over your erection.

For men who ejaculate too quickly, an additional useful exercise is to stop all stimulation once you are fully erect and near the point of ejaculating and do a 20–0 Countdown. Then resume stimulation. When you're near the point of ejaculating again, stop again and do a 20–0 Countdown. The Countdown will usually take about a minute and a half. Doing it will help you relax and gain more awareness of the sensations in your genital region.

Week Eight is a good time to assess your progress. Turn to the chart in Singles Week One, page 360, and record your times and numbers there.

You may be interested to compare these numbers with those that you recorded in Week One. If they represent more time in erection or orgasm, or number of contractions, that's obviously a clear benefit and bonus. If these numbers remain approximately the same, you will probably at least have found the process of practicing a pleasurable one.

Using condoms. Practice using a condom while you're erect. Experiment with slipping it on and then lubricating it on the outside. Notice the difference in sensation with a condom compared to sensation without one. Many men find that condoms can add variety and additional pleasure to the experience of self-stimulation and with a partner. Rather than a handicap—as in the old complaint that wearing a condom is like taking a shower with a raincoat on—condoms can actually enhance your love-making.

Purchase several different varieties of condoms at a drugstore. They come in different colors and textures and even with some variation in length, diameter, and thickness. Try using a lubricant inside a condom also. The feeling of the latex sliding on the penis can be pleasurable. Obviously, this practice wouldn't be a good idea during intercourse, since it might cause the condom to slip off.

Becoming comfortable with the use of a condom is important in this era of increased risk of sexually transmitted diseases. If you are single, you need to be cautious with partners in your sexual practices. We suggest making it an absolute rule to use a condom with any sexual partner whose sexual history you don't know with certainty and in whom you don't have a high level of trust.

Condom use is an important, proven protective factor in preventing transmission of a variety of diseases, including AIDS. The more comfortable you are about using condoms in your regular sexual practice, the more protected you'll be.

The unfailing use of a condom can save your life. That's why we strongly advise you to learn to find pleasure in condom use.

THE ECSTASY PROGRAM FOR WOMEN WITHOUT PARTNERS

The history of sex is centrally the history of controlling women's sexuality. Historical and anthropological studies of the world's many different cultures supply plentiful evidence to validate this statement. It isn't surprising that a woman who wishes to claim her right to sexual intimacy and pleasure has much unlearning to do. One of the most efficient ways to learn to improve your experience of orgasm is self-stimulation. A woman without a partner, therefore, is still excellently positioned to learn to increase the length and intensity of her orgasms by following a deliberate program of self-stimulation exercises. We offer such a program here, an eight-week agenda of exploration and conditioning that benefits most of those who follow it, from inexperienced beginners to sexual sophisticates.

Week One

1. 20–0 Countdown Exercise (2 times per day). (To review this exercise, see page 138.)

2. Sex Muscle and Breathing Exercise. (To review this exercise, see page 141.) There are three parts to this exercise: (a) Contract your P.C. muscle as if you are stopping the flow of urine; do so 20 times, approximately 1 contraction per second. If 20 repetitions feels difficult, do the maximum you're comfortable with. If you can go beyond 20, do so. Use the number you can do comfortably as your baseline. (b) Next, do 20 push-outs (more or less), bearing down and then relaxing. (c) Finally, do 15 slow clenches; hold each clench while you inhale and then release and relax the same muscles as you exhale. Repeat this exercise 2 times per day. (For a full discussion of how to evaluate the condition of your sex muscles, see page 144.)

3. Monitoring and Tracking Your Sexual Response. During the first week we'd like you simply to observe and time certain aspects of your sexual response. If you want to control and enhance response, it's useful to measure it first. To learn any skill, it's critical to get feedback about how you're doing. With that information, you can correct and make changes. It will also motivate you to improve.

Assuming that you practice some type of self-stimulation from time to time, set up your environment as you normally would and proceed to stimulate yourself in your customary manner. Follow this procedure three different times during the week. Pay attention to your reactions so that you can answer the following questions:

MONITORING YOUR SEXUAL RESPONSE: WOMAN

	Pre-program	Post-program
1. Approximately how many minutes elapsed from the start of stimulation to the beginning of orgasm?	_____	_____
2. Were you aware of having contractions in your pelvic area during the time you were having an orgasm?	_____	_____

	Pre-program	Post-program
3. How many contractions did you experience during orgasm?	_____	_____
4. How many seconds (approximately) did your orgasm last?	_____	_____
5. Did you have any subsequent orgasms after the first? If so, how many? How long did each last?	_____	_____
6. Based on a rating scale of 0–100, where 100 is the best orgasmic experience you've ever had at any time, how would you rate your orgasmic experience at this session?	_____	_____

At the conclusion of your seven-week program, we will ask you to record your experiences in the "post program" column.

Week Two

1. 20–0 Countdown Exercise (2 times per day).

2. Sex Muscle and Breathing Exercise. Do 10 percent more repetitions than last week. If you've been practicing at the average baseline number of 20, increase the number of each set to 22 flutter clenches at about 1 contraction per second; do 22 push-outs at 1 per second and 22 repetitions of the slow inhale/clench—exhale/relax. Do 2 sets of each of these groups every day.

3. Appreciating Yourself. 2 sessions of 1 hour each.

Arrange a comfortable, sensual environment. If you have satin sheets, put them on your bed. Pour yourself a glass of wine or a special drink. Provide something special for the occasion, such as flowers, and have soothing music playing in the background. Make sure the room is a comfortable temperature. Undress. Treat yourself to a leisurely bath or shower.

During the early portion of this session, touch parts of your body that you probably don't ordinarily think of as being arousing. Put your fingertips together, close your eyes, and feel the connection between your fingers. Slowly move your hands together. Caress each hand lightly, then your wrists, then move up your arms to your elbows, slowly and lightly over your elbows, caress your upper arms and shoulders, and move slowly to your neck and head. Search for the good feelings in this process. Let any judgment thoughts pass by redirecting your attention, as you're learning to do in the Countdown Exercise, to the smooth feeling of your skin. Lovingly stroke your forehead, your hairline, your scalp, enjoying the sensation of the hair passing through your fingers. Move your fingertips very slowly on your head and allow yourself to feel tension draining away. Lightly stroke your skin but avoid massaging or moving it. Stroke your eyes and ears and face down to your neck and the back of your neck. Feel the tension draining away under your fingers.

Continue to run your fingertips lightly down your arms, then down to your waist, then down to your thighs, outlining the outside of the thighs, the tops and the inner areas of the thighs. Avoid touching your genitals and your nipples. Observe the sensations that you feel from your fingers and notice how the parts of your body that you're touching react.

Extend your touch down to your calves and your toes.

In front of a full-length mirror, examine your body carefully from head to toe. Imagine that you're looking at yourself for the first time. Observe yourself kneeling, bending, moving around. Admire yourself. Focus on your good points rather than on aspects you dislike or wish to change. Do you like your polished toenails? Your clean, smooth, hairless legs (or your unshaven, furry legs)? The hair on your head? Your nose, your eyes? Stand and then sit with your legs separated and then together. Look over your shoulders, one side and then the other, to observe the curve of your back and how your buttocks appear.

Now lie down in a comfortable place with a hand-held mirror. Hold the mirror between your legs and examine your vulva. Regardless of what your earlier conditioning may tell you, your genitals are beautiful! Many women have never objectively examined their genitals because of shame or guilt. The female labia are like flowers, and just as with flowers, they come in an amazing variety of colors, shapes, and sizes. And also just as with flowers, all are beautiful.

Open the outer lips of your vulva and begin to explore the inner lips. Sometimes these are as sensitive as the clitoris. Some women have larger inner lips than outer lips.

Below the vagina is the perineal area, between the vagina and anus. Touch this area. If you've borne a child, you may have a scar in your perineal area from the episiotomy your obstetrician performed to prevent accidental tearing during childbirth. If you contract your P.C. muscle, you may be able to see your anus draw inward and your perineum pull upward.

Now part your inner lips to reveal your vaginal opening. By now you may have lubricated somewhat, moisture that will allow you to insert one or more fingers comfortably into your vagina (if not, you can moisten your fingers with saliva). Do so. Explore the variation and sensitivity inside your vagina. Nearer the opening will usually be more sensitive than deeper inside.

Explore your clitoral area. The sole function of your clitoris is to create pleasure. As you move your finger gently around it, you may feel it swelling. Pull back its hood and use the mirror if necessary to look at it more closely. Notice the color at the top. Is it pink or reddish? How freely does the clitoris itself move? Even indirect stimulation on the clitoris through the outer vaginal lips or the mons can be sufficient to create an orgasm in some women.

Apply a lubricant such as Albolene cream to your clitoral region. Stroke the area around your clitoris, teasing it but not touching it directly for a tantalizing couple of minutes. Create an arousing fantasy. Then stimulate your clitoris directly with enough intensity and for sufficient time to bring yourself to an orgasm. Even if you do not have orgasm, proceed with the exercise.

Insert your finger about an inch inside your vagina. It feels both strong and soft at the same time. This is the area of your P.C. muscle, the pubococcygeus. The other end of this muscle is attached to the end of your spinal column, the coccyx. The P.C. muscle runs between the coccyx and the pubic bone that forms your mons in front. With your finger inside your vagina, deliberately contract this muscle. Visualize it becoming tight in a straight line. Your P.C. muscle begins approximately one finger-joint, or one to two inches, inside your vagina.

Notice the smooth texture of your vaginal walls, then rub across the tissue from side to side. The structure will feel ribbed or corrugated. The tissue itself feels soft. With pressure on the walls of the vagina you'll notice a firmer support structure beneath the tissue, which is muscle. If you rotate your finger, the ridges feel more distinct, and it is these ridges that are the P.C. muscle.

Keeping your finger in this position, relax and breathe slowly. Deliberately contract your P.C. muscle in the same way you do when you stop the flow of urine. The ridges of the muscle will then press against your finger and pull it upward toward your uterus. Now relax the muscle and feel the pressure lessen. Repeat this process.

If the muscle is well-toned and strong, it will squeeze against the finger so tightly that some women can almost push their fingers out of their vaginas. P.C. muscles that are not in such good shape will not be able to exert this much pressure. With practice, however, you can learn to increase the strength considerably. If you do have a strong grip, you can still increase the strength with more exercise.

Again, tighten the muscle and then release it. Feel the muscles loosen completely and then let go. Again tighten the muscles. This is the tightening and releasing that are the two muscle skills necessary for P.C.-muscle control.

Insert your finger deeper into your vagina until you come in contact with tissue. The firmer protuberance there is your cervix. Although it used to be thought that the cervix had no sensation, it's now known that the cervix is sensitive to pressure and can produce pleasure when stimulated. Voluntary push-outs help to push the cervix closer to the opening of the vagina, making it more accessible to penile stimulation. Automatic push-outs that occur with orgasm shorten the vaginal barrel and increase this stimulation.

The cervix is the opening to the uterus, which has a sexual function beyond that of childbearing. The uterus has been demonstrated to contract pleasurably during orgasm, particularly orgasm of the deeper, push-out variety.

Not all women are able to locate an inner trigger area in their vaginas. Those who do usually find it on the inside front wall of the vagina just behind the pubic bone, under the bladder, the G spot. You can exert pressure on your pubic area from above to locate the bladder. The G spot is about one to two inches behind the pubic bone. It's usually not detectable unless you're in a state of very high arousal, near orgasm. It's tricky to stimulate your own G-spot area effectively. Insert one or two fingers in the vagina and curl them forward as you press up inside. Sometimes squatting can make this easier.

It's sometimes possible, when you stroke the area of your inner trigger, to stimulate an uncomfortable urge to urinate. If you continue stroking, you may notice the sensations becoming erotic and pleasurable.

The size of the inner trigger area varies among women from about the size of a dime to that of a half dollar. With stimulation it swells, helping to create even more sexual arousal.

Keeping one or two fingers on one hand inserted in your vagina, bring your free hand to your clitoris. Stimulate your clitoris. Stimulate your clitoris lightly or firmly, whichever feels best. Does your inserted finger notice any change inside your vagina, such as more engorgement in the vaginal walls pushing outward? File the information that you learned for future practice sessions.

Stop when you're ready or finish with another orgasm if you are so inclined.

Week Three

1. 20–0 Countdown Exercise (2 times per day).

2. Sex Muscle and Breathing Exercise. Increase the number of repetitions by 10 percent. If you started at the original baseline, you will do 24 flutter clenches, 24 flutter push-outs at 1 per second, and 24 slow inhale/clenches—exhale/relax. Do 2 sets of these groups every day.

3. Self-Stimulation (3 sessions of 30 minutes to 1 hour each). Arrange a pleasant, private time for yourself, as before. Allow yourself to relax. Do a 20–0 Countdown, allowing all the tension to drain away from your mind and body. Shift your mental attention to erotic thoughts.

Now stroke your entire body from the top of your head down to your feet. Caress your nipples. If you feel comfortable doing so, try using saliva as natural lubrication, or apply lotion around your nipples and massage the nipples between your thumb and forefinger lightly, one by one. Recall times when you've enjoyed having your nipples caressed. Notice if they become engorged and erect.

Stroke your pelvic area with your hands. Stroke your pubic hair. Take up a quantity of a long-lasting sexual lubricant such as Albolene and open the lips of your vagina, apply the lubricant, and begin stroking your inner lips and clitoris. Insert fingers into your vagina and then withdraw them to stimulate the clitoris. Rhythmically clench and relax your P.C. muscles in rhythm with your breathing, clenching as you inhale, relaxing as you exhale. Continue to caress your inner and outer lips and clitoris.

Focus on stimulating your clitoris. Take your clitoris between your thumb and forefinger and massage it. Stop. Notice your clitoris becoming engorged with blood and feel it lengthen and swell. Resume stimulation for several massaging strokes and stop again and notice your increasing excitement. Continue to stroke your vulva and notice the changes taking place throughout your entire body.

Resume stimulating your clitoris, noticing it becoming even more erect. Continue this pattern of stimulation until you finally reach an orgasm. Trust yourself totally while you completely love yourself. When your orgasm starts, feel the involuntary orgasmic contractions of your P.C. muscle at about one per second, feel the warm surge of blood in your pelvic area, and notice the sensations of mental peacefulness. Take a mental snapshot and memorize the experience that you're having, recognizing that you can deliberately re-create this experience at will. Do this exercise at least two other times this week.

Week Four

1. 20–0 Countdown Exercise (2 times per day).
2. Sex Muscle and Breathing Exercise. Increase the number of repetitions by another 10 percent this week. Do 27 flutter-clench contractions; 27 flutter push-outs at 1 per second; and 27 slow inhale/clench—exhale/relax. Do 2 sets of these groups every day.
3. Self-Stimulation (3 sessions of 30 minutes each.)

This week we'd like you to use a vibrator. If you don't already own a good plug-in, hand-held, two-speed vibrator, they're easy to obtain. Large department stores and drugstores often carry them. The long-handled "wand" type, the short-handled, interchangeable-head type, and the Swedish hand-strap type all have their own advantages. (Consult the Sources section in the Appendix for reliable mail-order outlets.) Battery-operated vibrators are not as effective as plug-in vibrators for self-stimulation; the batteries run down. Such vibrators can be useful for exploring inner trigger areas, though.

Imagine that you're preparing for the arrival of a special guest with whom you anticipate a special sexual experience. Prepare your room to receive your guest with attention to lighting, candles, scent, plants, flowers, music, comfortable pillows, and of course undisturbed privacy. Take a leisurely hot bath if a tub is available. How about a special bubble bath? Sip your favorite drink. Feel the wonderful sensuousness of the heat and the water dissolving tensions and putting you in the mood for lovemaking. If you're using a shower, direct the stream of water to different parts of your body and focus your attention on the pleasurable experience the water creates on your skin. Take at least ten minutes for this activity. You deserve it. Then dry yourself slowly and sensuously, noticing the feeling of the towel rubbing on different parts of your body and awakening your skin to sensation.

Now lie back on the bed or other area that you've selected. Touch and caress yourself as you'd like a lover to do. Imagine that your lover is exploring your body with appreciation and wonder at the discovery. Lubricate your genitals slowly and sensuously. Distribute the lubrication over your clitoris and your outer and inner lips. Notice the engorgement that comes to this area with stimulation.

A man, at this point, would be noticing and enjoying the development of his erection. You're probably experiencing just as much engorgement as a man, but yours is internal and is easier to feel than to see.

Stroke your clitoris and inner and outer lips, slowly building engorgement and arousal. After several minutes, apply your vibrator at the slowest speed. Start with the area around your genitals, rather than directly on them. Notice the sensations as you move your vibrator around the central "target" area. Tease yourself. Anticipate more direct stimulation.

Now move the vibrator onto the clitoral area briefly and then move it away. Use light pressure at first. Hold it on the area of your vaginal opening and then move it away, teasing. Now hold your vibrator head on a single location on or very close to your clitoris. Without moving it around, deliberately practice your sex-muscle contractions. Do a set of repetitions of each of the three types—squeezes, slow clenches, and push-outs. Notice the sensations and what happens to your level of arousal.

Don't allow yourself to have an orgasm yet. Move your vibrator around, varying pressure and location, and you'll discover a wide variety of pleasurable sensations.

Move your vibrator back to a single location on or close to your clitoris. Now do a 20–0 Countdown. If you get distracted in counting your exhales, remember to return your attention to the last number that you recall counting. Notice the kind of thoughts you have that may cause you to lose your concentration on counting numbers. The highly pleasurable sensations in your genitals are likely to be an important distraction. That's to be expected and it's useful to learn to switch your attention to the neutral process of observing and counting your breaths as a method of managing distracting nonsexual thoughts.

When you've completed one cycle of the Countdown, switch your attention back to fully experiencing your level of arousal. Has it increased, remained the same, or decreased?

Experiment with switching your vibrator to a higher speed. Notice what effect this has on your arousal. What's the difference? Place something between the head of the vibrator and your clitoris such as a fold or two of towel, a small pillow, or your other hand. What effect does this padding have on your arousal? Set your vibrator to whichever speed you prefer.

After about twenty minutes of genital stimulation with your vibrator, allow yourself to have an orgasm. As you start to have your orgasm, please do three things simultaneously:

1. Deliberately push out (bear down) and hold your push-out as long as you can. If you relax your pushing out, resume again after one or two seconds.
2. Counteract the reflex tendency to hold your breath during orgasm by deliberately breathing slow, deep breaths in and out.
3. Count your sex-muscle contractions from the very first, no matter how subtle, to the very last contraction, no matter how subtle.

After the last contraction, rather than putting your vibrator away, investigate how and where you can apply it to increase your arousal. Placing it directly on the head of the clitoris will probably be somewhat uncomfortable immediately following orgasm. However, you may find that applying it very lightly around the clitoris or directly above the clitoris or the pubic bone, or placing a towel or washcloth between the vibrator head and your genitals creates another round of increasing stimulation. You may find that stimulation after orgasm is very pleasurable. If so, know that it may be possible for you to have another orgasm. This second orgasm may require you to explore ways of applying your vibrator and directing your thoughts to allow this possibility. Another orgasm may occur again within a minute or less, or after a number of minutes of further stimulation.

If you begin to have another orgasm, again deliberately push out, breathe in and out, and count the number of contractions.

Although becoming aware of the number of contractions and counting can be slightly distracting from the experience of orgasm itself, the usefulness of monitoring and knowing what is happening objectively during your orgasmic process is worth this slight and temporary inconvenience. When your orgasm is over, jot down the number of contractions you experienced.

After your orgasm, spend several minutes reviewing and appreciating the experience you just had. This review helps to store your orgasmic process in your mind's permanent memory, allowing you to draw on it and re-create it in the future.

Week Five

1. 20–0 Countdown Exercise (2 times per day).
2. Sex Muscle and Breathing Exercise. Increase the number of repetitions by 10 percent. If you started at the basic initial rate, do 30 flutter clenches, 30 flutter push-outs, and 30 slow inhale/clenches—exhale/relax. Do 2 sets of these groups every day.
3. Self-Stimulation (30 sessions of 40 minutes each).

Prepare your space for your comfort and privacy. Settle back and with your eyes closed, do a 20–0 Countdown to allow your body to let go of accumulated tension and your mind of routine processing.

When you've finished the Countdown, think of a fantasy. Use one of your long-standing favorites or create a new one. You can consult page 94 for ideas. Try picturing scenes of romance and lovemaking that are a little different for you. Allow yourself to be adventurous. It's all in your imagination and it's perfectly safe. Try out pictures of situations that are extremely erotic, maybe with more than one lover, or being swept off your feet or rendered temporarily helpless, or in an unusual or risky situation. Remember, simply picturing scenes or situations does not mean you will ever want to carry them out.

Stroke, touch, and stimulate your body in the ways that you picture and imagine your fantasy lover doing. Perhaps there are different ways of touching or stimulating you that one particular lover in the past has done, or that only you know about. Imagine his warm kisses. When you're feeling sensual and at least partly aroused, apply lubricant to your genital areas. Approach your clitoris as a musician might approach his/her instrument. Explore your clitoris: the shaft, stroking on either side, the tip, retracting the hood. Begin with a very light stroke and gradually increase the pressure. You'll find you can use more intense pressure comfortably if you rub through folds of the skin on one side or the other of the clitoris, rather than directly on the glans. Try to increase and decrease sensation by varying the pressure.

After about thirty minutes of stimulating yourself clitorally in this way, allow yourself to have an orgasm. Be deliberate about trying to stretch it out in time and intensity. You don't have to leave better orgasms entirely to chance. Tense your pelvic and thigh muscles. Push out and bear down; hold your breath; increase the rate and pressure of your clitoral stimulation—then let yourself go. As you start to have the automatic contractions of orgasm, start to breathe and begin mentally to count the number of contractions. If, at the end of the series of contractions, you've lost count, estimate the amount of time the contractions took or estimate their number. It's understandable if you sometimes allow yourself to be distracted by being caught up in the experience of your orgasm. You can create lots of opportunities to take these mental measurements in the future.

Experimenting with Multiple Orgasm

While you're having orgasm, notice the type of stimulation that feels best on your clitoris. Some women like very light, slow stimulation during orgasm, others prefer more intense, rapid stimulation. At the end of their orgasmic contractions, most women find that their clitoris has become very sensitive, often too sensitive for continued stimulation.

Experiment with providing extremely light stimulation to the clitoral shaft and/or hood. If, in the seconds immediately after your first orgasm, even this stimulation is too much, stimulate the area around the clitoris, including the inner and outer lips and the mons. Make sure you have enough lubrication on these areas. Focus your mental attention on the sensations you feel. Thoughts in the form of resistances are likely to crowd into your mind, thoughts such as "Once is enough," "It's too sensitive," "This isn't going to work," "I'm losing control," "I should stop now." Order yourself to stop these negative thoughts and immediately switch your attention to the pleasurable sensations that you are experiencing that emanate from your genitals. Stroke and stimulate around your clitoris for fifteen or thirty seconds, then edge back to direct stimulation on your clitoris. Discover what type of stroking feels pleasurable and adds to your arousal.

Whenever you are very highly aroused, or after an orgasm, the most sensitive area may be a very tiny spot, smaller than a pea, on one side of the clitoris or the other, under the hood. Experiment with locating such a spot and continuing your stimulation to that area alone for several minutes.

As long as your clitoris continues to be too sensitive to touch, keep stimulating around it. Discover the appropriate time for you to focus your attention again on direct clitoral stimulation, then experiment with the type, rate, and pressure of stroking that allow you to experience an increase in arousal that may lead to another orgasm.

Many women who are singly orgasmic can learn by this procedure to experience a second or even a third orgasm, or to extend the length of orgasm. Don't be discouraged if additional orgasms don't occur the first few times. Sometimes months are required. Remember, not all women will desire to have more than one orgasm.

Week Six

1. 20–0 Countdown Exercise (2 times per day).

2. Sex Muscle and Breathing Exercise. Increase the repetition number by 10 percent. Do 33 flutter clenches using more contraction force than in previous weeks; do 33 flutter push-outs using more force than in previous weeks; and 33 slow inhale/clenches—exhale/relax with as much muscular strength as you can muster each time. Do 2 sets of these groups every day.

3. Self-Stimulation (3 sessions of at least 40 minutes).

Start this week's exercises by doing something a little different to vary your arousal process. You might choose a sexy nightgown, bra, slip, or underpants to wear at the start of this session. Feel the texture with your fingers. How does it feel to touch your breasts and genitals through this material?

After a while, undress yourself (or continue partly dressed if you like the feeling). Use erotic visual or reading materials. Reading about other women's fantasies can be a distinct source of arousal. Some X-rated videotapes are also enjoyed by women, particularly when viewed alone and without the concerns of a partner's response to the video materials. Femme Productions has videos produced by women that may be more likely to appeal to women. (See Appendix under Sources.)

Begin your self-stimulation process now, doing something a little different than you usually do or have done in the earlier weeks. Use your imagination and creativity. Consider using different textures to stimulate yourself, such as a silk scarf, velvet, or a piece of fur, and rub yourself sensuously. Use a different location or a different position. If you normally lie back, sit in a chair this time, lie on the floor, or kneel. Or lie on your stomach with a pillow between your legs. You may consider getting out your vibrator and putting it inside the pillow and moving your pelvis against the vibrator rather than holding the handle and applying it to your genitals. Be creative and a little daring.

After a few minutes of this warm-up arousal, put aside your props and get in a comfortable position, lying back with your lubricant conveniently available. Lubricate your genitals, clitoris, inner and outer lips, vagina, and anal area generously. Proceed to stroke and arouse yourself in the ways you've learned are the most effective.

Change positions several times during this process and notice the difference in your stimulation pattern. Get on your knees, on the bed, using one and then two hands to stimulate your genitals. Try resting your head and chest on a pillow. Or try lying on your side, or on your back with your legs up. Try various body movements, such as rocking your pelvis up and down while on the bed. Experiment with holding your breath during this time, as well as with rapid breathing (panting).

When you're near orgasm, experiment with stimulating the area around your anus, lightly around the opening. If that feels good to you, try slowly and gently inserting your finger a short distance inside. Observe the tendency of your anal muscle to contract. When you notice the sphincter starting to contract automatically, concentrate on overriding the contraction reflex and allowing the sphincter to relax as you stimulate the clitoral area with your other hand. Such relaxation allows additional engorgement to occur and can add pleasure. It may also allow you more comfortably to insert your finger. If you have long nails, insertion should be done cautiously if at all. Remember not to insert this finger in your vagina without first washing it.

Experiment now with stimulating your vagina. Insert your forefinger a short distance and sweep it around the vaginal opening, a full 360 degrees, about an inch inside the opening. You may find this easier to do with your right hand if you're right-handed. Notice which areas are most sensitive. Insert your finger another inch and begin to circle the vagina, exerting some pressure at each position of the clock face. Finally, insert your finger full distance and sweep around, first in one direction, then the other. With the other hand you may continue some clitoral stimulation to maintain your high arousal level.

Now take your inserted finger and, starting at twelve o'clock (up just below the clitoris), slowly move your finger deeper in the vagina. Have your finger curled upward and notice whether you can locate a distinct inner trigger area. It may be easier to locate in your current state near orgasm. Try rhythmic, firm pressure. If you notice an urge to urinate, or an uncomfortable feeling, you're probably on the area. You may need to go deeper to locate this area. It can be awkward for a woman to stimulate this area by herself, because of the need to curl her fingers up and inward. Try several different positions, with your legs over your head and in a squatting position on the floor. A battery-powered, penis-shaped vibrator may help you locate and stimulate your inner trigger area. Insert it only part way for this purpose and tip the head forward.

Now lie back on your bed and allow yourself an orgasm. As usual, deliberately push out, breathe, and count your contractions. As you start contractions, insert your other hand into your vagina and stimulate your inner trigger area. If doing so feels awkward at first, recognize that the more practice you have with this kind of two-handed stimulation, the easier it will become. You may find it helpful to keep your legs separated as much as possible, which shortens the vaginal barrel. Experiment with different rates and pressure for internal stimulation. Note the number of contractions you experience and the intensity. Did the contractions feel more intense, the same, or less intense than without the internal stimulation?

After you've cooled down, be sure to make a note about your observations and findings.

Multiple Orgasm

As in the previous weeks' exercises, don't stop stimulation as soon as your contractions stop. Focus your attention this week on continuing vaginal stimulation. If your clitoris is very sensitive immediately after orgasm, experiment with stimulating only your vaginal area. Particularly focus on the inner trigger area. It's usually most responsive just before, during, and immediately following orgasmic contractions. Provide rhythmic stimulation with one or two fingers curled up against the front wall of your vagina. Pressure that is medium to fairly firm, about one stroke per second, is a good basic pattern.

Continue stimulating your inner trigger area for at least several minutes after your orgasm. Even if you don't find yourself becoming aroused again, this stimulation should still feel quite pleasurable to you. Regularly practicing internal stimulation following your orgasm, you may be very pleasantly surprised and pleased to have a second orgasm.

After several minutes of internal vaginal stimulation, add clitoral stimulation with your free hand. Often the combination of clitoral stimulation and internal vaginal stimulation will provide the necessary impetus for a second orgasm. Even if it doesn't happen, you'll have fun trying.

Week Seven and Beyond

Continue to practice self-stimulation at a weekly frequency that seems to satisfy your needs. This may be one, two, or three times, or even more. Allow sufficient time, preferably at least thirty minutes. When you reach orgasm, push out with your sex muscles and press down firmly on your pubic bone with your four fingers directly on top of your clitoris without moving your fingers. Periodically, count the contractions. You may find they're extending to thirty seconds or more. This pattern is a good basic regimen and should satisfy your basic sexual needs. It will also allow you progressively to increase your sexual potential and build a solid foundation for sex with a partner.

You can be creative by combining various methods and procedures that you've practiced in the previous weeks. Remember that the guidelines in this program are simply that—guidelines. We hope you'll supply creativity and spontaneity during your self-stimulation experiences.

Record your experience in the "Post Program" column of the chart you did during Week One, page 373. Has there been any change in the length of your orgasm? Has there been any change in the number of contractions that you experience with your orgasm? Have you experienced a repeated orgasm for the first time? Have your orgasms at times been stronger than usual? The contractions more intense? Don't be concerned if your answers to these questions show little or no change. No orgasm is incorrect. Every orgasm is a moment of magic. However, better and longer orgasms are always possible as you continue deliberate practice, and attention to pleasure is always worthwhile.

The knowledge you obtain about yourself from your experience can be invaluable in improving sexual interactions with a partner. The more you know about your own sexual preferences and responses, the easier it is to guide and teach your partner, and the more sexually compatible you can be.

We wish you success in your quest for a suitable lover or spouse.

APPENDIX

SOLVING PROBLEMS

Although the Ecstasy Program in its entirety is not intended for those with longstanding sexual problems, specific parts of it can be helpful. Some men and women will be able to work through their particular problems with the information we supply here. Some won't. For them we advise consulting other self-help books we recommend here that focus more on dysfunctions, or seeking counseling with a competent sex therapist.

Solving Sexual Problems

You have a sexual problem if there's a significant gap between what you expect your experience should be and what it actually is. That's a much more accurate description than some esteem-diminishing labels that many authorities still use, labels such as "frigid," "impotent," "incompetent." Sexual functioning isn't fitted to some universal standard. The range is enormous. So is the potential, as we've seen. Most people never attain their full sexual potential. In that sense, we all may be considered to have sexual problems.

The only person who can validly identify a problem area in your sexual functioning is you. A man might define himself as an early ejaculator if he ejaculates sooner than he and his partner wish and doesn't know how to delay orgasm. A woman might define herself as situationally nonorgasmic if she can stimulate herself to orgasm but doesn't know how to have an orgasm with her partner during intercourse, and wants to.

388

Medical Problems

Not all sexual problems are psychological. Some are medical and physical. Diabetes can cause sexual problems. So can prostate surgery, chronic infections, torn ligaments, excessive alcohol, chronic illness, chronic pain, and many physical difficulties. A variety of medications can interfere, particularly tranquilizers and drugs for high blood pressure. If you suspect your problem is predominantly medical, visit a physician for a thorough examination.

Even if you have a physical condition that can affect you sexually, deliberate effort to improve your sexual functioning, such as following the exercises and programs described in this book, can improve your sexual experience. There are very few people, even with severe medical disabilities such as diabetes or paraplegia, who cannot learn to have better-quality sex than they now think possible. Unfortunately, their doubts are sometimes reinforced by their doctors, family, and friends. Our advice: don't necessarily believe prophets of sexual doom. Follow a reasonable program for enough time to experiment with your potential, regardless of your physical difficulties.

Traumatic Early Experience

Some sexual problems can be worked through best in long-term therapy —psychotherapy or psychoanalysis. These are usually problems that go back to childhood: a background of severe punishment for sexual behavior; severe conflict about sexual behavior; traumatic incest; molestation, or other traumatic earlier sexual experiences. These experiences can produce anxiety that may be too deep-seated to give way to the self-training methods we discuss here. If you find yourself unable to make progress by these methods, you may want to work with a competent psychologist or psychiatrist. But most people can greatly improve their sexual skills without long-term therapy.

In the last few years, those who have been molested as children have increasingly been willing to come forward and talk about their problem. In various areas of the country, mental health professionals have organized groups to deal with these difficult issues in a supportive environment. This process of sharing one's most painful experiences with a group of individuals who have experienced similar feelings is often surprisingly useful.

MALE PROBLEMS

Erection Insecurity (Impotence)

A small percentage of men have had a lifelong history of inability to have erections during intercourse with *any* partner. Erections for such men are usually possible with masturbation and sometimes manual or oral stimulation by a partner. Often what's called "primary erection dysfunction" originates in deep-seated emotional conflicts about sex or about women. Although the program described below is frequently helpful, men who experience this primary erection problem may benefit from longer-term psychotherapy.

Erection insecurity is a term we've devised to replace the more common and, in our view, less satisfactory label "impotence." Erection concerns usually involve either getting erect or staying erect, particularly during intercourse. A substantial majority of the male population has had the experience of not being erect when the man or his partner wished or expected him to be. Almost all men have had the experience of losing an erection during intercourse. The erection mechanism isn't that reliable.

Physical or psychological? There are a variety of reasons why a man may experience less frequent or less reliable erections. These are either physical or psychological in nature, sometimes both. It's relatively easy to determine in a general way how important the physical elements may be. At least once a week do you find yourself moderately to fully erect when you awaken from sleep? If you think not or don't know, try the postage stamp test. Stick together a ring of postage stamps snugly around the base of your (flaccid) penis at bedtime. If the ring is broken open in the morning, you probably had an erection during sleep. If the stamp ring is intact, you probably didn't. Can you get a reasonably firm erection when you self-stimulate? If the answer to both of these questions is no, then you should consult a medical doctor. He will check you for possible physical or medication factors that could contribute to diminished erection functioning. If the answer to both of these questions is yes, the problem is more likely to be psychological or interpersonal.

The three most common reasons why a man whose erection mechanism is basically intact has erection insecurity are: (1) his own performance anxiety; (2) insufficient sexual arousal in his partner; (3) insufficient direct stimulation of his genitals.

It's important to recognize that in any sexual interaction, the man's erection is a *shared* responsibility. It's not necessarily sufficient for a woman simply to be unclothed and in passive agreement with the sexual interaction. The woman may need to be more direct in her stimulation of the man with her hands or orally. It's a common misconception that the man should automatically be erect without additional direct stimulation from his partner. If the woman allows herself to have an orgasm before intercourse, she'll probably be more interested and patient in helping her partner achieve and maintain an erection. The erection mechanism is highly sensitive to subtle and even unconscious emotional cues. The more each partner can be aware of the doubts and subtle mental resistances at a particular moment, the more it's possible to change the attitude to one of greater agreement. When this happens, a man is more likely to be erect.

The following exercises from the Ecstasy Program may be helpful.

The Exercises

1. The 20–0 Countdown Exercise (see page 138). The skills learned by regular practice of this exercise will help a man improve the concentration necessary to focus his attention on pleasurable, sensual feelings and exclude negative and intrusive doubts and anxieties. Regular practice in nonsexual situations will also assist in reducing the buildup of stress and anxiety that interfere with erection functioning.

2. The Sex Muscle and Breathing Exercise (see page 141). This exercise is extremely important for improving awareness of sensations in the genital region and also for enhancing erection strength.

3. Follow the program for Men Without Partners, in the Singles Chapter, beginning on page 355. Note that this singles program incorporates both of the above exercises and emphasizes an extensive self-stimulation program.

4. Follow the Twelve-Week Ecstasy Program exactly as described, omitting every exercise that includes intercourse. If you are currently having intercourse, such an agreement to stop having it may at first seem unreasonable. In our experience, however, the variety of new kinds of sexual interactions and experiences that a couple has by following the program more than compensates for the absence of intercourse. The couple will likely be pleased to discover the man's erection becoming more reliable and his sexual self-confidence enhanced.

How long the ban on intercourse should be needs to be agreed upon as a function of how long and frequent the erection insecurity has been. Generally, we suggest maintaining the prohibition on intercourse for at least eight weeks. If the man experiences only occasional problems getting or keeping an erection, a shorter ban period, such as four weeks, may be sufficient as a minimum.

At the end of the prohibited intercourse period, the couple gradually reintroduces intercourse for brief periods of time. This may start with less than a minute of penetration for the first few times, increasing to several minutes. This gradual reintroduction of intercourse is particularly important for those men who experience erection insecurity at the start of or during intercourse.

For improving erection insecurity, partner exercises that are particularly useful in the Twelve-Week Program are:

a. Sensual Focus Exercise, Steps 1 through 4, in Weeks Two through Five.
b. Soft-Penis Exercise, Week Seven.
c. Learning to Extend Orgasmic Response I, Week Nine.
d. Learning to Extend Orgasmic Response II, Week Ten.
e. Learning to Extend Orgasmic Response III, Week Eleven.
f. Learning to Extend Orgasmic Response IV, Week Twelve.

5. If you don't have a regular sexual partner of if your sexual partner can't be included in your decision to delay intercourse for a month or two, you can unilaterally decide not to have intercourse. Then give your partner more attention in other ways sexually so that she won't miss intercourse as much and won't pressure you to have intercourse. This unilateral ban isn't as desirable as your partner's agreement, but it's better than no restriction at all. It may be to your advantage not to tell your partner in the beginning what you're doing. With a ban on intercourse you may notice that your erection begins to return. You shouldn't expect erections to return all at once, but eventually, combined perhaps with additional direct sexual stimulation, they will. It's important that you don't try immediately to use your erection for intercourse. Waiting for a future interaction builds pleasurable anticipation.

Most men need their penises directly stimulated for erection. This need increases with age. A partner is the best source for that stimulation, so you should continue self-stimulation training as we describe it through the stages when your partner watches you learn how and then takes over the process.

You are responsible for arranging enough stimulation. You have to make sure your partner gives you enough or you give yourself enough direct genital stimulation. Then, even if you don't begin a sexual encounter with an erection, you can produce one with self-stimulation. If you've done that in front of your partner in training, then you won't be embarrassed to do it again when it's needed. And it's okay. Many men stimulate themselves in order to achieve a working level of arousal. It's more fun if your partner does it for you, but not all women are willing to agree. It's your penis, your pleasure, and ultimately your responsibility.

6. Make a list of times when your penis rises to the occasion and the times when it doesn't. You may identify a pattern. Perhaps it's related to alcohol use or time of day or whether you or your partner are the initiator of an interaction. Some men find they have no difficulty with a familiar partner, but difficulty with a new partner. For other men it's the other way around.

Especially with a familiar partner, you can probably solve your problems by finding ways to make sex feel new, different, and more exciting. Change the time, setting, or position. One certain new adventure that you and your partner might arrange for yourselves is agreement to follow the Twelve-Week Ecstasy Program.

7. You need to learn how to reduce anxiety. Practice changing your thoughts—cognitive restructuring. Practice breathing exercises. Do visualization and fantasy. Have your partner use positive suggestion.

Just as you are responsible for arranging enough stimulation, so you are also responsible for deciding when you feel up to lovemaking. Don't have sex just because you think you ought to. If you're feeling pressed, if you have a deadline the next morning, you should recognize you're in conflict and aren't likely to give pleasure your full attention. It's good to agree never to say no to sex, but if you have an erection problem, you're not yet ready for that agreement.

Men have more trouble saying no than women do. It's important to say no in a way that won't hurt your partner's feelings. Be honest. Don't tell her you have a headache. Admit you have a deadline the following day and you're preoccupied. Offer an alternative: "Can we agree to make love tomorrow night instead? Because then I'll be more attentive."

Early Ejaculation

Rationale

Early ejaculation is a timing problem. You ejaculate before you want to or before your partner wants you to. In sports we admire quick reflexes. In bed they can cause difficulties. But it's not farfetched, in the context of the potential of extended orgasmic response, to say that all men are early ejaculators. Very few of us can or even wish to make love for three hours at a stretch.

It's possible to learn to extend your sexual endurance. You only have to want to. You'll be able to give your partner more pleasure in lovemaking if you can last longer. That's the traditional rationale. It's true and valid. But less often emphasized is another reason for learning to delay ejaculation, equally valid and perhaps even more in your interest: you'll give yourself more pleasure, too. Go back to page 110, Chapter VI, and look at the graph of male orgasmic response. It demonstrates that the longer your erection can last, the higher your arousal and the more total pleasure you'll have. If erection insecurity persists despite following the above suggestions, consider using one of the erection enhancement products listed in the Sources section.

The Exercises

Men without partners, follow the Eight-Week Singles Program.

Men with partners who agree, follow the Twelve-Week Ecstasy Program. Take as many weeks as you need to complete each week's exercises.

Solo Exercises

1. 20–0 Countdown, twice per day
2. Sex Muscle/Breathing, twice per day
3. Self-Stimulation I–IV, Weeks Three–Six or
4. Singles Program, Weeks One–Seven

Partner Exercises

1. Sensual Focus, Steps I–IV, Weeks Two–Five
2. Sexual Exploration, Week Six

3. Simultaneous Partner Stimulation, Week Six
4. Partner-Assisted Stimulation, Week Eight
5. Learning to Extend Orgasmic Response I–IV, Weeks Nine–Twelve. These are the key training exercises. The woman should concentrate on creating multiple peaks for the man when she's stimulating him.
6. Intercourse I–V, Weeks Eight–Twelve. The couple emphasizes slow, very gentle strokes and movements. Woman Above, Rear Entry, Scissors, and Laptop are positions that more easily allow the woman control to create multiple peaks. The man adopts a passive, receptive attitude. Man-above positions tend to be less desirable for training the man since they create muscle tension which increases ejaculatory urgency and give his partner less control.

Delayed Ejaculation

Delayed ejaculation is a relatively less common problem. If you often have vaginal intercourse with an erection for thirty minutes or more but then are unable to ejaculate vaginally even if you want to, you may have a problem with delayed ejaculation. Delayed ejaculators can usually ejaculate in other situations—when self-stimulating, for example. The problem is almost always caused by a severe resistance to allowing semen to enter the vagina, and it's often best dealt with in psychotherapy.

Relaxation techniques can help. So can self-stimulation exercises fitted to intercourse. Those work this way: you stimulate yourself almost to the point of ejaculation and then insert your penis into your partner's vagina at the final moment to finish. When you can ejaculate inside the vagina that way, then at later sessions of lovemaking, insert yourself at earlier and earlier stages before ejaculation. After a month or more, you may find you won't need to stimulate yourself at all prior to intercourse, except possibly to achieve an erection.

Another approach to delayed ejaculation is by way of Sensual Focus I–IV, Weeks Two through Five and Partner Stimulation. Your partner should do Sensual Focus with you. Follow Self-Stimulation I–IV in Weeks Three to Six. When your partner has learned how you like to be pleasured, she should practice stimulating you by hand to orgasm. Then, at a later session, she should take you up to the point where you're ready to ejaculate and then insert your penis into her vagina with you on your back and her kneeling facing you, astride. At successive sessions she should insert you progressively earlier. She can also help by doing rhythmic push-outs to increase penile stimulation.

FEMALE PROBLEMS

Women experience two basic kinds of sexual difficulties: problems with orgasm and pain with intercourse. Problems with orgasm divide between those women who have never had orgasm and those who have it only in some situations but not in others.

Preorgasmia

If you have never learned to have orgasm, either with a partner or alone, by any means, you're preorgasmic. Preorgasmia is the easiest of all female sexual problems to correct. More than 90 percent of preorgasmic women can learn to have orgasm through a directed program. The key is self-stimulation. To learn to have orgasm you need to be willing to practice regular self-stimulation. All the advantages of sexual pleasure, for yourself and for your partner, follow from that decision.

You can learn to have orgasm, and then have orgasm during intercourse, by following a twelve-step program. Practice each step until you complete it successfully before going on to the next step.

Do these exercises every day.

Twelve-Step Training Program for Preorgasmic Women

1. Practice the 20–0 Countdown twice per day. (See page 138, Partner Week One)

2. Sex Muscle/Breathing Exercise (See page 141, Partner Week One)

3. Stand nude in front of a full-length mirror. Look at your body as if you were another person. Be neutral, not critical. Assess yourself. Find your good points. Very few women ever take time to look at their bodies. See if you can agree to appreciate your body as it is, as worthy of pleasure. Look over your genitals. Examine them. Learn where things are.

4. In a comfortable, private place, such as lying alone in bed, touch yourself for pleasure, not sexual arousal. Include your genitals in your touching, but with no expectation of arousal. Enjoy touching and being touched. Notice what feels good.

5. In a comfortable, private place touch yourself for arousal. With your eyes and your hands, explore your body and your genitals to discover the areas that are most sexually sensitive. Touch your scalp, your neck, your shoulders. Touch your nipples to see what feels good. Does firmness feel best? Does rolling your nipples between thumb and forefinger feel best? Touch your belly. Touch the insides of your thighs, your labia, your clitoris. Learn what feels good so that later you can teach your partner. He won't know what you like unless you teach him. You can't teach him if you don't know yourself.

6. In a comfortable, private place, stimulate yourself for arousal (without seeking orgasm) in the areas you identified in step five as sexually sensitive. Use a lubricant when you stimulate your genitals (see "Lubricants," page 79).

7. Stimulate yourself more intensely over a longer period of time, at least thirty minutes or more every day. Allow orgasm to happen naturally. If, after two weeks of daily stimulation, you haven't had an orgasm, go on to step eight.

8. Using a vibrator, stimulate yourself in turn on each of the sensitive areas you've identified, working your way to your genitals. (See "Vibrators," page 175. Also "Sources" for ordering information.) Include clitoral stimulation and bring yourself to orgasm. If one type of vibrator doesn't seem to work for you, try another kind. If the vibrator feels too intense, put a towel between it and your genitals. Or use water from a tub faucet or flexible shower hose. A flexible shower hose with the head removed is a superb tool for sensual pleasure. Relax in the bathtub and adjust a warm, soft flow from the hose. Direct the flow all over your genitals, then focus on the flow and later experiment with greater pressure.

If, after two or three weeks of daily exercises, you are unable to have an orgasm using a vibrator, consult a sex therapist or a training group. Many women's organizations offer group counseling for preorgasmia. That's the least expensive form of treatment, and it gets results. Call around.

When you achieve orgasm with a vibrator (congratulations!), see if you can learn to have orgasm without a vibrator. Use the vibrator to get close to the point of orgasm. Then switch to your hand. When you can take over orgasm with your hand, stop using a vibrator a little earlier each week. Eventually you may be able to give yourself orgasm using your hands alone.

9. Stimulate yourself to orgasm with your partner observing. Vibrator is optional.

10. Allow your partner to stimulate you to orgasm as you demonstrated in step nine. Vibrator is optional.

11. During intercourse, stimulate your genitals to orgasm. Vibrator is optional.

12. During intercourse, allow your partner to stimulate you to orgasm as he learned in step ten. The best position for this exercise is the rear-entry position with both of you kneeling (see illustration, page 253) or with the man standing beside the bed. He can reach around in this position to stimulate your clitoris with his hands. Vibrator use is optional.

Additionally, you may follow the Singles Program (Seven Weeks) or the Self-Stimulation Exercises I–III, Weeks Three to Five.

Orgasm Sometimes, but Not with Intercourse

Women who have orgasm with self-stimulation or partner stimulation but not with intercourse need first to consider how assertive they are sexually. They are often women who have been taught to believe that the man's pleasure always comes first. One practical problem with that conviction is that when a woman encourages a man to ejaculate before she's had orgasm, she no longer has an erect penis available to work with. First of all, then, be sure you're taking what you need. You may want to extend the time you spend in foreplay and intercourse. You may want to make sure the conditions of lovemaking suit you. You may want to choose a more arousing position for lovemaking. Subservience doesn't work in bed. Your needs are just as important as your partner's.

Another approach is to assign yourself the pleasure of having orgasm in ways different from what is usual for you. Find a different position or make subtle changes in the angles and movements within positions you are already using. If you haven't been using a vibrator with intercourse, try it. If you've been making love only in bed, make love somewhere else. Deliberately alter some habitual patterns. Focus on the pleasurable sensations you do feel during intercourse rather than on the ones you think you should be feeling. This will encourage sensations to grow.

If you have a partner who agrees, follow the Twelve-Week Ecstasy Program.

Learning to Extend Orgasmic Response, Exercises I–IV, Weeks Nine through Twelve, is an excellent way to deal with this problem. Your ability to experience orgasm with manual and/or vaginal stimulation is enhanced. If you are able to experience an orgasm by manual and oral stimulation, your vagina will become heavily engorged with blood and pleasurably sensitive. It's much easier then to continue the orgasmic experience with a thrusting penis. The stronger and longer is your orgasm prior to intercourse, the more likely it will be to continue or restart an orgasm with intercourse.

Shift to intercourse as smoothly as possible soon after a period of orgasm by manual and/or oral stimulation. Emphasize the positions that give more stimulation to the inner trigger area: woman-above, rear-entry, and laptop.

Despite their own or their partner's interest in doing so, some women do not succeed in having an orgasm during intercourse. In fact surveys repeatedly confirm that more than 50 percent of women do not have orgasm with intercourse. Many of those women feel no less sexually fulfilled. The key to your sexual satisfaction is to enjoy within your own ability the experiences you do have.

Situational Nonorgasmia

If you've had an orgasm in the past, but are presently unable to have an orgasm by any means at all, this is your category. Situational nonorgasmia usually signals a change in your health, your relationship, or your attitude.

Has your physical condition changed? Do you have an infection? Have you started to have a problem with drugs or alcohol? Are you taking any regular medication? Some diseases can develop silently that affect your sexual functioning. Diabetes is the most common. You may want to arrange a complete examination to rule out physical causes.

If health isn't a problem, then you and your partner need to talk about what's changed in your lives. You may not be getting what you want from your relationship. Maybe you've moved. Maybe you've added children to your life. You may be feeling isolated and angry. Use the Communication Exercises we discuss in Chapter III, page 53, and each Week in the Twelve-Week Partner Program to help work through some of the feelings you may be holding in. Also use the Dumping Exercise, page 59, Chapter III. Twice daily, practice the 20–0 Countdown Exercise, described on page 138, Week One of the Partner Program; twice daily, practice the Sex Muscle/Breathing Exercise, described on page 141 of Partner Program Week One. These will help with relaxation and thought control as well.

Self-Stimulation practice is likely to be quite useful. Follow the Self-

Stimulation Exercises I–III described in Weeks Three through Five, or the Singles Program Weeks One through Seven.

Following the Ecstasy Program will be good training and should maximize the possibility of becoming orgasmic again. In order to reduce performance pressure in exercises referring to reaching orgasm, substitute in your mind the words "climax" or "release" to refer to your highest arousal peak. Omit sections of the exercises that refer to multiple or extended orgasm.

Pain with Intercourse

An early step when intercourse is painful is examination by a gynecologist or other physician. If your pelvic area is normal, then you need to take more control of your lovemaking. Painful intercourse very often occurs because your partner is controlling the timing, position, and depth of thrusting in intercourse. The vagina lengthens and enlarges with sexual arousal to accommodate almost any size penis, but it doesn't respond instantly. You need to be properly stimulated and engorged first.

1. You should be thoroughly lubricated. (See "Lubricants," page 79.)

2. Have your partner insert a lubricated finger into your vagina. You should push out against his finger. Pushing out opens up your vagina for easier penetration. Your partner can start with a smaller finger and work up to a larger finger. At first he should insert a finger without moving it. Then he should begin moving it, imitating the thrusting of a penis, slowly increasing depth of penetration and speed.

3. Allow yourself to be the receiver, totally. Have your partner stimulate you manually/orally to the best and longest orgasm possible. He should stimulate you vaginally as well as orally. If possible, locate and have your partner stimulate your internal trigger area or G spot. Don't allow this important step to be rushed. See Sexual Exploration Exercise, page 212, Partner Week Six, and the Learning to Extend Orgasmic Response Exercises I and II, Weeks Nine and Ten, for more instructions.

4. Now take charge. If your partner is not erect at this point, stimulate him manually/orally until he is. See Sensual Focus, III and IV, Weeks Four and Five; Sexual Exploration Exercise, Week Six; Partner-Assisted Stimulation, Week Eight; and Learning to Extend Orgasmic Response I–IV, Weeks Nine through Twelve, for appropriate techniques.

5. Choose a position for intercourse where you have a greater degree

of control. Rear-entry, woman-above, scissors positions, and laptop are usually best. You control the speed and extent of penetration. You determine the amount and type of thrusting, ranging from none at all to vigorous. Feel perfectly free to stimulate your clitoris at the same time. Remember to keep pushing out against your partner's penis.

6. Practice this exercise until you have an orgasm with your partner's penis inserted. You need your partner's cooperation. He should realize that this problem can be solved more easily if he's helpful and nonjudgmental. The process can be as enjoyable for him as it is for you.

PROBLEMS COMMON TO BOTH SEXES

Discrepancy of Desire Between Partners

The most frequent common sexual problem is a discrepancy of desire between partners. One partner wants to make love more often, or in a different time pattern, than the other.

All couples have a discrepancy of desire to some extent. It may be a relatively minor difference, where they are both satisfied, for instance, with a frequency of three times a week, but one prefers to have a sexual interaction in the morning, the other at night. The discrepancy becomes a problem if it results in frequent, unresolved disagreements, which interfere with the quality of other areas in the relationship.

Communication is crucial when there's a difference of desire between partners. Often the problem isn't sexual at all. It's a problem in some other area of the couple's lives. One partner may be angry with the other. Both people need to talk. Both carefully reread Chapter III, Better Communication, beginning on page 32, and follow the exercises described. The Communication Exercise is particularly vital. You may need to arrange to focus more attention on sex. You can do that by deliberately creating sexual times together, as we discussed in that chapter.

Agreeing to follow the Ecstasy Program can be an excellent way to equalize differences in desire. Both of you need to first understand the content of this book by reading it thoroughly and discussing it.

The keys to success are:

1. Your willingness each to compromise 50 percent.

2. Keeping agreements. Only make agreements that you intend to keep. Write down each agreement. Keep every agreement you make.

Doing the Exercise Planning Agreement and the Exercise Completion Agreement for each program week you do is essential. Use the Communication Exercise to express any disagreements or uncomfortable feelings you may have about the manner in which your partner is compromising or making and keeping agreements. Using these tools successfully will help build trust. Trust increases willingness to make further mutually beneficial compromises and agreements. It can strengthen love.

Men should work to understand and apply the information in "Hidden Sexual Energy," page 48, Chapter III. Both partners will benefit from rereading and applying suggestions from Chapter V, "In the Mood for Love," particularly the section on Romance, page 85. Sections from Chapter IV, "Space and Sounds," page 72; "Hygiene and Bathing," page 75; "Warm Up—Deliberately," page 76; "Lighting," page 78; and "Erotic Videos," page 78, may be particularly helpful.

How many weeks you may spend on completing any program week is much less important than doing the exercises as described and at the times you agree upon. Some couples with significantly discrepant desires have taken up to three months to complete the first week or other weeks, with eventual success. It's okay also if one of you enjoys the experience more than the other.

Extended Orgasmic Response is ideally *not* the major goal. If either of you finds your orgasmic response is improving, that's a major benefit. Another important benefit is sometimes the reappearance of lust reminiscent of the feeling of sexual "chemistry" that couples may have experienced at an earlier time in their relationship.

LEARNING ORAL LOVEMAKING

Many men and women resist oral lovemaking. They've been taught that it's dirty or wrong. Or they're afraid they'll be rejected. They're concerned about the taste of their partner's secretions. Women may be afraid that they'll gag.

Oral lovemaking is another way to pleasure. It can add to arousal and to intimacy. It's sad but true that prostitutes find eager and nearly universal interest in oral sex among their clients. That's because it's intensely pleasurable, and too often, because the men's sexual partners reject oral lovemaking at home. If you don't know how to do it, you can learn. If you're anxious about doing it, you can gradually free yourself from anxiety.

Begin by *imagining* oral lovemaking while you're making love or during self-stimulation. Imagine you are kissing and licking your partner's genitals. Imagine your partner is kissing and licking yours.

Agree with your partner that you both want to learn oral lovemaking. Agree further that while you're learning, if either of you becomes too uncomfortable, you'll return to familiar lovemaking for the rest of that period of time. Agree to take turns and to proceed in small, incremental steps.

Cunnilingus

Cunnilingus (kun-ih-*ling*-us), the man orally pleasuring the woman, can begin with both partners smelling and tasting the woman's natural lubrication when she's clean and fresh. Many women (and men) are concerned about genital odor. The best way to resolve that concern is to bathe or shower together before making love, paying special attention to washing the genitals. If odor continues to be a concern, the man can apply scented oils or scented lubricant to his partner's genitals. He can adjust to the oil by applying it first to a nongenital area of his partner's body and licking it off.

We suggest you do a Sensual Focus Step III Exercise (page 192) followed by the man's briefly brushing his lips over his partner's genitals. From session to session he then slowly increases the time and the intensity of his stimulating.

He should experiment with different kinds of oral stimulation: brushing with his lips, licking, light suction. Regularly alternating tongue pressure on and around the clitoris and clitoral hood with sucking the clitoris into the mouth can be highly arousing. Men usually err in the direction of excessive force. Women generally like lighter, more regular, predictable, rhythmic stimulation. Let your partner's responses guide you.

At first, orgasm shouldn't be a goal. Later, when both partners are comfortable with oral lovemaking, it can be.

Some women find their partner's physical position during cunnilingus unmanly. They can help themselves through that resistance by deciding it's mistaken and by applying the techniques discussed in Week I, "Discuss Resistances", page 145. The kneeling-over position (see illustration, page 262) or the position for mutual stimulation (see illustration, page 219) can help alleviate this concern.

Fellatio

Women often resist fellatio (fuh-*lay*-she-oh) because they don't like the idea of their partners ejaculating in their mouth. They may dislike the taste of semen. They may feel the penis is dirty because it's also used for urination. They may be afraid of gagging, possibly from previous experience.

Bathe or shower together to assure each other of cleanliness. Uncircumcised men should draw back their foreskins and carefully wash the area. Begin with Sensual Focus Step III, page 192. The woman then kisses the penis without taking it into her mouth. When she's comfortable doing that, at the same or a later session, she can begin taking the erect penis into her mouth. She should position herself above the penis, her partner on his back, so she can control any thrusting. She can also place her hand around the shaft of the penis to limit its movement into her mouth. These controls help her avoid gagging.

Suction isn't necessary. Simply moving the glans penis in and out of her mouth, making sure her lips cover her teeth, is highly arousing. So is licking the glans and the shaft.

Women who fear accepting their partner's semen into their mouth and who don't trust their partner's ejaculatory control can desensitize themselves by practicing fellatio with a condom over the penis. Later, when they gain confidence in themselves and their partner and learn to recognize the signs of approaching ejaculation, they can pleasure their partner without using a condom. (If you are practicing safer sex, however, use a condom for all oral sex.)

Some women may choose never to receive their partner's semen orally. They can still give him the pleasure of fellatio, returning to manual lovemaking or intercourse for ejaculation. An excellent alternative is for the woman to take her mouth off her partner's penis just before he begins to ejaculate but keep her warm, lubricated hand moving on the glans. Under those circumstances the man may not even know the difference. She may catch the semen in a towel or tissue, wipe it up later from the man's body, or simply not worry about it.

A woman who wants to learn to enjoy fellatio to ejaculation has to accept the taste and texture of semen in her mouth and throat without gagging. The mere thought of swallowing semen can trigger the gag reflex in some women. Others find that the taste and texture of semen has the same uncomfortable effect. A woman who wants to avoid swallowing semen can practice pressing her tongue against the back of the roof of her mouth. This arrangement closes and blocks her throat. She may then spit the semen onto a tissue or a towel.

Our experience, however, indicates that most men would prefer their partners not to spit out their semen. A woman can learn to hold both semen and penis in her mouth. Saliva begins to collect after a few seconds. It dilutes the semen, changing taste and texture to make it more acceptable and pleasurable.

Some women who accept the taste of semen still have trouble swallowing it. Another way to get used to semen—taste, texture, and swallowing—is for the man to ejaculate into the woman's hand. She can then place a small amount of ejaculate in her mouth. She should savor its texture and flavor and gradually increase the amount she tastes and swallows until she can enjoy all of it.

A woman who finds it impossible to like the taste of her partner's semen can at least disguise it with flavored oil or by preparing her mouth with a flavor she prefers—a sip of wine, a piece of chocolate, a swallow of fruit juice. Semen may taste slightly sweet or slightly bitter. It may have hardly any taste at all. Alcohol, even drunk in moderation, most frequently causes bitter semen. If bitterness is a problem, a man can experiment with changes in diet.

A woman should recognize that swallowing her partner's semen can be an intensely intimate act for both partners. It can be a significant symbolic gesture of love, and many women find it a meaningful and even a spiritual experience. It can strengthen your relationship. If this possibility appeals to you, you can both train yourselves toward it.

FURTHER READING

If you wish to read more about managing sexual problems and dysfunctions, you may find the following books useful. They are more completely referenced in the bibliography, page 410.

Male Problems

1. Zilbergeld, Bernie. *Male Sexuality.*
2. Hartman, William, and Fithian, Marilyn. *Any Man Can.*

3. McCarthy, Barry. *Male Sexual Awareness.*
4. Nowinski, Joseph. *Becoming Satisfied: A Man's Guide to Sexual Fulfillment.*
5. Berger, Richard and Deborah. *Biopotency: A Guide to Sexual Success.*

Female Problems

1. Barbach, Lonnie. *For Yourself.*
2. Heiman, Julia, and Lopicollo, Leslie and Joseph. *Becoming Orgasmic: A Sexual Growth Program for Women.*
3. Ladas, Alice; Whipple, Beverly; and Perry, John. *The G Spot.*
4. Friday, Nancy. *My Secret Garden.*
5. Britton, Bryce. *The Love Muscle: Every Woman's Guide to Intensifying Sexual Pleasure.*

Self-Help for Men and Women

1. Castleman, Michael. *Sexual Solutions.*
2. Yaffé, Maurice, and Fenwick, Elizabeth. *Sexual Happiness: A Marital Approach.*
3. Rosenthal, Saul. *Sex over 40.*
4. Williams, Warwick. *Rekindling Desire.*
5. Pearsall, Paul. *Super Marital Sex.*

SHARE YOUR EXPERIENCES

One of the ways we develop, improve, and verify the methods and information of our training programs is to respectfully request feedback from participants. A copy of the "Evaluate Your Satisfaction with Your Relationship" questionnaire would greatly assist us in our continuing research on methods of improving intimate relationships and sexual response. Please feel free to attach additional pages to add to or clarify your answers. We invite those who have followed the singles' program to send us a copy of the chart on their pre- and post-program experiences (men, page xxx; women, page xxx. You need not include your name and address with the questionnaire. We will, of course, protect the confidentiality of your communications in any reports we may prepare. Although we try to answer individual correspondence and questions, we are not always able to do so personally.

We would also like to hear from men and women who started to follow any part of the Ecstasy Program, but whose resistances, fears, or conflicts interfered. A discussion of your experience would greatly help us with our work.

Everyone who responds can take satisfaction in the knowledge that the information you send us may specifically benefit research that may increase the health and happiness of many other men and women.

Any reader who wishes to be included on our confidential mailing list for material that may be of interest, and for specific information on weekend training seminars, which we conduct several times a year in different parts of the U.S. and Canada, write to:

> Brauer Medical Center
> Box 6050
> Stanford, California 94309

SOURCES

Abco Research Associates
Box 329
Monticello, IL 61856
High-technology stimulation machine for women.

Astro-lube
Box 9788
North Hollywood, CA 91609
Distributor of Astro-glide, a moderately long-lasting, water-soluble lubricant.

Condoms—selected manufacturers:

Carter Wallace
767 Fifth Ave.
New York, NY 10022

Circle Rubber Corporation
408 Frelinghuysen Ave.
Newark, NJ 07114
The Gold Circle Line was voted "best overall" and "easiest to use" by
the Stanford University AIDS Education Project, 1987. Foil package
can be opened with one hand; micro-thin latex.

Mellow Mail
P.O. Box 811
Cooper Station
New York, NY 10276-8011
A large distributor of sexually oriented products.

Mentor Corporation
1499 W. River Rd. North
Minneapolis MN 55411
Generally considered the best condom available. Unique, slip-resistant
"safety seal," with unusual two-part, easy-application system. Expensive.

Creme de Femme
Especially Products
Box 547
Playa del Rey, CA 90296
Physician-designed sexual lubricant—reported safe with thick latex
condoms.

Eve's Garden, International, Ltd.
119 W. 57th St., Suite 1406
New York, NY 10019
Reliable direct source of sexual products.

Femme Productions
588 Broadway, Suite 1110
New York, NY 10012
Erotic films by a female producer.

Fun Ways, Inc.
15424 Cabrito Rd.
Van Nuys, CA 91406
High-technology stimulation machines for men.

Good Vibrations
3416 22nd St.
San Francisco, CA 94110
Reliable source of broad selection of vibrators.

Institute for the Advanced Study of Human Sexuality
1525 Franklin St.
San Francisco, CA 94109
Safe-sex kits.

Osbon Medical Systems
1246 Jones St.
P.O. Drawer 1478
Augusta, GA 30903
Erection-enhancement system—physician prescription necessary.

Revive System, Inc.
156 Broad Street
Box 790
Lake Geneva, WI 53147
Erection-enhancement system.

BIBLIOGRAPHY

Alman, Isadora. *Aural Sex and Verbal Intercourse*. Burlingame, CA: Down There Press, 1984.

Araoz, Daniel. *Hypnosis and Sex Therapy*. New York: Brunner/Mazel, 1982.

Bakos, Susan. "Double Your Orgasm Time." *Forum Magazine*, 1987.

Bancroft, J. H. *Human Sexuality and its Problems*. New York: Churchill Livingstone, 1983.

Barbach, Lonnie. *For Yourself: The Fulfillment of Female Sexuality*. Garden City, NY: Doubleday Anchor Press, 1975.

Barbach, Lonnie. *Women Discover Orgasm: A Therapist's Guide to a New Treatment Approach*. New York: Macmillan, 1980.

Beck, Deva and James. *The Pleasure Connection: How Endorphins Affect Our Health and Happiness*. Anaheim, CA: KNI, 1987.

Benson, Herbert. *The Relaxation Response*. New York: Morrow, 1975.

Berger, Richard and Deborah. *Biopotency: A Guide to Sexual Success*. Emmaus, PA: Rodale, 1987.

Bohlen, J. G., and Held, J. P. "An Anal Probe for Monitoring Vascular and Muscular Events During Sexual Response." *Psychophysiology 16* (1979), pp. 318–323.

Bohlen, J. G.; Held, J. P.; and Sanderson, M. D. "The Male Orgasm: Pelvic Contractions Measured by Anal Probe." *Archives of Sexual Behavior 9* (1980), pp. 503–521.

Botwin, Carol. *Is There Sex After Marriage?* New York: Simon and Schuster, 1985.

Boylan, Richard. *Orgasm: The Ultimate Experience.* New York: Dell, 1973.

Brauer, Alan P. and Donna. *ESO: How You and Your Lover Can Give Each Other Hours of Extended Sexual Orgasm.* New York: Warner, 1983.

Britton, Byrce. *The Love Muscle.* New York: NAL, 1983.

Brooks, Marvin. *Lifelong Sexual Vigor: How to Avoid and Overcome Impotence.* Garden City, NY: Doubleday, 1981.

Campbell, H. J. *The Pleasure Areas: A New Theory of Behavior.* New York: Delacorte Press, 1973.

Castleman, Michael. *Sexual Solutions.* New York: Simon and Schuster, 1980.

Cohen, H. D.; Rosen, R. C.; and Goldstein, L. "Electroencephalographic Laterality Changes During Human Sexual Orgasm." *Archives of Sexual Behavior,* 5 (1976).

n.a., *Condom Sense.* San Francisco, CA: Eroticus, 1988.

Covington, Timothy. *Sex Care: The Complete Guide to Safe and Healthy Sex.* New York: Simon and Schuster, 1987.

Deangelis, Barbara. *How to Make Love All the Time.* New York: Rawson, 1987.

Debetz, Barbara, and Baker, Samm Sinclair. *Erotic Focus: The New Way to Enhance Your Sexual Pleasure.* New York: New American Library, 1985.

Dodson, Betty. *Sex for One: The Joy of Self-Loving.* New York: Harmony Books, 1987.

Everett, Jane, and Glanz, Walter. *The Condom Book: The Essential Guide for Men and Women.* New York: New American Library, 1987.

Fisher, Seymour. *The Female Orgasm.* New York: Basic Books, 1973.

Flemming, Paul, ed. *Sex over 40.* Chapel Hill, NC (Newsletter).

Franklin, Steven and Jacqueline. *The Ultimate Kiss: A Guide to Oral Sex.* Los Angeles: Media Publications, 1982.

Friday, Nancy. *Men in Love: Men's Sexual Fantasies.* New York: Dell, 1980.

Friday, Nancy. *My Secret Garden*. New York: Pocket Books, 1983.

Gabbard, Glen O. "Out of Body States." *Psychiatric Times*, Jan. 1988, pp. 5–6.

Garrison, Omar. *Tantra: The Yoga of Sex*. New York: Causeway, 1964.

Goldstein, L. "Time Domain Analysis of the EEG: The Integrative Method." In G. Dolce and H. Kunkel, Eds., *C.E.A.N.—Computerized EEG Analysis*. Stuttgart: Gustav Fisher, 1975.

Graber, Benjamin, ed. *Circumvaginal Musculature and Sexual Function*. New York: Karger, 1982.

Graber, B.; Rohrbaugh, J. W.; Newlin, D. B.; Varner, J. L.; and Ellingson, R. J. "EEG During Masturbation and Ejaculation." *Archives of Sexual Behavior 14*, pp. 491–503.

Hartman, William, and Fithian, Marilyn. *Any Man Can: The Multiple Orgasmic Technique for Every Loving Man*. New York: St. Martin's Press, 1984.

Heiman, Julia, and Lopicollo, Leslie and Joseph. *Becoming Orgasmic: A Sexual Growth Program for Women*. New York: Prentice-Hall, 1976.

Hite, Shere. *The Hite Report: A Nationwide Study of Female Sexuality*. New York: Dell, 1976.

————. *The Hite Report on Male Sexuality*. New York: Ballantine, 1981.

Kaplan, Helen Singer. *The Evaluation of Sexual Disorders: Psychological and Medical Aspects*. New York: Brunner/Mazel, 1983.

————. *The New Sex Therapy: Active Treatment of Sexual Dysfunctions*. New York: Brunner/Mazel, 1974.

————. *The New Sex Therapy, Vol. II: Disorders of Sexual Desire*. New York: Brunner/Mazel, 1979.

Kinsey, Alfred. *Sexual Behavior in the Human Female*. Philadelphia: Saunders, 1953.

Kinsey, Alfred; Pomeroy, Wardell; and Martin, Clyde. *Sexual Behavior in the Human Male*. Philadelphia: Saunders, 1948.

Kitzenger, Sheila. *Woman's Experience of Sex: The Facts and Feelings of Female Sexuality at Every Stage of Life*. New York: Penguin, 1985.

Kolodny, Robert C.; Masters, William H.; and Johnson, Virginia E. *Textbook of Sexual Medicine*. Boston: Little, Brown, 1979.

Kroger, William, and Caprio, Frank. *How to Solve Your Sex Problems with Self-Hypnosis*. New York: Citadel, 1964.

Ladas, Alice Kahn; Whipple, Beverly; and Perry, John D. *The G Spot*. New York: Holt, Reinhart, and Winston, 1982.

Legman, G. *The Intimate Kiss*. New York: Paperback Library, 1969.

Leiblum, S. and Rosen, R. *Sexual Desire Disorders*. New York: Guilford Press, 1988.

Levin, Linda, and Barbach, Lonni. *The Intimate Male*. Garden City, NY: Doubleday, 1983.

Liebowitz, Michael R. *The Chemistry of Love*. Boston: Little, Brown, 1983.

Lief, Harold, ed. *Sexual Problems in Medical Practice*. Monroe, WI: American Medical Association, 1981.

Lowen, Alexander. *Love and Orgasm*. New York: Collier, 1965.

Masters, William, and Johnson, Virginia. *Human Sexual Response*. Boston: Little, Brown, 1966.

———. *Human Sexual Inadequacy*. Boston: Little, Brown, 1970.

Masters, William; Johnson, Virginia; and Kolodny, Robert. *Masters and Johnson on Sex and Human Loving*. Boston: Little, Brown, 1986.

McCarthy, Barry. *Male Sexual Awareness*. New York: Carroll & Graf, 1988.

McIlvenna, Ted. *The Complete Guide to Safe Sex*. Beverly Hills, CA: Specific Press, 1987.

McKay, Matthew; Davis, Martha; and Fanning, Patrick. *Messages: The Communication Book*. Oakland: New Harbinger, 1983.

Meshorer, Mark and Judith. *Ultimate Pleasure: The Secrets of Easily Orgasmic Women*. New York: St. Martin's, 1986.

Nowinski, Joseph. *Becoming Satisfied: A Man's Guide to Sexual Fulfillment*. Englewood Cliffs, NJ: Prentice-Hall, 1980.

Otto, Herbert and Roberta. *Total Sex.* New York: Signet, 1972.

Pearsall, Paul. *Super Marital Sex.* Garden City, NY: Doubleday, 1987.

Pietropinto, Anthony, and Simenaut, Jacqueline. *Beyond the Male Myth.* New York: Signet, 1977.

Raley, Patricia. *Making Love: How to Be Your Own Sex Therapist.* New York: Avon, 1980.

Ramsdale, David Allen, and Dorfman, Ellen Jo. *Sexual Energy Ecstasy: A Guide to the Ultimate, Intimate Sexual Experience.* Playa Del Rey, CA: Peak Skill, 1985.

Reich, Wilhelm. *The Function of Orgasm.* New York: Simon and Schuster, 1975.

Richards, Brian. *The Penis.* New York: Valentine, 1977.

Robbins, Mina, and Jensen, Gordon. "Multiple Orgasm in Males." *Journal of Sex Research 14:1* (Feb. 1978), pp. 21–26.

Rosen, Raymond C., and Beck, J. Gayle. *Patterns of Sexual Arousal: Psychophysiological Processes and Clinical Applications.* New York: Guilford, 1988.

Rosenberg, Jack Lee. *Total Orgasm.* New York: Random House, 1973.

Rosenthal, Saul. *Sex over 40.* Los Angeles: Tarcher, 1987.

Schwartz, Kit. *The Male Member.* New York: St. Martin's, 1985.

Sex: A User's Manual. New York: Putnam, 1987.

Simenauer, J., and Caroll, D. *Singles.* New York: Simon & Schuster, 1982.

Whipple, Beverly, and Ogden, Gina. *Safe Encounters: How Women Can Say Yes to Pleasure and No to Unsafe Sex.* New York: Barber Hill, 1989.

Williams, Warwick. *Rekindling Desire: Bringing Your Sexual Relationship Back to Life.* Oakland, CA: New Harbinger, 1988.

Womack, William, and Stauss, Fred. *The Marriage Bed: Renewing Love, Friendship, Trust and Romance.* Seattle: Madrona, 1986.

Yaffé, Maurice, and Fenwick, Elizabeth. *Sexual Happiness: A Practical Approach.* New York: Holt, 1988.

Zilbergeld, Bernie. *Male Sexuality.* New York: Bantam Books, 1978.

BRAUER WEEKEND SEMINARS

The Brauers offer weekend seminars for individuals and couples on expanding sexual potential for optimum relationships and health, two times a year at eastern and western U.S. locations. For specific information, or if you wish to be placed on a confidential mailing list to receive information that may be of interest to Ecstasy Program readers, write to:

Brauer Medical Center
Box 6050
Stanford, CA 94309

INDEX